Advance Praise for *The Transformative Power of Family Wealth*

Too often, wealth is seen as a pathology that ipso facto causes destruction to our individual, relational and collective well-being. Seasoned experts, such as Philip Marcovici, however, know that the power inherent in great wealth can be used to create exceptional returns when properly understood and channelled. In his most recent contribution to the field, Mr. Marcovici provides an honest, clear and well researched roadmap for families of wealth and the professionals who serve them to use their wealth in ways to maximize their individual, relational and financial well-being.
—**Dr. Paul Hokemeyer**, Author of *Fragile Power: Why Having Everything Is Never Enough* (Hazelden, 2019) and *Fragile Power 2.0: Wealth, Narcissism & Mental Health* (2024, in print)

Thank you for reaching out and sharing your superb new book *The Transformative Power of Family Wealth*. I read it and find, as I expected, that the depth of your experience and the wisdom you have earned from your career, sing out. I am sure that for families and advisors all over the world the book will be a classic, a Rosetta stone that clarifies in a field of opacity. Please use this statement as an encomium from me for your career, not only the book.
—**James(Jay)E, Hughes, Jr**, Author of *Family Wealth: Keeping It in the Family*; co-author of *The Cycle of the Gift* and co-author of *Family Trusts*

For wealth and business owning families and their advisers, this is the ultimate guide to getting it right.
—**David Chong**, Group President, Portcullis (Singapore) Pte. Ltd., described by the Singapore Academy of Law as *The Guru of Asian Family Offices*

This fluent guide, outlining the many challenges to the successful transmission of family wealth and a variety of constructive solutions, should be helpful reading for wealth and business owning families and their advisers.
—**Paul Stibbard**, Former Co-chair of Baker McKenzie's Global Wealth Management Group

In this, his latest offering, Marcovici brings his many years of experience and deep expertise to an overview not only of how families with complex wealth challenges may navigate the many issues that arise for modern wealth management but understand how individual family issues sit within a dynamic, changing world of tax policy, asset management, structured investment opportunities, and long-term planning for inter-generational wealth stewardship. By outlining a vision of strategic wealth management at the family level while connecting that vision to the global context of today's families, Marcovici walks the reader through a variety of aspects and opportunities to be considered not only by families but those advisors and professionals working to ensure the challenges of wealth are well addressed to the benefit of today and tomorrow's generations.

—**Jed Emerson**, Chief Impact Officer, AlTi Tiedemann Global

It is timely to address the "purpose of wealth" as author of *The Purpose of Capital* Jed Emerson said: "Human societies are now dominated by financial capitalism" and the implications of that dominance reminds us that financial capital is a social construct.

As social and environmental challenges grow, the role of wealth is evolving. Often, investors and philanthropists tend to focus on investing with returns with lesser attention to how such investment will create impact in their own, the community and the world lives. Realizing the need to first define one's wealth with purpose, integrating in how they make investment that create the right impact, aligning it to the philanthropic endeavours is an awakening to recognise how best to using their resources for lasting impact thus shifting and reflecting with new vision and role of wealth as a tool for change and not being the servant of one's wealth.

Philip is best placed with his vast knowledge in tax and advising global families in wealth planning over his long career and this would be another book not just a worthy reading but an inspiring tool to provoke your thinking to reconsider how you would like to set your pathway in a purposeful, mindful way in managing your wealth.

—**Anthonia Hui & Leonardo Drago**, Singapore

It is trite to say that our world seems more complex today. The challenges for many families (and not just the wealthy) involve a myriad of factors, including wealth preservation, succession planning, family responsibility and involvement in societal and economic development, and they are increasingly apparent.

It is not often that we read a book where what should be self-evident truths, in this instance relating to family wealth and responsibility, are highlighted and explained in a way that peels back unconscious bias that too often obscures such truths and vigorously challenges adherence to the maxim "if it ain't broke, then don't fix it."

If the reader is looking for a roadmap in this context, Philip Marcovici's book emphasises clearly that one size does not fit all. But Marcovici does, through informed argument and numerous practical examples, provide guidance and a comprehensive structure to deal with those matters which should inform family members and their advisors of the means and actions they may take to realize the ultimate goals that the family wishes to secure for its ongoing prosperity and happiness.

In short, this book is not just about money (although finance considerations inform many decisions made in relation to family business and relations). Rather, Marcovici's book ultimately aims to guide families in their efforts to strive towards a better life for all of their existing and future members and to consider the role they may play in helping develop a better and fairer society from which we all may benefit.

—**Andrew Halkyard**, Adjunct Professor, Law Faculty (retired), Hong Kong University

Building on his previous work, Philip Marcovici's *The Transformative Power of Family Wealth* is packed with insights and offers wealth owners powerful tools for channeling their resources into a force for good. Must reading not only for those stewards of family wealth, but for all those striving to serve them.

—**Amaury Jordan, CFA**, Co-founder of Avalor Investment (Switzerland) and TriLake Partners (Singapore)

Philip's book is a very worthwhile read for those who work with wealthy families. In particular, the paradigm of the Theory of Change as a mechanism to help to shape a succession planning strategy is fascinating. It is also refreshing to read a positive exposition of the role that private businesses can play in regenerating society.

—**John Riches**, Partner RMW Law and President of the International Academy of Estate and Trust Lawyers

The Transformative Power of Family Wealth is the perfect guide for wealthy family, wealth managers and family offices. Philip is a man of paradox, not a man of prejudices, which makes his views and advice unique and extremely valuable. After having identified the "Destructive Power of Family Wealth," he is showing us the silver line where wealth and public good are no longer incompatible.

—**Pascal Saint-Amans**, Former director of the OECD Centre for Tax Policy and Administration, Professor at HEC Paris and Lausanne University

Unlike most sequels, Philip Marcovici's second volume on family wealth does not disappoint. This time he focuses on the regenerative power of wealth for families as opposed to the destructive power covered in the first volume. And this time he broadens the scope to include countries as well as families, all with a rich intellectual underpinning in theory of change and the circular economy. It's a compelling handbook for all those involved in building businesses, creating wealth or managing and advising on it.

Drawing on his lifetime's experience in advising global wealthy families there is both an optimistic vision of how positively things could turn out, as well as cautionary warnings on the inevitable pitfalls
—**Michael Morley**, Independent Non-executive Director
Financial Services and Luxury Brands

With his extensive experience and deep insights, Philip's latest book is required reading, not only for wealthy families and their advisors, but also for policy makers and thinkers as they ponder the role of wealthy families in tomorrow's world.
—**Edmund Leow S.C.**, Senior Partner,
Dentons Rodyk & Davidson LLP, Singapore
Senior Partner

Here is a book full of wisdom for wealth holders, their families and even the countries in which they reside. How fortunate to have the thoughts, strategies, and insights of a person who has had a remarkable career spanning generations of clients, a multitude of cultures, and situations as diverse as families of wealth can find themselves addressing. He addresses the fundamental questions of figuring out what your wealth is for, dealing with the dynamics of family, and recognize the benefits wealth can bring not only to families but to communities. I recommend this book to any family looking at how it can prosper and any advisor or government trying to understand the challenges and benefits of wealthy clients and citizens.
—**Charles A. Lowenhaupt**, Chairman & Partner,
Lowenhaupt & Chasnoff, LLC, St. Louis, Missouri

An impressive work, reflecting Philip Marcovici's deep knowledge and experience. It offers a comprehensive understanding of the broader context of policy making, the needs of wealth owners and their advisors, and proposes thoughtful, practical solutions for the systemic changes needed to create a more just and equitable world.
—**Stefan Liniger**, Founding Partner, Conduct, Zurich

Another Tour de Force by the author, this book comprehensively addresses all relevant issues international wealth owners and their families face. Its clear language and powerful illustrative story telling make the topics not only highly digestible but actually fun to read. Wealth owners and their advisors alike will be grateful for the existence of *The Transformative Power of Family Wealth*.
—**Dr Britta Pfister**, Founder, Britta Pfister Advisory

Wealth and business owning families, and their advisors should keep this important book close at hand. It will serve as a precious and practical guide as to how to do things the right way. Thank you Philip Marcovici for this thoughtful and comprehensive work.

—**Gary J Gartner**, Managing Director, Alchemy Capital Planning LLC

Philip's new book *The Transformative Power of Family Wealth* is a logical continuation of his former book *The Destructive Power of Family Wealth*. Highly inspiring and constructive Infotainment for wealth and business owning families, their advisors and policy makers.

Wealth means responsibility – this book is perfect to get you up to speed, both technically and philosophically. A very nice read.

—**Benedikt Kaiser**, Kaiser Partner, Vaduz, Liechtenstein

An insightful, thought-provoking and eminently readable traverse of the key issues surrounding family wealth succession and structuring. For anyone with an interest in this area, definitely worth reading.

—**Bernard Rennell**, Principal, InterGen Capital Partners Limited. Former CEO HSBC International Trustee Limited and former Regional Head, Asia-Pacific, HSBC Private Bank

For wealth and business owning families and their advisors, this is the ultimate guide to getting it right. And for policy makers interested in the transformative power of family wealth an invaluable resource.

—**Jefferson VanderWolk**, Former Head of Tax Treaty, Transfer Pricing and Financial Transactions Division, OECD Centre for Tax Policy and Administration and former International Tax Counsel, US Senate Committee on Finance

This book is an ultimate guide to how to get it right. It is a must read for business owners, private wealth advisors, tax and estate practitioners. The book is an excellent refresher for practitioners who have been practicing for decades and a primer for young practitioners who are just starting out.

—**Jacqueline Loh**, Global Head of Private Wealth, Ogier Global

I have had the privilege of knowing Philip for over two decades, dating back to the early days of my legal career at Baker McKenzie. When I first heard him speak at a conference, it was clear that Philip is far more than a lawyer—he is a true thought leader. His remarkable ability to transcend the confines of his expertise in wealth management, tax, and law allows him to connect disparate ideas and anticipate emerging trends with a visionary perspective. Even then, I recognized him as a futurist, someone who

intuitively grasps what lies ahead. This same foresight makes his latest book both compelling and thought-provoking yet pragmatic and helpful.
—**Elena Zafirova**, Founder & CEO, Dionz

Through working with wealth owning families and governments over many years, Philip shares his unequalled experience by providing a roadmap towards the goal of sustainable family models. In showing the interdependency between these families and society, Philip makes a compelling case as to how they can contribute to a better society for all, addressing issues which include wealth inequality. This book will undoubtedly serve as an enlightening guide to both professionals in the wealth management industry but also young inheritors of wealth who seek to identify the purpose of their wealth and in so doing, pursue their own sense of self-fulfilment.
—**Xavier Issac**, Chief Executive Officer, Accuro Trust Group

For wealth and business-owning families and their advisors, this is the ultimate guide to getting it right... By offering practical strategies and introducing frameworks such as the Theory of Change, Marcovici shows how to navigate the complexities of wealth while focusing on long-term family and societal goals. From addressing governance challenges to understanding tax systems and much more, this book provides a comprehensive roadmap for ensuring that wealth supports the family's legacy and helps accomplish their most important objectives across generations.
—**Suchi ("Shi-Chieh") Lee**, Senior Business Advisor, Retired PwC partner and former Global Leader of PwC's International Tax Services Network

The Transformative Power of Family Wealth is a magnificently written book addressing the specific areas and needs wealthy families must address to create their Theory of Change.

Marcovici outlines the legal and practical approaches to sustain families and their business interests. Plus, and most importantly the different characteristics reflective of high functioning families.

Each chapter communicates a guide for families to embrace the sustainability of all individuals, family values and the family Road Map, including the necessary planning tools.

This is a must read to all advisors seeking to fulfil the holistic needs of the families they serve.
—**Lesley Lewis**, Founder, Culture3Counsel

Wealth is a magnifying glass! It shows up our weaknesses and, sometimes, our strengths. Wealth can be a positive or a negative but is never neutral. *The Transformative Power of Family Wealth* does not only demonstrate how wealth can be protected by reasonable means but provides a lot of advice on how families can ensure that their wealth will be uplifting. However, *The Transformative Power of Family Wealth* is not only for the rich. Political decision-makers and anybody interested in how tax systems can be made simpler and fairer, loopholes closed, and constructive dialogue with wealth owners undertaken, should read this book. It is an extraordinary work by an extraordinary expert! There are lessons for us all!

—**Peter Hulsroj**, Co-author of *Essays on the Optional Society - and a Letter Concerning Inclusion*

The Transformative Power of Family Wealth brilliantly captures the dynamics shaping family wealth today. With candour and insight, Marcovici thoughtfully addresses how wealth management must evolve to meet contemporary needs, offering practical strategies for resilience and prosperity in an ever-changing landscape. It is a must-read for those dedicated to effective and responsible wealth stewardship!

—**Gina M. Pereira**, B.A.(Hons), LL.B., TEP, Founder & Principal, Dana Stewardship Advisory

Philip Marcovici's *The Transformative Power of Family Wealth* offers a compelling and practical roadmap for families to leverage their wealth in ways that benefit both their legacy and the broader society."

—**Veit de Maddalena**, Former CEO of Rothschild Private Wealth and Global Partner, Non-Executive Board Member/Chair for Family Enterprises, Zurich, Switzerland

This book is the ultimate guide for all wealth and business owning families and their advisors. A dispassionate view on how to avoid the pitfalls and dangers of wealth

—**Adrian Braimer-Jones**, Ensof Advisory Group, London

This is an important, constructive book both for families of wealth and the societies they live in. Following its guidance will help business and wealth-owners thrive, contribute and be sustainable.

—**Tom McCullough**, Chairman and CEO, Northwood Family Office, and Adjunct Professor, Rotman School of Management, University of Toronto

To navigate a world of uncertainty and rapid change, a wealth and business owning family needs both a north and a compass to guide its decisions. This new book offers constructive advice as well as an innovative "Theory of Change" approach that can help both the family and their advisors to gain clarity on both the here and now.

—**Etienne Eichenberger**, Managing Partner, WISE Philanthropy Advisors

Complementing Philip's previous book (*The Destructive Power of Family Wealth*), *The Transformative Power of Family Wealth* explores the symbiosis and positive potential of private wealth both for wealthy families as well as functioning society. Borne from a career of experience working with some of the wealthiest global families as well as governments, Philip's easy writing style combined with frank analysis, references to real-life situations and (importantly!) humour, makes his book not only invaluable reading for industry professionals but also (and perhaps more critically) to members of wealth and business-owning families themselves.

—**Simon Michaels**, Vice Chairman, CEO and shareholder of Camelot Trustees, Singapore

I cannot imagine a more complete, authoritative and common sense overview and guide to all the key issues and challenges facing wealth and business-owning families and their advisors around the world, and how to address them.

—**Markos Komondouros**, Founder and partner, Investing For Purpose

For wealth and business owning families and their advisors, this is the ultimate readable in depth guide to getting it right. Unlike other publications in the field, it's truly all embracing, covering not just the essential legal and tax factors but even more importantly the vital steps needed to make sure that the family's collective aims and members' well-being are properly determined, articulated, implemented and protected. It truly is a tour de force.

—**John K. Connor**, Former long-time Baker McKenzie International partner, Sydney, Australia

A must read for wealthy families and their advisors, especially where impact goals and supporting strategy is not yet clearly defined. We have applied the approach of the author with a number of families and it is simply a game-changer.

—**Roman Marti**, Zurich, Switzerland

The Transformative Power of Family Wealth

The Transformative Power of Family Wealth

HELPING FAMILIES AND THEIR COMMUNITIES CAPTURE ITS REGENERATIVE POTENTIAL

Philip Marcovici

WILEY

This edition first published 2025

© 2025 Philip Marcovici. All rights reserved

All rights reserved, including rights for text and data mining and training of artificial intelligence technologies or similar technologies. No part of this publication may be reproduced, stored in a retrieval system, or transmitted, in any form or by any means, electronic, mechanical, photocopying, recording or otherwise, except as permitted by law. Advice on how to obtain permission to reuse material from this title is available at http://www.wiley.com/go/permissions.

The right of Philip Marcovici to be identified as the author of this work has been asserted in accordance with law.

Registered Office(s)
John Wiley & Sons, Inc., 111 River Street, Hoboken, NJ 07030, USA
John Wiley & Sons Ltd, New Era House, 8 Oldlands Way, Bognor Regis, West Sussex, PO22 9NQ, UK

For details of our global editorial offices, customer services, and more information about Wiley products visit us at www.wiley.com.

Wiley also publishes its books in a variety of electronic formats and by print-on-demand. Some content that appears in standard print versions of this book may not be available in other formats.

Trademarks: Wiley and the Wiley logo are trademarks or registered trademarks of John Wiley & Sons, Inc. and/or its affiliates in the United States and other countries and may not be used without written permission. All other trademarks are the property of their respective owners. John Wiley & Sons, Inc. is not associated with any product or vendor mentioned in this book.

Limit of Liability/Disclaimer of Warranty: While the publisher and authors have used their best efforts in preparing this work, they make no representations or warranties with respect to the accuracy or completeness of the contents of this work and specifically disclaim all warranties, including without limitation any implied warranties of merchantability or fitness for a particular purpose. No warranty may be created or extended by sales representatives, written sales materials or promotional statements for this work. This work is sold with the understanding that the publisher is not engaged in rendering professional services. The advice and strategies contained herein may not be suitable for your situation. You should consult with a specialist where appropriate. The fact that an organization, website, or product is referred to in this work as a citation and/or potential source of further information does not mean that the publisher and authors endorse the information or services the organization, website, or product may provide or recommendations it may make. Further, readers should be aware that websites listed in this work may have changed or disappeared between when this work was written and when it is read. Neither the publisher nor authors shall be liable for any loss of profit or any other commercial damages, including but not limited to special, incidental, consequential, or other damages.

Library of Congress Control Number: 2024950282

Hardback ISBN: 9781394280506
ePDF ISBN: 9781394280520
ePub ISBN: 9781394280513

Cover Image: © Good Gnom/Getty Images
Cover Design by Wiley

Set in 11pt ITC New Baskerville Std by Lumina Datamatics
SKY10094356_122024

To my own family and to the many families I have been fortunate to work with and learn from over the years.

Contents

Preface		xvii
Acknowledgements		xxiii
About the Author		xxv
Introduction		**xxvii**
Chapter 1:	The *Theory of Change*—Starting at the End and Working Back	1
Chapter 2:	Applying Circular Economy Principles to Family Business and Wealth Stewardship	17
Chapter 3:	Understanding the World of Taxation and the Realities of Tax Transparency	51
Chapter 4:	Is Society Optional? Better Ways to Tax Wealth and Business Owners and Moves Towards Global Taxation	113
Chapter 5:	Any Amount of Wealth Is Enough to Destroy a Family—Some Thoughts About the Psychology of Wealth	151
Chapter 6:	The Derailers—Addressing the Many '*What-ifs?*'	181
Chapter 7:	Bridges and Tunnels—Using the Tools of Wealth Planning to Navigate the Derailers	253
Chapter 8:	Advisors—We Need Them but Need to Control Them	287

Chapter 9:	**Getting It Right**	**309**
Chapter 10:	**The Apple, Bird and Crane Families—and Dagland—Their *Theories of Change* and the Process to Get There**	**333**

A Few Extracts From *The Transformative Power of Family Wealth*	365
Glossary	373
Index	387

Preface

Eight years ago, I completed a book entitled *The Destructive Power of Family Wealth: A Guide to Succession Planning, Asset Protection, Taxation and Wealth Management*.[1] Published by Wiley, the publisher of this new book, my earlier book was my opportunity to share my experience in working with wealth owners around the world and their advisors. *The Destructive Power of Family Wealth* was also an opportunity to put into writing some of the thoughts that I had been sharing with students in my teaching over the years.

This book is designed to provide both an update to my earlier work and a roadmap to not only how the destructive power of family wealth can be avoided but how family wealth and business ownership can be *constructive*—for the families involved, for their business and wealth interests, and for their communities, firms and planet. In relation to the latter, my focus is not only on how wealth-owning families can themselves navigate towards a happy and successful future, but how our societies can benefit from the ability of wealth-owning families to contribute to a better world.

I strongly believe that *holistic sustainability* can be achieved by both wealth and business owners and the societies with which they interact. If planning focuses on the longer term and specific steps are taken by stakeholders, not only can the destructive power of family wealth be contained, but benefit can be achieved for individual family members, families as a whole (including their business and investment interests) and society.

While this book retains content from *The Destructive Power of Family Wealth*, it purposely provides less of a technical focus on tax and other regulatory areas—leaving my earlier book as a resource on these, among other, topics.

Now retired from practising law, I spent my career as an international tax and private client lawyer, working with families, businesses and the wealth management industry, first in New York and Vancouver, and then in Hong Kong and Zurich. I have also worked with governments seeking to address the global problem of undeclared funds, and have taught widely in Asia and Europe, learning while sharing my views on the potentially destructive nature of wealth and the failings of the wealth management industry and of advisors to truly help the families they are meant to serve.

Since retiring, and from bases in Hong Kong and London, I have continued to work with global families on their holistic continuity planning. This involves helping families to formulate their vision for the future and take the steps necessary to help make that vision a reality.

I have also continued to work with governments, now more on approaches that might be taken to better engage with wealth-owning families to the benefit of society. In my teaching, I have, among others, been collaborating with Cambridge University and the Cambridge Institute for Sustainability Leadership (CISL) on programmes oriented to helping wealth and business-owning families identify the roles they can play in the development of sustainable economies and how a focus on sustainability can help families and their business and investment interests be better positioned to achieve long-term continuity and success.

A concern I have had for many years relates to the misunderstandings that exist in relation to the positive role wealth and business owners can and do play in society. I have observed a number of countries, particularly in recent years, failing to evidence an understanding of the benefit effective engagement with and support of wealth and business owners can result in. My teaching and writing are increasingly oriented to the considerable opportunities that are being missed. It is my hope that this book will be read not only by wealth owners and their advisors, but also by those concerned about growing inequality and sustainability generally, and who might benefit from a better understanding of the positive contributions wealth and business owners can make to societal wellbeing.

Journalists, governments and many others can themselves contribute to a better world through an appreciation of the force for good that wealth and business-owning families can be. It is easy to bash the wealthy, but it is more effective to harness their ability to contribute—and not only financially.

I began working with wealth-owning families on their succession and other needs early in the 1980s, in Hong Kong. Having studied law in both Canada and the United States, I had started out as a corporate tax lawyer in New York, and then moved to Hong Kong where I spent twelve years practising law. The 1980s and early 1990s were interesting times in Hong Kong. Pretty much the most capitalist place in the world was soon to revert to pretty much the most communist place in the world. China was negotiating the return of Hong Kong to China by the United Kingdom, which had been governing Hong Kong under treaties that, in part, were coming to an end after a term of ninety-nine years. The handover of Hong Kong to China was ultimately agreed between Margaret Thatcher and Deng Xiaoping and took place in 1997.

In the run-up to 1997, many of Hong Kong's wealth-owning families began restructuring their businesses in view of perceived political risk and sought second (and third and fourth) citizenships and places of alternative residence. My work moved from being work for companies on their tax affairs to work for the owners of companies looking more comprehensively at their situation, mixing in issues of political risk and asset protection with tax exposures in the United States and elsewhere associated with cross-border investment and new residences and citizenships. Many of the wealth owners in Hong Kong came from families who had fled China on the arrival of the communists and who suffered the expropriation of their businesses and many other challenges. They were not about to let themselves lose everything again.

My work with families in relation to their personal and business assets and the protection of wealth led me to work with the wealth management industry—the providers of asset management services, trusts and other 'tools' of wealth planning. Something I learned early on is that the industry all too often does not meet the comprehensive needs of the clients it serves. This led me to become active in training and education and to work on strategies for private banks and others interested in greater alignment with the needs of their clients. But overall, I was working in a major growth industry that was to me surprisingly chaotic (and often unethical) in its management and delivery of services.

In the mid-1990s, I moved to Switzerland, where I spent 15 years working with private banks, trust and insurance companies and the global families that use their services. With young children, we were looking for a clean place to live given growing pollution in Hong Kong. A partner of an international law firm, I had the opportunity to look at a map and broadly choose where I wanted to spend the next years of my career. We arrived in Zurich and found the clean place we were looking for—air that was broadly unpolluted, a lake that could be swum in and a population surprisingly obsessed with cleanliness. One of our many challenges in adapting to Switzerland related to the complexities of throwing out garbage, navigating a system that combined charges for unsorted waste and the encouragement of free recycling.

But while Zurich and Switzerland were certainly clean places, this was pretty much only from the point of view of the environment. While I was not naïve when arriving in Switzerland, I was still shocked at the *unclean* nature of the Swiss financial centre and, in particular, its wealth management industry. Now forced to change, the Swiss were, to me, clearly abusing their role as global champions of privacy, ignoring the real needs of their clients, which in my view include ensuring that families *play by the rules* of their home countries of residence and investment—including by the tax rules of those countries. While tax evasion is a global problem and the role of the wealth management industry in facilitating tax evasion is and was by no means limited to Switzerland, I believe that Switzerland, as the dominant player in the wealth management industry, had the opportunity to take leadership in addressing the issue. Instead, Switzerland and many other secrecy centres misled their clients into believing that secrecy could be the solution to all problems.

Today, we are in a changed world. Not only in Switzerland, where tax compliance and transparency are (or certainly should be!) at the top of the agenda in the wealth management industry, but around the world. Data leaks have contributed to change, but the shift from an opaque world to one that is increasingly transparent is taking time, and the road for many wealth owners continues to be a rocky one. Switzerland failed to take the global lead it could have on the issues of undeclared money, and today there remain, surprisingly, advisors and other intermediaries who continue to mislead families into thinking that hiding money is good planning. The United States is a particularly egregious offender, particularly given the way it has sought to protect its own tax revenues through aggressive attacks on Switzerland and others while preserving the ability of its banks and corporate service providers to market secrecy over substance. In the years that have passed since the writing of my earlier book, the misuse of the United States by those seeking to hide wealth has, in my view, only increased, to the detriment of the countries the tax laws of which are being evaded.

I believe that the misuse of bank secrecy and the now somewhat historical focus on tax evasion practised by key wealth management players globally has cost our society dearly and in many ways. Rather than helping to focus attention on the benefits societies can achieve through close collaboration with wealth and business-owning families, the interests of each diverged. The wealth owners increasingly feared governments and the political landscape moved increasingly to a bashing of the wealthy and to a focus on the realities of growing income and wealth inequality. Would a more transparent world and one where wealth owners could really trust governments have produced a better result? Are there ways to get on to the right track to more effective collaboration and the symbiosis that can be achieved through alignment of interests of wealth owners and society?

In my experience, too many families have failed to understand their own planning needs and the conflicts of interest their advisors and banks have. Many of the families I have come across have neglected to focus on the critical issue of succession—in part due to an obsession with secrecy and an over-emphasis on tax exposures. Tax enforcement is a reality, with many developments that have changed the ways of the past and continue doing so. Notwithstanding these changes, I continue to have a real concern that families do not put enough emphasis on the key issue they need to address—will wealth destroy their family?

In the 1980s, a common line of thinking among my clients and friends in Hong Kong and the region was that things were different for Chinese families. I was told that I did not understand that the Chinese were close and loving families, where succession would never be something that would end up destroying the family and relationships, unlike the case of litigious Westerners lacking the respect for the older generation that the Chinese have. I later ran across Latin American families arguing a similar theme of love and devotion (and music) making them different. The sad reality, proven over and over again by the many disastrous fights among Asian, Latin American, Middle Eastern and other families of late, is that *all* families are the same—the children, holding hands, arrive at their parents' home for dinners and lunches, and after the passing of their parents all too often end up enriching lawyers happily fuelling the flames in disputes over murky succession arrangements left by the older generation.

There is no question that religious and cultural issues impact how families work and the succession process ensues. But no family is immune to the dangers that wealth can result in, or the relatively new challenges associated with all of us living longer and the demographic changes that result. If Mum or Dad lives to 105, does that mean I inherit when I am eighty? And what of the growing incidence of dementia and all the problems that come with it?

Are these only a problem of the 'wealthy'? For me, the answer is no—**all** wealth owners, meaning anyone who owns anything of value that may pass to the next generation or to others, have the potential to destroy their families through the succession process. In fact, families who have relatively little in the way of assets have a particular responsibility to ensure that what they have and hope to use to enhance the lives of the next generation does not end up in the wrong hands or result in the destruction of family relationships.

Who really is wealthy is, in any case, a very subjective thing—what is a fortune to one person may be a pittance to another. And there is a sad reality that human nature seems to make people think they always need more than they have to really be 'rich'. In the end, we do need money to survive, but how much is ever enough? Does wealth really create happiness? Or does it too often create unhappiness?

Perhaps the comedian Spike Milligan was right in saying '*money can't buy you happiness... but it does bring you a more pleasant form of misery*'.

Was Spike Milligan too cynical? Is there a way to avoid the destructive power of family wealth? This book will explore possibilities for success—not only for the families involved, and for their businesses and investments, but for society as a whole.

Note

1. *The Destructive Power of Family Wealth: A Guide to Succession Planning, Asset Protection, Taxation and Wealth Management* (Wiley, 2016).

Acknowledgements

I have many to thank for their support and input in my writing of this book. Over the last forty odd years, I have enjoyed a career that has allowed me to learn from the wisdom and experience of others and for this I am most grateful.

I shared an early draft of this book with a number of friends and colleagues and am most appreciative for the time and attention that was invested in providing me with comments that helped shape this book. While I have reflected many of these comments in this book, any errors are mine alone.

I have to particularly thank Peter Hulsroj, my law school classmate and himself an author, for his very careful review of my draft and the precise and useful input he provided. Good to know that Danes are better at writing English than Canadians like me.

Among others who provided me with great insights and edits were Stefan Liniger, with his emphasis on the need to explore the necessity for wealth-owning families to critically reassess their social role and responsibilities; Jed Emerson, for his plea that I turn the book into a call to arms for change and a reflection on the connection between how families experience the world and how the world policy framework is established; Jay Hughes, for his inspiring leadership in the field of family business and his insightful comments; Sammy Lee, for his brilliant ideas on how family businesses can learn from each other and from Asian perspectives in particular; Paul Stibbard, for his clear explanations of Islamic law; Pascal Saint-Amans, for his friendship and for his work in helping to address the challenges in fair taxation for our world; my childhood friend, Gary Gartner, for his thoughtful insights and deep knowledge of international taxation and for inspiring me to take up tax law; Amaury Jordan, for complaining about the length of the book (and more seriously, for the value of his input); Adrian Braimer-Jones, for his emphasis on the importance of families keeping it simple; Tom McCullough, for his helpful edits and advice; and Dr Paul Hokemeyer, for sharing his experience in dealing with the complex mental health issues families of wealth face.

Markos Komondouros, Britta Pfister, Andrew Halkyard, Simon Michaels, Lesley Lewis, Suchi Lee, Edmund Leow, Charles Lowenhaupt, Benedikt Kaiser, Bernard Rennell, Jeff VanderWolk, Jacqui Loh, Elena Zafirova, Xavier Issac, Roman Marti, Etienne Eichenberger, Veit de Maddalena, Gina Pereira, David Chong, Anthonia Hui, Leonardo Drago, John Riches, Michael Morley and many others also provided input on my early draft of this book.

John Connor, a mentor and friend, provided me with the opportunity to develop as an international tax lawyer and I thank him for this as well as for his insightful comments on my draft of this book. In 1982, John, an inspirational leader and the founder of a number of Baker McKenzie's Asian offices, had me join the Hong Kong office of the firm and embark on my journey as an advisor to wealth and business owning families.

And particular thanks to my wife, Peggy, for not only reading and commenting on my drafts, but for her well-founded challenges to some of my thinking. Peggy, and my sons Joshua and Luca, are inspiration and support.

About the Author

Philip Marcovici is retired from the practice of law and consults with governments, financial institutions and global families.

Philip practised in the area of international taxation in Hong Kong and Zurich as well as in New York and Vancouver.

The author of numerous publications, Philip is also the author of *The Destructive Power of Family Wealth*, published by Wiley.

A graduate of Harvard Law School and the law school of the University of Ottawa, Philip is a member of the Advisory Committee of the Hong Kong University of Science and Technology's Roger King Center for Asian Family Business and Family Office and a founding advisor to the Cambridge Institute for Sustainability Leadership in relation to programmes oriented to business and wealth-owning families and the contributions they can make to a more sustainable society.

Philip is a consultant to the CFA Institute in relation to private wealth management matters and is a co-author of readings on the subject in the CFA curriculum.

Introduction

This book is designed to share my experience in working with families and their advisors around the world. The book also reflects my work over the years with governments on tax and other policies relating to wealth and business owners and is designed to assist in necessary conversations about how our societies might better engage with wealth and business owners to help address, among other things, the realities of income and wealth inequality. The symbiotic relationship between wealth ownership and society is under constant challenge and questioning—something that is unhealthy in the absence of a clear vision of the end goal and what can be achieved if outcomes are optimized.

Wealth and business-owning families have much to contribute to society and where the family itself is strong and sustainable over generations, this contribution can be all the greater. The synergies that can be enjoyed where a family works on its own sustainability through a focus on what the family can do for others—stakeholders including employees, community and society—are exciting and real.

While my professional experience has been primarily oriented towards families at the upper end of the wealth spectrum, I am absolutely convinced that wealth can and does destroy *any* family, no matter what the level of wealth involved. A single asset, whether a piece of jewellery, a sum of money or a small property, can carry with it enormous importance to the younger generation—whether due to its value or for sentimental and emotional reasons or, as is more likely, both. How wealth transfers from one generation to the next, who gets what and when, carries messages that are remembered, rightly or wrongly, as being what the transferor 'meant'. Gifts of one asset to a son and another to a daughter may be well intended but may also end up leaving one of the children with a wrong sense that they were less loved than their sibling.

I hope that this book will also be a guide to those beginning their careers in the wealth management industry, and that it will help them understand the real needs of their clients, leading them to become effective, trusted advisors. For the more experienced advisor, this book will, hopefully, help make them even more effective in their work with families. And for advisors to wealth-owning families, I hope to encourage a way of thinking that supports the notion that wealth-owning families have responsibilities to society that go along with the benefits of wealth. This does not need the resistance that the idea might give rise to: wealth-owning families can come to the realization that a focus on what they can contribute to societal wellbeing can be critical to the family's own long-term success and sustainability.

This book begins in **Chapter 1** with an introduction to the *Theory of Change* as a methodology that can be used to help address the destructive power of family wealth. The *Theory of Change* is about working hard to develop a clear vision for the future and then work backwards to identify the steps necessary to ensure that the desired outcome and destination will be reached. In the context of families, this means developing clarity on the envisioned ecosystem for both the family and its business and investment 'engine' in the future. We then work *backwards*, identifying the derailers that can block the progress of the family—internal disputes, political risk, taxation, lack of adequate preparation of family members for their roles, poor succession planning and many other challenges. The focus is then on the *actions, inputs and outcomes* that can lead to long-term positive outcomes for both the family and its wealth and business interests.

The *Theory of Change* can also be a methodology for governments to use to help focus on what can be done to capture the symbiosis that can be achieved between society and wealth and business owners. A focus on the end goal can provide a clear roadmap to the inputs and actions that need to be put in place today.

Once I have introduced the *Theory of Change* as a methodology, the balance of the book fits into discussion of some of the relevant actions, inputs and outcomes that might be considered. This begins in **Chapter 2** with a look at how circular economy principles can be applied to family business and wealth. The circular economy, in large part, is about focusing on manufacturing processes and ensuring that resources are not only not wasted, but that value be found in resources that might otherwise go unused. This chapter of the book discusses how this thinking can apply to families and their wealth and business interests and how important it is that a family focus on its own sustainability before considering how the family can best contribute to society and wider community sustainability objectives.[1]

In **Chapter 3**, the book then addresses the world of taxation and the realities of tax transparency—an area that is often so complex that, despite its importance, those affected do not sufficiently understand how tax systems work. My intention is not to turn readers into tax experts, but rather to help them better understand not only how tax systems affect them, but how tax systems could evolve, for better or for worse. There are risks for wealth and business-owning families given the direction of tax systems. And there are even bigger risks, in my view, for our societies if more effective (and simpler) ways of taxation that respect the constructive power of family wealth are not developed.

A discussion follows in **Chapter 4** on the possibility of there being better ways to tax wealth and business owners given, among others, the realities of growing inequality and the need for responsible wealth and business stewardship. Here the question of whether society is optional for anyone comes up. While it is true that those with meaningful resources can choose where to live and work, there is a reality that our small planet does not allow society to truly be optional, even for the wealthiest among us. But optionality is a critical check on governments that must be maintained—how do we find the right balance and determine what is and what is not optional?

In this book, I attempt to address the topic of taxation in a less technical way than I did in *The Destructive Power of Family Wealth*. I also extend the discussion to outline the past, present and possible future of taxation, with suggestions for both those owning wealth and governments seeking better ways of addressing their policy and revenue needs. But in a discussion of taxation and more effectively taxing wealth and business owners, the important question of whether governments are failing to meet the needs of these taxpayers, to the detriment of their economies, arises. Tax policies might benefit from thoughtful approaches to providing value to the wealth and business-owning community in exchange for that community's important contributions to a well-functioning society and economy.

International taxation was the primary focus of my career, and clearly tax issues are relevant to most families considering the succession process and the protection of their wealth. Tax laws are ever changing, and in too many countries unfair approaches to taxation are part of the political risk, making the navigation of the tax world a critical thing for any wealth owner. My view, however, is that all too often tax is a distraction in the succession planning process. An over-focus on tax minimization leads to the neglect of what may be more important issues to the family. Where the wealth owner does not fully understand the tax planning being implemented, dangerous losses of control and other consequences result. All too often it is the tax advisor, obsessed with taxation and ill-equipped to address other areas, who handles succession planning for a family. The inevitable result is an insufficient focus on the many other needs of the family.

In relation to taxation, it is also important to highlight that families of wealth have moral responsibilities. It is often the younger generation that supports deep thinking on social responsibility and Chapter 4 is designed to help families see how important it is to *them* to be part of a fair and thriving ecosystem that includes employees, community and planet. Families need to align their actions with their values and be part of a paradigm shift in how wealth is managed and taxed.

Following the chapters on tax is a discussion in **Chapter 5** about the reality that any amount of wealth is enough to destroy a family, accompanied by some observations on the psychology of wealth and the mental health issues that can come into the picture for wealth and business-owning families. Among others, I consider the psychological issues that arise in and around wealth, and how these impact the thinking of wealth owners as they get older and their life circumstances change. I also discuss the effect of gifts on the recipients of the gift, as well as the effect of not receiving wealth that one may expect to receive. Gold-diggers, mistresses, paramours, illegitimate children and many more interested players come into the mix.

I am sometimes playful in relation to the messy relationships that enter the picture, but I do believe that there are some very practical lessons to be learned by all reading this book. Not everyone is as evil as I might suggest, and there are many nuances to the complexity of human relationships. But protecting wealth, businesses and families requires me to approach things in a frank and practical way. These psychological issues are often referred to as being part of the 'soft' issues in wealth planning—but the reality is that they are not so soft and certainly are not unimportant, despite their neglect by many associated with guiding wealth owners through the asset-protection and succession process.

When should the older generation discuss succession with the younger generation? Should details on assets be provided, and if so, when? Should in-laws be involved in family retreats that are organized to allow the older generation to communicate matters relevant to succession to the family? Will wealth destroy the dreams of the younger generation, or are there ways to avoid this happening? Are there ways to avoid wealth coming in the way of family relationships or is it normal for a parent to encourage their child to call their elderly aunt on her birthday because '*if you don't, your cousin will get her money when she dies?*'

As wealth owners age, is there a risk of their becoming paranoid about staff and family members stealing and are they afraid that if they give up their wealth, their family will no longer visit? Do failing memories put assets at risk? At what age should the younger generation come into wealth, and how do decisions their parents and grandparents make affect their life? Is it fair for a grandparent to spoil a grandchild with money, destroying a parent's attempt to help their children lead a fulfilled life?

There are no right and wrong answers here, but what is clear is that the soft issues count. The families that get it wrong on dealing with the many issues that come up are the families that allow wealth to destroy relationships and enrich lawyers who live from disputes among the younger generation.

In **Chapter 6** I then go on to discuss the *derailers*—the '*what ifs?*' that families need to think about if long-term sustainability of the family is among their goals. Despite being a tax lawyer, I have come to the deep appreciation that tax advice is only one of the many needs families have. These other needs, reflecting events that can derail a family's plans, range from protecting assets from political risk to dealing with second (and subsequent) marriages, divorce and the many other challenges to wealth and family harmony that can and do arise. All wealth owners have needs, but many of these needs are *latent*—needs the wealth owner has but does not know he has. And if the need is latent, and the right questions are not asked, the succession and asset-protection plan may fail a family that neglected to address a need, or derailer, that only comes to the surface when it is too late.

Following a discussion of the derailers is a review in **Chapter 7** of the *bridges and tunnels* that can help navigate around and avoid these events—a look at how the tools of wealth planning (trusts, foundations, partnerships, insurance strategies and more) can help address the derailers. Communication and planning are part of the process, and this chapter highlights a number of important planning opportunities that many families fail to take advantage of. Among the areas addressed is political risk minimization. We are living in unprecedented times of economic, social and political disruption, and the potential ramifications for political interference with international investments are great. There are approaches wealth and business owners can take to reduce risks associated with seizure, confiscatory taxation, asset freezing and other challenges, including taking advantage of bilateral and multilateral investment protection agreements. The discussion links this kind of planning to the earlier themes of focusing on the long-term desired outcome and on ensuring that resources (both human and capital) are not wasted—and how new ways of thinking and planning can deliver resilience to families.

But how does the wealth owner address their needs? This is done using the help of advisors—lawyers, accountants, private bankers, trustees and others. Advisors who, in turn, use the tools of wealth planning to address the needs of their clients. The toolbox is a big one, containing trusts, foundations, onshore, 'midshore' and offshore companies, partnerships, insurance strategies and many more structures and approaches that can be mixed and matched and adapted to meet diverse and changing circumstances. It is these too that the wealth owner and their family need to understand to be able to ask the right *'what ifs?'* and to make sure that the succession plan will do its job in addressing the holistic needs of the family. What is a trust, and how does it work? What are the right checks and balances to protect the interests of the family for the long term? Not every trust or foundation is the same—there are huge differences from one to the other, given how they are set up and maintained and because of who is involved. **Chapter 7** discusses the various ways the tools of wealth planning can be used, and also how they are all too often misused.

Relevant to the use of wealth planning tools and how they work is an understanding of the business of wealth management. Private banks, insurance companies, trust companies, lawyers, accountants, family governance advisors, asset managers and many others participate in the process. Advice and help for many families are a real need, but key is to understand the conflicts of interest that inevitably exist, and how those advising families should best be managed by the families taking up their services. **Chapter 8** is about advisors and how they are needed, but need to be controlled. I try to shed light on an opaque industry, hopefully helping families to ask the right questions and make the right choices.

The world is a complex one and the challenges for wealth and business owners are such that advisors are a critical need. How to choose and work with advisors is something that needs careful consideration and in **Chapter 8** I endeavour to discuss how advisors can prepare themselves for the future and the needs of responsible wealth and business owners. I address how advisors work, and the importance of the consumer of advisory services understanding how advisors charge and working to manage the many conflicts of interest that almost always arise.

Chapter 9 explores how it is possible to get it right—for countries, families, advisors and others interested in ensuring that wealth is positive for the families involved and the societies they live in.

Again, reflecting on the *Theory of Change* as a methodology, I come towards the end of the book with a summary roadmap to success in **Chapter 10**—working backwards from the goal developed to achieve family, business, investment, philanthropic and societal objectives. My conclusion is in a summary of how the *Theory of Change* can help families, and governments, navigate to a positive destination with aligned interests supporting the family, employees, communities and planet.

At the end of this book is a short glossary designed to help readers in their understanding of some of the terms that are used in dealing with succession and planning approaches taken—what are trusts and foundations, and what is the role of the settlor or protector? What are retrocessions (a nice word for kickbacks an asset manager may get for introducing an unwitting client to an investment). Hopefully the glossary will provide some help in allowing the owner of wealth to ask the right questions and demystify the succession process.

Note

1. The author, together with Professor Kenneth Goh and Iraj Ispahani, wrote a mini-book on the topic entitled *Circular Economy Principles for Family Business and Wealth Stewardship – A New Governance and Sustainability Framework* (Society of Trust and Estate Practitioners, 2022). Elements of that publication have been used in this book.

CHAPTER 1

The *Theory of Change*—Starting at the End and Working Back

I was first exposed to the *Theory of Change* at the Cambridge Institute for Sustainability Leadership (CISL) in England. Iraj Ispahani, a family business consultant I collaborate with, and I are founding advisors to CISL on programmes oriented towards wealth and business-owning families. In our teaching, we endeavour to help families appreciate the importance of social, environmental and economic factors to their own family, business and investment interests.

A key objective for me in my work with CISL relates to the importance of bringing all stakeholders, including governments and wealth-owning families, to an understanding of the contributions families can make to society and the important synergies a focus on impact can achieve for the families involved.

Use of the *Theory of Change* as a planning methodology is common in social change projects but has been little mentioned as an approach that can be useful in addressing planning needs for wealth and business-owning families. What I have begun to do is to use the *Theory of Change* to help families in their planning. My collaboration with Iraj Ispahani in this area has helped me develop my thinking on how the *Theory of Change* can be particularly helpful to families seeking to plan for the long term.

I also believe that the *Theory of Change* can help those serious about addressing the failure of countries to find the right way to align interests with wealth and business owners. I am hopeful that readers of this book will include policymakers, wealth and business-owning families and their advisors, as well as others interested in the important value family wealth and business does and can bring to society. This does mean, however, that some elements of my thinking on the *Theory of Change* will be more relevant to one reader over the other. It is also the case that not all aspects of using the *Theory of Change* in planning for families will be meaningful for every family. No two families are alike, and the complexity and volume of assets involved, among other factors, will affect how the *Theory of Change* can best be used.

In simple terms, the *Theory of Change* is a structured way to address programme planning and evaluation that teases out underlying assumptions, causal connections and anticipated outcomes, helping to guide and design a *roadmap* to change. One of the more important things that can result is clarity on the logic and rationale behind particular initiatives expected to bring about a desired result.

For me, the most important thing about the *Theory of Change* is the focus on the ultimate impact sought—the destination of the planning to be undertaken. In other words, the idea is to start at the end—what are we trying to achieve? Once the ultimate destination is clear, the approach is to then work back and ensure that steps are taken to reach the desired destination.

A typical *Theory of Change* can be set out in a diagram, starting with the ultimate *impact goal*, and then moving to the components that can help lead to that successful outcome. These components start with the *inputs and resources* that will be needed—in a sense, the investments that will have to be made and including funds, people, skills and delivery partners.

Most importantly, there are then *activities and strategies* that the programme needs to undertake. These are specific actions and interventions that can form an action list for those involved in running the programme. These *activities and strategies* then lead to *outputs*—the direct and immediate results of the programme activities, outputs that can be tangible and measurable. These outputs, in turn, lead to *outcomes*, which are the short and intermediate changes that occur as a result of the programme's outputs. These outcomes can include changes to how people think and interact and how things are done. Ultimately, these outcomes lead to *impacts*—the long-term overarching changes and goals that are aimed to be achieved.

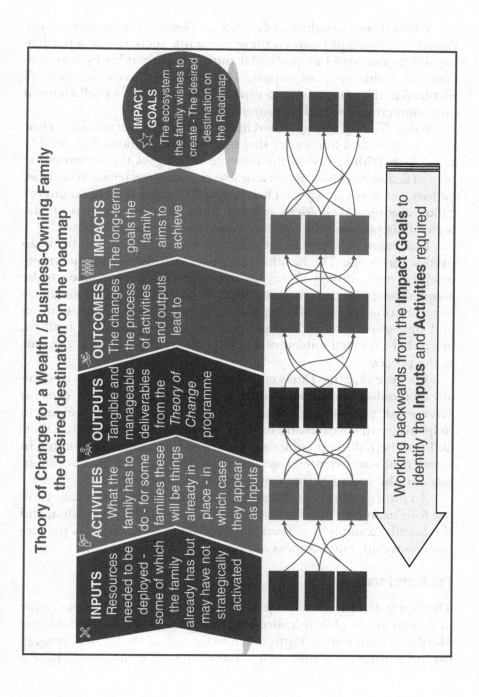

When shown visually in a diagram, a *Theory of Change* sets out the causal relationships between these elements, such as how a particular activity can lead to a particular output that then leads to an outcome and ultimately an impact. The *Theory of Change* can help all involved in the programme to understand the logic of each element and align efforts towards common goals.[1]

If the *Theory of Change* is used in the right way, it can provide a clear strategic plan and framework that sets out interventions that need to take place. With clarity on the ultimate *impact goal*, the design of the plan of action can show the measurable relationships between *activities, outputs, outcomes and impact*. The approach can also help in communication among stakeholders, helping those involved to focus on the logic of the plan and the outcomes and impacts that are achieved.

Evaluation is helped as the effectiveness of the plan can be measured at each stage. The fact that the *Theory of Change* is a very learning-oriented methodology allows for the approaches undertaken to be adapted based on ongoing evaluation and feedback. Resource allocation is clarified as critical components of the plan requiring attention and investment are highlighted. Further, accountability is built in, given that expected outcomes and impacts are articulated at the start of the process.

I believe that the *Theory of Change* can be used effectively by virtually all families undertaking future-oriented planning. The *Theory of Change* can also be helpful to governments and others seeking to help ensure that wealth and business-owning families maximize their ability to benefit their communities not only through taxation but in a variety of ways oriented towards recognizing the symbiosis of interests and the synergies that can result.

To illustrate how the *Theory of Change* can work practically, I will use four examples that I will return to. Three are family related, and the fourth example is a government looking to develop its policies towards wealth and business owners.

The Apple Family

The Apple family is made up of Reginald Apple and Martha Apple and their three children, Brenda, Susan and David. Reginald and Martha did not start out with much in the way of wealth, but through careful savings they now own a home free of a mortgage, have a comfortable lifestyle, and have put aside somewhere in the range of US$500,000 in savings. Now in their early sixties, Reginald and Martha are considering their estate planning and particularly how they might best ensure their own retirement needs and then help their children in their lives as much as they can. Both Reginald and Martha are employed and working full-time, though they do anticipate moving to part-time work in the coming years.

The Apple children range in age from twenty-eight to thirty-three and while all three are unmarried, Brenda, the eldest, is in a long-term relationship with Alex that is looking to become more serious.

All of the Apple children are working, but only Susan, who is thirty, is earning enough on her own to cover her living expenses. Reginald and Martha provide supplemental allowances to Brenda and David to help them cover their housing expenses, something they have had to do since Brenda and David left home a year or two after graduation from university.

The Bird Family

Alfred Bird is a third-generation Bird, at least in his estimation. Alfred's father, George, claims that Alfred is actually G-2 (second generation) given that it was George, in George's view, who saved the family business from certain collapse.

The family business, a chain of fifteen retail hardware stores, had its origin with the first Bird Hardware operation established by Alfred's late grandfather, Alexander.

Alfred is sixty-five and George is ninety-one. Alfred has three children, Emily, Doug and Frederick, and seven grandchildren. Alfred recently divorced his wife, Sheila, and has since developed a relationship with Sophie, who is younger than each of Emily, Doug and Frederick.

George is widowed and has just started a relationship with Giselle, 50, whom he met on a cruise he took two years ago with some friends.

The Crane Family

Sara Crane is a uniquely gifted and widely respected entrepreneur. Now seventy-five, Sara, three years ago, sold the tech company that she had established and eventually built into a globally recognized brand. The family wealth is now well over US$4 billion and is invested in a broad range of private equity and portfolio holdings.

Sara's husband, Sid, died five years ago, and Sara's three children, Ed, Sam and Syd (a name similar to her father's but with a different spelling) are all in their thirties and early forties, and married.

Dagland

Not a family, Dagland is a country that has been through tough economic and political times. Grappling with trying to increase its tax revenues, tax policies towards those considered 'rich' have become a political football. Traditionally a country that attracted global wealth and business owners, today most advisors to such families are encouraging their clients to look elsewhere to establish taxable residence.

Dagland is reviewing its policies and trying to come up with the right balance between what it would take to attract and retain wealth owners to the Dagland economy while ensuring that it can demonstrate fairness and a focus on the interests of the majority, many of whom have an instinctive scepticism about the benefits of wealth owners to society.

The First Step—Developing the Impact Goal Timeframe

Most of the planning that I have been asked to help families with over the years tends to be reactive. A change in a tax law affecting the family or a changing circumstance, such as a member of the younger generation moving to another country or getting married, triggers a review of the asset protection and succession plans of the family. What the *Theory of Change* envisions is that those involved in the planning process **start at the end**—where do we as a family, if it is a family doing the planning, see ourselves at a certain point in time? The approach is proactive and not reactive—the question is, where are we headed? If a roadmap is to be developed, we need to identify our destination.

In the context of the Apple family, maybe an appropriate date to set for developing the family's impact goal would be to project forward to when the parents, Reginald and Martha, will be in their 90s, so thirty years from now. That might be a time that reflects well the planning horizon of the family—they would like to ensure that, among others, Reginald and Martha are financially secure during their later years and retirement, and that all is set for a smooth transition to the next generation.

For the Bird family, planning might be somewhat more long term. The family business has been in the family for three generations, and maybe the family might choose a future date of fifty or sixty years from now for considering the family's impact goal.

In the case of the Crane family, an even longer-term approach might be appropriate. Some wealth and business-owning families consider things over decades; others think in centuries.

In the case of Dagland, and its hope to find ways to benefit its economy, a shorter-term focus, perhaps looking ten years ahead, would make sense.

Of course, the timeframes are rolling ones and can and should be adjusted over time. As steps are taken to put the plan in motion, the families and their business and investment interests will evolve. The *Theory of Change* can adapt, and the vision for the future will always change. And the same will apply for Dagland, the vision for which will evolve over time.

Developing the 'Impact Goal'—What Is Our Destination?

The *Theory of Change* contemplates having the stakeholders relevant to a project start the process by together clarifying long-term goals. In the context of a family and its wealth and business interests, this might involve family members participating in agreeing on the destination for the family, and then working out the pathways linking activities that might be needed to help the family reach its agreed destination.

The *Theory of Change* is both a process and a methodology, and has been used mostly in relation to social change projects. But there is much to be gained by families adopting the approach for their own asset protection and succession planning. The family can benefit from the process itself—working together to agree long-term goals and planning the journey to the destination by identifying and articulating the *inputs* and *activities* necessary to achieve the *outputs* and *outcomes* envisioned. The *Theory of Change* can provide a structured approach to planning that sets out a form of 'action list', identifies the resources that will be needed to reach success, and sets out ways to measure progress. Connections between resources and activities and the outputs and outcomes are identified and monitored.

So far, the Birds and the Cranes have worked out that their fifty-year vision for their families and their business and investment interests would be to have happy and healthy families that are supported by employees, partners, community and planet, and with an investment and business engine that runs on 'autopilot',[2] with prepared family members steering the way forward.

A bit more detail now, and maybe a bit more detail later, on the family ecosystems. In addition to an extreme balance between family and business, a similar balance between *I* and *we* can contribute to reaching the goal of having a happy and healthy family with family members well prepared for their roles. In many business and wealth-owning families, there is a neglect of the individual family member and the preconditions for his or her ability to become a confident and successful individual, in addition to their participation in the greater family. Having a part of the fifty-year vision focus on *extreme balance* here might therefore be of value.

Where the individual is truly independent, financially and otherwise, they may be better placed to commit to long-term stewardship of family assets. Creating this independence will again attract *activities* and projected *outputs*, all with a view to leading to the envisioned *impact goal*. More simply put, if the Birds and the Cranes want the next generations to steward their investment and business interests for the long, long term, maybe ensuring that each individual is fully financially independent and confident will help ensure an effective stewardship mindset and a commitment to the preparation for future roles that might be necessary.

The Impact Goal for Dagland

For Dagland, a country rather than a family, the *impact goal* will be different. Perhaps for now it might be articulated as Dagland, in a set number of years (say ten), having established itself as the country of choice for global wealth and business owners seeking not only a place of residence, but a place to establish holding companies and both non-operating and operating investment and management vehicles. Importantly, apart from the economic contributions wealth and business owners would be making by virtue of this activity, there would be taxing and related approaches in place that provide for a long-term synergistic collaboration between the country and wealth and business owners, including cultural and philanthropic leadership.

Taxing policies, among others, would seek to achieve, again, *extreme balance* between ensuring taxation that is fair, not only to the wealth and business-owning families involved, but to the overall population, addressing present and real income and wealth inequality, together with maintaining the country, with its focus on the rule of law and assurances that policies will not chop and change, as a destination of choice for well-advised wealth and business owners. How Dagland can develop a truly *regenerative* tax system that is focused on encouraging family-owned businesses and wealth is developed in later chapters.

A Snapshot of the Full *Theory of Change* Approach in the Examples

As mentioned earlier, developing a *Theory of Change* will involve laying out and developing on an ongoing basis the key elements and causal relationships that can show a pathway from where things are today to the *impact goal*—the positive outcome that is sought to be achieved. This will usually involve the creation of a diagram that lists, perhaps in individual boxes in a chart, the elements of each of the following.

Inputs and Resources

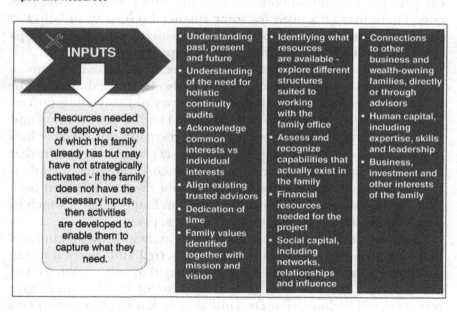

The starting point, of course, is the *impact goal*, which for now has been briefly described for each of the Apples, Birds, Cranes and Dagland.

The *Theory of Change* then involves moving from the end—the *impact goal*—to the beginning. What *inputs and resources* are going to be needed? This sets out the resources—financial, human and otherwise—that will be needed to undertake the steps that will lead to the *impact goal*. This can include financial resources that may need to be dedicated to the project: human capital in terms of expertise, skills and leadership from the family and those supporting the family (or from Dagland and those involved in helping Dagland to develop the relevant policies); social capital in terms of networks, relationships and influence; and more. The inputs and resources will adjust over time, reflecting additional needs and also reflecting that resources, in terms of human capital, for example, will increase as efforts are made to build such resources within the family through activities undertaken as part of the *Theory of Change* and otherwise.

In the case of the Apples, the inputs and resources to be lined up at the outset might focus on Reginald and Martha—the older generation—making time available to dedicate to the planning process. The resources of the family might or might not include all of the younger generation contributing time and thought to the process. There may be a need for some financial resources to help the family, perhaps with the help of advisors, to identify some of the steps that may need to be taken to get to the impact goal.

In the case of the Birds and the Cranes, more substantial inputs and resources may be available and may also be needed. This might include existing advisors and more in the way of financial resources. Family values may already be well developed and be part of input and resources. If not, the development and articulation of family values might be part of the next step in the *Theory of Change*—an activity that needs to be undertaken, the output of which (the values) can then lead to a desired outcome (perhaps clarity for the family in their decision-making process, which can be based on family values), which in turn leads to impact and ultimately the impact goal.

For Dagland, inputs and resources might include identifying and mobilizing the right human resources, internal and external to the government, as well as the time and money that will be required to develop the theory of change and implement it. The inputs and resources will include what Dagland already has to offer wealth and business owners, but likely these have not been well identified. Doing so would then be part of the next step—the activities that Dagland undertakes towards the impact goal.

Activities

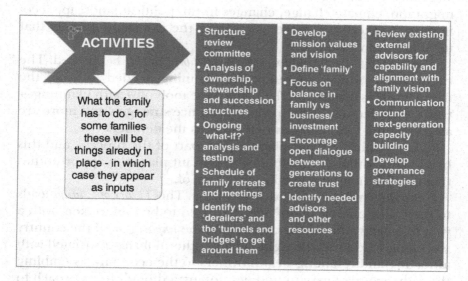

The *activities* that are needed are ones that are supported by the *inputs and resources* identified, and are designed to help achieve the ultimate *impact goal*. The activities become a kind of action list, helping the project managers, whether in a family or government context as in the examples, achieve the impact goal and ensure that the activities undertaken, which will be using inputs and resources, have the causal outputs and outcomes that will lead to the impact goal.

For the Apples, among the *activities* to be undertaken might be one or more family meetings to discuss the *impact goal* of the family and to have the *output* of a well-articulated plan that has as its *outcome* alignment of the family with the *impact* that disputes will be avoided and the ultimate *impact goal* supported. For the Birds and the Cranes, additional activities might include identifying advisors who can help the families create a schedule of family meetings, some focusing on family and others on business and investment interests, helping the family to move towards the extreme-balance objectives of their impact goals.

And for all three families, identifying and addressing the derailers will be key. The derailers are internal and external challenges to wealth and business-owning families—challenges that can derail the journey to the ultimate destination the family would like to reach. Divorces, dementia, family disputes, mistresses and paramours, fraud and more are among the internal challenges. Taxation, political risk, migration, climate change, changes in the political landscape, economics, markets and more are among the external derailers that need to be navigated.

To address the derailers, *tunnels and bridges* will be needed. The tunnels and bridges represent the planning needed to avoid the derailers. This brings into the picture the tools of wealth planning—trusts, foundations, partnerships, insurance strategies and more are all part of the tools that can help address the derailers.

Communication and planning are part of the process, and this book will highlight a number of important planning opportunities that many families fail to take advantage of.

For Dagland, the process is the same. The *Theory of Change* leads to the consideration of *activities* that need to be undertaken, with a view to *outputs* and *outcomes*, leading to the *impact goal*. If the country is seeking to identify the right tax and other policies associated with attracting and retaining wealth owners to the economy, assembling the right group of experts and developing a thoughtful approach to the development of solutions that can be explored with stakeholders would be important. For example, part of the set of activities to be undertaken might be a benchmarking of other countries and their approaches to attracting and retaining wealth and business owners to their economies.

Outputs and Outcomes

The *activities* that are undertaken as part of the *Theory of Change* will have *outputs*, and in mapping the journey to the *impact goal*, predicted *outputs* are set out and then reviewed as *activities* take place. If regular family meetings to review the asset protection and succession plan are an activity, a contemplated output might be alignment of interests among family members and an improvement in communication.

The *outputs* then lead to *outcomes*. The alignment of interests that are an output may have the outcome of family members having awareness of the planning in place and being equipped with the ability to consider and agree further planning approaches to be implemented to support the impact goal.

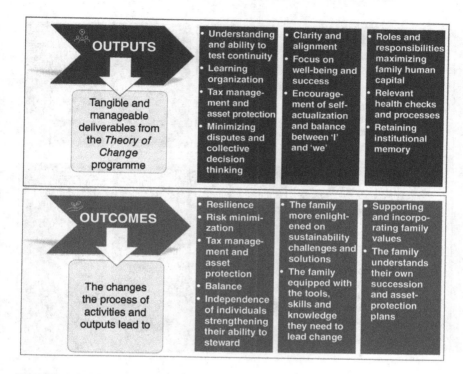

Impacts and the Impact Goal

Multiple activities will lead to multiple outputs, outcomes and impacts, and a well-developed *Theory of Change* diagram can show the causal connections that are expected. The collective of impacts achieved are all in support of the ultimate impact goal.

In the following chapters, I will use the *Theory of Change* as a methodology that can be employed. The key is to begin at the end—developing an understanding of the destination—the *impact goal* for the family or the government involved in the examples provided. The impact goal can and likely will itself evolve over time, and successful families will be adjusting their *Theory of Change* to take into account different and moving timelines. The steps necessary to achieve a 500-year vision for a family and its business and investment interests can be quite different from a ten-year vision. In the former, just the number of potential future 'family' members will be an important factor the family will have to plan for.

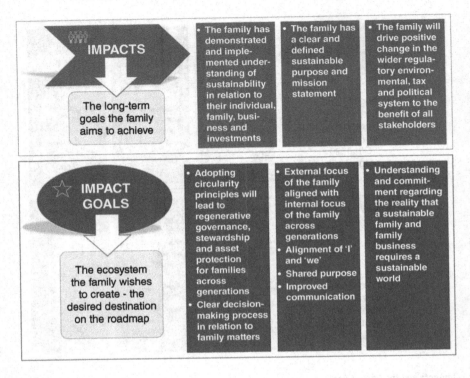

Notes

1. The diagrams that I have used in this book were developed with the kind and thoughtful help of Nicolette Fourie, the Chief Administrative Officer of Ispahani Advisory (https://www.ispahaniadvisory.com/the-team/leadership/nicolette-fourie-2/). I have worked closely with Nicky and her colleague, Iraj Ispahani, in teaching and consulting engagements involving the *Theory of Change* and the diagrams reflect our collective thinking.
2. Autopilot leadership is one of the many great ideas I have learned from Sammy Lee, in my view a top thinker on family business. Sammy is a fourth-generation member of the Hong Kong-based Lee family, with interests in a variety of sectors including the manufacture and distribution of delicious Chinese sauces and Chinese health products carrying the Lee Kum Kee and Infinitus brands. Sammy is Executive Chairman of the Lee Kum Kee Group. Among Sammy's writings are Lee, S., *The Autopilot Leadership Model* (McGraw-Hill Education (Asia), 2016) and Lee, S., *We Are Greater*

Than I: The Path to a Happier Life (Co-Creating Happiness Limited, 2021). I use many of Sammy's ideas in my work and writing, including in my development of his ideas on autopilot leadership and on the need for *extreme balance* in managing the interaction between family and business. As Sammy says: '*Discover the secret to sustaining wealth across generations: the art of achieving extreme balance between family and business.*'

CHAPTER 2

Applying Circular Economy Principles to Family Business and Wealth Stewardship

Together with two friends and colleagues, Professor Kenneth Goh and Iraj Ispahani, I collaborated on a mini-book discussing the application of circular economy principles to family business and wealth stewardship.[1] Elements of that book have been incorporated in the content of this chapter, and I thank Kenneth and Iraj for allowing me to share some of their words and ideas.

The use of circular economy principles in planning for the future in the context of wealth-owning families (and in the context of governments that might be interested in better achieving the symbiosis possible with such families) fits in well with the impact goals described earlier. Examples of this will be made in coming chapters of this book.

While wealth and business-owning families increasingly embrace sustainability as an area of focus, most of the dialogue on sustainability relates to areas *external* to the family and the governance of family and business interests. Climate change and other environmental issues, the need and benefit of considering the social and economic interests of all stakeholders in decision-making and much more come into conversations and actions around sustainability.

But, is enough thought being given by families and their advisors to the sustainability of the family itself, both as a family and in relation to the family's wealth and business interests? In developing

Theories of Change for the Apples, the Birds and the Cranes, would sustainability of the family, for the long term, be an appropriate element to add to the impact goal? If Dagland could offer, through its policies and laws, ways for wealth owners to achieve *greater* sustainability for their families, would this not be an attraction for such families to make Dagland their home and the place from which they conduct their investments and business? If Dagland offers this value to families, would this not help Dagland to sustain higher taxation than other countries that do not offer the same benefits?

Applying circular economy principles to family business and wealth stewardship can provide a new approach to governance frameworks for wealth and business-owning families. Circularity, in broad terms, means avoiding waste—not only of natural resources, but also of the human resources within families, including family members not directly involved in the family business, but who have a stake in the future and who need to support those in more active roles. Such family members highlight the kind of dilemmas families face—should a family member be channelled into working in the family business or allowed (indeed encouraged) to pursue their own career, reflecting their personal interests and aspirations?

The term 'waste' is misleading, however. As Gary Gartner—a close friend and trusted advisor to families in business—pointed out to me, my concepts of circularity are really about not only the re-use of important assets within the family (the common understanding of the term) but also the use of resources too often considered extraneous to the family business and investments. Overall inclusiveness, Gary emphasizes, is the key to ensuring that resources otherwise considered extraneous are used to extend the life of and enhance the family and its business and wealth interests.

As my co-author Professor Kenneth Goh says, the answer may not be *either/or*—perhaps *both/and* can be the outperforming decision—supporting family members on the path to self-actualization and exciting them about, and taking advantage of, the possibilities for them to support the family business and family members involved, and to contribute their personal knowledge, skills and experience in new areas the family business may expand to.

Wealth and business-owning families are aware of an increased focus in society on responsible and regenerative capitalism. But families must in parallel address internal issues that can become greater derailers than the challenges of the external environment. *Families must ensure that they themselves are sustainable.*

Embedding circular economy principles into the family system often involves confronting opposing or contradictory logics. Paradox thinking allows participants to see bridges between these opposing logics through the emergence of unimagined possibilities, allowing circular principles to be incorporated into the family system. Self-actualization is a good example. Can a family get fully behind preparing a talented member of the younger generation for a career that appears to have nothing to do with the family business? Or is the temptation to come up with rewards for those family members who comply with encouragement to live in certain geographies and take on certain roles? The paradox of the individual's ambitions versus what the family thinks it needs may well be an opportunity that has been misinterpreted. The notion of self-actualization is far from new, and much in the way of the current work of those teaching and writing about family business focuses on this. But the opportunity to achieve self-actualization of individual family members in a way that enhances the objectives of the family and its business and investment interests is what can be exciting to consider.

Families do not need to fear that self-actualization for each and every family member will compromise collective interests. Quite the opposite may occur if the hidden opportunities afforded by paradoxes are taken advantage of.

The Opportunities Afforded by a Circular Approach to Family Business and Wealth Stewardship

Family businesses and wealth owners must contend with manifold challenges today, including increased government interventionism, geopolitical risk, business disruption, technology-driven change, international conflicts and the climate crisis. These are some of the external derailers to the journey to the *impact goal*. More of these are addressed later in this book, together with possible tunnels and bridges to navigate them.

Wealth and business-owning families are aware of an increased focus in society on responsible and regenerative stakeholder capitalism. Families must in parallel address internal issues that can become greater derailers than the challenges of the external environment. Family continuity can be undermined without adequate preparation for asset protection and succession, and to be sustainable, and ensure continuity, increasingly the family should embrace circularity principles.

It is clear that the vision of the circular economy brings to light the important role of wealth and business-owning families to achieve this through their stewardship of family assets and their ability to make long-term decisions and commitments. Circularity principles, as defined by the Ellen Macarthur Foundation,[2] are eliminating waste and pollution, ensuring products and materials are kept in constant circulation, and regenerating nature. Through the application of circularity principles to the assets and investments owned by families and by the application of these same principles to the families themselves, the vision of a circular economy can be achieved—an economy that works for all.

The rising next generation should be encouraged to listen, learn and act as needed. To make the choices that are right for them. To take responsibility for their futures by engaging with their families' expectations. The rising next generations are the future of families and of our world. They should be better understood and supported so that family human capital is not taken for granted, wasted or overlooked. It is this next generation, however, that is already thinking this way and who are challenging earlier generations to get with the programme. It is actually often up to the older generations within the family to modify their thinking.

It is critical to have dialogue within families. The encouragement of the next generation to listen, learn and act does not mean that there is no need for lifetime listening, learning and action by all generations in the family. Learning within the family is a mutual undertaking.

It is also important to develop clear roles for 'family elders', whose experience can help in mentoring the younger generations. Families define themselves in different ways, some narrowly driven—perhaps by the family constitution—and some much more broadly.

Circularity encourages inclusion and optimal deployment of all family members, irrespective of whether there is a family business or not. One of the main objectives of a circular approach is not only to ensure that there is no waste—meaning that a family elder and their experience are channelled into effective roles—but that the family and its business and wealth interests truly regenerate as a result of the strength and resilience that the combination of a more effective younger and older generation can provide. This allows families to focus on their business and wealth creation, alongside maximizing their impact on communities and society.

In working on their *impact goals*, each of the families I am using as an example in this book can reflect on whether a focus on circularity would be of help.

In the case of the Apple family, the wealth of the family is owned by Reginald and Martha, and their impact goals include ensuring their own retirement needs and, as may be expected, their own health and happiness. Among their children are Brenda and David, both of whom are early on their paths to financial independence and are still relying on allowances from their parents. Having the impact goal include an objective of *not wasting resources* would mean planning for a time when all three children in the family can be financially independent, and when Reginald and Martha have enough for a comfortable retirement for themselves. To avoid wasting human resources, no early decisions in the family should be made to consider any family member as non-contributing—perhaps there are *activities* in the *Theory of Change* the family adopts that can help lead to the impact goal of all the next generation being financially independent. These activities might include additional training and education and simple encouragement—and careful financial management of family resources.

In the Bird family, Alfred Bird, a third-generation family member, recently divorced his wife and has developed a relationship with Sophie, who is younger than each of his children. Elaborated on later in relation to the *derailers* that can affect the plans of a family, second marriages can often be problematic, particularly where money is involved. Maybe Sophie is not well accepted by Alfred's children and, apart from keeping her away from family wealth, there are concerns if Sophie is being involved in the family business in any way. But is this not a potential waste of resources? What if Sophie has skills that would be useful to the Bird Hardware operation? What of the possibility that Sophie can help bring out the best in Alfred, helping him to not only be happy, but to outperform as a father and as a leader of the family business? And can this be achieved in a way that is not *either/or*?

Perhaps in the activities the family undertakes there is clarity about the financial position regarding Sophie and what could happen, whether or not the marriage lasts, using one of the *bridges and tunnels* to navigate *derailers,* such as a divorce, while finding roles for Sophie in the family business that help her to self-actualize and both be happy and secure and contribute to the family. And could clarity regarding Sophie's financial position and avoiding any risks to the main family wealth and business help create better relationships between her and Alfred's children?

For the Cranes, the transition has been from a business-owning family to a wealth-owning family. Are resources being wasted if the family does not consider ways to again become a business-owning family through engaging in *activities* that might allow this to happen? This could include developing the skills of the next generation, Ed, Sam and Syd, and perhaps adopting some of the approaches to funding private equity and entrepreneurial initiatives, as discussed later in this book. Success may not necessarily require that the next generation include entrepreneurs—yet perhaps setting the stage for the long-term preparation and encouragement of future generations will be what can create not only continuity for the Cranes, but a *regenerative* ecosystem for the family and its wealth interests that allows the next Sara Crane in the family to not only match the entrepreneurial success of the founder of the original family business, but use the resources of the family, both financial and non-financial, to outperform in ways that Sara Crane may never have been able to imagine.

One of my friends kindly helping in the review of my book, Peter Hulsroj, is mentioned in a later chapter. Peter correctly pointed out to me that families should also learn from the reality that many a fortune has been lost because a son or daughter felt obliged to try to match the achievements of others in the family. Peter suggests that while there should be plenty of opportunities given to the younger generation to show what they can do with resources that can be lost without pain, there is great benefit to allowing and encouraging family members to develop themselves in ways that may have little to do with the family business and wealth and which avoid their having to live in the shadow of others. I certainly agree, but do believe that there are roles supportive of the family and its business interests that all in the family can be developed to fulfil.

Dagland should also be considering its policies in the context of circularity. Are there *both/and* ways for Dagland to address the needs it has for revenues to put approaches in place that protect the vulnerable while also championing the interests of the wealth and business owners it seeks to attract? Can *extreme balance* be a way to guide Dagland along a path of understanding the value that wealth and business owners can bring to the economy, not just through taxation, but by virtue of the economic activity they create? Short-term, politically motivated statements that frame policies as attacks on the wealthy suggest an *either/or* approach. *Let's take away tax benefits for the wealthy to pay for a shortfall in our healthcare budget* as against *simplifying the tax system to broaden the tax base and enhance the attractiveness of Dagland to global wealth and business owners.*

Creating a High-Functioning Family

Not all high-functioning families are the same. For some, the family is defined by the person who created the fortune and all subsequent generations are included, regardless of their involvement in the business. For others, only those who have a financial stake in the family business are included, perhaps extended to their heirs and possibly a further generation. Clear tensions arise when the family grows and dilution of wealth occurs. Sharing a name, blood and heritage becomes more difficult to coalesce around. How a family is defined is critical to how the family operates, and aligned with this are the values that the family espouses and adheres to.

A circular approach can apply in all cases to maximize the human capital component of the family and its wellbeing. Simply put, unless a family is itself sustainable, it will not be able to fulfil its potential as a force for good over generations. A family that is able to achieve true sustainability for itself will be in the best position to contribute to the communities to which the family and its businesses and investments are oriented, and to the world at large.

Perhaps for the families in the examples presented, there are approaches that can embrace a growing family without diluting wealth. Here, stewardship of assets for the benefit of generations as against individual ownership can help, particularly when combined with clarity on the benefits (financial and otherwise) to be obtained by family members who support the generational stewardship of family businesses and wealth. This support might range from simply qualifying as a family member and not going against principles agreed by the family to taking on leadership roles that help regenerate family wealth. With clarity on rewards for different roles and outcomes, family members may not become *wasted family resources*.

Sustainability and High-Functioning Families

But what does sustainability mean in the context of a family itself? And how can a focus on circular economy principles help families navigate an increasingly challenging world of *derailers*—evolving political, economic, legal, tax and other risks that can compromise the ability of families to protect their assets against both internal and external challenges? How does the celebration of paradoxes and *both/and* versus *either/or* decision-making help families use circular economy principles to inform decision-making?

It often appears that there are only two choices—*either/or*—meaning that one of the choices will by necessity mean forgoing some form of other opportunity. Can both available choices be made at the same time and in a way that reflects true sustainability? Are families particularly well-suited to celebrating paradoxes and enjoying the benefits of a *both/and* decision-making process, providing yet another advantage family businesses can benefit from?

Families and family businesses need to be self-regenerative to contribute to society and sustainability initiatives—what does this involve? And are there ways for families to succeed beyond all expectations?

Wealth and business-owning families are uniquely placed to contribute to a better world. First, they are able to take a long view, putting them in a strong position to take action in complex areas in a way that can have real impact. A family business, for example, transitions through multiple political regimes. But unless the family and its own wealth and business interests are sustainable and regenerative, the longer-term ability of the family to contribute to society is at risk.

Second, a family business puts risk and control in broadly the same hands. Decision-making has the potential to be safer and more reflective of the interests of a broader group of stakeholders. Stability in leadership and authenticity can result.

Third, the opportunity is there for wealth and business-owning families to enlist the ingenuity of the next generation to achieve things that the older generation may not have even been able to dream of, and in ways that reflect lower costs—given the ability of the family to support investment and the efficiencies afforded by the volume of the family's assets, the availability of the family's advisors and otherwise. Unleashing this is a key part of a family being able to succeed beyond all expectations. In developing their impact goal, focus should be on this opportunity.

It is interesting to observe the frequency with which business founders instil a sense of inadequacy in the younger generation, creating a fear of taking the chances that entrepreneurship requires. As families work towards their impact goal, addressing this can be important. And there may be more to it than that, as Peter Hulsroj also pointed out to me. The feeling of inadequacy can also lead to inadequate risk assessment and deliberation, with deliberation itself misleadingly reinforcing a sense of inadequacy.

Many wealth and business-owning families have sustainability on the agenda. Discussions are held about the focus of the family on stewardship versus ownership, the thought being that the family business or wealth will be stewarded by current generations for the benefit of further generations of the family. This is a true value proposition, for it leads to a focus on the *we* over the *I*. But how many families undertake regular holistic continuity audits designed to review how family assets are owned, with a view to ensuring that continuity on all fronts can be achieved, notwithstanding ongoing change in both the internal and external environment affecting the family? Families need to consider the importance of ensuring economic independence of family members, something that can be achieved in a number of ways, with a view to helping family members develop the confidence to truly take a long-term view and focus on what is best for the *we*—the family as a whole and the wider circles of employees, community, society and beyond. Asking the right '*what-ifs*' on a regular basis is key, as is taking action to address areas of internal and external risk that could compromise the longer-term objectives of the family.

Looking at the three core principles of circularity, we can begin to see how these can be translated to the family level, and how these fit into the *Theory of Change* plan.

- *Eliminate waste and pollution*: In broad terms, waste and pollution are created by design flaws—it is not inevitable that waste and pollution have to be consequences of production. For families, the key is to focus on how the *design* of family governance structures, education and mentorship and more can address, upfront and transparently, the 'waste and pollution' of the family unit and the resources of the family. This includes non-family resources such as advisors and employees, who also may be a critical part of the family's 'plan B' if non-family support is needed at a variety of junctures.
- *Circulate products and materials*: Keeping things in circulation for longer periods is key to circularity. In the context of the family, this brings to light the importance of developing meaningful roles for all family and non-family members (i.e., trusted advisors, employees, family friends and otherwise). Stewardship of assets versus ownership of assets is a key element of internal circularity.
- *Regenerate nature*: Regeneration is about restoring balance and equilibrium. Equilibrium in the family can mean ensuring equal input—adequate voice from all generations, including the next generation and family elders.

Creating Alignment Between *I* and *We*

How does one create alignment between *I* and *we*? There is often tension between the personal agenda and the family agenda. It can be a significant issue for rising next-generation members who wish to pursue causes or hold beliefs that are not consistent with those of their families or family foundations, which often provide the funding.

To optimize family functioning, there has to be accommodation of *I* and *we* if families are to co-exist happily and flourish. Why should individuals in a family simply subscribe to collective responsibility because it is expected? Individuation is to be expected and respected as a source of identity. As Jay Hughes observes: '*The whole family's intention being to enhance that individual's process of individuation of happiness—toward the whole family flourishing.*'[3]

This definition of the common interest is vital and it being embedded during one's childhood, adolescence and early adulthood is fundamental. What the common interest is will vary from family to family, but each family must manage its own context by asking two simple questions: *Where did we come from?* and *Where do we want to go?* As Alex Haley, the author of *Roots*, said: '*In every conceivable manner, the family is link to our past, bridge to our future.*'[4]

The alignment of *I* and *we* can be relatively simple to achieve, and requires recognition that the '*I*' cannot be neglected—strong, confident and diverse family members can and do contribute more than family members constrained into a focus only on '*we*'. Related to this is recognizing the risk of the family developing what is, in essence, a fake '*we*'. Is the family's vision genuine and reflective of both what the family has achieved and where it hopes to go? It is often important for families to realistically evaluate what they really stand for and whether individual family members are aligned in understanding and championing what the '*we*' really is.

Incentive mechanisms come into the picture here, as do conflict-resolution procedures. In both areas, the right approaches can support the alignment of *I* and *we*. How the rules are set, what is done to get buy-in and more need to be considered, and the role of ownership and governance structures—such as trusts and shareholder agreements—need to be carefully drafted to provide the required alignment.

Achieving *extreme balance* between *I* and *we* can be an important impact goal for families to consider. And in terms of actions that might be undertaken, families might consider ensuring that the younger generation has a feeling of independence and that can likely best be achieved through clarity regarding finances.

In the case of the Birds and the Cranes, families with business and investment interests that they will be thinking about having future generations steward rather than own, having part of the wealth of the family pass to individual ownership might be part of what will ensure safe and committed stewardship. Clarifying the financial rewards associated with such stewardship, both in terms of compensation for work performed and added rewards for success, can be part of this approach. Further, recognizing that all family members—including those who may not be directly involved in operating or even supervising the management of investment and business interests—will be contributing to the family reaching its impact goals, perhaps periodic generational harvests can be implemented. This would involve sharing some of the growth in financial values achieved with family members individually, something that again strengthens the '*I*' and, hopefully, in turn the individual's commitment to a strong '*we*'.

While Valuable, Individualism Can Threaten Family Unity

At what point does the insistence on individualism threaten family unity? For example, if there is a family business, to achieve cohesion, everyone involved needs an understanding of the values that underpin the family business. Sometimes these values have to be updated and redefined, so that successive generations feel their relevance, or are at least reminded of them. You can base your strategic decisions on these values and use them to encourage the right behaviours. The grandparents' and parents' generations and their advisors must try to ensure that everyone is singing from the same hymn sheet. Embedding circular thinking in a family's mindset and modus operandi will encourage this cohesion. And, more simply put, not having to choose between the individual and the family as a whole, but rather choosing *both*, provides a refreshing approach to unity—a celebration of the individual and of the group.

Values may evolve and change: not so long ago, the world was very patriarchal and hierarchical; but today we have a flatter, more democratic structure, which allows and encourages more questioning. This, of course, is more the case in some cultures than in others. The younger generations are not as easily accepting of the approach of previous generations and must buy into any planned transitions within a family enterprise. If they are not listened to and their needs are not accommodated appropriately, they may vote with their feet and become detached from the family. Families that are clearer on their values, and whose governance frameworks embed and endorse these values—together with true respect for the evolving values of the younger generation—will be more successful in holding their family and business together.

It is also important to note that families do not need to agree on everything. What is critically important is for all to have a sense that their voices will be heard and respected, and that there are processes to take all views into account. And once a decision is made, the ideal is that the family as a whole agrees that whatever the decision made, all will back the decision and work towards making the decision the right one for the family.

Time to Rethink Family Constitutions and Related Governance Approaches

Disruption is likely to increase through geopolitical instability and technological advances. Family legacies in this fast-evolving environment will likely be more difficult to maintain, but a shared sense of purpose can add much-needed cohesion and glue. Families with longevity inherently do have an adaptive mindset because they have lived through and survived system shocks. However, the pace of change requires an element of rethink. Simply relying on thinking and behaviours that have served the family well in the past is not likely to be enough to thrive. Adopting a non-linear, circular approach is likely to better prepare families to cope with future system shocks and underpin living the family purpose.

In many wealth and business-owning families, discussion takes place on the development and maintenance of family constitutions and other means of documenting vision and governance. But all too often, what is in the family constitution does not find its way into the actual ownership vehicles that are put in place for the family. Complex trusts and other arrangements, possibly designed for other purposes—such as tax minimization—may not actually reflect the better-thought-out governance approaches covered in a family constitution (or the dynamic nature of family life). In the event of a family dispute, will the non-binding constitution have any impact on litigation that relates to a particular trust deed or other arrangement? Does the family really understand and uniformly buy into the family constitution?

Real sustainability for families requires that there be consistency between the objectives of the family (e.g., *We want to be a family in business for the next 100 years and more*) and what the family actually does in terms of how assets are owned and structured and how family assets, including human capital, are developed and protected. As families work back from their impact goal to consider the activities, outputs and outcomes needed to get there, a review of constitutions and governance is necessary.

Finding Value in 'Waste'

Circular economy principles involve eliminating waste to the extent possible and ensuring that resources are fully utilized. And the elimination of 'waste' includes maximizing the usefulness of resources, and uncovering the value and opportunity in 'waste'. This thinking can be applied to any industrial or other activity and increasingly is. But how can a wealth or business-owning family apply this thinking to their family and family assets? Are family members resources that are inadequately developed, supported and taken advantage of? Are underperforming family members excluded or encouraged to excel? Are mental health, addiction or other issues addressed with a view to a full-on recognition of the balance needed between *I* and *we*? Best practice would involve early interventions—mentoring and educating the younger generation; identifying individual talents and making sure that the resources the younger generation offer are being properly taken advantage of. These resources can include not only areas of interest and ability of the younger generation, but also their desire to be physically located in certain geographies.

It makes little sense to force someone who wants to become a doctor into studying business, considering the wrong signals on personal development this may give. A frustrated family member with a business degree may well be compromised and add much less value than a well-educated doctor with the right mindset to support the objectives of the family.

Maximizing the usefulness of resources comes into many elements of planning for families—but using a circular economy lens in addressing some of the issues wealth and business-owning families face can help ensure that planning is holistic and comprehensive. Early education within the family about the responsible and sustainable use of financial resources is important.

In evaluating the resources of a family, these extend well beyond physical assets such as interests in wealth and businesses. The experience of the family, its reputation and standing in the community, connections to those who support the family (e.g., employees, governments and others) are all part of the resources a family seeking real continuity needs to avoid waste. Most importantly, human capital within the family needs to be developed and preserved. Understanding and developing socioemotional wealth is an important objective that wealth and business-owning families should have. This relates to the non-economic wealth of a family, to which insufficient attention is often given. How socioemotional wealth is developed, protected and passed through the generations needs at least as much attention as economic wealth.

Adopting circular economy principles in family governance goes beyond perpetuating the family unit, but also means realizing value in 'waste': recycling 'waste' and extending the lifespan of resources through repurposing and regeneration. These concepts can apply to wealth and business-owning families themselves, but all too often are not thought about as legal advisors develop 'exit' mechanisms in trust and shareholding arrangements on the basis of valuing the 'pruning of the family tree'. Family business advisors often advocate the retirement of family elders to make room for the younger generation. Tax advisors may discourage the participation of family members holding particular citizenships, such as that of the United States. But is this all a waste of a family's human capital? Can inclusionary approaches achieve more than exclusionary ones? Importantly, families are well placed to lead by example and to demonstrate to their peers and to non-family businesses the value of inclusion versus exclusion.

For a wealth or business-owning family, adopting circularity means going beyond sustainability practices in the business—it means applying similar concepts to the family unit itself.

How Paradox Thinking Supports Circular Economy Principles

Embedding circular economy principles into the family system often involves confronting opposing or contradictory logics. Paradox thinking allows participants to see bridges between these opposing logics through the emergence of unimagined possibilities, allowing circular principles to be incorporated into the family system. Families must resist the instinctive belief that the way they have always done things is the best way to proceed today. Intransigence, or narrow thinking, can limit a family's ability to develop into an effective and impactful organization. Focusing on the *both/and* framework will encourage less rigid and more creative and pragmatic thinking.

In some prominent families, patriarchies by and large, little planning has been done for those in the younger generations who were not expected to enter the family business. Therefore, these multi-generational families often have more family members who are pursuing lives outside the family fold in an unstructured way, often enabled by the family dividend, which, while keeping them connected to the business, makes some individuals unhealthily dependent on the family shilling. They may have taken the off-ramp, but where is the on-ramp should they so wish, or be required, to join the business?

The most evolved single-family offices today proactively pay a good deal of attention to family education in the widest sense, recognizing that for the majority of the children of wealth and business owners, the best future is one beyond the family business and that the wellbeing of all family members is equally important. For too many wealth-owning families, the default position in the past was simply making sure that children went to the right schools and universities.

Career development and mentorship apply equally well to those who are seen to have a future within the business and to those who, at the outset, are not. Education is also critical in addressing a key concern raised by many families: to make sure that wealth does not become a disabler for the younger generations. Some families ensure that younger family members are educated in both understanding the key operating businesses but also, and more importantly, in financial matters to help them become 'better owners'. Most do not rely on future generations' abilities to run operating businesses, but they do need them to be able to make the right investment and divestment decisions to maintain and grow the family's wealth.

The natural tensions within a family over factors such as increased size, diverse interests, different risk appetites and geographic spread have also led to operational challenges, which inevitably bring fragmentation. A key differentiator is whether the family is still involved in an operating business or not. Many families see the operating business as synonymous with the history and core of the family; others see it as a chapter in the history of the family. The existence of an operating business usually creates a stronger emphasis on family cohesion, and this has often impacted the family's commercial decisions, in particular around very mature assets seen as iconic for the family.

For example, family members pursuing an independent career may lead to concerns about their separation from the family enterprise. *Either/or* thinking may lead the family to think about who is in or out. *Both/and* thinking gets people to consider possibilities for how to allow family members to re-enter or contribute to the business and family, regardless of their immediate area of focus and interest. They may come up with an inviting **revolving-door** policy and other approaches designed to embrace the reality that family members may move closer to, or further from, the family business from time to time, but even in periods of distance may be able to contribute to the family and its interests in a variety of ways. With this perspective, rather than splitting up the business, independent family members can strengthen the family business.

Instead of choosing option A or option B, adoption of circular principles allows families to uncover possibilities—different combinations of A and B and a broad range of variations between the two. This goes beyond a family being inclusive—it allows a family to be generative, thriving on the diversity of skills, interests and backgrounds of family members through the generations, including geographical diversity, which can be increasingly important in tax and political risk-minimization planning. A family can leverage divergent interests rather than being forced to draw the line between in and out. A family can move from mediating conflict to thriving on conflict.

How can wealth and business-owning families be sensitive to the opportunities for applying circular principles? Embracing paradox thinking, shifting from an *either/or* mindset to a *both/and* mindset, is an opportunity to move to circularity. This involves finding the connections, bridges and other points of integration between seemingly contradictory positions or imperatives. For example, a member of the next generation wants to become a veterinarian instead of joining the family business. Applying *either/or* thinking may involve the patriarch trying to convince his son to drop his plans and join the family business. A *both/and* perspective may involve looking into ways that veterinary expertise, knowledge and networks could benefit the family. For example, the member of the next generation might work with the family on a corporate social responsibility programme while being well prepared to support siblings or professional staff who are involved in running the family business. And if the veterinarian eventually develops a business relating to his or her profession, a 'family bank', as touched on below, might allow the main family business to capture a new area of growth for the longer term.

Families are complex systems and can benefit from parallels that appear in other complex systems, whether in nature or otherwise.

The more choices that arise, the more flexibility is needed in how things are regulated if success is to be achieved. Ross Ashby's introduction of the concept of 'requisite variety' can be helpful in supporting the idea that the more choices that are embraced by a family, the more likely the family and its business interests will adapt and survive.[5]

If the family constitution is, for example, the regulatory framework for the family, the more it can keep pace with growing variety within the 'system'—the family and its business and investment interests—the more likely successful outcomes can result. A family can and should be able to keep its goals constant, but to achieve these by varying and flexible behaviours, many of which cannot be predicted or fully controlled. A 'command and control' approach to family governance may not be fit for purpose if the objective is circularity and long-term success. Circularity can also alter perceptions of time. In the corporate world, time is usually linear, fast-paced and narrowly focused on the short-term present. Circular principles involve seeing time as cyclical, following the pace of regeneration and broadly focused on distal past/futures.

Having the right mindset is the first step—adopting circularity in governance and other structures the wealth or business-owning family uses is what it is all about.

Changing Demographics and the Roles That Family Elders Can Play

The good news is that we are all living longer. The fact that family members can live well into their eighties, nineties and increasingly over 100 brings a number of challenges—and opportunities. For wealth and business-owning families, there are many areas that need consideration in light of changing demographics. These include dealing with the dangers of dementia and the need to consider living wills and other protections associated with the challenges that ageing can bring. Protecting against varieties of elder abuse is also critical, though not always easy, particularly where a powerful but ageing family member falls into the clutches of villainous caregivers and others.

But in addition to addressing risks associated with ageing, the fact that family members may live much longer presents a number of other challenges and opportunities. If the matriarch or patriarch remains in a leadership role for decades, will this stifle the development of younger family members and even non-family executives? Will a forced handover of duties and responsibilities not only create friction, but also compromise the happiness and sense of fulfilment a deserving older-generation family member could otherwise achieve? Do decisions regarding the role of family elders have to be *either/or*—with either a fixed retirement age set or no retirement age and an elder being allowed to continue in what may be a dominant role for the long term? Among the issues that an *either/or* approach gives rise to is that it is pretty inevitable that resources will be wasted. Retirement that is premature will waste a valuable family elder's ability to contribute; retirement that is postponed may waste an opportunity to bring in the younger generation to take on a leadership role.

If the wealth or business-owning family shifts to a *both/and* mindset and uses circularity as a framework for decision-making, the contradiction between the family elder remaining in their role and a member of the younger generation taking on the role might be resolved. A commitment to finding a solution that provides both a meaningful role for the family elder that is one family elders will cherish and aspire to, while allowing for the mentorship and early entry into leadership of the younger generation, is a simple example of how circularity works: all resources are maximized and celebrated—not as compromises, but as carefully considered and crafted approaches to uncovering possibilities and developing them into lasting value for both the family as a whole and the individuals involved.

Circularity and Succession Planning

Good succession planning is a need that every family has. No family can avoid the changes that take place in the event of death or incapacity—changes that affect the governance of assets as well as their ownership. Yet it is all too often that succession planning is inadequate, resulting in wasted resources on any number of fronts, including that resulting from the costs (financial and emotional) of family disputes.

Succession planning involves many, many elements if it is to be holistic and reflect good continuity planning for a wealth and business-owning family. Here are some short examples of how a circular economy mindset can help in a variety of areas.

Dividing Things Up

Good succession planning means knowing what assets are to pass on death, disability or at earlier stages, ensuring that these are subject to a solid inventory, so everyone knows what they are looking for and is clear on who gets what. Lots of complexities arise here, including working out what assets should not be divided up and in this case how such assets are to be governed and employed.

A circular economy mindset may bring with it clarity that circularity can be achieved through a combination of ensuring that each family member is financially secure and understands how family assets can support their personal success. This clarity might include an understanding of what freedom there is in relation to the consumption of assets, as well as clarity on assets that are truly circular, belonging to no one in the family but being the subject of stewardship that ensures continuity. Coming into this will be the mix of financial independence of the younger generation, mechanisms to 'capture' successful endeavours for the long-term good of the family (e.g., through a 'family bank' approach as described later), as well as approaches to how shared assets will be enhanced, enjoyed and stewarded. Is it better to leave valuable and meaningful jewellery to one child, perhaps a daughter, injuring the feelings of another, perhaps a son; or to divide the jewellery among the children as a whole, with one then gifting a family heirloom to a temporary love who runs off with the item? Perhaps more circular is to have the jewellery be held in trust for the family for the long term, with a mechanism allowing for the use on loan of the jewellery to family members over generations. Will this ensure that a wider group of family members will enjoy the family heirlooms and preserve them for future generations?

At What Ages Should Family Members Benefit—Managing Expectations

There is much that can be said about the pros and cons of family members receiving meaningful assets at a young age. As in many areas of succession and asset-protection planning, there are no hard and fast rules. But what is clear is that younger family members receiving too much, too soon can compromise their enjoyment of the successes we all may enjoy at various stages of our development. Worse, mismatched expectations can result in unhappiness and, in the extreme, ruined lives and destructive litigation.

A circular mindset that embraces a *both/and* approach allows for the idea that one can benefit the younger generation earlier and hold back access to assets at the same time. Managing expectations is best achieved through early communication with the younger generation on the succession and related plans of the family. It is not important to discuss the value of assets, but it is good to let the younger generation know early on the principle that they will be taken care of in terms of health, education, housing and other basics, while not getting much more until much later. This information may well impact their drive to study and create their own success and get themselves ready for whatever role they may play in or out of the family business in future. And the more financially independent family members are, the more their thinking may move away from *I* to *we*—effective stewardship of family businesses and assets is much easier to implement where this occurs. When family members are forced to be dependent on their parents for money even into their adulthood, the likelihood is that on the passing of their parents, they will be clamouring for ownership (and not celebrating stewardship) of the assets their parents leave behind. This gives rise to a wasted opportunity to develop true stewardship that could be circular and regenerative, benefiting the family and those around the family.

Instead of thinking of financial independence as strengthening individual members at the expense of the family, embracing a paradox mindset surfaces solutions for how financially independent members can strengthen the family business and facilitate the shift to '*we*'. This adaptive mindset, which allows families to define success in a more comprehensive, open-architecture manner, is likely to lead to all the family's capabilities being harnessed in support of the family purpose in an optimal way for the family and for the business.

Governance

A family's adoption of a circular economy mindset, coupled with paradox thinking, goes beyond avoiding the waste of family resources to leveraging on 'waste' as a source of new opportunity. Leadership selection moves to an inclusive collaborative process that emphasizes the celebration of diverse perspectives and skillsets through shared leadership and roles, rather than an exclusive competitive process that emphasizes the selection of one leader and the exclusion of others. This opens the possibility of a number of family members rotating through important roles, which could fundamentally alter the dynamics of how family members prepare themselves and support each other. In a family business where new skills and experience are needed to deliver on the evolving strategy, it may well be that the best-qualified family talent is not working in the family business. In a supportive operating environment and culture, it is more likely that this external family talent can be attracted to, and brought into, an executive or non-executive board role.

Incapacity, Ageing and Dealing with the Realities

We are fortunate to be living at a time when we all have the chance of living longer, healthier lives. But changing demographics also brings with it challenges for wealth and business-owning families. Will opportunities for the younger generation to develop be closed by the older generation being able to discharge their duties for longer? Do increasing risks of dementia and other disabilities increase risk for the family business?

On the issue of ageing, there is a strong tendency to think in *either/or* terms. The term 'ageing' refers to an unchangeable, inevitable human condition brought about by the passage of time. People only grow old—they do not grow young. The past and future are distinct and separate. In the future, people decline and become less relevant. The past matters less, further into the future.

An *either/or* approach requires very difficult decisions—when should Mum or Dad hand over the reins and retire? Do we take away Mum's ability to sign things and handle her wealth at the first signs of dementia? Early retirement might waste a hugely valuable resource; not putting the younger generation in key roles may waste an opportunity to keep the younger-generation family members interested in being part of the business. Taking away Mum's signing authority may accelerate her feelings of ageing and uselessness, wasting decades in which she might continue to thrive despite the onset of dementia.

A *both/and* perspective surfaces practices that support circularity principles—practices that build interdependencies between the past and the future. A family elder moves into a new role at age 65—a role that better fits an active, experienced leader, now able to spend more time sharing and mentoring. The younger generation moves into the right leadership role at the right age. In the case of Mum, and the onset of her dementia, early on, even before anything manifests itself on this front, Mum is part of key decisions. For example, these might include that, at various stages in the ageing process, abilities to sign and manage assets move from *I* to *we*—and much like the thinking for the younger generation, there is maintained, for as long as possible, a true sense of independence for the ageing family member. Mum has access to reasonable funds and can make her own decisions on those funds for a long, long time—but not over chunks of assets that can compromise the longer-term interests of the family as a whole.

Divorces, Second Families and More

There is no end to the distress and destruction of family relationships and businesses that the realities of life bring. Divorces are destroyers of wealth (or, depending on your perspective, creators of wealth—particularly for the spouse entering a business-owning family, and exiting the marriage with a healthy chunk of the family business and wealth in hand).

Living longer and healthier lives is increasingly giving rise to more romances between participants who may have decades between them in age. And among the romances are any number of shades of grey—relationships that are in varying degrees driven by the economics at least perceived as being associated with connecting to someone wealthier and part of a wealth or business-owning family.

There is an industry around these relationships, and even litigation-funding firms that are now specializing in financing spouses seeking to detach themselves from a relationship in an exceptionally profitable way.

There are many issues to address in this area, but a circular economy mindset allows for approaches that are circular, and not *either/or* in approach. Clarity on the financial picture associated with relationships is part of a circular approach—an approach that is focused on avoiding the waste of family assets of any kind, including emotional wellbeing.

Early conversations with children about pre-nuptial agreements and the importance of communication with a potential spouse about the economics of the relationship are vital. Waiting until your son or daughter comes home holding the hand of the love of their lives to insist on a pre-nuptial agreement is a recipe for unhappiness, at least in part based on a right or wrong assumption that the discussion has arisen because of the parent's view of the wife or husband to be. Much more effective and meaningful is to have this conversation way ahead of any romances—ensuring that children understand the value to their future relationship and to the family and family business of having clarity on the financial deal associated with relationships, whether in marriage or otherwise.

A similar approach is vital for family members of all ages. All too often the focus is on the children and their marriages—but what of the 70- or 80-year-old patriarch who thinks the 30-year-old he is in love with is interested in him only for his charm and good looks, and not in any way for his wealth? And is this cynical view itself not circular in that it short-changes that 30-year-old in terms of what they can contribute to the wellbeing of their new husband and possibly to the family as a whole? Indeed, it is wrong and anti-circular. A better and more circular approach is to openly discuss and plan things with the involvement of *all* stakeholders. Perhaps the new, younger spouse needs financial independence and clarity regarding what they will get (and what they will not get). And this before the relationship is formalized. And the patriarch in love, perhaps through the family constitution or otherwise, will know that well before the relationship ever started he agreed that in the case of such new relationships, he would not only have a pre-nuptial arrangement, but he would part with a good chunk of his assets in favour of his family.

Could such a circular view avoid the waste of not only financial resources, but also the human resources lost through the mismatch of views that all too often occurs when there are second marriages or other similar situations?

These are only examples of the highly emotional and sensitive areas that come up within families. Sustainability and a circular approach may require work for a family to be in a position to address and speak about emotional issues, something that is by no means easy. Courage is needed, together with the ability to act with respect and develop a sense of goodwill in the family system. We see mediation and arbitration on legal principles and issues—why not on behavioural and ethical ones too?

A 'Revolving-Door' Mindset

Many family business advisors focus on the need to 'prune' the family tree. The rationale for this practice is that where a family member may be dissatisfied with how the business is being run, or is not interested in the business, it is important to have an 'exit' procedure that can avoid disputes. But buying out family members is not only expensive, it can also be wasteful. On the expense front, this can be managed through carefully drafted buy-out provisions in shareholders' agreements or elsewhere that allow for payments over time, and reasonable valuations. However, pruning denotes a permanent separation. Once a family member is out, this may mean a loss of a human resource asset—and not only of that family member, but the entire branch of the family involved.

The *'revolving-door'* approach reflects circularity and celebrates the *both/and* choice that can be made; it allows family members to temporarily distance themselves from the family business with terms for how they can return or be involved in the future. Perhaps this is backed by clear financial arrangements that give some level of financial support to all family members, regardless of involvement in the family business or other functions, with increased financial participation based on additional contributions. And the revolving door is always open in an enticing way—for the family member to return, perhaps on a buy-in basis, and to all of that family member's children and further issue—avoiding the loss of human capital that 'pruning' the family tree and an exit would result in.

It is encouraging to see the change in the way family members collaborate when they know that the exit sign over the door is not accompanied by a locked security gate keeping them and their children out of the family business forever. The revolving door encourages *we* over *I*, and an approach to conflict resolution and more that favours the family business being protected over the long term.

The 'Family Bank' and Its Relationship to the 'Revolving-Door' Mindset

A family may be celebrating the third generation coming into the ownership of a meaningful family business. Like most business-owning families, work is done on developing continuity and governance frameworks designed to protect the family business and to ensure effective family oversight, perhaps as non-operating owners of the family business. But how much work is done by the family to encourage and support the diverse interests of the younger generation? And is there clarity regarding how the family might support and capture the entrepreneurial endeavours of the younger generation? If there is no discussion and clarity on these issues, what happens when a child approaches her parents with a business idea that might be worthy of support? If the parents decide to make funds available for the business venture, who enjoys the success of the investment if the business does well? Who suffers if the business fails? The other children in the family may be resentful if their sibling is supported in an investment that then produces enormous success for that sibling, given the family investment involved. If the business fails, and the funds are lost, the reduction in the wealth of the parents will affect all the siblings, not just the one involved in the investment.

A circular mindset would question whether neglecting the possibility of capturing the entrepreneurial endeavours of family members is sensible. And, importantly, if assets are idle, is it not wasteful to not use them to support good ideas among the younger generation (or indeed coming from any generation)?

A better way might be for the family to develop a 'family bank'[6] mindset. This can be an informal approach that is made part of the family succession plan, reflected in trusts, foundations, wills and other tools used in the succession process. The approach can be more formal, and might involve the establishment of a family investment vehicle, and even in some cases an actual 'family bank'. But the main objective is to discuss and agree, within the family, an approach to be taken to encourage and support entrepreneurial activity in the younger generation. And, where appropriate, to have a formula that might allow for such entrepreneurial activity to be 'captured' by the family.

Among the approaches a family might consider would be:

- Funds are set aside and made available to support entrepreneurial activities in the younger generation. An approach to evaluating investment possibilities is developed and agreed. This might involve links to third-party valuers and business consultants to help guide investment decisions.
- A family member with a business idea presents the idea to the 'family bank'. If an investment is to be made, it follows an agreed approach—this might, for example, involve the 'family bank's' investment taking the form of debt and equity—say 80% being in the form of debt, carrying an agreed rate of

interest, and 20% being equity. If the investment made by the family member promoting the project is successful, the 'family bank' owns a 20% interest in the business and will be repaid the 80% debt. If unsuccessful, the 'family bank' has lost its 20% equity investment, but the debt portion is taken out of the relevant family member's future share in family assets. The percentages and approach matter less than coming to a clear understanding within the family, in advance, on the economics of investments made by the family in the endeavours of any individual family member.
- In order to 'capture' the business for the long-term endeavours of the family as a whole, the investment by the 'family bank' might carry with it options for the family to purchase the business in different circumstances including, likely, first-refusal rights.

The 'family bank' can be used for more than just fostering entrepreneurship. The approach can be used to provide financial support in the case of incapacity, ageing and otherwise. There may be foundations or trusts used for this type of family support, but with financing provided by the 'family bank', perhaps operating as a feeder fund distributing certain revenues to support the structures that protect family members as they move through life's transitions.

Using Circular Economy Principles in Conflict Resolution

Embedding circular principles in the context of conflict can lead to generative outcomes. For example, sibling rivalry could be harnessed by having different siblings rotate their leadership of different businesses. Disagreements about dividend payouts could lead the family to work out a way for family shareholders to value their holdings and cash out, or to set up new vehicles that cater to different stakeholder needs. Importantly, underlying these principles is the acceptance that family members have different needs and motivations.

Differences need not lead to relational disharmony and separation. A *both/and* mindset helps one see the importance of putting in place structures and processes that allow differences to exist while maintaining relational harmony.

Political Risk and Asset Protection

In simple terms, political risk has to be considered at three levels. First, attention needs to be paid to political risk in the country of the citizenship and/or residence of the wealth owner. This may involve dealing with more than one country, given that there may be multiple citizenships and places of residence involved. Second, political risk needs to be considered in the location where investment structures are maintained. A wealth owner may live in the United Kingdom, for example, but there may be trusts, companies, partnerships, investment funds or other holding vehicles located somewhere else. The jurisdiction in which the structure is maintained is also highly relevant to any political risk-minimization strategy. Third, of course, is the country in which an investment is made.

Compared with commercial risks, political risks can be amorphous and hence difficult to predict and manage. Moreover, the political risks in the country of investment are likely to be different from those of the home country. Political risks can manifest themselves in varied and challenging ways. Examples range from circumstances of revolution, civil unrest and civil war to politically charged changes in regimes or governments, or—more prosaically—marked policy and regulatory changes or discrimination. Moreover, recent and wide-ranging international changes to tax and transparency frameworks are related to political risk. As mentioned above, risks can exist in the countries of intermediate structures, such as investment vehicles, partly due to ongoing challenges to traditional offshore centres.

A circular approach to de-risking includes taking advantage of the geographic diversity of family members and assets, and here making use of a number of de-risking techniques, including the careful use of investment protection agreements and otherwise. But a focus on diversification of ownership—simply not having all of your eggs in one basket—is an important step.

Diversification typically breeds complexity, which reinforces the importance for a clear vision, strategy and governance. A huge part of that vision is the overarching purpose. Diversification is not only about a diversification of the family business or assets, but also about diversification of ownership. Most families understand the need to diversify their investments—less of a focus for many families is the desirability of diversifying how assets are owned and by whom within the family. All too often, there is one holding company, possibly owned by a single trust, which holds all family investments. But in a world of considerable risk, political and otherwise, diversifying ownership can be important. This might involve having different family members own different portions of the family business and investments, possibly within understandings between family members on how they will support each other in times of crisis. Ownership diversification can also involve using different vehicles to own different assets—having more than one trust, and using partnerships, insurance strategies and other structures to hold assets, creating a diversification of ownership. The ownership of the 'family bank' can be part of this diversification. And for some families, the actual ownership of a bank, regulated in its ability to return capital, may be part of an overall asset protection strategy.

Cultural and Religious Approaches to Succession Planning and a Circular Economy Mindset

It is interesting to learn from wealth and business-owning families and to observe their varying perspectives on the role of culture and religion on succession planning and other approaches affecting the governance of family businesses.

In very broad terms, the reality is that there are more similarities among families around the world than there are differences, and culture is often overplayed as something that will reduce family disputes and the pitfalls of inadequate holistic continuity planning. Being a Chinese family, or an Indian family, or a Jewish family, or a Catholic family or a family following *Sharia* principles is not a guarantee that the all-too-regular roadblocks to smooth transitions will not arise. This said, there are elements of circularity in some religious and cultural approaches to succession planning that we can all learn from. There are also circular economy mindset principles that can enhance the way in which cultural or religious approaches are applied to the succession process. This may also serve to protect a family's spiritual capital.

In a number of cultures, the family business has been viewed as something that transitions to the eldest son, and with only family members carrying the family name (the sons of sons) participating in the family business. While this approach runs entirely contrary to the circular mindset given the 'waste' of family resources it results in, there are elements of circularity in the historical elements of the approach that are sometimes forgotten.

Potentially wasted resources include, of course, the female line in the family as well as the males who do not carry the family name—the sons of the daughters in the family. Other potential wastes of resources include capable in-laws, and the males in the family younger than the oldest son—which males may well be better business leaders than their older brother, something suggested by studies by, among others, Professor Roger King of the Hong Kong University of Science and Technology's Roger King Center for Asian Family Business and Family Office.

But a model of succession that clarifies governance has positives—the elder son knows his responsibilities and if the family buys in to the overall approach, the roles of all family members are clear, to support the elder son and to adopt roles for themselves (and to prepare themselves and their children for these roles). In the modern world, it is all too often the case that the imposition of traditional approaches to succession represents a historical family mindset that does not fit with the westernized modern mindset of the younger generation—meaning that the family does not buy into the way this was all meant to work. Those left out—whether daughters, in-laws or younger brothers—fail to prepare themselves for and fulfil the roles they could have played in supporting the success of the family business.

There are elements of traditional succession approaches that are circular and might provide useful guidance. A clarity of roles can be critical to successful succession planning—as can objective versus subjective approaches to the selection of leaders. If we know that the elder son will be the boss, the friction associated with selection is avoided. If we know that we are not one of the members of the family who will be running the show, we know we should be out there making our own way in the world. If we know we are the elder son, we should also know the full range of responsibilities this brings—not only responsibilities for the family business, but responsibilities for the family as a whole, including the responsibility to ensure that all family members have opportunities to develop themselves independently.

Properly applied (which in the modern world it is all too often not), there can be benefits to a traditional succession approach.

More exciting is where some of the thinking behind traditional succession approaches is combined with a circular economy mindset and modernized. Rather than having the elder son run the show, there is recognition that success will come from a move away from an *either/or* mindset to a *both/and* approach. Maybe the ultimate leadership of the family business correctly goes to the most capable in the family—which might be a daughter who is not the eldest of her gender. But a clarity of role of the elder son and the responsibilities for the family overall is also in the mix—together with the traditional approach of having all family members fully support each other (the '*we*' rather than the '*I*').

For Muslim families, *Sharia* principles can influence succession depending on the relevant connecting factor, such as the location of assets, domicile, nationality and residence. Broadly, and this varies considerably between different schools of *Sharia*, daughters get half of what sons do, and, interestingly, succession rules require that assets be divided and distributed at death. On this latter point, this can be highly destructive of a family business, as it requires that the business be divided on death. There are tools and approaches that can be used to manage this, including the use of shareholders' agreements and lifetime gifts, but the often-used western concept of discretionary trusts, which can keep assets out of direct ownership of the younger generation, is generally not acceptable under *Sharia*.

First, those governed by *Sharia* can learn from the circular economy mindset and use a variety of approaches that are *Sharia*-compliant to achieve the benefits of circularity—the avoidance of wasted resources, including daughters and including implementing ways of succession that focuses on *we* versus *I*. Second, those observing *Sharia* from a distance, together with families committed to *Sharia*, can benefit from the learnings *Sharia* provides. A clarity of who gets what and the requirements on succession that are objective rather than subjective do much to avoid the mess that families often get into when they seek to communicate with their wealth—making subjective decisions on succession rather than being guided, as *Sharia* does, into treating all sons equally between them, and all daughters equally between them. The *Sharia* approach avoids assets going into 'suspension' on death, as they often do in the discretionary trust model—a concept described later in this book. This can result in the younger generation being detached from their personal connection to the family business or family wealth, which may well bring less successful outcomes.

In the context of families seeking to use a circular economy mindset, combining the idea of having each family member have financial independence, as is assured under *Sharia*, can help each member of the younger generation feel, given their financial security, that they can now focus on the '*we*'—not only the family, but also the community, the world and the greater good.

Elimination of waste and pollution; circulation of products and materials; regeneration of nature—the principles of circularity can help wealth and business-owning families to develop governance, stewardship and asset-protection strategies that are regenerative and align the external focus of the family with its work on the internal. Where there is alignment, there is potential for much more than continuity and stewardship—there is potential for true self-actualization of all family members, ensuring emotional well-being and alignment with the objectives of the family for its own businesses and wealth, and for how these can benefit all stakeholders for the very long term.

Notes

1. *Circular Economy Principles for Family Business and Wealth Stewardship—A New Governance and Sustainability Framework,* Philip Marcovici, Kenneth T. Goh and Iraj Ispahani, with illustrations by Emma Nesset, published by the Society of Trust and Estate Practitioners (STEP), 2022 with editorial support from Louise Polcaro of STEP. A free download of this book is available on the STEP website (https://www.step.org/research-reports/responsible-stewardship-wealth). Iraj Ispahani is the founder and principal of Ispahani Advisory and Professor Kenneth Goh is Associate Professor of Strategy & Entrepreneurship and Academic Director of the Business Families Institute at the Lee Kong Chian School of Business at Singapore Management University.
2. https://ellenmacarthurfoundation.org/topics/circular-economy-introduction/overview. Note that the Macarthur Foundation has sought to simplify concepts on circularity that have been the subject of considerable original and foundational analysis.

3. Hughes, J. E., Massenzio, S. E. and Whitaker, K., *The Voice of the Rising Generation: Family Wealth and Wisdom* (Bloomberg/Wiley, 2014).
4. Haley, A., *Roots* (Vintage Books, 1994). Quote sourced from https://www.goodreads.com/quotes/search?utf8=%E2%9C%93&q=In+every+conceivable+manner%2C+the+family+is+link+to+our+past%2C+bridge+to+our+future&commit=Search
5. See Dilts, R., *The Law of Requisite Variety* (NLP University Press, 1998).
6. The notion of a 'family bank' was introduced in Chapter 7 of the first edition of *Family Wealth: Keeping It in the Family* and reprised in the second edition published by the publishers of this book. Hughes, J. (Jay) E. Jr, *Family Wealth: Keeping It in the Family – How Family Members and Their Advisers Preserve Human, Intellectual, and Financial Assets for Generations* (2nd Revised and Expanded Edition) (Wiley, 2010). Jay reminded me that the idea of a family bank was one developed by Jay's father and which Jay then used in his further research and writing.

CHAPTER 3

Understanding the World of Taxation and the Realities of Tax Transparency

The art of taxation consists in so plucking the goose as to obtain the largest possible amount of feathers with the smallest possible amount of hissing.[1]

A growing number of families are international. Family members may live in different countries or hold different citizenships, and investments are increasingly likely to be maintained cross-border. Ever-changing tax laws are part of an almost unlimited number of other threats to wealth, adding to the burden for those seeking to maximize what can pass from one generation to the next.

Navigating a world of growing complexity and transparency is increasingly difficult, forcing wealth owners into the hands of private bankers, trustees, accountants, lawyers and a variety of other specialists who make their living from the needs of the wealthy. But does the wealth owner and his or her family really understand the planning and structures that are imposed on them by their advisors, and the many hidden charges and risks associated with typical wealth-planning devices? Is it safe to rely on outsiders whose interests may be starkly different from those of the family involved?

A wealth owner has responsibilities—and one of the most important of these is to really understand how one's own wealth is owned and how the structures implemented work—both in terms of their suitability to address the objectives for which they were created and in terms of their real costs and what security, if any, they provide against known and unknown risks. Even more critical is to understand what succession plan is actually in place, and its potential consequences for the younger generation.

In relation to the *Theory of Change* and the examples of the Apple, Bird and Crane families, understanding tax systems and their impact is part of the process of working towards the impact goals the families have identified. Relevant, of course, is to take steps that will protect family assets from taxation that could derail the hopes of the family for the future. But also relevant, and in need of careful consideration, will be how the families can responsibly ensure that the interests of all stakeholders are protected.

Simply put, is the impact goal for each family to avoid all taxation and not to participate in the obvious needs of society—to pay for the many costs of an effective government? In the ideal world, taxes are something that wealth and business-owning families should be more than comfortable to pay, recognizing the value they receive in return from the communities to which they are connected. This is part of what applying a circular economy approach to family business and wealth stewardship, the topic covered in the last chapter, would involve. Unfortunately, there is a reality that tax laws are often overly complex and outright dangerous for those who do not obtain the right guidance. An inheritance tax of half or more of the value of assets can be destructive for the impact goals of a wealth-owning family seeking to ensure succession over generations—but also disturbing is the reality that where countries have an inheritance tax at such levels, there are often planning techniques that are accepted to avoid the tax. *Derailers* on the road to a family's impact goal are addressed in Chapter 6, and tax can certainly also be an important derailer requiring the use of wealth planning tools and approaches to be navigated.

I am an advocate of low tax rates and simplicity. But this is not the way our tax laws around the world work. So, for the Apples, the Birds and the Cranes, understanding how tax systems work will be critical. And for Dagland, seeking to establish itself as a country of choice for wealth owners to live and work in, the opportunity to attract those who can contribute to the economy is outstanding.

Avoiding the Tax Tail Wagging the Dog

Before embarking on explorations of the world of taxation and its potential complexities, it is critical to highlight the dangers of letting the tax tail wag the dog. All too often, planning decisions for wealth and business owners are driven by tax-minimization objectives, the benefits of which may be far outweighed by other issues that should have been addressed by the family early on.

For those who put off their succession planning, understanding that *no plan is a plan* is also vital. In the event of death or disability, something will happen to your assets regardless of whether appropriate planning has been done. Have you worked out what will happen if you pass away? Who actually knows about the assets you have and where they are?

Fast-forward to a World of Tax Transparency

The tax landscape for wealth-owning families has been fast changing. Transparency and tax compliance are now much more the norm than was the case a decade or two ago. This is a positive development, given the financial challenges faced by governments seeking to address the needs of their populations and the growing inequality of wealth. But the road to transparency has not been a smooth one.

Wealth-owning families need to understand how the world has been moving towards transparency and the critical importance of tax compliance. It is also critical for families to be aware of how tax laws work and develop, and how wealth owners can legally and properly take advantage of approaches that will help protect wealth and avoid unnecessary tax exposures. But there is one bottom line: a wealth owner only has two choices. *Play by the rules of your country, or get out of your country.* There is no choice, despite the ways of the past, that allows for sitting in your country and hoping no one will find out about hidden assets and income. And the ability of tax authorities to find out about hidden assets and income is getting better and better.

And on the choice of getting out—something elaborated on later on—this is also a choice that is looking to become severely limited in the years to come. This raises the question of whether 'society' should be optional for wealth owners in the sense that they can just choose to leave if unhappy with, among others, the tax system of a country they are connected to. The *optional society* is a topic addressed later in this book.

For those involved in developing tax policy, particularly where, as is the case for Dagland in my example, there is a desire to come up with the right balance between what it would take to attract and retain wealth owners to the economy while ensuring fairness and focus on the interests of the majority, understanding how tax laws work internationally and the choices available to wealth owners is critical. For the families in my examples, developing an effective *Theory of Change* that leads towards the desired impact goal will require that family members understand how taxation will have an effect on their plans for the future. It is remarkable how the opportunities for countries to engage with wealth owners and benefit from what they can contribute to society are so often squandered.

Can We Blame It All on Bank Secrecy and the Ways of the Past?

For many years, the wealth management industry and a number of financial centres around the world directly or indirectly supported the misuse of bank secrecy to the detriment of both interested governments and wealth-owning families. These abuses have led to dramatic changes and often ones that go further than they need to go. Short-term thinking by those promoting *hiding the money* has led to outcomes that could have been avoided through a collaborative and open approach to balancing the privacy rights of wealth owners with their tax-paying obligations.

The United States took its first major step towards addressing offshore tax evasion when it introduced a regime known as the Qualified Intermediary (QI) system in 2001. America, through the QI system, successfully encouraged banks around the world to become their partners in tax enforcement, with virtually every meaningful bank involved in wealth management having become a 'qualified intermediary', required to identify and document US interests in bank accounts, whether directly owned or through, in certain cases, structures.

To avoid punitive withholding taxes on investments in American securities, even the most die-hard secrecy-based private banks signed on for a complex system that required banks *globally* to learn the nuances of US international tax rules. Backed up by independent audits, QIs made many promises to the United States under the system—and all under agreements that were written by the United States, could not be negotiated, and could even be changed by the Americans without the consent of the other contracting party, the bank involved.

And in case this is all getting too boring, a reminder. Under the QI system, information about the income and assets of affected taxpayers is passed on electronically to a relevant tax authority by an intermediary bank. This is the main message ... under the QI system, and under other regimes described later, it is nearly impossible to keep information about bank accounts secret. Clients are required to allow their banks to share information with their countries of residence and, in the case of the United States, citizenship.

Interestingly, rather than entering into negotiation and dialogue over the request of the United States to introduce the QI system, virtually every offshore centre and private bank took the defensive approach of simply agreeing to move forward with the QI system. In a sense, how the QI system came into existence is a good example of what happens when there is no focus on the ultimate impact goal, as would have been the case had jurisdictions with an interest in serving the needs of wealth and business owners adopted a thoughtful *Theory of Change*.

For many banks operating in the 'offshore' world, the thought was that the United States was a relatively small market for them, and they did not want to rock the boat when it came to the broader issues in and around misuse of bank secrecy for wealth owners from other countries. Had, however, a clear and reasonable request been made that whatever system the United States sought to implement would have to be reciprocal, perhaps the QI system could have been delayed by years. In other words, if a country were to say that it was prepared to provide information to the United States about US taxpayers using that country's banking system, but *in exchange* for information about its taxpayers using the US banking system, this would have made much sense.

It could also have been that a more thoughtful approach to ensuring tax compliance would have been put in place, better balancing the privacy and other interests of taxpayers and their banking intermediaries. The reality is that the United States would have been unable to deliver reciprocity given the operation of its own bank secrecy rules and accompanying tax laws, which severely restrict any exchange of information on non-US owners of bank accounts and structures in the United States. Interestingly, this lack of reciprocity continues today, with the United States being virtually the only serious country not participating in the Organisation for Economic Co-Operation and Development (OECD)'s common reporting standard (CRS), which is a global system of automatic information exchange.

For many, the QI system was not recognized for what it was—a *first* step in tax transparency ... not a *last* step. As can now be seen from the number of attacks on private banks by the United States, particularly in Switzerland, the reaction of some banks to the QI rules was to circumvent the efforts of the United States to stamp out foreign tax evasion by passively or actively working with American taxpayers to find ways to avoid reporting under the QI system. This was not a huge challenge given the clear limits under the QI reporting system in and around the question of 'beneficial ownership', which was determined under American tax principles rather than under local know-your-client or other rules. Under US tax principles, among others, the beneficial owner of a bank account, where the account was owned by a properly established and managed offshore company, was the company itself rather than its shareholders, even if those shareholders were Americans. While this did not change any other US tax principles associated with the tax and reporting requirements of Americans owning offshore companies, or rules in and around aiding and abetting tax evasion or otherwise, the limits of what the QI rules required banks to technically document were misinterpreted (or taken advantage of) by what appear to be many banks that used the QI system as a roadmap for how to perpetuate offshore tax evasion by Americans.

Abuses by Banks and Others of the QI System with Consequences That Continue Today—and Led to FATCA

The abuse of the QI system became clear in and around the United States' attack on Switzerland's largest bank, UBS, facilitated by the information the Americans were able to obtain from whistle blowers and others. After US$780 million in fines, and the turning over of thousands of US depositors, the United States scored further tax-collection successes with its various voluntary disclosure programmes. But were these voluntary disclosure programmes real wins for all stakeholders, including banks, families and interested governments? Could dialogue amongst stakeholders have led to more effective results, and perhaps results that were less destructive of lives and businesses?

Information obtained by the United States through the UBS case played a big part in the next steps taken by America, including its successful rollout of the heavy-handed *Foreign Tax Compliance*

Act—or FATCA—broadly, a reaction to the abuses discovered in relation to the QI rules, and from a timing perspective, well placed to become the new global standard in automatic exchange of information between countries.

As with the QI system, the United States is still unable to deliver real reciprocity, despite reciprocity having now been documented as at least an objective in bilateral agreements that the United States has entered into. And because of its early move with FATCA, the United States has so far managed to stay out of the more recent system of automatic exchange of information, which involves even broader reporting requirements under the *common reporting standard*. Perversely, the United States has managed to navigate itself into a position where the world's banks have become their policemen, ensuring that those with connections to the United States are tax compliant, while the United States enhances its position as the best place to maintain privacy for international families, given the limited information it collects and provides to other countries.

The United States has strong bank secrecy, and there are very limited requirements regarding the information that US-based banks have to obtain from their clients and, particularly, what of that information actually goes to the US tax authorities. In the case of complex structures, where beneficial owners are not direct account holders, but rather use companies, trusts and other intermediate investment vehicles, very limited information finds its way to the US tax authorities—meaning that there is no information for the US tax authorities to exchange with other countries. Attempts to change these rules have largely failed, with the US Republican Party particularly resisting change, in part encouraged by lobbyists representing the Florida and Texas banking associations and others involved in providing wealth management and related services to families from Latin America and elsewhere seeking to hide their money.

Information obtained by the United States led to further attacks on private banks, primarily in Switzerland, leading to the destruction of Switzerland's oldest private bank, Bank Wegelin, and significant financial and other challenges for a very long list of Swiss banks, including the Swiss operations of many well-known international banks.

Along the road, the US Department of Justice introduced, in effect, a voluntary disclosure programme for banks in Switzerland, and was itself surprised at the significant sign-on to this, with over 100 banks (about one-third of the Swiss banking community) applying for non-prosecution agreements in exchange for disclosures of activities and data in and around undeclared accounts and the payment of significant penalties based on the value of accounts not disclosed to the United States on certain key dates linked to the UBS case. Penalties were reduced where clients of the relevant bank applied for voluntary disclosure, meaning that the arrangement had the effect of banks encouraging their undeclared US clients to come clean with the tax authorities.

But with penalties of between 20% and 50% of account *balances*, was the Department of Justice 'agreement' with Switzerland a fair one for the private banks involved? The Swiss Bank Program ended up resulting in more than US$7.5 billion being paid by banks in Switzerland (including non-Swiss banks operating in Switzerland) to the United States.

From the website of the US Justice Department[2]:

> The Swiss Bank Program, which was announced on August 29, 2013, provides a path for Swiss banks to resolve potential criminal liabilities in the United States. Swiss banks eligible to enter the program were required to advise the department by Dec. 31, 2013, that they had reason to believe that they had committed tax-related criminal offenses in connection with undeclared U.S.-related accounts. Banks already under criminal investigation related to their Swiss-banking activities and all individuals were expressly excluded from the program.
>
> Under the program, banks are required to:
>
> - Make a complete disclosure of their cross-border activities;
> - Provide detailed information on an account-by-account basis for accounts in which U.S. taxpayers have a direct or indirect interest;
> - Cooperate in treaty requests for account information;
> - Provide detailed information as to other banks that transferred funds into secret accounts or that accepted funds when secret accounts were closed;
> - Agree to close accounts of accountholders who fail to come into compliance with U.S. reporting obligations; and
> - Pay appropriate penalties.

Swiss banks meeting all of the above requirements are eligible for a non-prosecution agreement.

While other countries, such as France, Germany and Italy, have also successfully attacked Swiss banks involved in evasion of their taxes, the United States and its structured approach to shutting down tax evasion remains the most successful, from the perspective of a government.

Attacks on Enablers of Tax Evasion Continue

But further erosion of bank secrecy and attacks on enablers of tax evasion are by no means over. When will a well-advised government in Latin America or elsewhere turn the tables and go after the United States and its banking community for their role in hiding the assets and income of their taxpayers?

Dialogue and negotiation, with a view to coming to approaches that benefit all stakeholders, may have brought a different result, and maybe there remains room for approaches that recognize that undeclared money is a *global* problem. There is still significant undeclared money around the world, and the financial centres involved extend geographically from Europe to the Caribbean to Singapore and Hong Kong, and to the United States itself, where Miami, New York and other centres provide international private banking services to clients from Latin America and around the world, and often without meaningful checks on whether the relevant earnings are declared in the home countries of beneficial owners.

Lack of an *impact goal,* strategy and cooperation has resulted in other lost opportunities for the wealth management industry as a whole. For Dagland, in my example, there are lessons to be learned from countries that have failed to adopt effective policies.

Once under challenge for its bank secrecy-based tax-evasion strategies, Switzerland sought to address some of its difficulties by introducing its 'Rubik' strategy. A failure from the outset, even the name of the strategy apparently came under challenge from the owners of the rights to 'Rubik's Cube'.

What Switzerland attempted to do, was to introduce a very complex (and costly) withholding system designed to allow it to provide confidentiality to account holders while accommodating the tax demands of the countries of residence of the account holders involved. Among the weaknesses of this strategy was Switzerland's approach to Germany and the United Kingdom as first-takers (with Austria, a bank secrecy centre itself, an easier bet to negotiate with). At this period in history, with governments focusing on their legitimate rights to tax residents and address income inequality, it was hugely provocative to propose a solution to undeclared money that would keep secret the names of taxpayers—particularly in the case of countries, like Germany and the United Kingdom, whose tax laws are well developed, and reflect a first world system of protections of taxpayer interests. While some may not like the UK and German tax systems, the reality is that both are generally free from corruption and provide significant taxpayer protections.

The deal with Germany eventually never came to pass because of resistance within the German political system. In relation to the United Kingdom, which had gone forward with the agreement with Switzerland with a view to enjoying short-term tax revenues, Switzerland *guaranteed* CHF500 million in taxes to the United Kingdom. Ultimately, the ambitious tax-collection estimates were not met, and even the guarantee figure was not covered by tax withholdings, meaning that the Swiss bank community, which had shared in the responsibility of meeting the guarantee, had to bear part of the cost.

A complex, costly and failed system, the 'Rubik' approach evidences yet another lost opportunity for governments interested in protecting the interests of wealth and business owners to show global leadership on a global issue—undeclared funds. Switzerland's provocation of the United Kingdom, through its insistence on maintaining confidentiality for UK taxpayers, led to an expensive deal for taxpayers and, ultimately, for Swiss banks.[3]

Secrecy-Based Financial Centres Have Not Helped

Secrecy-based financial centres have caused great harm to both the world's wealth owners, by misleading them for too long regarding the misuse of bank secrecy, and to the countries whose tax laws were evaded. Instead of leading the way to change, these financial centres focused on short-term profits. The emergence in a very public way of the misuse of bank secrecy by Swiss-based banks in particular resulted in an over-reaction by onshore governments and a critical focus on even very legitimate tax-planning approaches wealth owners have adopted.

Open, strategic dialogue between stakeholders may be a more effective way of addressing the needs of all—wealth and business owners and the societies to which they are connected. This dialogue continues to be urgent, and despite what some may think given the rapid move to transparency, there remain many, many issues to be resolved, meaning that the opportunity for a country like Dagland to take leadership remains. With a focus on its ultimate impact goal, a country can find the right balance between what it would take to attract and retain wealth owners to its economy, while ensuring that it enhances the interests of the majority.

It is interesting that given the focus on Switzerland in many of the initiatives of a decade or so ago by the United States and others, Switzerland has in many ways benefited from the shifting landscape, allowing it to build on its historical success in the provision of sophisticated, knowledge-based, tax-compliant wealth management services. Given that it was a target of many of the initiatives attacking the misuse of bank secrecy, Switzerland and its wealth management industry learned from its mistakes. Not all financial centres have joined Switzerland in this progress.

Tax Compliance Works Better than Tax Evasion

Today, families are increasingly realizing that apart from being the right thing, tax compliance can be far cheaper and safer than tax evasion. There have, of course, been a number of voices pushing for transparency and compliance over the years, but the approach of too many in the industry has been to resist change and to perpetuate the ways of the past—which ways are inappropriate in today's world. Transparency in relation to taxation continues to develop, and families and their advisors have much to do to be prepared for the changes that have taken and will be taking place.

Wealth-owning families need to hear the truth, and to be guided by their advisors as how best to navigate a fast-changing and increasingly transparent landscape. And for the wealth owner, critical is to understand how tax systems work and change, and how to be in a position to understand the advice they receive and make their own decisions on the right approaches to take. For wealth owners still following the advice of those encouraging them to hide, it is urgent to become very sceptical, and to seek better guidance.

In the case of the private banking and trust world, secrecy was all too often the historical basis for planning, with aggressive or outright evasive approaches being adopted on the logic that *no one will ever find out*. Indeed, private banks and trust companies all too often marketed bank secrecy and, in effect, tax evasion, as a luxury product, available to those with the wealth and contacts needed to attract them offshore.

Switzerland and bank secrecy provided important protection to many families in and around the turmoil of wars, confiscations, corruption and more. But bank secrecy has been abused—and not only in Switzerland. Data leaks in a number of tax havens and other offshore centres have made it easy for the press and others to bash offshore 'tax havens' and those involved in promoting the use of opaque structures designed to hide assets. Not enough is being done, however, to have an open dialogue about the reality that the United States is one of the best places for money to be hidden, given its lack of regard for the needs of countries other than the United States to get information on companies, trusts and assets connected to the United States.

Not All Countries Are Ready for Tax Transparency

There is also not enough dialogue about the reality that not all countries are ready for transparency. Countries with tax systems that cannot be trusted, in a world of transparency, are facing a reality that the wealth-owning entrepreneurs they need for their economies to survive are being forced to relocate, creating a tax refugee crisis that negatively impacts those countries most in need—countries that are still developing and where tax revenues are critical to address poverty and starvation.

With the tax landscape having changed dramatically, many banks and trust companies now look to protect themselves ahead of looking to address the needs of their clients—wealth owners need to be aware of this. For advisors to families, understanding that compliance is a *client need*, and that there is huge value to helping families navigate a changing world, may help to provide an edge to not only retaining clients, but also building new relationships as clients realize that they need something different from what they received in the way of help and advice in the past.

The wealth management industry and the jurisdictions in which it operates have not done a good job of proactively leading on issues in and around growing transparency. To a large extent, the industry has been reactive, defending the past rather than working out how best to cooperatively address the needs of all stakeholders. This lack of strategy has resulted in the future of the wealth management industry and financial centres being dictated by others, including onshore governments, which themselves are not necessarily achieving what they set out to achieve. The leaders of private banks have been among the worst offenders, looking more to short-term profits than to the long-term best interests of their clients and society. Governments interested in perpetuating the ways of the past did far too little, when they had the opportunity to do so, to show the way forward.

Forced to change, financial centres are adapting to new rules on exchange of information and otherwise. But they have failed, for the most part, to play a role in helping to address the real needs of our societies, to the detriment of all involved, including their own economies.

Similarly, the wealth-owning community has not taken leadership in showing responsibility and being proactive in shaping how tax laws should work to fairly address the needs of governments for revenue and the need to address poverty and inequality. But are governments to be trusted when led by populists thinking of their own short-term interests? Are wealth owners safe in a world where corruption, political misuse of tax systems and unfairness in tax systems abound? How much tax is a fair amount of tax, and at what stage does a tax actually become confiscation of assets?

For many years, arguments on behalf of offshore centres seeking to preserve the past have focused on the notion of a *level playing field*, pointing to bank secrecy and the use of opaque structures in countries such as the United States as a rationale for continuing past practices. It is true that the United States is probably the best place in the world to hide money, given its own bank secrecy rules and limited ability to exchange information with other countries. The reality, however, is that onshore countries have every right to tax their residents (and sometimes citizens) as well as those who invest in their countries. The industry failing to recognize this reality, and its clear abuse of bank secrecy, has led to a *tsunami* of over-reaction—to the detriment of the wealth management industry and the families it serves.

Over-reaction by governments has ranged from punitive and intrusive reporting and taxpaying requirements associated with the use of trusts to aggressive attacks on private banks and others for past practices. Compliance requirements are out of control, and getting more and more complex, dangerous and difficult to deal with. Some wealth-owning families have been destroyed as the practices of the past have come under attack, with significant penalties, jail sentences and sometimes worse being the consequences of the sudden move from hidden money to transparency.

There is a need for wealth owners to understand the impact of global change in relation to tax enforcement and transparency and also to participate, with the wealth management industry, in helping to educate onshore and offshore governments and smooth out the continuing rough road to transparency. To date, not enough has been done.

The Need for a Proactive Approach

It is time to be far more proactive, to the benefit of all. It is also critical for wealth-owning families and their advisors to understand what is really going on. Many things have been happening to help move the world into transparency, and the secrecy landscape has been changing fast and in a very public way.

Interestingly, but not surprisingly, respect of tax laws seems to have carried greater sway when the laws involved were those of the jurisdiction of the advisor rather than those of another country. For example, it is not unusual to see American private banks having a history of being far more careful about US tax evasion than the evasion of taxes of other countries by their clients. Similarly, UK, Dutch, French and other banks seem to have greater sensitivity to what they do with clients from their own countries as opposed to others. This said, the dramatic end of Swiss bank secrecy as it relates to tax matters clearly showed that the Swiss private banking industry historically had particularly little regard for global tax laws in their short-term focus on easy profits. This led to many wealth-owning families realizing too late that they had been misled and mis-sold advice in relation to their tax positions.

What is particularly worrying is that the over-reaction of onshore governments has led to a problematic picture for wealth owners, forcing many out of their countries, to the long-term detriment of the economies properly seeking to increase their revenues. For Dagland, this may be part of the opportunity.

The adoption of varying standards of ethics on the issue of tax compliance has also extended to the community of advisors and others involved in the industry. In my experience, even top tax lawyers in Miami and New York tend to pay far more attention to the question of US tax compliance than the tax compliance of global families in their home countries. Today's advisor (and, frankly, yesterday's) must look at tax compliance as a *global* issue, meaning that when a Chinese, Venezuelan or Mexican invests in the United States and is guided by a US tax lawyer, that lawyer should properly liaise with Chinese, Venezuelan or Mexican advisors to ensure that the overall approach adopted is tax compliant—not only in the United States but in all relevant jurisdictions of residence and investment. The foreign investor has often been misled by advisors who failed to take the global picture into account, and in today's world, anyone failing to understand the fast pace of change relating to transparency is making a big, big mistake.

Undeclared funds are a global problem, and measurement of the amounts involved is very difficult. But it is worth thinking about these things in the context of the realities of growing income and wealth inequality.

These issues affect wealth owners, advisors to wealth owners and interested governments, both onshore and offshore. For the wealth-owning family, the explosion of transparency as a reaction to historical tax evasion conducted on an industrial scale is going to have more than just tax consequences in their future.

How Do Tax Authorities Find Out About Undeclared Money?

There are many ways that tax authorities get the information they need to enforce their tax laws, and this ability continues to increase. Automatic exchange of information has changed the global landscape, and is bringing an unprecedented level of transparency, for both better and (sadly) worse.

Information traditionally comes to tax authorities through many means, including the old-fashioned tip from jealous neighbours, friends, disgruntled employees and spurned spouses. Sometimes blackmail is involved, a trusted secretary or other employee fired, and then threatening to report the tax evasion they were aware of to the authorities if not paid off. In divorces, the threat of being turned in has too often led to settlements beyond those that would otherwise have occurred.

In some countries, such as the United States, the tax authorities actually reward those who turn others in to the authorities. Bradley

Birkenfeld,[4] an American private banker working for UBS in Switzerland, received a reward of US$104 million—an astounding amount, but actually lower than he might have been eligible for given the US$780 million fine paid by UBS for its activities in and around US tax evasion by a number of its American clients and the many, many millions of dollars recovered by the American tax authorities from wealth owners whose information came to light in the process.

Tips to the authorities can be about individual taxpayers on a one-on-one basis, but increasingly have come through stolen bank information, something that has affected banks ranging from Julius Baer to LGT, HSBC and many, many others. In some cases, governments actually buy the stolen information—in others, it is just given to them, sometimes by other governments who have received the information. Data leaks in a number of locations show only a small part of the extent of assets that have been hidden.

What of credit cards, and the role of technology in helping tax authorities to find things out? Many countries get and use credit card information to check on the expenditures of their taxpayers, reviewing whether reported income is sufficient to substantiate what people are spending. And information from credit card companies that a government gets may be shared with other countries through, among others, 'spontaneous information exchange' under tax treaties, meaning that a taxpayer in, say, Indonesia using a credit card on an undeclared account while travelling in the United States may well find that information on their spending activities and account relationship finds its way back to their home country. The lesson is not to avoid using credit cards and online payment services—the lesson is that in a world of technology, it is very hard to think that what one spends or owns cannot be discovered.

Unexplained wealth orders and other means of questioning how an individual comes to own assets are tools tax authorities can use to pursue a wealth owner for unpaid taxes. If a wealth owner owns expensive homes and cars and spends lavishly can they rationalize the values with the tax declarations they have filed? As transparency increases and countries can more easily and automatically, through technology and otherwise, gain access to information about global income and assets, enforcement of tax laws gets much easier. The younger generation within wealth and business-owning families need to be aware of the fast-changing landscape as it is increasingly their risk that arises through the sometimes misguided approaches of the older generation.

Many banks have come under attack by tax authorities for their role in the tax evasion of their clients. UBS, in addition to its US$780 million fine, found itself again under investigation by the United States for other possible misdeeds and at the time of writing has not resolved the fines and additional payments to France in relation to tax-evasion claims still being litigated. Credit Suisse, before being absorbed by UBS, settled with the United States by paying a fine of US$2.6 billion.

But what does all this mean for the wealth owner?

First, it is important to understand that not every bank can afford the fines that are doled out for misdeeds, meaning that some will close their doors. Institutional risk associated with working with wealth owners holding undeclared assets and income means that legitimate banks and other intermediaries are refusing to be involved, and in a number of cases will be the source of information provided to governments.

For those who advise wealth owners, whether from within the financial services industry or outside of it, understanding the real needs of families is what it is about. A time of change is also a time of great opportunity, as wealth owners are more clearly able to articulate what they are looking to their asset managers and advisors to help them with.

For those who spend time in countries but pretend they don't, it is important to understand that governments are improving their ability to track the time people spend in the country, through both technology and greater alignment between border entry controls and the tax authorities. Most are not there yet, but it is only a question of time—and not too much time—before it will become totally clear that there really are only two choices: *play by the rules, or get out.*

Automatic Exchange of Information Backed Up by Anti-money Laundering Rules—But Do Wealth Owners Understand How Far the Rules Go?

There has now been widespread adoption of global approaches to automatic information exchange, a dramatic departure from the methods of information exchange of the past, such as information exchange upon request. What does 'automatic' exchange of information actually mean?

The global community has moved towards a system that has financial intermediaries, such as banks, obtain information on the residence (and sometimes citizenship) of their clients, which information then results in details on earnings and assets being reported directly to the client's country of residence—automatically, and without any request for such information having been made.

The rules and procedures are well developed, and implementation is well in progress, with over 100 countries (excluding the United States) having implemented the approach. It is not information about the companies or trusts that hold accounts that is being exchanged, but rather information about 'beneficial owners'—the individuals behind structures that have, in the past, sometimes been misused to obfuscate ownership. The approach to reporting that is being developed involves the CRS, coordinated by the OECD.[5]

For a wealth-owning family, it is absolutely critical to understand who has what information on their family and wealth, and to whom that information will go. With banks and other financial intermediaries seeking to ensure that they do not expose themselves to fines and other sanctions, some have compliance approaches that may go beyond what they are actually required to do; some wealth owners may find that the information their financial intermediaries hold is inaccurate or out of date. Just leaving things to chance is a dangerous approach, given that information on income and assets may simply find its way into the wrong hands. Tax compliance is a given, but the road to transparency is a rough one.[6]

The United States and its implementation of FATCA, which was designed to ensure tax compliance by US citizens and residents maintaining financial arrangements outside the United States, provided the model for the OECD. Participation by the global community in FATCA made it easier for the OECD, with the support of the United Kingdom and others, to develop a global standard for automatic information exchange. The European Union had been successful in closing loopholes on exchange of information that were already in place in Europe, and has now moved to fully automatic exchange of information in a very comprehensive way.

Tax transparency and automatic information exchange is no longer just something affecting Americans—we are now in a world of global tax transparency, and one where information exchange takes place without the taxpayer necessarily being aware of it.

The ability of automatic information exchange to address the global issue of undeclared funds is substantial. An important, but sometimes overlooked, element of tax enforcement relates to the move to have anti-money laundering rules include tax crimes as 'predicate' offences, something that has already been introduced in many countries, including the United Kingdom, Singapore and Hong Kong. Through initiatives of the Financial Action Task Force, among others, we are ever closer to comprehensive anti-money laundering rules in key financial centres that include tax offences as anti-money laundering offences.

What do anti-money laundering rules that include tax offences as predicate offences do? If a wealth owner approaches an advisor, be it a real estate broker, an accountant or a banker, that advisor, on learning that monies being handled are tax undeclared, may have a legal obligation to turn the wealth owner in, filing a 'suspicious activity report' to the authorities, and with an obligation to *not* tip off the wealth owner that the report is being made.

Combining the impact of anti-money laundering rules that are effectively enforced with automatic information exchange arrangements, undeclared money is clearly being significantly reduced. A bank in a traditional bank secrecy country, where the anti-money laundering rules so provide, has to be comfortable that monies on deposit are tax declared in the home country, failing which anti-money laundering reports will need to be made. Parallel to this are automatic exchange of information agreements, whether or not part of comprehensive tax treaties, that require information to be automatically exchanged regarding the earnings and assets of taxpayers connected to countries that have entered into automatic exchange agreements. It is important to understand that anti-money laundering rules can apply even where there is *no* automatic exchange of information yet agreed with the relevant home country.

Developments towards global transparency include growing initiatives to require the creation of public registers on beneficial ownership. While the debate continues, there are moves towards this for companies, trusts and other investment and asset-holding vehicles—and even in the United States, a continuing secrecy champion.

Importantly, beneficial ownership of assets such as real estate is also being targeted for full disclosure in a number of countries. This links closely to automatic exchange of information, and data leaks in several offshore centres which led to massive global press coverage and new calls for transparency. New and sometimes duplicative approaches to information exchange and disclosure are being discussed, and some of the proposals are certainly over-reactions and may carry with them many problems over and above the challenge to the human right to privacy. But where things are going is clear, and wealth owners need to be ready for the substantial changes that have taken place and the further changes that are to come.

Something many are not aware of is that automatic exchange of information will include information that goes far beyond the information governments actually need to enforce their tax laws. For example, among the information that is exchanged is information on the total value of assets held in a bank account—not only the income from investments, and this even where the country receiving the information does not need information on the assets involved or their value to enforce their tax laws. And countries whose tax laws do not include reference to overseas income will be receiving information that they do not necessarily need. Are wealth owners aware and prepared for this?

There are now many countries obtaining information automatically and developing ways to process this information with a view to benefiting their tax systems.

But Again—Are All Countries Ready for Automatic Exchange of Information?

Automatic information exchange is being implemented on a global scale. However, the reality is that not all countries are *ready* for the full tax transparency that the world is working towards.

What happens where a taxpayer is a resident of a developing country, the tax system of which does not respect privacy, meaning that information the tax authorities have is improperly made available to journalists and others, perhaps including kidnappers interested in knowing who has what? What if there is corruption in the tax system, and tax proceeds are, maybe in part, diverted improperly? What if information on an individual's assets and income leads to corruption and to a bribe to avoid a full tax audit? And what of countries that use tax information to attack the political enemies of those in power?

Taxpayers connected to countries whose tax systems are not ready for full transparency will be forced into finding ways to avoid new reporting and compliance systems. In some cases, taxpayers will be encouraged to abandon their residence to avoid being resident taxpayers, something that contributes little to the local economy. In other cases, untaxed assets might well be converted into investments that do not yet attract the tax compliance that passive investment portfolios with banks now attract. For example, instead of holding a bank account that earns interest, and which holds equities producing capital gains and dividends, the wealth owner might be tempted to hold a safe deposit box with diamonds and gold. Unlike the bank account, the safe deposit box, at least under present rules, does not attract automatic information exchange.

Again, not something that encourages investment into the home country which needs it most. It is the entrepreneurs who can hugely benefit a home economy, with their knowledge and experience of the country, who are encouraged to invest abroad and find ways to distance themselves economically and otherwise from the place they know best. Meeting the tax laws of many developing countries may simply not be an option given the practicalities of how the tax system operates.

Wealth owners and the wealth management industry have a key role to play in helping the world address the issue of undeclared money. A continuation of a reactive approach to change serves badly both the industry and wealth-owning families. There is a need for leadership and dialogue, with a focus on outcomes that can benefit all stakeholders.

Most important, though, is for the wealth-owning family to understand enough about the changing tax world and how tax laws work if they are to avoid the many challenges to preserving and enhancing wealth, and most importantly, the financial and non-financial best interests of their families.

For Countries That Are Not Ready for Transparency, What Kind of Alternative Tax System Could Work?

The simple reality is that wealth owners need to accept the realities of tax transparency. For many, the risks are enormous, particularly where they are connected, by residence, investment or otherwise, to countries that are not themselves ready for transparency given the political and legal framework of the country involved.

I believe that there are approaches that the global community could take to improve the situation, and perhaps, for Dagland, the country in my example, considering ways to assist can be a way to help itself.

Dagland, as part of the activities it conducts, might advocate more openness and discussion on the reality that not every country is ready for full transparency. Dagland might cooperate with a suitable non-governmental organization, perhaps Transparency International, to evaluate the tax and legal systems of countries, measuring levels of corruption, misuse of taxpayer information and other characteristics relevant to the determination of what countries are actually ready for full tax transparency.

Where countries are not ready for full transparency, Dagland and its banks and trust companies could agree to ensuring tax compliance by identifying the relevant owners of assets and income for itself, and agree to withhold tax on initial capital and annual income, say at a figure of 10%. The proceeds of the withholding tax would be maintained in a fund that would be made available to the home country involved under certain conditions. Because the taxpayer would be considered tax compliant in the financial centre involved, no anti-money laundering or other reports would need to be filed.

This would be very different from Switzerland's failed 'Rubik' strategy discussed earlier—a weirdly complex system of withholding requiring the input of mathematicians, and oriented to precisely the wrong countries—the United Kingdom, Germany and others clearly *ready* for automatic exchange of information. Again, you may or may not like the UK or German tax systems, but the reality is that both countries have tax and legal systems that protect taxpayer rights and are generally free from corruption and political misuse.

Dagland might advocate a simple and transparent approach to anonymous withholding that is attractive to taxpayers and which reflects the reality of tax collections rather than 'headline' tax rates. Should there be withholding at 40% if the effective tax collections in the relevant country are at 10%? Most importantly, unlike Switzerland, which focused its now abandoned withholding thinking on the United Kingdom and Germany, two examples of first world tax systems fully ready for automatic exchange of information, the withholding approach would be used for countries that are *not ready* for automatic exchange of information—countries that do not properly protect taxpayer information, countries where tax proceeds are corruptly converted to incorrect use and where information on financial affairs is used for political or other wrongful purposes.

On agreeing to accept the funds held for it as settlement of tax due in relation to assets subject to withholding, the withheld amounts would be paid over to the home country. It would also be possible to have withheld amounts be the subject of disbursement with international oversight, something that may be particularly appropriate for countries where tax revenues are improperly applied. In some cases, the tax withholdings might have a role in repayments of outstanding international loans.

The idea would be to allow a wealth owner resident in a country not ready for transparency to be tax compliant without putting their assets and families at risk. If I live in a country that uses tax information to achieve political objectives, or where such information leaks out to kidnappers, I will not remain a resident given the risks this will give rise to. If there is corruption in my tax system, information my government gets may simply result in my being subject to additional blackmail by low-level or other tax officials. Rather than being forced to leave my country, what if there were an alternative system, designed to operate until such time as my country cleans up its act? The alternative system might actually accelerate the ability of countries to root out corruption and put in place proper legal and practical approaches to protecting taxpayer information and rights.

Short term—immediate, released revenues that can be applied as they need to be given the circumstances of the country involved. Medium and long term, the system may influence what the country needs to do to establish an effective and fair tax system that can operate in the interests of the country and its taxpayers.

But will issues relevant to countries not ready for automatic information exchange be smoothly addressed in the years to come? Or will the industry and relevant financial centres again fail to take leadership? Are international organizations like the International Monetary Fund, the OECD, the United Nations and others more focused on the longer-term need to establish effective tax administration systems in developing countries and neglecting the shorter-term need to ensure that there are tax revenues which are applied appropriately to those in need?

For the wealth owner, there is no choice but to be ready for continuing chaos.

Tax Competition, Mobility, and Countries Not Ready for Full Information Exchange

Like most competition, tax competition is healthy and necessary to ensure that countries are imposing tax fairly and efficiently. This statement is, however, controversial, and there have been and will continue to be steps taken regionally and internationally that seek to eliminate such competition. As with other areas of taxation and how these will develop over time, understanding moves that seek to address tax competition is critical for wealth-owning families and their advisors to understand.

In relation to countries not ready for full information exchange, if something is not done to address the reality of the dangers to families that result from transparency, wealth owners faced with a corrupt or otherwise defective home-country tax system will be encouraged to relocate, taking advantage of the tax savings and privacy protection afforded by this. One element of the reality of tax competition is that countries with attractive and reliable tax systems will be safer for wealth owners to be connected to than countries lacking the basic legal and political protections a proper tax system should provide. This, of course, is an opportunity for Dagland and can guide the activities that it can initiate towards its impact goal of attracting wealth owners to its economy, but it is a sad loss to the countries that have lost and will continue to lose their best entrepreneurs.

For example, a wealth owner who has international business activities and who is based in a country that is unstable and developing may fear having the local authorities be aware of global wealth. With growing transparency, and anti-money laundering rules that include tax evasion as a predicate offence, a wealth owner may be forced to relocate to avoid putting their family at risk by complying with home-country disclosure requirements. Relocation may be to a country that 'competes' with its tax system—for example, as was historically the case, the United Kingdom, which had, at least for a set period of time, not taxed the unremitted foreign earnings of those who were 'resident' but not 'domiciled' in the United Kingdom. While the United Kingdom at the time of writing this book is in the process of eliminating this system and replacing it with one that only provides very short-term benefits to new residents and overly complex and unfair solutions for wealth owners who would have considered making the United Kingdom their home, similar, simpler and more strategic benefits can be achieved by relocating elsewhere. Wealth owners have choices of more tax-attractive places, including Hong Kong and Singapore, given their territorial tax systems, and Italy and Greece, given the straightforward tax regimes offered to new wealth-owning residents.

This competition is healthy as it encourages home countries to review their tax systems and to ensure that they are fair ... but this process can be a long one, particularly in the case of fragile, developing economies—another attraction of an interim withholding-based taxation regime or other approach designed to both retain wealth owners to countries that need them and produce sorely needed revenues for governments.

But is society optional for those who can afford to take advantage of the benefits of mobility? Are countries putting up barriers to this mobility and are there coordinated efforts to tackle even healthy tax competition? More on these topics to come.

Should Tax Be the Driver in Asset Protection and Estate Planning?

Historically, there has been an over-emphasis on taxation in asset and succession planning, something fuelled by advisors focused more on tax minimization than on understanding the real needs of their clients. These real needs are varied and include three kinds. First, some needs are particular to the family involved, such as where there is a child that would benefit from special protection. Second, there are needs of wealth owners that are driven by the laws and structure of their home country and of the countries in which they invest. Here, issues such as forced heirship, political risk and many others come into the mix. Third, there are needs that apply to all families, such as how to best deal with succession of assets and the many other issues all wealth owners face as they age.

The over-emphasis on taxation notwithstanding, it is important that wealth-owning families understand their tax position, learning from advisors and being guided by them, but not allowing them to 'kidnap' the family's wealth and keep the family in the dark about how their own ownership structures really work. If the wealth owner understands the tax systems of his countries of residence, citizenship and investment, he is in a better position to guide advisors and make the right decisions.

For advisors to wealth-owning families, it is important to understand that it is of huge assistance to your clients to just be able to help raise the right questions, and to help wealth owners identify the right advisors to address their concerns. In an increasingly complex world, no one has all the answers. Being able to ask the right questions is the first step to really being of help and value. Even a top tax specialist will be unable to address all the tax issues typical wealth owners face given the international nature of families, the structures they use and where they invest.

An important overlay to how tax systems and planning work is to also understand the changing world of tax enforcement, and the reality that the luxury product offered by the private banking industry in the past—secrecy without much more—has fallen and continues to fall away. This has real importance not only for families connected to countries at the forefront of tax enforcement, such as the United States. In some ways the issue is of even greater importance to families connected to countries whose tax systems are just developing, and where corruption and misuse of tax information is rife. The combination of anti-money laundering rules and heightened institutional risk is driving advisors and intermediaries, such as banks, insurance companies, accountants and others, to turn their clients in to the authorities. A wealth owner needs to understand these developing risks. And in a world where disparities of wealth are increasingly at the forefront of the political and social agenda, is 'hiding the money' an option or ever the right thing to do?

I have worked with many wealth owners who are in the younger generation, and who, on inheriting assets from their parents, have negotiated 'voluntary disclosure' arrangements with tax authorities, essentially coming clean on the past tax evasion undertaken by earlier generations. The costs for this are often higher than the costs would have been to the older generation had they paid their taxes, and undertaken legitimate and legal ways to reduce exposures. Was the older generation right in believing that they were doing the younger generation a favour by salting the money away in secret accounts and opaque structures?

And for those who do not take advantage of tax amnesties or voluntary disclosure, what is the consequence of getting caught? In many cases, tax authorities and those involved in prosecuting tax cases are looking to make examples through severe penalties and jail sentences. It is not always only about punishing tax evasion, but also about making an example to scare others into compliance. Is it worth the risk for a wealth owner who has spent their life building their business and their wealth? Is this the legacy to be left to the younger generation?

The move to tax transparency also brings with it the question of privacy, and whether privacy of one's financial affairs can be legally achieved. I am a believer that privacy is a human right, and that privacy and tax compliance can go hand in hand. But it is not always straightforward, and the approaches open to wealth owners very much depend on their countries of citizenship, domicile and residence. We are in times of enormous change, and in times where headline tax rates are probably much higher than they should or need to be—in a world of full tax compliance, governments would be collecting enough revenue to permit tax rates to decline substantially—but we are likely several decades away from this being able to happen.

Many countries have misleadingly high 'headline' tax rates, allowing politicians to claim that they are adequately taxing the wealthy. But actual tax rates reflect deductions and other tax reliefs, and faulty collection systems further influence the huge gap between the headline or published top tax rate and what countries actually collect.

We are also decades away from all governments having tax systems that can be trusted; tax systems free of corruption and of political misuse of tax information; tax systems where information the tax authorities hold is truly kept confidential. We are also, perhaps in some ways fortunately, far from having a global tax system—meaning that tax competition is, for the most part, alive and well. This said, the recent implementation of global minimum tax rules for large multinational interests is a step in the direction of a global tax system and there are already calls mentioned later in this book for a global and coordinated approach to taxing wealth owners.

Countries compete for investment and business on the basis of their tax systems, and as the world moves to greater tax transparency, the role of mobility in tax and privacy planning becomes increasingly important. Interestingly, the world is also getting smaller, with wealth-owning families becoming more and more international. Mobility therefore becomes an important element of planning—carefully choosing where to be resident and how to manage time spent between different countries. Citizenship can also be an issue here, and one that in the years to come may be more and more significant.

While tax is important, and in succession and asset protection planning is a key issue to be managed and minimized, it is critical to keep tax in its place—and to *not* allow tax planning to compromise what should be holistic continuity planning.

Tax laws are difficult for anyone to understand. Even the most sophisticated tax advisor will not have all the answers. Today's wealth-owning families are, for the most part, international families. Family members may live in different countries, the family is likely to invest in a number of places and citizenship can sometimes play a critical role in the tax picture. Where grandchildren are born, and the citizenships of children and their spouses, can all have an impact. And the only certainty in the tax world is one: *the laws will change, and constantly do.*

The wealth-owning family does not need to become expert in the tax laws of every country that affects them and their investments. Rather, the wealth-owning family needs to be able to understand the advice they receive from experts, and needs to be able to challenge that advice, and ask the right questions. Being aware of how tax systems work can help families stay in control of the succession and asset-protection planning put in place for their families.

There also remains much that wealth owners, the wealth management industry and the financial centres involved can and need to do to address the sometimes conflicting needs of wealth owners with the needs of governments to enforce tax and other laws.

Tax is also a form of political risk. As the world moves towards ever increasing tax transparency, governments will be getting hold of much more information than they actually need to enforce their existing tax systems. What will they do with this information? Will populist governments impose new 'taxes' as a means of confiscating the assets of wealth owners as a way to address perceived inequality? Will corruption in tax systems be helped by the massive amount of information that will now be available to governments that are in many ways not ready for automatic information exchange?

Wealth owners need to understand these risks, and also the opportunities to legally address risks by choosing which countries to live and invest in. Sad to say, but transparency, in many cases, will not result in developing countries receiving more in the way of tax revenues. I fear that wealth owners who create jobs and economic activity will be forced to exit countries that others are not keen to invest in.

This book is not designed to turn the wealth owner or their advisors into tax experts, but is meant to help them ask the right questions, and to be in a better position to understand and evaluate the advice they receive.

Tax Evasion, Tax Avoidance and Tax Planning—and the Years to Come

Attitudes and approaches in relation to tax evasion and aggressive avoidance are fast changing.

Tax evasion, the illegal non-payment of taxes due, is something that is usually pretty clear. A rule applies, and one actively fails to comply with that rule, breaking the law and committing the offence of tax evasion. Bank secrecy, opaque ownership structures and non-compliance with reporting made tax evasion a pretty easy thing for wealth owners to commit, sometimes with clear intent, but sometimes unwittingly, perhaps encouraged by those 'selling' bank secrecy and opaque structures, and sometimes by accident or neglect.

Mobile wealth owners connected to multiple countries may wittingly or unwittingly become taxable residents of the countries they spend time in, but may not tell anyone, particularly the tax authorities of that country, that they have been present in the country for a sufficient number of days to be considered tax resident. This, one of many forms of tax evasion, is becoming increasingly dangerous as authorities are becoming much more able to track where people actually are. And tax authorities are always motivated to severely punish tax evaders they catch as a means of scaring others into compliance.

Tax avoidance, once largely considered to be legal, is different from tax evasion. Avoiding tax by skirting a rule in place is increasingly under attack under a range of 'anti-avoidance' rules that countries put in place to address arrangements that lack commercial substance and which take advantage of unintended loopholes.

There are many grey areas in and around tax avoidance and what works and does not, and what is right and what isn't. A wealth owner needs good advisors, and the ability to make their own judgement about what advice is safe to follow. Denis Healey, a former UK Chancellor of the Exchequer, was quoted as saying that the difference between tax avoidance and tax evasion is the '*thickness of a prison wall*'.

Today, perceptions of inequality and abuse of tax laws by corporations and individuals are leading to new tax rules, new transparency through reporting and other requirements, and an environment where wealth owners and businesses face negative perceptions and publicity when found to have taken aggressive advantage of (albeit legal) 'loopholes' to reduce or otherwise avoid taxation. In other words, it is no longer enough to just ask whether a tax strategy is legal. One must also ask whether it would be considered acceptable in the current environment and what the consequences might be if the approach, as is likely, comes to light.

Tax planning, which refers to understanding the tax rules that have application and navigating them so as to legitimately pay the minimum of tax that is actually required, is perfectly legal, and what a well-informed wealth owner seeks to do. The tax laws of countries may be designed to encourage investment in certain areas, providing tax advantages as an incentive; wealth owners can choose where in the world to live and to invest; giving away an asset to children before it increases in value may result in lower tax on a gift of the asset than the inheritance tax that might arise if the asset is given away years later—these are all simple examples of legitimate tax planning. In a world of transparency, good tax planning is particularly important.

But the tax world is fast changing, and in the next years, more and more difficulties will be faced by the world's wealth owners as the rough road to transparency leads to governments being better able to enforce their tax laws. I have a vision of a world in which tax laws can be simple and predictable, with modest tax rates, and where full compliance results in a significantly higher level of tax revenues for countries which can efficiently and transparently administer a tax system that addresses income and wealth inequality and the needs of a fair society, while attracting to it for the long term wealth and business owners who invest and are otherwise locally active.

But moving from a world where the wealthiest often pay much less in the way of tax than they should, to one where there is real fairness, will be a long and rocky road, and one where the human right to privacy is compromised, and where populist and sometimes corrupt governments will destroy wealth and lives. And complexity leads to the wrong people getting the revenue—accountants, lawyers and other advisors rather than governments seeking to cover social and other costs.

A wealth owner needs to be well equipped with the knowledge required to know how best to proceed.

Different Kinds of Tax Systems

Different countries have different tax systems, and these vary significantly, both in terms of complexity and in terms of the tax rates that apply. Understanding how a tax system that one is subject to works, is a first step to understanding the input tax advisors provide in relation to asset protection and succession planning. Also key is to understand which tax system actually applies—for many wealth owners, it is not only one tax system that is relevant. A wealth owner may live in one country and invest in another, and this in and of itself may attract the application of the tax laws of two countries. Usually, however, it is even more complex—a wealth owner may spend time in several countries, and the question may arise as to whether he is resident, for tax purposes, in more than one. And investments are increasingly global, and the structures used to hold assets may themselves be located in yet other countries, the tax laws of which come into play.

Will There Be One Global Tax That Applies or Will Tax Competition Survive?

I did not think that we would see one global tax system for many, many decades and this despite the rush towards increased tax information and enforcement cooperation between countries. But more recent developments suggest that elements of a global tax system are now already with us and that global approaches to taxation, particularly as they might affect wealth and business owners, will be increasing.

I believe that tax competition is important and beneficial, keeping governments in check in relation to their policies, and allowing taxpayers to choose where to live and to invest, reflecting not only the services and protections different countries provide, but also the cost, benefit and risk of living or investing there.

There have been moves, however, to address what governments and others see as unfair tax competition, and this can be seen in the European Union in particular, as the practices of Luxembourg and other countries that have used their tax systems to attract business have come to light. Evidence of the abuses of bank secrecy, tax havens and opaque structures by companies and individuals has encouraged governments to do things that may not be the best in relation to wealth owners, and perhaps not even in the best economic interests of the countries involved. But there are clear realities about abuses that wealth owners and businesses have committed. And growing income and wealth inequality needs to be addressed. The world of taxation is changing and needs to change.

Short-term politics often wins out over long-term good planning, and this will increasingly have a negative effect on the tax laws wealth owners need to navigate.

For Dagland, there are opportunities to see through the fog of reactionary approaches to change and be strategic. Wealth owners need a safe home and are willing to pay for this.

Countries That Do Not Impose an Income Tax

The simplest tax system of all is where a country does not impose income tax. Such jurisdictions do exist, and among these are Dubai, where there is no personal income tax. Other kinds of taxes do apply, but for an individual who resides in Dubai, there is, simply, no income tax at all.

There are other countries that also impose no income tax, and these include a number of offshore Caribbean and other centres, such as the Bahamas.

Countries that impose no personal income tax often do have other taxes designed to raise revenues for the government. These can include taxes on particular business and other activities (as is the case of Dubai), taxes designed to force pension savings for individuals, sales taxes and others. Later on, some of the kinds of taxes that can apply are discussed, but where a country does not impose an income tax, it generally leaves a wealth owner free of the main taxes that affect wealth, including taxes on capital gains, salaries, dividends and other revenues, as well as transfer taxes, such as gift or donation taxes and estate or inheritance taxes.

Living in a tax-free country sounds attractive, but this does not mean that the taxes of other countries do not apply. If a wealth owner invests in other countries, tax exposures may arise, and depending on residential and citizenship connections, other exposures to tax can arise, based on these connections.

Territorial Tax Systems

Next to countries with no tax on income at all, jurisdictions that impose tax on a territorial basis are the next simplest to understand. The definition of what constitutes a 'territorial' tax system can vary dramatically, but for my use, I refer primarily to jurisdictions that tax only income that is locally sourced—meaning that income from outside the country involved is generally tax-free. Good examples of territorial tax systems are Hong Kong and Singapore, though there are a number of others that also impose tax on this basis, in full or in part.

Where a jurisdiction imposes tax on a territorial basis, the focus is not on where the taxpayer lives, is domiciled or has citizenship, but rather on the *source* of income. In the case of Hong Kong and Singapore, whether or not someone actually lives in Hong Kong or Singapore is not generally relevant to determining tax exposures—the tax question is simply whether the income involved is of a Hong Kong or Singapore 'source'. In the case of Singapore, residence can affect the tax rate, but the main issue remains the question of where the income is sourced.

Many rules and interpretations apply in relation to what constitutes Hong Kong or Singapore 'source' income, but in simple terms, earning a salary from working in Hong Kong or Singapore would clearly produce locally sourced and taxable earnings. Similarly, if a business is conducted in either place and the revenues are all earned from activities that take place only in the jurisdiction involved, tax will arise.

Most important in relation to territorial tax systems is that there is no tax on income that is foreign sourced, meaning that earnings properly earned through activities conducted outside of, for example, Hong Kong or Singapore are entirely free of taxation. In the case of Hong Kong and Singapore, tax rates on even locally sourced income are relatively low, generally around or under 20%. In Hong Kong, there is no relevance to whether tax-free foreign-sourced income is 'remitted' or brought into Hong Kong. In the case of Singapore, this also has no relevance for individuals, but is an issue in the case of corporate taxation, where remitted income can become taxable—but keeping that income out of Singapore, even in the corporate context, can retain tax-free status in Singapore for foreign-sourced income.

Something to note about both territorial tax systems and the tax systems of countries imposing no taxes on income: things are changing, with complexities and tax exposures being introduced to counter international pressure against the perceived negatives of tax competition. More on this later.

As outlined below, there are varieties of taxes that countries can impose ... and in the case of Singapore and Hong Kong, many of these do not apply, even if the income involved is locally sourced. Hong Kong and Singapore do not impose tax on capital gains or dividends, and also do not impose tax in relation to gifts or transfers made on death.

Linked to the benefits of living in a jurisdiction with no taxes or with a territorial system of taxation is the privacy regarding foreign income that this gives rise to—privacy that is now compromised by the approach of automatic information exchange and how it applies. Under domestic tax laws, the general principle is that where there is no tax on foreign earnings, there are also generally limited reporting requirements on foreign earnings. A resident of Hong Kong or Singapore who has a bank account in, say, Switzerland, has not had to report the capital in the account or the earnings from the account given that there is no tax on foreign-sourced income.

But what is the effect of automatic exchange of information on the privacy benefit of residing in a place that imposes tax on a territorial basis? Something that a wealth owner needs to understand is that automatic exchange of information results in the sharing of information that often goes well beyond what information a tax authority actually needs to enforce its tax laws. For example, given that Hong Kong has entered into automatic information exchange agreements with Switzerland and the United Kingdom, this results in the Hong Kong government receiving information on the assets, income and gains associated with a Swiss or UK bank account of a Hong Kong resident. Under Hong Kong tax law, this information may not be strictly needed by the Hong Kong authorities to enforce the territorial tax system in place in Hong Kong. And what of moves to ensure disclosure of beneficial owners of high-value real estate in London, New York and elsewhere? How does this fit into the picture, along with new beneficial ownership registers and other transparency initiatives? What if the taxpayer at issue would prefer that information on their foreign assets not find its way to mainland China's tax authorities? Is there an ability for this information to be shared by the Hong Kong government with the authorities in mainland China? Of course there is.

Worldwide Taxation on the Basis of Residence

The most common system of taxation is that based on residence, and where the tax that arises is then imposed on a worldwide basis. This means that if the wealth owner lives in a particular country, that country will tax all of the wealth owner's income, wherever in the world that income may arise.

This form of tax system applies in countries throughout the world. But there are significant differences in how these tax systems work.

A first question in relation to a tax system that imposes tax based on residence is whether or not the individual taxpayer is a resident for tax purposes. If I own a house in the United States, for example, but spend little time there, am I a resident of the United States? The United States has separate tax rules that apply to citizens and 'green card' holders, discussed later, but if I am neither a citizen nor a green card holder, does having a house in the United States or just spending time there each year cause me to be a resident, subject to American tax on my worldwide income?

In the case of the United States, the question of whether an individual who is neither a citizen nor a green card holder is resident there for tax purposes is based on a purely *objective* test, meaning that tax residence has little to do with intention, and much to do with how much time one physically spends in the United States. Like many things to do with American tax laws, the rules are not simple, but the bottom line is that if an individual never spends more than four months a year physically in the United States, they will NOT be resident for tax purposes, meaning that exposure to tax on a worldwide basis will not arise.

More technically, the residence rules in the United States count days of presence on a rolling three-year basis. To know whether I am resident in, say, 2024, I count my days of presence in 2024, add to those my days of presence in 2023, divided by three, and my days of presence in 2022, divided by six. If I spent at least 31 days in the United States in 2024, I will be a resident for tax purposes if the total under this formula comes to 183 days or more. Many exceptions can also apply, including exceptions for qualifying students and others. It is also possible to overcome being considered a resident under what is known as the 'substantial presence' test by showing closer connections to another country and spending less than 183 days in the United States in any year. This requires, however, the filing of a tax form, among others.

It is not the detail of how the US residence rules work that a wealth owner needs to focus on. With the help of advisors, a wealth owner can be guided on the residence rules of any country. What is important is to realize that when one spends time in different countries, it is critical to understand how that country's tax laws work in terms of determining whether taxable residence arises. While the American approach is objective in looking at the number of days of presence in the country, other countries include subjective elements to their residence tests, making it tricky to determine whether residence does or does not arise.

In Canada, for example, spending 183 days or more a year in the country gives rise to resident status, an objective test. But Canada also considers as resident those who 'in the settled routine of their lives regularly, normally or customarily live in Canada'. This rather *subjective* test makes it tricky to know for sure whether one is resident in Canada for tax purposes, given that many factors come into the picture, including residential, personal and other ties. And the question of residence is critical from a tax perspective—someone who is resident in Canada is taxable in that country on their worldwide income, and at combined federal and provincial tax rates that can reach 50% or more.

Other countries have very sensitive residence rules in the sense that even minimal presence, under some circumstances, can give rise to taxable residence and tax exposures on a worldwide basis. In Germany, for example, just having a home available there can result in an individual being considered to be domiciled in Germany, and thereby subject to worldwide taxation.

Tax Treaties and the 'Tie-Breaker' Rules

A very important exception to the residence rules of countries and their application comes up where there is a tax treaty that applies. Tax treaties, which are either bilateral or multilateral agreements on taxation between countries, can provide critical tax benefits to wealth owners, and one important such benefit relates to how they apply in the area of determining tax residence. Most comprehensive tax treaties contain what are known as 'tie-breaker' rules, which avoid the possibility of the countries that have entered into the treaty both treating the same individual as resident in their country.

In the absence of a tax treaty, there is nothing that stops two or more countries treating the same person as a tax resident. Subject to applicable credits or deductions, double or triple or more taxation could arise on the same income. Application of a tax treaty in the case of multiple residence can therefore be critical.

Here is an example of how a tax treaty can work to help deal with the possibility of being treated as a tax resident of more than one jurisdiction. If the wealth owner is a Hong Kong native and has lived and worked in Hong Kong his whole working life, he will have been 'ordinarily resident' in Hong Kong under Hong Kong's determination of who is and who is not resident. This test of 'ordinary residence', which also applies in Hong Kong's tax treaties to determine whether someone is a resident of Hong Kong, does not look at the days of physical presence in Hong Kong, but rather at many factors, including where one has chosen to establish residence for settled purposes. The wealth owner in the example has always lived in Hong Kong, has close personal and economic connections to Hong Kong, perhaps has planned to be buried in Hong Kong and maintains club and other social memberships in Hong Kong.

If, after retirement, the wealth owner establishes a second home in Canada, perhaps close to where children and grandchildren live, and spends substantial time in Canada (maybe even more than 183 days a year), there can definitely be exposure to Canadian tax on the basis of Canada treating the wealth owner as a resident under Canada's domestic tax rules. This would result in worldwide tax at significant tax rates. If the wealth owner, however, continues to maintain a home and strong residential and other connections to Hong Kong, as would often be the case, taxation in Canada as a resident may be avoided, something that would provide substantial tax benefit given that Hong Kong does not generally tax on a worldwide basis, and taxes even Hong Kong source income at moderate rates.

The way the treaty works, only *one* of Canada or Hong Kong can treat the wealth owner as resident. If, under their rules, both do so, 'tie-breaker' rules apply to work out the answer. First, the question is where the individual maintains a permanent home—if in both locations, as is the case in the example, then the question becomes where the individual's personal and economic relations, or centre of vital interests, is closer. As often the case for wealth owners, this would, in the example, be in both countries. The next test is the location of the individual's 'habitual abode'—and again, this may exist in both Canada and Hong Kong, or not be clearly determinable. Finally, if this is the case, if the individual is not a citizen of Canada, but has the right of abode in Hong Kong (a formal designation in Hong Kong), then the individual is NOT tax resident in Canada.

Most tax treaties, for the final tie-breaker rule, focus on citizenship, but in the case of Hong Kong, the formal right of abode is used in place of the citizenship test. Only if the individual is a citizen of both countries, or if, in the case of Hong Kong, they have the right of abode in Hong Kong AND citizenship in Canada, is the question referred to the authorities to determine between them which of the two jurisdictions have the ability to tax on the basis of residence.

The impact of a tax treaty tie-breaker rule can be substantial, as can be seen from the Hong Kong–Canada example. If the taxpayer is considered resident in Hong Kong, but not in Canada, then the tax benefit is meaningful, particularly given that Hong Kong does not tax a wide range of income, including foreign-sourced income, capital gains, dividends and more. While not all tax treaties involving jurisdictions that do not tax certain income provide full protection where a tie-breaker rule applies, understanding the role of tax treaties is critical. In the case of the treaty between Canada and Hong Kong, specific protection is given for income that is not of Canadian source, and which is earned by someone determined to be resident in Hong Kong and not Canada—only the country of residence has the right to taxation.

This is all very complex, and enough to give the wealth owner a headache. But the headache is more pleasant than being taxed on worldwide income at substantial tax rates. Understanding how residence rules and treaties work can help the wealth owner establish a way of living that legally and effectively minimizes their global tax exposure.

It is also critical to remember that in an increasingly transparent world, it is not a question of whether a country will know how much time you spend there. You need to assume that they will. The only planning that a wealth owner can adopt is to *play by the rules or get out.*

There Are Many Differences Between Worldwide Tax Systems Based on Residence

Each country has its own tax system, and the fact that many countries have in common the approach of taxing residents on a worldwide basis does not mean that there are not important differences between tax systems. Tax rates, of course, vary widely, and many other factors can be relevant in determining just how much tax a worldwide taxpayer actually has to pay. Very relevant also is the question of how the problem of possible double taxation is dealt with. Where a country taxes its residents on a worldwide basis, what happens if the taxpayer is also subject to tax in another country on the same income?

Whether or not one is a resident of another country, tax exposure in that country can arise if income sourced in that country arises. Virtually all countries that have an income tax will tax at least some forms of income that arise in their country, regardless of whether the person earning the income is or is not resident there. In very general terms, if an individual lives in one country, but earns income in another, say by working in that other country or investing there, that income may be taxed in the country in which it was earned. If the individual is resident in a country that taxes on a worldwide basis, both countries will be seeking to tax the same income. This potential for double taxation is dealt with in a number of ways, and avoiding double taxation, needless to say, can be a very important (and legitimate) objective in tax planning.

Back to tax treaties. Where a tax treaty applies, one of the areas commonly covered is assurance that double taxation will not arise. This is achieved in different ways, including through assurance of the availability of foreign tax credits or exemptions. In simple terms, tax treaties will usually make it clear which of the two countries involved have the right to tax any particular item of income and, in the case of the source country, often to what extent.

An example would relate to income from real estate investment. Treaties generally protect the source country in the sense of allowing the country in which the real estate is located to tax income relating to the real estate under its own rules, and then requiring that the country of residence of the taxpayer, if it is going to tax the income under its worldwide taxing approach, provides a 'credit' for the tax paid, thereby avoiding double taxation. If the country of residence taxes at 45% and would charge a tax of $45 on $100 of net income from real estate, a credit would be provided for the tax imposed by the source country—say a tax of $35 on the same income. The final tax payable would be $35 to the country where the real estate is located, and $10 to the country of residence ($45 less the credit for the $35), thereby resulting in the final collective tax rate being the higher of the tax rates of the two countries involved.

Even in the absence of tax treaties, most countries that impose tax on a worldwide basis provide tax credits for taxes paid on income earned in other countries. How these credits work can be very different, and important steps may need to be taken to ensure that the credit can be obtained. In some countries, rather than a credit for foreign taxes, a deduction is provided. This can work out to be less valuable than a credit, resulting in an overall tax rate higher than the highest rate of the two countries involved. In other countries, Switzerland being an example, certain foreign income that is allocable to a foreign permanent establishment, as would be the case where a Swiss resident owns foreign real estate, is entirely exempt from Swiss taxation. This is highly attractive, as the exemption does not require that the income from the investment in the foreign country actually be taxed in that foreign country. As with tax credits, making sure that the availability of the exemption is maintained can be a critical element of legitimate tax-minimization planning.

A mistake that many wealth owners make, sometimes based on the legacy and incorrect approach of not properly disclosing foreign income and assets, is to own an income-producing investment through a company or other intermediate entity without having made sure that this does not result in double taxation. For example, a wealth owner may live in a country that taxes on worldwide income at a rate of 40%, but only provides tax credits on foreign taxes that are directly imposed on the wealth owner. If the wealth owner earns $100 of income in a foreign country, and pays $25 of tax in that country, that tax would be credited against the $40 of tax on the income in the home country, resulting in a total tax of $40–$25 paid to the foreign country, and $15 to the home country. If, however, the wealth owner owns the shares of a company that makes the investment in the foreign country, it is the company that may then pay the $25 in tax in that foreign country. When the remaining $75 is paid to the wealth owner as a dividend, it may then be that the full $75 is taxed at 40% in the home country, resulting in a tax payment to the home country of $30. The total tax paid in the home country and the foreign country comes to $55, meaning that the total tax is higher than it would have been had the wealth owner held the investment in the foreign country directly, and obtained a foreign tax credit.

This example is one of many that begin to point towards a topic dealt with later, tax-advantaged investing. This means thinking carefully about the tax effect of how investments are made and focusing not only on the potential of return and risks taken, but the reality that returns are very much affected by tax. It is key to focus on the *after*-tax return, and not the *pre*-tax return, and to do so by looking at tax not only in the country of investment, but in the country in which the wealth owner lives (and/or maintains citizenship, which may also be relevant).

Offshore Companies and Worldwide Tax Systems

Individuals living in countries imposing tax on a worldwide basis have long looked for ways to 'defer' or delay their tax exposures, allowing them to accumulate income and reinvest it on a pre-tax basis, enhancing returns, before exposing the earnings to tax in their home countries. If, for example, an individual is living in a country that imposes tax on a worldwide basis at a rate of 40% and invests $1000 in another country that does not impose tax on the type of investment being made, if the individual earns $100 of income from that investment, there would be $60 left to invest after the 40% tax is paid. But what if the activity or investment is not conducted by the resident individual, but rather by a company that the individual sets up? The individual could contribute the $1000 to a company in a country that imposes no tax, say the British Virgin Islands, and that company can then invest the $1000 in the country where the income is to be earned. If the income of $100 stays in the company and is not distributed to the individual shareholder by way of a dividend, is the full $100 then available to reinvest, as opposed to only $60, which would have been all that was left after the home-country tax of 40% was paid?

The answer is that it depends. Some countries that impose tax on a worldwide basis allow for the deferral, or delay, in tax the example suggests. Switzerland, which (subject to limited exceptions for some foreigners) taxes its residents on a worldwide basis, is an example of a country where tax can, if certain steps are taken, be deferred in this way.

Other countries have a number of 'anti-deferral' rules that can apply, including what are sometimes referred to as controlled foreign corporation (CFC) rules. These rules focus on the use of foreign corporations and limit the ability of a taxpayer to 'defer' or delay tax exposure. If an individual resident in a country that has these rules owns a bank account in another country, tax cannot be delayed by having the bank account transferred to a corporate vehicle. The individual, if taxed on a worldwide basis, would pay tax in his home country on the income earned from the account, despite the account not being located in his home country. If the individual transfers the account to an offshore company owned by him, while the offshore company itself may not be taxed in the individual taxpayer's country of residence, the individual shareholder can be treated as taxable on the earnings of the company, even if the company does not distribute a dividend and holds onto its earnings.

Generally, CFC rules look at the nature of the activity of the offshore company. Where it is involved in passive investments as opposed to independent active business, the controlled foreign corporation rules can apply to tax the income on a current basis. Even where active business is conducted, some countries have complex rules to evaluate circumstances where tax can be deferred, making review of the issue complex.

CFC rules tend to focus on companies that are 'controlled' by taxpayers from the country whose tax laws are the issue. However, even where such control does not exist, anti-deferral rules can have application where a country focuses not only on 'controlled' foreign corporations, but also on 'passive' foreign investment companies, where the anti-deferral effect arises even where the taxpayer owns only a small part of a foreign passive investment company.

In simple terms, an individual living in a country that taxes on a worldwide basis needs to understand how their tax system generally works, as only then can the wealth owner begin to be in a position to understand their own succession and asset-protection plans, asking advisors the right questions and guiding them in the planning process.

Also relevant to wealth owners living in countries that impose worldwide tax based on residence is the question of where the foreign company they have established is itself resident. While where a company is incorporated is a very important element in determining tax residence, many countries also treat companies as resident where the company is 'managed and controlled'. A Swiss-resident wealth owner who owns shares of a British Virgin Islands company that, in turn, owns assets outside of Switzerland, will not be taxable on the earnings of the British Virgin Islands company as Switzerland does not have CFC rules. But if the British Virgin Islands company is viewed as being 'managed and controlled' in Switzerland, as would be the case if the wealth owner, from Switzerland, 'calls all the shots', then the company itself would become taxable in Switzerland, losing the ability to help in achieving tax deferral. Careful planning, and ensuring that management and control takes place outside the home country, will be critical to avoiding current tax exposure.

'*How will anyone find out?*' has been the basis of defective and historical tax 'planning'—advisors and taxpayers asking themselves how, in a world of bank secrecy and opaque ownership possibilities, anyone will know about offshore companies used by taxpayers, or of other cross-border structures that might be taken advantage of. The move to transparency has been an unstoppable one, and the amount of information that tax authorities (and others) are receiving is unprecedented. For wealth owners seeking to manage their tax exposures through legitimate tax planning, it is key to navigate ever-changing tax laws and ensure that the structures they use have the substance they need to withstand full scrutiny.

The opportunity for Dagland, the fictitious country I have used as an example, might be to offer simplicity in a world of complexity to wealth owners. More on what Dagland might do to take advantage of this opportunity is discussed later.

Moves to transparency are not limited to a focus on the taxation of individuals, and automatic information exchange implemented through a focus on the banks and other financial intermediaries they work with. In parallel, there is a focus on ensuring transparency in relation to the corporate tax world and, in particular, the use (and possible abuse) of 'offshore' companies and inappropriate transfer pricing. In broad terms, governments have moved towards requiring information from taxpayers, from tax authorities abroad and from other sources, all with a view to understanding the full global tax picture for corporate groups, whether or not owned by individuals.

Simply allocating a portion of income to a company in a tax haven is not tax planning—it never really was. But what if no one ever found out, and there were positions that could be taken that the planning was legitimate? The 'offshore' world of tax-haven companies developed in the shadows of an opaque world, where the main countries of residence of individuals and corporations would not have a full picture of what was going on globally. In a world of transparency and focus on transfer pricing—the allocation of earnings and profits between related entities—this has and continues to be fast falling away. The possibility of allocating earnings and profits to an offshore company with little substance or activity and not paying any tax on this in the home country is becoming part of history. While the use of tax havens and offshore companies will continue, and for many legitimate uses, the shift is to **substance**, and increasingly to the use of jurisdictions that can offer real infrastructure that supports substance, as well as favourable tax rates, a wide network of tax treaties and more. Such locations are not often found in the offshore world of the Caribbean but rather in the 'midshore' world of locations like Singapore and others offering infrastructure, treaties and moderate taxation.

The starting point in any tax analysis is always to understand how the home country taxes the wealth owner. If a wealth owner is investing abroad, a mistake often made is to start the analysis in the country in which the investment is made. The right first step is to first understand how the home country, through its tax laws, affects the wealth owner and to then marry the tax planning that might be possible in the country of investment with the rules applicable in the home country. Relevant here will be, among others, whether the home country taxes the overseas income; whether dividends from foreign companies are taxed; are there CFC and are there issues that can arise in relation to 'management and control'? Effective tax planning means putting together the rules applicable in all relevant countries.

The United States and Worldwide Taxation of Citizens and 'Green Card' Holders

The United States, in addition to taxing those who are resident in the United States on a worldwide basis, taxes its citizens and permanent residents (known as 'green card' holders) on a worldwide basis, regardless of physical presence in the United States. A number of countries in the world look at citizenship as a factor in some taxes that are imposed, but the United States is the only country in the world that imposes its taxes comprehensively on those who hold citizenship or green card status virtually regardless of their physical presence in the United States.

In the case of a permanent resident of the United States, full taxation on a worldwide basis can sometimes be avoided if the green card holder is also resident in a country that has a tax treaty with the United States and the relevant treaty 'tie-breaker' rules apply. Treaties, however, do NOT generally protect US citizens from worldwide taxation.

Citizenship of the United States has long been viewed as a great benefit by wealth owners, particularly those linked to countries with political risk and uncertainty, and where home-country passports do not make travel easy. Many wealth owners in India, Pakistan, Indonesia, China and other places have sought to obtain US citizenship to provide them with a passport that allows travel without a visa to many countries, and to afford their families the possibility of 'escape' to the United States in the event of political or other problems in their home countries. Some families have gone to great lengths to obtain American citizenship for themselves or their children, but many of them have not been clear about the tax effects of having US citizenship. Under US tax law, exposure to tax (and numerous reporting requirements) arises when a wealth owner is a citizen, and this regardless of where the wealth owner actually lives and whether they spend any time in the United States. This is also regardless of whether the wealth owner has a valid US passport or multiple citizenships.

Becoming a US citizen can be remarkably easy, and automatically includes those born in the United States, as well as many circumstances of those born outside the United States to a US parent. There are certainly situations where one may be a US citizen but not be aware of it!

Boris Johnson, Mayor of London at the time, found out about the difficulties faced by American citizens living abroad the hard way. A British national born to British parents, Boris Johnson was also a US citizen as his mother gave birth to him in New York. Despite the fact that he was living in the United Kingdom at the time of selling his house there, he discovered that dealing with UK tax on the sale and navigating principal residence tax exemptions was not enough. As a US citizen, he was subject to hefty capital gains taxes in the United States on his sale of a home in England, and this reportedly outraged the outspoken then mayor, resulting in his stating that he simply would not pay. It did not take long for Boris Johnson to learn that you really only have two choices: *play by the rules or get out*. And in his case, he was reported to have had to do both. First, to pay the taxes due in the United States, playing by the rules, and then to give up his US citizenship in a formal way, getting out of the US worldwide tax system going forward.

Historically, it has been difficult for the United States to ensure that its citizens, particularly those living outside the United States, meet all of their tax and reporting obligations. This, however, has been fast changing, as banks in particular have been brought into the picture through reporting requirements backed by tough tax and penalty rules designed to ensure compliance.

For US citizens, whether living in the United States or not, getting out of the tax system means not only not spending more time in America than the US residence rules allow, but also giving up citizenship. And before giving up citizenship, key is to sort out any tax issues of the past, meaning that if tax and reporting requirements have not been complied with, *voluntary disclosure* is the only way to go.

When a tax authority catches a wealth owner who has not been compliant with tax and reporting requirements, it is often not just about punishing the taxpayer, but about making an example of them to scare others into compliance. Voluntary disclosure, which means going forward to the tax authorities to sort out historical non-compliance, can often avoid many of the penalties associated with tax evasion, and in the case of the United States, like other countries, there are from time to time procedures in place in relation to voluntary disclosure that can provide very favourable results to wealth owners seeking to 'come clean'.

For those who do not come clean with the American tax authorities in relation to undeclared income, even if they do not get caught in their lifetime, there is generally no time limit that applies to tax claims in and around undeclared situations. 'Transferee liability' may also apply, meaning that if my mother was an American citizen, regardless of whether I am or not, I may be responsible for her unpaid US taxes if I inherit from her.

Wealth owners need, in my view, to leave a clean slate to the younger generation, and it is not only in the context of untaxed monies owned by American citizens at death that this is of relevance.

There Are Many Kinds of Taxes

Countries impose a wide array of taxes, and for the wealth owner it is critical to understand which do and do not apply. And for Dagland, an appreciation of the challenging complexities faced by wealth owners will help it to discover the opportunities afforded by helping to address a real need of the wealth-owning community: simplicity, consistency and long-term trust in one's country. This is something that I believe wealth owners are ready to pay for, and in a way that can comprehensively benefit the society to which they connect.

Indirect taxes, being taxes that are applied on goods and services rather than on income and gains, are increasingly relied on by governments as an easier way of collecting taxes. The most common of these are 'value-added' and other sales taxes imposed on consumption. For wealth owners, indirect taxes can be important, and this particularly in relation to real estate, with a number of countries increasingly focusing on stamp duties and similar levies as a means of raising income.

Of even greater focus for wealth owners are direct taxes on income and gains.

Income taxes generally include taxes on salaries and other income, but with considerable differences in how countries tax different items and at what level. For example, in some countries, dividends may be subject to income tax, while in others some or all of a dividend may be exempt from tax. Investment income in the way of interest income is usually taxed, but some countries provide exemptions for certain interest income earned by non-residents as a means of encouraging investment into the country.

Capital gains are different from normal income and in the case of some countries, capital gains may be tax-free. In other countries, capital gains may be taxed at lower rates than ordinary income. What constitutes a capital gain can, therefore, be a very important thing to determine. An occasional sale of a real estate investment may give rise to a capital gain; a trader in real estate selling a piece of real estate may be considered to not be earning a capital gain, but rather fully taxable trading income, given that they are in the business of buying and selling real estate.

Transfer taxes—taxes on gifts and on death—can be very important to wealth-owning families. While some countries do not tax transfers made during life or at death, many do, and at sometimes very high tax rates that are not based, like an income tax, on profits, but rather on the value of assets that are transferred. An increasing global focus on income and wealth inequality is suggesting that we may see more in the way of transfer taxes being imposed in the future, albeit the rules vary country by country.

For example, in some countries the tax is imposed on the giver of the gift or the estate of the person whose assets pass on death; in other countries it is the recipient that is taxed. A common mistake made by wealth owners and their advisors is to not enquire about the tax residence of the recipient of a gift or bequest. A resident of the Bahamas, for example, may assume that the gift made to a child is tax-free given the absence of gift taxes in the Bahamas, but in certain jurisdictions, such as France, Ireland and Spain, a recipient resident there may become taxable on receipt of a gift.

In cross-border gifts and inheritances, avoidance of double taxation also becomes an issue, and here too tax treaties can have an impact, with a number of countries having in place bilateral estate and gift tax or similar agreements designed to help avoid double taxation.

Wealth taxes are imposed by some countries, and these taxes are of particular concern to wealth owners given that taxes can exceed income. If, for example, the wealth owner owns a particular asset, and the asset does not produce any income, then the *value* of the asset will still be part of the tax base for determining exposure to the wealth tax. Tax will be payable, regardless that the asset does not produce any income. Wealth taxes are also of concern given the disclosure that providing information on one's net worth results in. In a world of populist or authoritarian governments and changing regimes, it is not always a safe option for wealth owners to provide this kind of information to the government of the country they may live in.

But wealth taxes are increasingly on the agenda and even potentially in a global way, as is addressed later. And for Dagland, if it can prove itself a trustworthy home for wealth owners, wealth taxation may be part of a broadening of its tax base and its move to balancing the interests of wealth owners with the needs of the broader community.

There are many other taxes that can also be critically important to wealth owners, and which will affect how assets are owned for succession and asset-protection purposes.

Increasingly, countries are focusing on the taxation of real estate, both through indirect taxes, such as stamp duties, and direct taxes, such as income and inheritance taxes. There are ever-changing rules on how high-value property is taxed and on how different ownership structures used by wealth owners affect the tax position. Real estate is an immoveable asset, and for countries seeking to raise revenues, taxing owners of real estate is an increasingly attractive taxing option. Canada has taken the opportunity to impose a number of taxes that apply in relation to real estate owned by non-residents of the country, in part with a view to dampening real estate prices (which have risen beyond the reach of most Canadian taxpayers).

Real estate is also coming under scrutiny as an investment class that permits an opaque approach to ownership, with the frequent use of offshore companies and other vehicles as owners, masking beneficial ownership. This is resulting in new beneficial ownership reporting requirements both inside and outside of the world of automatic exchange of information, and is likely to intensify.

Mobility and Citizenship Planning, and Fixing Historical Tax Non-disclosure

Play by the rules or get out. These are the only choices wealth owners have—the third choice of staying connected to a country by residence, domicile, citizenship or otherwise and hoping that no one will find out is simply not an option in a world of growing transparency and where tax laws are increasingly and more aggressively enforced. Tax laws are laws, and there is no choice but for compliance with them.

Getting out means sorting out any historical tax liabilities, and then moving on to exiting a tax system and finding a new one, and ideally a more favourable one, to become subject to.

In addressing historical tax liabilities, a first and important step is to work out what they are. This may not be easy, given the difficulty of finding historical records on the income involved, and the forensic work necessary can sometimes be difficult. Where someone inherits undeclared funds, working out the past can be even more complex.

Sadly, where assets and income have been hidden, steps may have been taken that make tax exposures higher than they would have otherwise been, and more difficult to calculate. This is particularly the case where offshore companies, trusts, foundations and other structures come into the picture. In other words, had the older generation played by the rules, less in the way of tax would have been payable than what the younger generation has to pay to come clean when they come into the money. This highlights the need for the older generation to take charge and not leave a legacy of problems to those who may inherit from them.

A next step in figuring out tax exposures associated with undeclared money is to determine whether there is an applicable limitations period that may apply. In some countries, statutes of limitations may prevent a tax authority from having the ability to look back more than a few years in relation to undeclared and untaxed income. In other countries, no limitations on time may apply. The effect of death and the existence of 'transferee liability' will also be relevant. If my father died and left me assets that he did not declare to the tax authorities, am I responsible for the taxes he did not pay? There are few things my father may have done wrong that I am legally responsible for, but tax may be one of them. Again, the answer to this question will vary country by country and will have a major impact on my determination of how much tax, if any, I owe in relation to undeclared income and assets.

Different countries, at different times, offer programmes designed to encourage taxpayers with historical non-disclosure issues to come forward voluntarily. These can be forms of amnesties or voluntary disclosure procedures, all designed to encourage compliance. Related to growing transparency and the moves to automatic information exchange is that more in the way of voluntary disclosure procedures have occasionally been on offer. In most cases, these facilities provide much more efficient, safe and inexpensive ways for taxpayers to 'come clean'. Failing to take advantage of these opportunities is often a mistake, particularly given that when countries catch a tax evader (as opposed to when one voluntarily seeks to come clean), it is not just a question of punishing the taxpayer, and imposing taxes, interest and penalties, but making an example that will scare other taxpayers into compliance.

The more wealth involved and the better known the taxpayer is, the more risky it may be, given the good example their punishment may provide. Increasingly, governments seek to name and shame those who break the tax laws with a view to making it clear to other taxpayers that tax compliance is their only choice. Rather than becoming an example for the tax authorities, voluntary disclosure can be an important way to put the past behind you in a safe, predictable and confidential way.

Given the ever-increasing automatic exchange of information between countries, many countries are moving to ensuring that there are reasonable means for taxpayers to regularize their historical tax affairs, recognizing that this will increase revenues and help ensure longer-term tax compliance.

Golden Rules of Undeclared Money

Despite huge increases in global transparency and tax enforcement, undeclared money remains a major issue around the world. Assets and income remain hidden in any number of ways, including where—among families and between friends—ownership is obfuscated through false filings and declarations. I have seen and continue to see, sadly, many wealth owners falling into the trap of putting assets in the names of others—whether within their family or not—who may be living in more benign tax jurisdictions and assuming the money will end up where it belongs. Apart from this being illegal tax evasion with serious criminal and financial consequences, all too often the money ends up in the wrong hands as relationships change, people die or become incapacitated, or other circumstances of life intervene.

For years, I have put forward a set of three 'golden rules' in and around undeclared money.

- *Don't make someone else's problem your problem.*

    Whether you are a banker or other advisor or simply being asked by a family member, friend or business associate to help, it is important to understand how easy it is for someone else's problem to become your problem in the area of undeclared money. Tax evasion is a crime, and helping someone to commit a crime is itself a crime.

    In the tax area this can come up in any number of ways, including through a conspiracy to tax evasion, aiding and abetting or otherwise. If a banker or other advisor assists a client to disguise the real source or ownership of income or assets, this can easily turn into a crime. A wealth owner living in one country may be asked by a friend from another country to hold assets in their name with a view to a future gift to the

children of the real owner or otherwise—lots of variations on a theme, and all examples of easy ways that someone else's problem can become your problem. In today's transparent world, the only option for the real owner of the assets or income is to play by the rules, and where there is historical non-reporting, to regularize this through voluntary disclosure or similar procedures.
- *In today's world, no new undeclared money.*

Looking back in time, it is understandable, in many circumstances, why wealth-owning families may have had undeclared money. This may have arisen through inheritance or otherwise, or because of historical issues faced by the family given their background or countries to which they are connected. During the Second World War, many families lost everything through confiscation and, not trusting governments, took advantage of bank secrecy to protect a portion of family wealth; in many countries corruption, political risk and other factors forced wealth owners to keep a portion of their income and wealth undisclosed. But in today's increasingly transparent world, the wealth owner risks more by keeping things undeclared, and other, legitimate approaches to wealth protection need to be undertaken. While there may have been a historical rationale to keeping money hidden, there is no room for this today, and in respect of new flows of income, legal approaches to achieving confidentiality and tax minimization need to be adopted.
- *No new bad guys—keep the younger generation innocent.*

Today, the best approach for a wealth owner to take where there are historical non-disclosure or other issues is to undertake voluntary disclosure—making unprompted contact with the relevant tax authorities and seeking to address the issues of the past. Where a taxpayer makes such an approach, in the case of most countries the position is hugely different from where a taxpayer gets caught with undeclared money. And in many, many cases, the more innocent of wrongdoing the person coming clean is, the less in the way of penalties and other negatives arise.

Where the older generation has an ownership interest in undeclared funds, likely the older generation has signing authority and other incidents of ownership over the relevant funds. They may have a history of using the funds and may even have been involved in steps taken to disguise the ownership of the funds—all steps that turn them into 'bad guys' in the sense of their having broken the laws of the country whose taxes are in issue. Keeping the younger generation of the family out of any wrongdoing can be critical if it is the younger generation, on inheriting the assets involved, who will have to come clean with the relevant authorities. Do not add your children as signatories to the account; do not have your children access the funds or be involved in structures that may wrongly be used to disguise actual ownership.

If those in the younger generation are innocent of wrongdoing, on inheriting the assets they may be in a much better position to undertake voluntary disclosure in a way that will result in a minimum of penalties.

Getting Out—Exits May Become Increasingly Costly

Once historical tax issues are addressed, and the wealth owner is clearly 'playing by the rules', they can consider the important question of whether 'getting out' is a good option.

Mobility, and taking advantage of the ease with which a wealth owner can move from one country to another, is an important element of not only tax planning, but also the achievement of a number of other objectives the wealth owner may have. The reality is that different countries have different tax rules, and where someone lives (and in some cases, where one holds citizenship or is domiciled) may drastically affect tax exposures. Apart from tax, residence choices will affect the question of what information which government will hold about a wealth owner's income and assets, an important issue in a world where challenges to wealth are only increasing, and where it is not always safe for information about wealth to be in the hands of governments (where such information can fall into the hands of bad actors or be misused politically or otherwise).

Achieving the objectives of mobility does not necessarily require that the whole family relocate. Sometimes just having one or two members of the family take up residence in an appropriate country may facilitate a solid tax-minimization and asset-protection plan for the family. For example, a family living in a particular country may have a business there, and a number of family members involved in various aspects of the business, both in the home country and abroad. If one or two members of the younger generation relocate to a more tax-advantaged country and become the owners of new family businesses established there, they may be able to own the new businesses, and even transfer them to tax-beneficial structures that benefit the entire family. Ownership of the new assets may not be part of the reporting requirements of the country that has been exited, and a number of tax and non-tax objectives of the family may thereby be met.

The first step in mobility is the question of how to exit the country you are currently connected to. Those looking at mobility almost always begin by asking the wrong question—how long do I need to spend in Monaco or the Bahamas or wherever to be a resident there? The reason that this is the wrong question is because the key first step is to work out how to exit the country you are currently connected to, whether by residence, domicile or citizenship, or a combination of them.

As discussed, many countries impose tax on a worldwide basis on those who are resident in that country. A first step in mobility planning is to understand the residence rules and to work out how they apply to those giving up residence, and how much time going forward you will be able to spend in the country you are leaving without continuing to be a resident, or resuming residence once residence has been given up. Usually, this involves carefully monitoring the number of days of physical presence in the country one seeks to exit, though in some cases also relevant will be whether accommodation is retained in the relevant country and what personal and economic ties continue to exist after a departure.

Very relevant to exiting a country may well be the presence of a favourable tax treaty between the country one is departing from and the country one is moving to.

Touched on earlier, tax treaties contain residence 'tie-breaker' rules that prevent an individual being considered to be a tax resident in both countries at the same time. If the conditions of the treaty are met, domestic tax rules—which might otherwise cause the individual to remain taxable in their original country of residence—may be supplanted by the application of the treaty, which provides protection against the individual still being considered to be a resident of the country involved. A good example would arise in relation to Germany, where a long-term resident seeking to leave Germany and give up residence may find that the maintenance of accommodation in Germany, even if accompanied by minimal physical presence, will result in taxable domicile in Germany, and continued tax exposure on a worldwide basis. This domestic rule, however, can be overcome if the individual involved establishes sufficient connections to their new country of residence and that new country of residence has a suitable tax treaty with Germany. Exposures to gift and inheritance taxes apply similarly in many cases, and inheritance and gift tax treaties can also be of importance.

A growing issue relevant to leaving the taxing jurisdiction of a country is the question of whether *exit taxes* apply. An increasing number of countries impose an exit tax on those who give up taxable residence (and in the case of the United States, citizenship or long-term 'green card' status, elaborated on below), often through a deemed sale of assets at fair market value on the date of departure. Canada, for example, has long had an exit tax that operates in this way. A resident who leaves the country is taxed on their departure, on the basis of their being considered to have sold their assets when they leave. If the individual owns appreciated assets, exposure to capital gains taxes thereby arises.

Basically, exit taxes of this kind seek to tax the appreciation in assets that occurred during the period of residence, ensuring that a departure from the country does not permit this 'pregnant' gain to avoid taxation.

A number of European countries also impose exit taxes, though in recent years how these taxes apply has had to be adapted to ensure that the taxes remain valid in light of freedom of movement assured under agreements that form the European Union. Even with such freedom of movement, a number of European countries, such as France, do have exit taxes that are now compliant with EU rules, and which require careful planning and navigation where mobility planning is underway.

One simple guideline on mobility planning, however, is that the best time to consider leaving a country is *before* that country begins to impose an exit tax. As the world moves to greater tax transparency and tax laws are enforced more vigorously, it is likely that more wealth owners will be using mobility as part of their planning, attracting more high-tax countries to consider barriers to mobility, including exit taxes and tougher rules in relation to the question of who is and who is not a tax resident, particularly among those who were previously taxable residents of the country.

Where exit taxes apply and there are rules that deem the sale of assets on a departure, it is useful to consider an exit when asset values are low, such as during an economic downturn. In a wealth-owning family, it is also relevant to consider having those in the younger generation of the family undertake mobility planning before and not after they come into wealth.

In relation to the United States, it is not only the giving up of taxable residence that is important in mobility planning, but also the giving up of citizenship or 'green card' status. The reason for this is that the United States is virtually the only country that currently taxes citizens and permanent residents on their worldwide income regardless of how much time they spend in the United States. In the case of citizens and long-term green card holders, giving up citizenship or green cards can result in an exit tax applying, depending on, among other things, the individual's net worth and income and certain other factors. Giving up citizenship before a family member in the younger generation comes into wealth can often be an important thing to consider.

When one considers giving up citizenship, the question of what replacement citizenship can be obtained comes up. Citizenship planning is also relevant to wealth owners seeking second, third and further nationalities, something of interest to those whose existing citizenship gives rise to political risk or inconvenience. There are many wealth owners from countries that are politically unstable and whose passports do not afford easy travel. Here too, interest in obtaining second or further citizenships arises.

Pre-migration Planning

Once planning in relation to getting out of a country has been undertaken, the question arises as to where the wealth owner can go. A sometimes related question is where a wealth owner can obtain a second or further citizenship.

Where mobility planning is undertaken, there are often many choices regarding where a wealth owner can move to. Obvious tax-advantaged choices include jurisdictions that impose virtually no tax at all, such as the Bahamas or Dubai. Other choices can include countries that impose tax on a territorial basis, such as Hong Kong or Singapore, where a resident (or non-resident) only pays tax on their locally sourced income, not on worldwide income. There are also a number of countries that offer special 'deals' on taxation for specific groups of taxpayers. In Switzerland, in some cantons, it is possible to negotiate a 'lump sum' tax arrangement where taxes are imposed on the basis of a fictitious income figure that is calculated on the basis of expenditures in Switzerland for housing rather than on the basis of actual worldwide income. In Thailand, retirees can avoid being taxed on their non-Thai-sourced income. And in Italy and Greece, a straightforward annual payment for a set number of years, replace worldwide taxation, exempting foreign-sourced income from taxation.[7]

For Dagland, in its consideration of how to move forward as a destination of choice for responsible wealth owners, the United Kingdom is an example of lost opportunities and a lack of vision by its government.

Historically, many wealth owners had found themselves in the attractive position of being resident in the United Kingdom, through physical presence, but not domiciled in the United Kingdom, either because their father was domiciled outside of the United Kingdom or because they established a 'domicile of choice' outside of the United Kingdom. A resident, non-domiciliary of the United Kingdom, rather than being taxed on a worldwide basis, was able to choose, more recently at a cost after a set number of years, to be taxed in the United Kingdom only on their UK-sourced income and on that portion of their foreign income that they 'remitted' or brought into the United Kingdom. This attractive tax regime has, for a number of years, been the subject of focus and review, first resulting in limits to, among others, the number of years beneficial non-domiciled status could be retained. Most recently, non-domiciled status was limited to fifteen out of twenty years.

The United Kingdom has, however, announced the end of the non-domiciliary system. In many respects a good thing, given how poorly the system operated in terms of fairness. But the rules replacing the system, at least as outlined so far, fail to take advantage of the opportunity the United Kingdom had: to establish itself as the country of choice for responsible wealth owners. The United Kingdom had the opportunity to do what is later outlined as Dagland's opportunity.

In all these cases, care needs to be taken in planning one's affairs to reflect the way in which one's new country imposes tax, and it is critical to do this on a 'pre-immigration' basis—taking steps before one becomes a resident of the new country.

While many countries offer tax advantages to wealth owners establishing residence, it is important to pay attention to the reality that where a tax system discriminates against 'locals' as against 'foreigners', political and other pressures can result in many changes to the rules and increasing costs to the new resident. Good examples here would include Switzerland and the United Kingdom, where those on 'lump-sum' tax arrangements in Switzerland and who qualified as 'resident, non-domiciliaries' in the United Kingdom have found their status to be under constant review and change, with costs increasing and uncertainties regarding long-term reliance on the special taxing regime arising. The United Kingdom has been particularly egregious in constantly changing its already complex tax rules, fuelling distrust in the tax system as a whole.

Pressures from other countries are increasingly inevitable, as more and more wealth owners choose to 'get out' as a means of managing their tax exposures. On this front, jurisdictions that impose virtually no tax on both local and foreign individuals—or which, like Hong Kong and Singapore, do not tax the foreign income of *both* local and foreign taxpayers—may have a longer-term future as interesting locations for wealth owners to move to. This said, the possibility of *global* taxation initiatives is on the rise, something expanded on later.

Demand in relation to mobility is increasing, and this is resulting in not only more in the way of exit taxes, but more difficulty in obtaining resident permits in places like Singapore, and higher costs for those seeking to take advantage of tax-advantaged locations.

Interestingly, there is much in the way of planning that an individual can undertake before a move to even what may be perceived as being a high-tax country. Here, pre-immigration planning again comes into the picture, and a variety of approaches—sometimes involving the use of trusts and other wealth-planning 'tools'—become relevant. In very simple terms, for a retiring couple, for example, some simple steps can reduce tax dramatically before a move to a new country. Gifting assets to children, directly or through structures, if properly done, may well result in the assets no longer being owned, meaning that tax in relation to income earned on those assets will be avoided in the new country of residence.

Citizenship is available in a number of circumstances, and a good starting point is often to consider what citizenships may be available as a result of family history or religion. A number of countries have laws that consider the children and further descendants of a citizen to be a citizen. So, if your mother or grandfather was born in a particular country, you may find that you are eligible to become a citizen of that country. In fact, you may already be a citizen, and it is only a case of proving your right to obtaining a passport as proof of that citizenship.

In the case of Israel, a right of 'return' open to all who are Jewish makes it possible for Israeli citizenship to be available to those who can prove they are Jewish and who establish residence in Israel.

There are also countries that, in effect, sell citizenship. This is often achieved through investment and other programmes, and in some cases the countries involved are even members of the European Union, affording their citizens freedom of movement within Europe and wide access to visa-free travel to many countries. Other countries require a considerable period of physical residence before citizenship can be obtained, and this includes countries like Australia, Canada and the United Kingdom. But unlike the United States, these are countries where, once citizenship is obtained, if one is no longer resident in the country, there is no exposure to worldwide taxation—like any non-resident, whether a citizen or not, tax only arises on locally sourced income when one is not resident there.

In the longer term, it is likely to become more and more difficult to obtain and keep second, third and further citizenships. As in the area of mobility, where there are an increasing number of countries that impose exit taxes and whose residence and related rules are getting tougher and tougher, it is likely that more countries will seek to limit the circumstances in which second, third and further citizenships are permitted. For now, however, multiple citizenships can be an important safety net for wealth-owning families, and not only from a tax perspective.

***

The world of taxation is not a simple one, but tax is an important area for wealth owners to navigate to reach the family's impact goal.

The only certainty in the tax world is one of change—tax laws rarely stay the same, and the complexity of cross-border investment and global families all too often results in wealth owners losing the ability to really understand their overall tax position and the structures that their advisors put in place for them. Most important, however, is for the wealth owner to have enough of an understanding of their tax position to be able to ask the right questions, and also to realize that while tax is important, it is only one of many needs that wealth owners have and must address in their succession and asset-protection planning.

Notes

1. Jean-Baptiste Colbert, Minister of Finance under King Louis XIV of France in the seventeenth century
2. https://www.justice.gov/tax/swiss-bank-program https://www.swissinfo.ch/eng/business/how-the-us-tax-evasion-crackdown-impacted-swiss-banking/49032750
3. Also relevant to the failure of the arrangement between the United Kingdom and Switzerland was the Liechtenstein Disclosure Facility, which came into effect in September 2009. Acting for the Liechtenstein government, I was able to initiate the Liechtenstein Disclosure Facility and related arrangements with the help of the OECD, and eventually a team of advisors to Liechtenstein and the United Kingdom. These arrangements recognized that countries, like the United Kingdom, whose tax and legal systems respect the human right to privacy, are entitled to ensure that the integrity of their tax systems remains intact. Under the arrangement, the United Kingdom provided attractive terms for the voluntary disclosure of tax undeclared funds and incentives for the use of Liechtenstein as a clean financial centre. Thousands of UK taxpayers found the terms of the Liechtenstein Disclosure Facility far more attractive than the Swiss 'Rubik' approach (see https://www.gov.uk/government/publications/offshore-disclosure-facilites-liechtenstein/yield-stats).
4. Birkenfeld, B. C., *Lucifer's Banker: The Untold Story of How I Destroyed Swiss Bank Secrecy* (Greenleaf Book Group Press, 2016).
5. For a clear and engaging outline of the road to implementation of the CRS, Pascal Saint Aman's book on the subject is perfect. As the director of the OECD's Centre for Tax Policy and Administration, Pascal Saint Aman led the tax world to where it is today. Saint Aman, P., *Paradis fiscaux: Comment on a changé le cours de l'histoire*, French edition (Seuil, 2023).
6. Stefan Liniger, one of the founders of a Swiss trust company, Conduct, pointed out to me in his helpful comments on a draft of this book: '*Recent regulatory pressures have sometimes pushed*

financial institutions toward a "report first" mentality. This means institutions may pre-emptively report their clients—some of whom were previously advised to set up certain structures—without being able to inform them beforehand. This shift creates a situation where institutions are delivering their own clients to supervisory authorities, which can erode trust and complicate long-standing relationships. Additionally, many institutions have "shadow management" structures in place, where legal and compliance departments oversee client onboarding and transactions. While their role is essential for risk management, these departments often follow a strict, checkbox-driven approach. As a result, they may prioritize their own compliance and legal exposure over the client's interests, especially when the client has been with the institution for decades. The fear of regulatory consequences can lead to overly cautious decisions that don't align with the broader, more relationship-driven service model that clients might expect. There's also the issue of disconnect between the front office (client advisors) and the back office. Advisors may promise a "tailored" or flexible solution to win the business, but once the deal is closed, clients quickly find that the reality is much more restrictive. What was initially presented as straightforward becomes increasingly complicated, which can lead to client frustration. This highlights the importance of being fully transparent about the limitations and implications of dealing with financial intermediaries before any engagement takes place. Lastly, it's worth noting that using financial institutions across different jurisdictions, each with their own regulatory standards, can lead to significant challenges. Inconsistent standards across borders can create confusion, particularly if clients engage low-quality service providers from unregulated industries. For example, some lawyers—even from prestigious firms—may offer planning advice without a thorough understanding of how regulated financial institutions operate. This can result in the institution filing suspicious transaction reports due to poorly conceived structures.'

7. At the time of writing this book, in the case of Greece, the annual payment was €100,000. Italy, given the success of its programme, increased the annual payment to €200,000 through rule changes implemented in 2024.

CHAPTER 4

Is Society Optional? Better Ways to Tax Wealth and Business Owners and Moves Towards Global Taxation

I was happy recently to receive a note from a law school classmate of mine, Peter Hulsroj, together with a copy of a book that he co-authored with Marco Aliberti, *Essays on the Optional Society – and a Letter Concerning Inclusion*.[1] The title of Peter's book alone interested me, as the question of whether society itself is (and should be) optional, particularly for wealth owners with the ability to easily plan where they are tax resident, is one that I have been thinking about for a long time.

While the book is more about the increasing options we are all exposed to and how these elements of freedom are shaped (and perhaps properly restricted) by our communities,[2] it contains many insights relevant to my exploration of tax systems and the options wealth and business owners have and should have and how some of these options are likely to be increasingly restricted, perhaps dangerously, in the years to come.

As discussed earlier, wealth owners have only two choices when it comes to the tax laws of their jurisdiction of residence (and sometimes citizenship)—*play by the rules or get out!* But is tax mobility a good thing? How does this fit with freedom and democracy and where does *responsible* wealth and business ownership come into the picture?

The reality is that the way tax laws work at present is not really fit for purpose, particularly when it comes to balancing the needs of wealth and business owners from society and the needs our societies have from them. There are ways that wealth and business owners and interested governments can work together to better address the interests of our communities and planet, but it is hard to find good examples of this really working. Singapore has benefited from a strategic approach, as have a few other countries, but there is much more that can be done to take advantage of the transformative power of family wealth.

In too many countries of the world, tax systems are overly complex and feature headline tax rates that simply do not apply to those who can afford to be well advised. This is not fair. A wealth owner living in a country with a 50% inheritance tax rate passes away without having adopted a tax-minimization plan, and half of their assets go to taxation. Yet in many countries, the adoption of legal planning approaches, including the use of trusts and other instruments (or, as I refer to later, *tunnels and bridges* that can help navigate the *derailers*), can bring that tax rate down to zero.

I was invited to lunch a while back by a friend who wanted to introduce me to a fifth-generation member of a family owning a globally known consumer brand. With double digits of billions in wealth, the family is highly respected for having done the work families need to undertake to ensure safe continuity of family and business. I asked what this individual, who had chaired the family business, felt was the most important accomplishment of the family in achieving success over five generations. I was initially surprised at the answer—that finding ways to legally avoid applicable inheritance taxes was key. My expectation was that the answer to my question would be the efforts the family takes to support its employees and communities; the focus of the family on developing good family and business values; the work of the family on developing the younger generation—and more along these lines. But there is a reality regarding the answer to my question—inheritance taxes (and other taxes) around the world have and continue to have the ability to destroy wealth and family wealth and business succession. And in my view this is not only not good for the family—it is not good for society given the value to our world that a multi-generational family business can provide.

Historically, inheritance taxes in the United Kingdom have been as high as 80% of the value of assets passing on death; in the United States, the historical highs were around 75%. Today, the 'headline' US and UK tax rates that can apply are still a high 40% and, in the case of the United States, state taxes can add to this. It is important to note that inheritance taxes apply to the **value** of assets—unlike an income tax, not just to income earned from investing assets. This means a dramatic change in the asset base of the family affected and could mean an inability to retain a family business over generations.

Despite the high headline tax rates, though, for both the United States and the United Kingdom, inheritance or estate taxes are almost optional given the planning opportunities there are for the well advised. And mobility in both cases, combined with avoiding the retention of assets in the relevant countries, can be another way of getting the figure down to zero. Mobility can be a particularly easy way of avoiding inheritance taxes given the many countries around the world, even high-income-tax countries, that do not impose inheritance taxes, particularly for intra-family transfers, or do so at very low rates.

Thomas Piketty, a well-known French economist, has, based on his analysis, concluded that 'optimal' inheritance tax rates might be 50% to 60% of wealth or even more.[3] Thomas Piketty is not far removed from those advocating even a *100%* inheritance tax rate. This has been regularly floated as an idea to address inequality. See, for example, an article by Abi Wilkinson, a freelance journalist, in a contribution to *The Guardian* on the topic.[4] From that article, entitled 'Why not fund the welfare state with a 100% inheritance tax?':

> *In contemporary times, most people agree that tax should facilitate transfer of wealth from those who 'have' to those who 'need'. Public spending is messy and complicated, but the overall redistributive flow is from the relatively rich to the comparatively poorer. Justifications for not totally eradicating income equality have both moral and practical arguments: it's argued that people morally deserve to be rewarded for being good at their job, and also that society needs to offer financial rewards to encourage people to work hard and be productive.*
>
> *Neither of these arguments really apply in the case of inheritance. Morally speaking, people who stand to inherit large sums haven't*

> *done anything to earn that money. An accident of birth placed them in a comparatively wealthy family and they've benefited from that their whole life. Some people who stand to inherit have struggled, true, but so have many people who won't inherit anything at all.*

I am **strongly** opposed to this kind of thinking—particularly in view of the reality that multi-generational wealth and business ownership has the evidenced capacity to be a force for good in our societies. As Peter Hulsroj pointed out to me, there is also a moral argument against confiscatory taxation of this kind and the notion that an heir has done nothing to deserve the inheritance—the accident of birth. Peter asks the right question: What about the rights and interests of the one who created the wealth (possibly generations removed)? Why should she be able to buy a superyacht or a sports team but not be able to donate her wealth to her children upon death? Peter went on to say that we are genetically disposed to want to take care of our offspring—it is often called love. Is it moral to bar a wealth creator from taking care of the next generation, even if that generation has done absolutely nothing to deserve it?

However, there are realities about income and wealth inequality and more that require us to rethink how tax systems should work for the benefit of all. And a way that does not work is to have misleading headline tax rates that might address the political objective of a government to show that it is tough on the wealthy while preserving only to the wealthy complex and costly ways to get out of paying that tax.

Tax systems can be simpler, fairer, more transparent and more accessible. And it is this that wealth owners and concerned governments need to work on together, with a view to achieving the balance that is possible. It is not about whether a country should or should not impose a tax on death, but rather how the collective taxes on income, on wealth and on transfers, are imposed. Lower rates and simpler systems do require a broader tax system and one that includes more than just a tax on income. And the question of fairness also raises the question of why those who earn from capital they have rather than from their labour often pay less.

Around the world it is common to see earned income taxed at much higher rates than capital gains. In some countries, capital gains are not taxed at all. A salary can be taxed at 45% in the United Kingdom; a capital gain at 20%. In Switzerland, depending on the Canton involved, the salary might also be taxed at 45% or even more and the capital gain be free of taxation entirely.

There are many reasons put forward to defend the different treatment of capital gains. One position is that capital gains reflect savings and, in effect, taxing a gain on savings is a double tax—the original investment would have been made with taxed funds. The reality, though, is that this may or may not be the case, depending on many circumstances. There is also the argument that lower or no capital gains taxes encourage savings and that taxing capital gains would need a mechanism to adjust for inflation of the value of capital assets.

The reality is that what really matters is the result—is the tax system a fair one that addresses the needs of all stakeholders? And for me, is the tax system one that also reflects **value** to the wealth and business owner? Perhaps the ideal is a system with low rates and simplicity but with broad coverage—including taxation of capital gains and income at the same level, a wealth tax, an inheritance tax and taxes on consumption of luxury products—but all in a range where the wealth and business owner is **content** to pay the tax as in exchange the wealth owner lives in a country offering the stability and protection the wealth owner needs to achieve their *Theory of Change* and support an impact goal that includes both a thriving family over generations and a thriving business and investment engine that supports what the family can achieve.

In too many countries, tax systems are used to co-opt wealth owners to dictatorships or near dictatorships—the underlying message being *support me and I won't mess with your financial interests*. And, again, in too many countries, the press and the masses are duped into thinking the tax system is fair because of the high headline rates that apply. The mind-numbing complexity of the tax system and the legal tax minimization that can be achieved for those with an appetite to pay high legal and accounting fees provide the smoke that keeps things murky.

But the solution is NOT to bash the wealthy and tax their income and assets away—the reaction that has always been among the many challenges faced by wealth owners. There is a better way, and a move to *regenerative* taxation is one way to think about this.

What Might 'Regenerative' Taxation Involve?

My inspiration for thinking about *regenerative* taxation comes from reading some of the work of John Fullerton and others on the concept of regenerative capitalism and the potential of regenerative economies.[5]

The idea of regenerative capitalism starts with a focus on learning from nature and from the realities of how interlinked each element of our world is.

In the cited article, 'Regenerative capitalism—how universal principles and patterns will shape our new economy', Fullerton describes eight interconnected principles that underlie the health of a stable and sustainable economic system. I have used some of Fullerton's words in setting these out.

1. *In the right relationship*: Humanity is an integral part of an interconnected web of life in which there is no real separation between 'us' and 'it'. We are all connected to one another and to all locales of our global civilization. Damage to any part of that web ripples back to harm every other part as well. Symbiotic collaboration is the key.
2. *Views wealth holistically*: True wealth is not merely money in the bank. It must be defined and managed in terms of the well-being of the whole, achieved through the harmonization of multiple kinds of wealth or capital, including social, cultural, living and experiential. It must also be defined by a broadly shared prosperity in that the whole is only as strong as the weakest link.
3. *Innovative, adaptive, responsive*: In a world in which change is both ever-present and accelerating, the qualities of innovation and adaptability are critical to health.
4. *Empowered participation*: In an interdependent system, fitness comes from contributing in some way to the health of the whole.
5. *Honours community and place*: Each human community consists of a mosaic of peoples, traditions, beliefs and institutions uniquely shaped by long-term pressures of geography, human history, culture, local environment and changing human needs. Honouring this fact, a regenerative economy nurtures healthy and resilient

communities and regions, each one uniquely informed by the essence of its individual history and place.
6. *Edge effect abundance.* Creativity and abundance thrive synergistically at the 'edges' of systems, where the bonds holding the dominant pattern in place are weakest. For example, there is an abundance of interdependent life in salt marshes where a river meets the ocean. At those edges the opportunities for innovation and cross-fertilization are the greatest. Working collaboratively across edges—with ongoing learning and development sourced from the diversity that exists there—is transformative for both the communities where the exchanges are happening, and for the individuals involved.
7. *Robust circulatory flow.* Just as human health depends on the robust circulation of oxygen, nutrients, and so on, so too does economic health depend on robust circulatory flows of money, information, resources and goods and services to support exchange. The circulation of money and information and the efficient use and reuse of materials are particularly critical to individuals, businesses and economies reaching their regenerative potential.
8. *Seeks balance.* Being in balance is more than just a nice way to be—it is actually essential to systemic health. Like a unicycle rider, regenerative systems are always engaged in this delicate dance in search of balance. Achieving it requires that they harmonize multiple variables instead of optimizing single ones.

The idea of a regenerative economy is one where, rather than featuring exploitation and destruction, the system is designed, like nature, to restore and build. The economy can be run in such a way that resources are wisely managed, with the economic system itself supporting renewal and development.

There is more here than just circularity—in simple terms and in relation to taxation, regeneration needs something more than governments just extracting taxes and putting the proceeds into public spending. In other words, regeneration needs more than taxing wealth and business owners heavily to redistribute to those in need. Regeneration would be considering, among others, how the tax system can **help** the wealth and business-owning family to achieve its long-term impact goal of sustaining the family and its business and investment engine, permitting the family to contribute to its employees and other stakeholders over generations. Regeneration would involve putting effort into supporting the emergence and growth of new wealth and business-owning families to the benefit of all.

The reality of this is that with an ecosystem that encourages family business and wealth owners to thrive and develop, and where all truly have the opportunity themselves to become business and wealth owners, the real needs of society can be effectively addressed. Investments in encouraging and supporting wealth creation can be far more effective than wealth redistribution on its own.

Achieving this simple idea would require wealth and business owners to work with governments and other stakeholders in ways that do not exist today. The discourse on taxation needs to change, as does the reactive view of many that the way to address income and wealth inequality is to take things away from wealth owners and reallocate. This only encourages those seeking to protect their businesses and wealth to separate from the country involved and perhaps society as a whole.

In my view, John Fullerton, in his vision of a regenerative economy, neglects to focus on family business and wealth ownership as one of the possible keys to a healthy economy. Fullerton even states that '*progressive income taxation and aggressive inheritance taxation*'[6] serve the purpose of releasing pressure from today's extreme inequalities. I believe in a different reality. Family business and wealth ownership can be at the **centre** of a regenerative economy and regenerative taxation can help make this happen. And it is the opposite of '*progressive income taxation and aggressive inheritance taxation*' that could get us there.

In a regenerative economy, large multinational businesses would honour community and place—operating around the world, but with values that reflect *home*. Family wealth and business ownership, large and small, could be at the core of the ecosystem. If the focus is the potential of each individual family, whether today a wealth and business-owning family or one that aspires to become one in future, this can help define the approach a country takes to maintaining the health of the economy. The answer is far from '*aggressive inheritance taxation*', which would be destructive of the family's plans for a multigenerational future and what it could contribute to the economy.

Just mentioning '*aggressive inheritance taxation*' chills the desire of a wealth and business-owning family to establish roots in a country championing this. Rather, the focus might be on cherishing and championing the interests of wealth and business owners and to do this through tax systems that help, not hurt, the family along its multi-generational mission. And key is also to encourage, at every step, the formation of new family business and wealth owners. Knowing that there is nothing to stop a family from moving into wealth and business ownership is an incentive important to a healthy and regenerative economy. And it is not every wealth-owning family that needs to immediately be a business-owning family. The children of a well-compensated professional may go on to inherit wealth and maybe it is only among their children that this wealth will be deployed to establish a family business. But whether or not a family business is ever established, the responsible stewardship of wealth, which might feature impact investing, philanthropy and otherwise, will be positive for the economy involved.

In a recent report from McKinsey, it was stated that family-owned businesses account for more than **70%** of global GDP and about **60%** of global employment.[7] Family businesses, according to the report, simply outperform non-family businesses. Among others, the reasons for this include: (1) purpose beyond profits; (2) long-term perspective and reinvestment in the business; (3) financial conservatism and caution about debt and high-risk investments; and (4) efficient decision-making.

Those promoting inheritance taxes approaching 100% fail to understand the transformative power of family wealth.

For Dagland, in developing its ideas on how to attract wealth and business owners to the country, understanding how regenerative taxation might work can be helpful. It is not *laissez faire* economics that will outperform and regenerate. Free-market capitalism that favours deregulation and 'freedom' over all else is not the road to regeneration and, if anything, has brought us to a difficult crossroads around the world. The impact on the overall system and place needs to be taken into account holistically. For Dagland, this includes environment, its entire population and its role in regional and global initiatives and needs.

As John Fullerton emphasizes, **place** is important. Dagland is not the same as other countries and has its own cultural and physical features that need to regenerate. And if Dagland is successful in doing this, it is already making a major contribution to the planet. In its design of a tax system that is truly regenerative, Dagland can focus on 'place' and preserving and enhancing the positives. This can include the physical aspects of Dagland—perhaps its cleanliness, its forests and waters. Tax policies should orient to enhancement. Dagland may also be a place where society functions through good healthcare, education and housing policies. A tax system that focuses on maintaining and improving these, using Dagland's focus on attracting and retaining wealth and business owners to its economy, can be a way to be regenerative, given that a functioning society is part of what will attract and retain wealth and business owners over generations.

Maybe in relation to health systems Dagland can learn from Singapore and Switzerland, countries with health systems that largely serve the needs of **everybody**. Those who can afford it can receive private care at the highest level; those who cannot afford it are ensured healthcare that is paid for by the government and is of high quality. In Singapore, the system is even designed to put the onus on the individual to keep healthcare expenditures under control, with incentives to shop for lower-cost, higher-quality healthcare. Money left over in health savings accounts maintained to cover insurance deductibles and other costs can ultimately be used for retirement or pass to heirs, encouraging the individual to be careful in their healthcare spending. And importantly, unlike Canada, with its limited private options in a public single-payer health system, it is not necessary for a wealth and business owner to travel to another country to get high-quality and timely private healthcare. On healthcare, Dagland can also learn from the United States—and how its lack of public healthcare is increasing inequality and hopelessness.

True regeneration will involve Dagland having its tax system not only help to keep wealth and business owners connected to Dagland, but also help to create new wealth and business owners. A stable, fair, broad and predictable tax system that reflects the realities of healthy global tax competition, combined with a focus on implementing policies that support wealth and business owners, is feasible. More on the opportunity for Dagland in the last chapter of this book, looking at a possible *Theory of Change* for Dagland.

Learning from the Lost Opportunities of Others—Again, the UK Example

The United Kingdom and its approach to wealth and business owners to the date of my writing this book is a good example for Dagland (and for others, particularly real countries looking to benefit their economies and societies) of the failure of a government to recognize opportunity and take advantage of it. It is the UK economy and UK society that lose out.

For years, successive UK governments failed to take the opportunity to encourage a review of UK tax policy and, for instance of whether the United Kingdom provided too warm (or too cold!) a home to wealth owners. The United Kingdom, over the years, managed to attract many thousands of global wealth owners to the country but squandered its opportunity to develop a regenerative tax system oriented to *retaining* these wealth owners for its economy and encouraging a two-way flow of value—to the United Kingdom and to the wealth and business owners connected to the United Kingdom.

Before its July 2024 landslide victory, the Labour party announced that if elected, it would eliminate what was known as the 'non-dom' system (reflecting what are known as the 'non-domiciliary' rules). Perhaps as a political move, this encouraged the then governing Conservative party to itself announce steps to eliminate that tax system and replace it—sadly, something that was announced with little preparation, planning or vision.

While elimination of the non-dom system makes sense for a number of reasons, I have been disappointed to see a failure of this being combined with the introduction of fresh and thoughtful approaches designed to truly benefit the UK economy. While the new Labour government may still announce something unexpected on this front (fingers crossed!), there is at the time of my writing this book great instability among wealth owners connected to the United Kingdom, with many already taking steps to relocate and otherwise detach from the United Kingdom.

Other countries can learn from the United Kingdom's strategic failure—and benefit from it by attracting the wealth and business owners who have left and will continue to leave, together with those wealth and business owners who would have considered the

United Kingdom a home and business base but who will now not even consider the possibility.

Both the now governing Labour party and the Conservative party indicated that in replacing the non-dom system, the country would focus on maintaining tax benefits for *short-term* residents in the United Kingdom. This, rather than explore policies designed to attract and retain an even more valuable group of taxpayers—wealth and business owners ready to make multi-generational contributions to the economy. And the new Labour government, while promising to be 'business friendly', certainly seems to have little appreciation for the benefits of multi-generational family businesses.

Tax reform designed to address the realities of inequality while recognizing the value of attracting and retaining wealth owners to the United Kingdom was long overdue. For decades, both the Conservative and Labour parties failed to recognize the importance to the economy of wealth owners and what they can contribute if the tax system were strategically orientated. Rishi Sunak, the former Prime Minister, seemed afraid of stepping into the issue given the criticisms he had faced about his wife (fully legally) availing herself of the non-dom system. And Labour, to be applauded for taking some leadership in making proposals that the Conservatives then kidnapped, wrongly focused on replacing the non-dom system with one oriented to encouraging short-term residence in the United Kingdom by 'high earners'.

On the latter, statistics apparently suggested that the majority of those benefiting from the non-dom system just before its demise were high earners in the City of London—salaried professionals and others outside of the community of major wealth and business owners. Perhaps it is these statistics that encouraged the focus on retaining to the United Kingdom the ability to attract high earners on short-term stays—think of a highly compensated New York-based banker moving to London for a few years. But this failed to recognize that past changes to the non-dom system and otherwise had not only sent packing many serious wealth and business owners from the United Kingdom (at least as tax residents as opposed to non-resident owners of high-value real estate in London and elsewhere in the country), but also discouraged many others from coming to the United Kingdom in the first place.

The United Kingdom also needed and continues to need an effective tax system for these important contributors to the UK economy—and ideally a system that would attract them to the United Kingdom for the long term.

In the real world, the missteps of the United Kingdom have benefited other jurisdictions, from Singapore to Dubai to Italy and Greece and others, all of whom have tax policies far more aligned to the needs of wealth and business owners. These countries have demonstrated how such policies can benefit their economies in meaningful ways.

So, both of the major political parties in the United Kingdom have gotten it wrong—at least from the steps they have taken so far. And as is the case with many countries in the world, politicians seem to be afraid of discussing a complex area that generates much in the way of encouragement to tax (and bash) the rich and raise headline rates. Playing to those who do not really understand how tax systems can and do work is not doing the United Kingdom any good—and other countries can learn from this. There are many opportunities to raise significant revenue for the United Kingdom—to fund the struggling national health service, to help with the housing crisis and to lower taxes for those at lower income and wealth levels.

Is it not time for countries to be smart about some of these opportunities? Is it not time to set a good example for other countries? And all this can be presented as what it is—*a way of ensuring that the wealthy are contributing their fair share.*

Recognizing the Needs of Wealth and Business Owners—and Among These Are Governments That Can Be Trusted

Today's mobile wealth owners need to live in countries, the governments of which can be trusted and where tax systems are fair and predictable. Given the many advantages of the United Kingdom, the country would not have needed the lowest tax burdens to achieve success.

The non-domiciliary rules had been changed over their over 200-year history so as to **reduce** the attractiveness of the United Kingdom to wealth and business owners. Chaotic and overly complex, the system resulted in revenues in too many cases going to advisors rather than to the government. Complexity and constant chopping and changing supported a perception that the United Kingdom does not welcome wealth owners. Meanwhile, for those with an appetite for paying professional fees, the UK system allowed for low or no taxation at all. Unlike competing offerings from Italy,

Greece, Switzerland and others, the UK system offered a virtually free ride for at least the first seven years of residence, which made little sense. The system was even perversely designed to *discourage*, rather than encourage, remittances to and investment in the United Kingdom.

What Could the United Kingdom Have Done and Lessons for Dagland and Its Opportunity

What the United Kingdom could have focused on is the importance of reducing 'headline' tax rates while taking steps that would, at the same time, raise substantially more revenue. Longer term, it would have made sense for both domiciled and non-domiciled taxpayers, if resident in the United Kingdom, to be taxed in the same way—but under a low-rate tax system with a dramatically simplified and broadened tax base.

While it is challenging to reduce rates and hope for more revenue, there may be ways of achieving this safely—perhaps through what could initially be set out as an alternative taxing approach the wealth or business owner can elect to be subject to—something Dagland can experiment with and which is discussed in the last chapter of this book.

There would have been (and remain) many options for the United Kingdom to adopt a simplified and fairer approach to taxation that would attract rather than repel wealth owners to the United Kingdom and permit benefit to the economy that can go a long way towards achieving a fairer society.

While the departure from the European Union was, to many (including me), a grave mistake, one could think that Brexit would help afford the United Kingdom an opportunity to carve out an important global role as the premiere location for **responsible** wealth owners reflecting the current and real needs of global wealth owners, UK society generally and our world. Perhaps a *regenerative* approach to taxing wealth and business owners could have been an option for the United Kingdom to implement.

How individuals live and work has been changing, and the basis on which wealth and business owners have been taxed in the United Kingdom was not fit for purpose if the United Kingdom were serious about achieving the benefits for its economy that it could achieve. The opportunity for the United Kingdom to emerge as the country of choice for global wealth and business owners was a very real one, particularly in a world of tax transparency where home governments are increasingly fully informed about the income and wealth of residents. Mobile wealth and business owners need to live in countries, the governments of which can be trusted with information about their assets and where tax systems are fair, predictable and straightforward. Wealth and business owners living outside the United Kingdom need to invest in and through countries they can rely on and whose tax and legal systems encourage such activity.

The United Kingdom would not have needed to offer the lowest tax burdens globally to achieve success. The United Kingdom could, and still can, simply rely on its existing strengths and build on a long-term strategy oriented towards *collaboration* with responsible wealth and business owners, reliance on the rule of law (and therefore certainty) and simplicity. In part, this strategy would focus on *place*, as emphasized in regenerative systems. A taxing approach that recognizes the unique elements of the United Kingdom and helps to build on its strengths would be one that is regenerative.

Again, it is challenging for any government to consider reducing tax rates in the hope that, even in combination with a broadening of the tax base, revenues will increase. For consideration by our fictional Dagland, these ideas are elaborated on in a discussion of Dagland's *impact goals*.

The Importance of Trust and Some Comments on Global Tax Systems

I have oriented my thinking towards longer-term changes to the tax systems of countries that can address the many reasons their current tax systems are not fit for purpose, particularly in today's globalized economy and where wealth and business owners have many options as to where to live, work and pay tax. A collaborative approach by government, and one which recognizes the value of wealth and business owners to the economy and the needs of this community, is critical to achieving the success I believe is possible.

Importantly, my recommendations reflect the urgent need for both government revenue and enhanced business and investment activity.

Governments need to be clear in their commitment to attract and retain wealth and business owners to their economy, and wealth and business owners need to feel much better than they do today about paying their fair share of taxes. This can be achieved.

The first move needs to be taken by governments, which need to consider ideas oriented towards lowering, not raising, headline tax rates. Tax systems need to be hugely simplified, and the sad reality of corruption in tax systems, particularly in developing countries, needs to be addressed—and where it cannot be immediately addressed, interim approaches to addressing this need to be adopted with a view to ensuring that tax revenues are captured and go where they need to go.

Governments also have to commit to providing more in the way of certainty on tax rules, stripping out of the system constant wholesale changes of approach and overdesign round the edges which are usually targeted at very few people and end up complicating the system immensely for the majority. On this latter point, it is unacceptable how much wasted cost and effort is undertaken by taxpayers to adapt to ever-changing tax laws only to find that the changes adapted to are themselves changed yet again. Particular issues are broken promises—where the government promises one thing but delivers another.

It is not unusual to find countries that have headline rates of, say, 45% on income. This may be imposed through a single tax, or through a combination of local and national taxes. Politicians seeking to address inequality are quick to discuss the possibility of increasing headline tax rates—but this is not the solution. The question one needs to address is what *actual* tax rates are collected and from whom? Low tax rates combined with a broadening of the tax base can be much more effective than raising headline tax rates. If the tax system is a complex one, which too many are, how much does a wealth or business owner actually pay? And on what? And are headline rates only paid by those who cannot afford tax advice?

It is disturbing how things actually work in many countries. An owner of significant passive wealth who does not need to work may pay virtually no taxes if guided by expensive tax lawyers and accountants who navigate tax systems filled with complex tax incentives permitting deductions for investments in particular areas, or for charitable donations that can include donations to one's own charity that is controlled by the individual involved and all too often benefits the individual and their business more than anyone else.

It is not that the idea of an incentive to encourage particular investments is bad. There may be good reasons to encourage investments in social housing or sectors that will bring needed employment and development. But we can now see that the good intention of encouraging such investments through tax deductions has failed. Complex rules need to be developed, and once they are, tax advisors are quick to work their way around the rules to find ways to achieve tax benefits for their clients while ensuring that the investment funds are not at risk, compromising the objective of the tax incentive in the first place. The role of lobbyists in the legislative process makes things worse, as more in the way of loopholes and complexity are introduced.

The tax law becomes so complex that only the wealthy can afford to take advantage of all the deductions that are available. What this means is that someone who works hard and earns a good salary may end up paying the top headline rate of, say, 45%. The wealthy individual, even the one who is not a tax evader, but happens (for example) to legally provide their labour through a company, may end up paying 25% or even less on their income. Is this fair?

Could inequality be tempered with those earning at the lower end of the scale paying no tax or very, very low rates of tax? The answer is obviously yes, particularly if government revenues increase and the increased revenues of governments are applied to address the need for health care, education, housing and more. But governments fear that not taxing the mass of low-income individuals would reduce government revenues drastically. This is true if the lost revenue is not recovered from those who can better afford to pay more and if the relevant government fails to retain and attract those who can pay more to their country. But paying more does not mean moving the 45% headline rate to 70%.

What if instead the headline rate moves to 20%? To ensure that tax revenues are not compromised, this is combined with stripping out of the tax system *all* tax deductions for things like tax-incentivized investments. This simplifies how taxes are filed and simplifies the tax system for all. Enforcement is easier, and things are clearer. And the country can attract, rather than repel, wealth and business owners.

Incentives for investments in social housing or other important areas can be addressed *outside* the tax system. This can allow the tax system to remain simple and pure, and allow any incentive programme to be supervised and administered by governments more carefully and thoughtfully than they are today.

Yes, there is much economic analysis needed to help a government gain the confidence to dramatically lower headline tax rates to achieve higher tax revenues. Finding the right headline rate can be achieved in stages if necessary. But thought should be given to doing this and focusing on broadening the tax base by attracting and retaining global wealth and business owners, ensuring that those who use government services actually contribute to them. Regarding this latter point, in too many countries there are too many who can avoid tax exposures by limiting their time in the country, leaving the cost of government services to those much less able to pay. And countries need to understand that for many wealth and business owners, there are justifiable questions as to what their tax dollars are actually paying for.

> *The digital revolution removes us from so many of the geographical and knowledge constraints that were used to force us into the arms of the nation state as the provider of essential services and safeguards. The digital revolution allows the privileged to replace essential social services with commercial ones, for instance. If you buy your books at Amazon, why not your health services, your retirement benefits, your security, your children's education. Why pay taxes if instead of asking what you can do for your country, you ask what your country can do for you—can do better than commercial service providers.*[8]

Taxpayers should be encouraged, through the tax system, to be happier than they are about paying taxes. A lack of trust in how governments spend tax revenues is among the reasons many wealth and business owners do everything they can to legally minimize their tax obligations while working hard to contribute to charities and otherwise benefit their communities. Trust needs to be earned, and while there are economic arguments against hypothecation of taxes (the earmarking of taxes for a particular expenditure purpose), knowing that at least part of the tax you pay will be used to provide education and healthcare to your community and to address climate change and other needs may help moderate feelings of governments wasting tax revenues. Some hypothecated tax programmes may also encourage *voluntary* tax contributions or the like, something that can and should be part of an effective reform of how tax systems work. And the word 'tax' in relation to some payments that wealth and business owners make might well be rebranded to better reflect a new collaboration between government and wealth and business owners—a collaboration where some of the tax dollars contributed by wealth and business owners are invested in providing what wealth and business owners need to thrive over generations.

Broadening the Tax Base—Examples of and for Hong Kong and Singapore and the Attraction of Returning to Gift and Inheritance Taxation

Key to the ability of a country to reduce headline tax rates while achieving the goal of funding initiatives in education, healthcare and otherwise to address income and wealth inequality and increase opportunities for all is to broaden the tax base. This relates to ensuring that a broad range of income, assets and expenditures are taxed, and all in a thoughtful way that balances the interests of all stakeholders.

It may seem that jurisdictions like Hong Kong and Singapore have it right through their primarily territorial tax systems and low tax rates. Indeed, both are in many ways havens for wealth and business owners, and Singapore has made particularly significant strides to this end in recent years. But both, like many other jurisdictions, have failed to address the needs of their broader societies—particularly Hong Kong with its stunningly poor supply of housing for those in need. And Hong Kong has been particularly guilty in ignoring the massive inequality that exists in Hong Kong society. For Dagland, this real-life example involving two relatively successful players in the world of offering wealth and business owners an attractive home can be instructive.

Both Singapore and Hong Kong have eliminated inheritance taxes (or, as known in those jurisdictions, 'estate duties'). Of course, elimination of these taxes was something welcomed by wealth owners. But maybe there is a role for such taxation as part of a strategy to broaden the tax base and move to a fairer society. And something to learn for other countries seeking to make themselves a long-term home for *responsible* wealth and business owners who understand that for their families and business interests to be sustainable, they need to be connected to sustainable societies.

Indeed, in looking at a new tax system for Dagland, the idea is to *broaden* the tax base and to tax, among others, gifts and inheritance.

If Dagland designs the system to permit it to offer *more* to the wealth and business owner in exchange for these taxes, regeneration results.

Looking at Hong Kong as an example, estate duty was abolished as of 11 February 2006. Maybe it is time for a return of not only estate duty to Hong Kong, but also a comprehensive accompanying donation tax. And given the similarity in tax systems between Hong Kong and Singapore, Singapore would benefit from a similar step.[9]

In a 2015 speech entitled 'Lifting the small boats'[10] delivered by Christine Lagarde, then Managing Director of the International Monetary Fund (IMF), Lagarde emphasized that the theme of growing and excessive inequality is not only a matter of newspaper headlines, but also a growing problem for economic growth and development. It is not immoral to enjoy one's financial success, said Ms Lagarde, but it is a reality that poor and middle-class families have not been able to stay afloat through hard work and determination alone. Reducing excessive inequality, according to Lagarde, is not just morally and politically correct, *but is good economics*, essential to the generation of higher, more inclusive and sustainable growth.

IMF research shows that if the income share of the poor and middle class is raised by one percentage point, GDP growth increases by as much as 0.38 percentage points over a period of five years. An increase in the income share of the wealthy by the same one percentage point results in a *decrease* of GDP growth by 0.08%, likely due to the lower fractional spending of income by the wealthy.

In most of the world, inequality is a sad reality. Inequality has become one of the most important political issues of our age, giving rise to populist governments and increasing risk of social unrest and instability.

For wealthy communities such as Hong Kong and Singapore, inequality is just not right and needs to be addressed. A new system of estate and donation duties would not alone eliminate inequality. But steps in the right direction need to be taken.

Government Policies and Action Are Critical

Before turning to the logic of why Hong Kong and Singapore need estate and donation (gift) duties, it is important to emphasize that taxation alone does not address inequality. Governments need to be creative and proactive in developing policies that address inequality in a real way.

Critical targets need to be set for ensuring access to education, healthcare and housing, and to address the environment and otherwise. Despite a variety of concerns about governments hypothecating taxes (earmarking particular taxes for particular expenditures), consideration might be given to linking new estate and donation duties to specific programmes oriented to addressing specific needs of the community as a whole—including wealth and business owners—and to specifically address growing inequality. This might help create a sense of real action on the part of the Hong Kong and Singapore governments and a sense of purpose and meaning for those subject to the new estate and donation duty regime. Again, possible examples for other countries interested in regenerative taxation.

Why Estate and Donation Duties?

Hong Kong and Singapore have tax systems that are among the most taxpayer friendly in the world, affording those living, working and investing in Hong Kong or Singapore the ability to accumulate wealth at a pace which is simply not possible in countries with high tax rates and a worldwide taxation base.

Top tax rates are well below 20% in relation to even the highest salaries and business profits. Further, taxation only generally applies in relation to Hong Kong or Singapore-sourced income, meaning that income sourced abroad is, subject to limited exceptions, totally free of taxation at home. And unlike many other jurisdictions, Hong Kong and Singapore do not generally tax capital gains, even when realized, or dividends. Indirect taxation, such as a value-added tax, does not, at least so far, apply on purchases of Hong Kong goods and services, something that contrasts with the approach of many other countries (even Singapore), particularly in Europe, where such indirect taxation contributes hugely to government revenues. Remarkably, even high-cost luxury goods are completely free from sales taxes in Hong Kong.

Governments need a broad revenue base, and Hong Kong and Singapore are not excluded from this, despite historic success in generating revenue through, among others, land sales and enjoying significant budget surpluses. The ability to rely on a narrow base of taxation for the long term would be a risky policy decision for any forward-looking government.

But apart from broadening the tax base, estate and donation duties would serve another very important need: they would introduce to Hong Kong and Singapore a sense that government cares about inequality and about those in need, and that those who have benefited from the enormous opportunity of being connected to Hong Kong or Singapore by residence, place of investment or otherwise are part of the collective effort to address the needs of the entire community.

In the case of Hong Kong, historically, estate duty contributed around HK$1 billion annually to government revenues, a relatively insignificant amount in view of historic budget surpluses. There is little question, however, that a more comprehensive approach to the imposition of estate and donation duties would add meaningful revenue. Broadening the base of revenue is important in view of the government's current narrow revenue base, and the reality that concentration on land sales and stamp duties associated with property transactions is not a safe, long-term way for government to fund the needs of Hong Kong and its ageing population. Indirect taxation, such as value-added taxes, may be part of the future of Hong Kong's tax system, but such taxation can be regressive if not well designed. An estate and donation duty system would help balance an approach to indirect taxation, and possibly allow for lower rates and additional exemptions for necessities, helping to alleviate many of the negatives of indirect sales taxes.

But Would Imposing Estate and Donation Duties Be a Technical Nightmare?

Fair taxation needs to be simple and transparent taxation. While there would be challenges in adopting the right approach to the imposition of estate and donation duties in Hong Kong or Singapore, these challenges can be met given the many examples worldwide of such regimes that work, and Hong Kong and Singapore's own experiences with their historic estate duty. In the case of Hong Kong, solid recommendations had been made regarding its retention and reform (albeit these were largely ignored).[11]

While it is not the intention of this book to propose a detailed new law to again implement Hong Kong and Singapore estate and donation duties, there are a number of points that can be made regarding the relative ease with which such laws could be developed, and some of the global dynamics that would make it easier to ensure enforcement today than was the case when Hong Kong and Singapore abolished estate duty. It is interesting to note that the abolition of estate duty in both jurisdictions may not have been particularly well thought out.

Can Estate and Donation Duties Be Imposed in a Fair and Effective Way with an Eye to Ensuring That Hong Kong and Singapore Do Not Jeopardize Their Attractions as Wealth Management and Investment Destinations?

A well-designed estate and donation duty system can raise revenue, be simple and fair. Hong Kong and Singapore can establish estate and donation duty systems that can be effective—systems that raise much more in the way of revenue than the cost of administration and otherwise, and which preserve the attractions of each jurisdiction as a place to live and work, to invest and in which to conduct a wealth management business.

When Hong Kong's estate duties were abolished more than ten years ago, some of the arguments made reflected a view that having estate duties could be harmful to Hong Kong's objective of developing itself as a wealth management centre. It was relevant that Singapore was also considering abolishing its estate duties, something it ultimately did. But Singapore, like many countries, has from time to time been reconsidering that decision, and the debate in Singapore regarding what it takes to create a fairer society is at least somewhat further in progress than is the case in Hong Kong.

But more importantly, there are really few reasons to believe that having a well-thought-out *low tax rate* estate and donation duty regime would chill any efforts to further develop Hong Kong and Singapore as wealth management centres and investment destinations. More important to these objectives are other factors, as can be seen from how other successful wealth management locations have managed to combine the imposition of such taxes with significant attractions to the international community to make use of their locations for wealth management—and here the United States would be but one example. Guidance from the experience of other jurisdictions would be instructive for Hong Kong.

Hong Kong and Singapore would have many choices for how to formulate their estate and donation duty so as to minimize any negative impact on choices investors make, or on their objective to compete as meaningful wealth management centres.

Information Exchange, the Common Reporting Standard and More

In an article published in 1991 in *Tax Notes International*, I advocated Hong Kong developing a wide network of tax treaties, agreements on taxation between countries, facilitating and encouraging cross-border investment and addressing, among other things, situations of double taxation and ensuring effective information exchange.[12] The ideas expressed were based on the view that in the run up to the return of Hong Kong to China in 1997, Hong Kong would have been able to negotiate particularly beneficial treaties with other countries. While I received an open ear from the Hong Kong government at the time, many tax professionals, from accounting and law firms and elsewhere, spoke out against the initiative, fearing that Hong Kong entering into tax treaties would compromise Hong Kong's ability to maintain secrecy, and retain and attract foreign investors seeking—for good and bad reasons—to hide behind opaque Hong Kong structures and investments.

Today, Hong Kong is still trying to catch up with Singapore and others in the tax treaty arena but does have a growing network of comprehensive tax treaties. But some of Hong Kong's treaties only deal with information exchange, Hong Kong having long lost its negotiating power in light of global tax transparency initiatives and the need Hong Kong has had to enter into a vast network of tax information exchange agreements. But the bottom line is that Hong Kong is now fully part of the global shift towards tax transparency.

The changing world has also resulted in the development and adoption by Hong Kong, Singapore and many, many other jurisdictions of new automatic information exchange rules, among which feature the CRS which, as mentioned earlier, was developed by the OECD. Under these rules, Hong Kong and Singapore both automatically send information to other countries regarding bank accounts maintained in their jurisdictions, and *receive* such information from other countries in relation to their own residents. Impossible for many to have contemplated fifteen or twenty years ago, today beneficial ownership information is being exchanged *automatically* in relation to bank accounts held directly or indirectly, through trusts, foundations, offshore tax haven companies and other previously opaque structures.

But even more is happening in the world of growing tax transparency. Registers of ownership of companies and other investment vehicles, transparency on the ownership of real estate and other assets and a growing range of tools based on technology and cooperation between governments is leading to a world where tax authorities, including those in Hong Kong and Singapore, have and will have at their disposition the information they need to easily enforce their tax systems.

For Hong Kong or Singapore to develop an estate and donation duty system that works is now a much easier task than it would have been even a few years ago.

Many Hong Kong and Singapore Investors Are Already Subject to Donation and Inheritance Taxes in Other Countries—Why Should They Not Have Home Jurisdiction Obligations?

Wealth owners in Hong Kong and Singapore invest globally, and when they do so, they become subject to taxation in other countries, which taxation is sometimes reduced or eliminated under tax treaties Hong Kong is a party to. In the income tax area, many countries impose withholding taxes on interest, dividends, rents and other payments, and in some cases other taxes, such as capital gains and otherwise. Where a Hong Kong or Singapore resident, as defined for treaty purposes, is the investor and an appropriate tax treaty applies, the foreign tax exposure is often reduced, and sometimes eliminated.

Countries also have estate and gift tax treaties, something that Hong Kong and Singapore do not have given that they do not tax either estates or gifts. A strategy under which Hong Kong and Singapore would develop new estate and donation duties would allow Hong Kong and Singapore to develop such a network of treaties, ensuring that their revenue base is protected, but also helping to manage the tax exposures abroad of those resident in Hong Kong and Singapore, adding to the many attractions of being a wealth or business owner resident in Hong Kong or Singapore. This is what paying attention to the needs of wealth and business owners involves—identifying things the government can do, ideally at little cost to the government, but which enhance the attraction to wealth and business owners to live there.

Why should an investor be subject to inheritance taxes at rates of up to 40% of the *value* of real estate investments in the United Kingdom but zero tax on the value of their real estate investments in

Hong Kong or Singapore? And in the case of the United Kingdom, the tax cannot be avoided by interposing a Hong Kong or other company between the investment and the beneficial individual owner.

The Beginnings of Global Taxation—The Future Is Here

Without a doubt, I will have lost a few readers along the way in my outline of taxation principles as well as in relation to my recommendations regarding the important dialogue needed about how future tax systems might work. And for a number of readers, my encouragement of broad taxation of wealth and business owners will not be a comfortable read.

For wealth-owning families, however, I believe it is *critical* for them to understand how tax systems work and how they are changing. One needs advisors, but to ensure a safe ability to absorb, evaluate and implement advice, the wealth-owning family needs to be able to understand the advice they receive and be able to ask the right questions. And for those readers upset at my suggestions of wealth taxes, inheritance taxes and more, I do hope that you will be open to my belief that a failure to address the realities of income and wealth inequality will lead to **more** in the way of tax and other changes unfavourable to wealth and business owners. And to a world that is not sustainable—meaning that the business and wealth interests of individual families will not be sustainable, at least in the longer term.

Optionality is key, as is the ability of a wealth owner to choose where to live and, as a result, where to pay tax. But this optionality is already being limited by, among others, exit taxes and strengthened residence and other tax rules. Interesting (and for many, frightening) is the development of **global** tax initiatives that are almost certain to become an increasingly important element of the tax landscape. These initiatives have the potential to severely limit mobility as a means of tax minimization.

If wealth owners do not engage in awareness building and dialogue on this topic, the changes will happen without their involvement. Having a country that champions the interests of wealth and business owners, such as my fictional Dagland, is a growing need for wealth owners. This is an opportunity for Dagland and other jurisdictions open to the constructive power of family wealth.

The Global Minimum Tax—Also Referred to as GloBE and Pillar Two[13]

Some readers may be aware of the almost worldwide move towards a 15% global minimum tax for large multinational businesses. However, not all wealth and business owners (or their advisors) have realized that this initiative affects private capital. The reality is that this new regime is relevant not only for large 'multinationals' but also for all wealth and business owners.

Trusts, foundations, family partnerships and holding companies can all fall into the scope of the global minimum tax. Although the tax is, at least for now, focused on multinational groups with sustained annual revenues of over €750 million, there is little assurance that in the years to come this revenue threshold will not decline. In other words, this new system of minimum taxation may become a model that extends to a number of areas and to lower thresholds of income. There is also little assurance that the 15% minimum tax rate itself will not increase over time.

Families based in many parts of the world, including Asia, the Middle East and elsewhere, have been used to low, single-digit levels of taxation given, among other things, the low or nil rates of tax in their home countries and/or the lack of taxation by the countries in which they have activities abroad. For these families, the global minimum tax may have significant and surprising impacts.

On 20 December 2021, the OECD issued model rules for a 15% global minimum tax on large multinational businesses. The model rules are called the Global Anti-Base Erosion rules (GloBE). Two days later, the European Commission released a draft EU directive incorporating the same rules.[14]

In October 2021, **137** countries in the OECD/G20 Inclusive Framework on base erosion and profit shifting (BEPS) had already agreed on the so-called Pillar One and Pillar Two proposals to change the taxation of large multinational enterprises. The new rules were meant to be implemented by the beginning of 2023. As it turned out, implementation was delayed, but now more than fifty jurisdictions have indicated implementation plans, with some beginning to apply the rules in 2024 and others in 2025, in whole or in part.

The origin of these rules relates to global concerns about the taxation of the digital economy and the realization that to do so would require a coordinated effort among countries. Pillar One works to distribute profits through the reallocation of taxing rights to market jurisdictions, regardless of the physical presence maintained in the market jurisdiction. In simple terms, these rules provide a mechanism to ensure taxation where digital services are consumed regardless of whether the supplier of the services is based in a tax-favoured jurisdiction outside the market country. Pillar Two, the part that extends to the interests of wealth and business owners, is aimed at reducing tax competition in, primarily, the corporate sphere, providing for a 15% minimum tax on *in scope* 'multinational' enterprises with annual group revenues of more than €750 million.

The first set of new rules to be unveiled were the model rules regarding Pillar Two's global minimum effective tax rate of 15% on the so-called 'excess profits' of multinationals with annual revenue of at least €750 million for two out of the four fiscal years immediately preceding the fiscal year in question.

The model rules provide for 'top-up' taxation with respect to the income of any group member taxed at an effective rate of less than 15% under globally harmonized income tax rules. The primary method for achieving this top-up taxation is an income inclusion rule (IIR), which requires the ultimate parent entity of the multinational group to pay to its home country all of the deficit for the entire global group. If a parent company is located in a country that has not enacted a qualifying IIR, then the undertaxed profit rule (UTPR) comes into play. The UTPR requires a country to deny deductions or otherwise adjust the tax liability of locally taxable group members to the extent necessary to increase their local tax liability to the amount of the total group top-up tax allocated to the country. A country's allocation of global top-up tax is based on the country's share of the group's total employees and tangible assets located in countries that have enacted the UTPR provisions.

The top-up tax computation for each country includes a substance-based exclusion that allows a certain amount of income to be taxed at less than the minimum 15% effective rate. The excluded income is initially 10% of local payroll costs and 8% of the value of tangible assets used locally, reducing steadily over ten years to 5% of each of those bases.

The model rules use financial statement income, with certain adjustments, as the globally harmonized base for computing group members' effective tax rates. The model rules also provide for the possibility that a country will enact a domestic minimum top tax using the 15% rate and the same computation method with respect to income from operations in that country, in which case no top-up tax attributable to low-taxed income from that country would be allocated to other countries.

There are many uncertainties in this new regime, including whether the US Congress will agree to amend US law to conform to the model rules. The United States has its own global minimum tax regime relating to *global intangible low-taxed income* (GILTI), but it is inconsistent with the IIR provisions of the model rules in a number of respects. The important thing to note is that the global minimum tax operates on the basis of multi-country agreements where those countries cooperate to ensure a minimum level of taxation on multinational activities. And the countries that are part of this include tax havens and other 'safe' havens around the world—including Hong Kong, Singapore, Switzerland and many others.

Private Capital and the Global Minimum Tax

From what has been published by the OECD to date, the model rules will apply to private investment structures that yield at least €750 million of annual investment income (e.g., a 5% return on €15 billion of invested assets). For wealth and business-owning families with this level of income, exposure to the global minimum tax was a surprise to many and even to their advisors, all of whom had assumed that the global minimum tax was going to be focused on active businesses and particularly the tech industry.

The rules contain carve-outs for non-profit organizations, government entities, pension funds and regulated investment funds and real estate investment vehicles that are owned by a number of unrelated investors. As there is no carve-out for other types of private investment structures, particularly those of a single family, the minimum tax rules can apply to typical family ownership or stewardship structures such as a holding company, trust or foundation for the benefit of a family.

Unlike the case of transfer pricing rules which require multinational enterprises to report country by country key information on their taxes and income annually for each jurisdiction in which they do business, the global minimum tax rules require a deemed consolidation of the income of all group members (other than those explicitly carved out) in the case of an ultimate parent entity (e.g., a family trust) that does not prepare consolidated group financial statements. This is the key to why family business and wealth ownership can unexpectedly fall into the scope of the rules.

Choices That Jurisdictions Will Be Making

Very important for private wealth and business owners will be how countries participating in the global minimum tax will actually implement the model rules. Also relevant will be the accounting rules that impact relevant financial statements. There is also flexibility for countries to elect to increase tax rates to at least 15% for all taxpayers or for only those in scope. More importantly, low-tax jurisdictions can choose to not increase their tax rates and leave it to the jurisdiction of the parent company to collect a top-up tax. Further, given that the rules do not apply if all of a group's activities take place in only one country, one must query whether there will be jurisdictions that seek to position themselves to attract investment and activity by not imposing the minimum rate, despite agreeing to be part of the OECD initiative.

It is not only wealth and business owners who will be reviewing their strategies in reaction to the global minimum tax; financial centres have much to gain or lose from how they go about developing legislation that is, for many, in progress.

For Dagland, there are lots of issues that it would need to consider given its objective to attract and retain wealth and business owners to its economy. And particularly interesting for Dagland and the families who choose to base themselves there, Dagland could choose to impose the global minimum tax rules insofar as groups are 'in scope' through their multinational structures but choose NOT to impose the rules for those families who fully trust Dagland and move all of their entities to Dagland itself, though still investing and operating internationally. If wealth and business-owning families trust Dagland, the global minimum tax can be a driver of localization—consistent with regenerative economies and the ultimate impact goal of Dagland.

More in the Way of Information Exchange

There is an obligation under the model rules to file an information return (the 'Return') that enables tax authorities to assess the tax due under the model rules. It appears that the Return is required to be filed even if no tax is actually payable, if the model rules apply to the group in question.

The Return will include certain information about the multinational group, including information about its constituent entities and a description of the overall structure of the group. The Return can be shared by the tax authorities where it is filed with the tax authorities of other jurisdictions applicable to any constituent entities.

There are still many uncertainties as to how these rules will apply to passive investment structures. In particular, where revenue arises principally from dividends and capital gains, consideration will need to be given as to whether, in calculating the €750 million target, it is necessary to mark to market investments and take into account unrealized gains. A further question is what is meant by 'cross-border'. It is not uncommon in private asset structures to form entities in one jurisdiction while they are effectively managed from another jurisdiction. If a group has entities established in more than one jurisdiction but they are all effectively managed from a single jurisdiction (where they are treated as tax resident), will they be treated as cross-border? In this regard the UK consultation paper on the implementation of OECD Pillar Two states[15]:

> *These rules are set out in Chapter 10 of the Model Rules. Broadly, most constituent entities will be located in the jurisdiction where they are tax resident. Where a constituent entity is not tax resident in a jurisdiction, it will be located in the jurisdiction where it was created, for instance where it was incorporated.*

Things to Consider

Given the uncertainty regarding the scope of the global minimum tax, those with an interest in large trusts or foundations need to consider the possible implications of being subjected to the new minimum tax rules and the filing and disclosure requirements involved.

Wealth and business owners, and their advisors, also need to consider carefully whether it makes sense, in view of the global minimum tax, to opt for the many advantages associated with *diversification of ownership*. Political risk minimization, creditor protection and many other objectives can be addressed, at least in part, through ownership diversification, something touched on in other parts of this book.

Separating the ownership of a family business from ownership of family investments would be a simple example—perhaps the family business itself has revenues of over €750 million and is 'in scope'. Having a single family trust that also holds interests in investment assets could well subject the entire structure to the global minimum tax. Having the ownership in two trust vehicles might well avoid the investment assets being in scope if the revenues involved are below the €750 million threshold. At the individual level of a settlor of a trust, consolidation is NOT required under the global minimum tax rules as they presently stand.

There is also much more to consider and much in the way of uncertainty that it is hoped further guidance will address. Are there risks of mark-to-market treatment being required in relation to investment assets, as opposed to just looking at actual revenues such as dividends and realized capital gains? Are anti-avoidance rules oriented to the restructuring of business groups meant to cover approaches families can consider, given the lack of consolidation required at the level of individuals? Is it clear that several trusts with a common trustee, even if such trustee is a 'private trust company', would not be treated as a single entity?

Most importantly, the direction of travel is clear. In a world where wealth and income inequality is a growing reality, tax regimes are changing and tax competition is increasingly viewed as a form of competition that is to be controlled, if not eliminated. All wealth and business owners, at whatever level of value or revenue, need to be prepared.

A Global Minimum Wealth Tax and/or Other Uses of the Global Minimum Tax Concept?

Wealth taxation (a tax on the value of assets owned as opposed to taxes on income and gains) continues to be controversial and only a few countries, like Switzerland, have shown an ability to maintain a wealth tax system that applies broadly and, generally, works. Not surprisingly, the global minimum tax rules, just coming into existence, have inspired thinking about how a wealth tax might be imposed through a similar multilateral approach. Just that this is being seriously considered is a dramatic step away from the taxing ways of the past—taxes being imposed unilaterally, country by country. Optionality on the part of wealth and business owners is restricted in a very meaningful way when taxes are imposed on a global basis. And reference to the multi-country approach that the global minimum tax rules take is being made beyond wealth taxation. Having minimum income tax rules that apply to wealth and business owners with designated levels of income is also something that is being thought about.

In 2022, initial discussions about a coordinated wealth tax took place within the European Union leading, in 2024, to the topic being addressed by the G20, with finance ministers giving the go-ahead to advance discussions about minimum wealth taxation. Commissioned to take the idea further was Gabriel Zucman, a French economist known for his work focusing on income and wealth inequality.[16]

The idea discussed by the G20 at its meeting in Brazil in February 2024 related to the possible imposition of a minimum wealth tax equal to 2% of the wealth of 'billionaires' who could otherwise avoid taxation in a number of ways. Building on automatic information exchange and now the global minimum tax on the income of certain multinationals, the idea is a coordinated minimum tax on the 'super rich'.

It is interesting that in a well-written report prepared by Gabriel Zucman, the proposals made do not focus only on 'billionaires' but would extend to 'centi-millionaires'—those with a net worth of over US$100 million.[17]

> *A minimum tax equal to 2% of wealth on global billionaires would raise $200–$250 billion per year in tax revenue from about 3,000 taxpayers globally; extending the tax to centi-millionaires would generate an additional $100–$140 billion. By construction, these revenues would be collected from economic actors who are both very wealthy and undertaxed today. Someone who pays more than 2% of their wealth in income tax would have no extra tax liability; only ultra-high-net-worth individuals with particularly low tax payments would be affected. This standard would effectively address regressive features of contemporary tax systems at the top of the wealth distribution. In the baseline proposal, the tax rate of billionaires would become no lower than that of middle-class workers. Beyond the revenue gains for governments, there would be benefits in terms of increased social trust and cohesion. Variations over the baseline scenario are also explored.*[18]

How all this develops remains to be seen. But the approach put forward would ensure that either or both of income and wealth taxes would reach a total of 2% of the **value** of wealth held. The super important thing to understand is that the move to coordinated taxation among countries is a very new approach for the tax world where, historically, tax has been the purview of individual countries which, through tax treaties and otherwise, coordinate with other jurisdictions. The global minimum tax represents, in simple terms, an agreement among countries regarding the minimum taxation of certain activities and for certain taxpayers, with a relatively elegant approach to determining which country gets the first bite at collecting the agreed minimum. Now that countries have already agreed to this kind of coordination in relation to the Pillar Two global minimum tax, it is inevitable, at least to me, that this approach will be used in other areas, including, as in the initiative of the European Union and the G20 discussed above, to address the taxation of those viewed as being the 'wealthy'.

France has indicated its support for moves to using the global minimum tax regime to influence new coordinated approaches to taxing the wealthy, work that French Finance Minister Bruno Le Maire wants completed within the next three years:[19]

> *By 2027, we should have a global agreement on ... taxation of the wealthiest people based on the sharing of information, transparency, and the fight against unfair practices.*

As reported in the cited article, in a press briefing, Le Maire said that he did not underestimate '*the challenges associated with taxing the rich*'. However, those difficulties are not a reason to give up, he is reported to have said, adding that countries must show political willingness and determination:

> *This is exactly what we did on digital taxation, and we have been successful. This is exactly what we did with minimum taxation on corporate tax, and we did it; we have been successful. It will be the same on the international taxation for the wealthiest individuals.*

Wealth taxation, the focus of some of the thinking on a global approach to taxing individuals, is not without controversy. But as mentioned, the same global approach to taxation can be something we begin to see in other areas than wealth taxation—income taxation being only one of the other possibilities. It is interesting to consider whether inheritance taxes could come into focus as something to be addressed globally given the different approaches today, with some countries imposing these at very high rates and others not at all.

Pascal Saint-Amans, the former director of the OECD's Centre for Tax Policy and Administration, was the driving force behind many global tax developments, including automatic information exchange and Pillars One and Two. In a *Financial Times* article,[20] Saint-Amans was reported to have said:

> *A wealth tax is a false 'good idea'—the tax which actually is the answer, and that doesn't have the same constraints, is inheritance tax.*

According to the article, it is relatively easy to collect inheritance taxes as assets can be liquidated on death to meet the cost. Saint-Amans, the report says, thinks it would make sense for countries to apply a global minimum tax on inheritances, for billionaires in particular. He says increased international tax cooperation, which has led to the end of bank secrecy and the automatic sharing of financial information between countries, would make it hard to avoid such a levy. He says that the template for getting international cooperation for such a policy would be the 15% minimum corporate tax rate agreement just introduced.

As possible 'global' approaches to taxing the wealthy are being considered, tying these to hypothecation and also to addressing what are global challenges might be something to be considered. Under the global minimum tax rules, there is coordination by governments and an agreement as to which government gets to tax what falls below the minimum. But maybe there is a need for taxes that go directly to funding needs that are less country specific and more global in nature. Extreme poverty worldwide, climate change, migration issues and many others are global challenges that perhaps need to be addressed globally. As initiatives to impose minimum taxes are developed, perhaps the revenues can and should be administered not by individual governments but by international bodies and maybe with input from those who actually pay the relevant tax.

Back to the Question of Whether Society Is or Should Be Optional?

There is a very simple reality that no wealth or business-owning family will survive for the long term if our planet does not survive for the long term. More specifically, the challenges of climate change, migration, instability, poverty, inequality and more are not ones that a family can escape for the long term by moving from one country to another. Success in navigating internal and external derailers is what can allow a family to be sustainable over generations—but the family is part of a connected ecosystem that also has to thrive for the family to thrive. This includes planet, community, employees and more. So no, society is not optional.

But wealth and business owners *need* optionality to survive the current rocky road of taxation as we move from a world of hidden funds and tax abuses to a world of tax transparency and taxation that better addresses income and wealth inequality. Wealth and business owners need governments they can trust, but too few governments have shown that they can be trusted. So, the ability to relocate is critical and needs to be championed. Survival, as in nature, has a better chance the more choices are available—and a well-prepared wealth or business owner will recognize this and ensure that he and his family adopt approaches that enhance their mobility.

But issues in and around inequality are not ones that wealth and business owners can ignore, except to their detriment and to the detriment of society. As we move to a world of technology and artificial intelligence, inequality is likely to increase, as traditional jobs fall by the wayside. New ways of addressing taxation of the wealthy will be on the agenda, and global, coordinated tax techniques will be developed.

> *But between sub-societies and in 'society' at large, anarchy will rule, unless humankind can find a way to effective global governance. That would require that a way also be found to re-invest the middle and lower class in community, and that can only happen if income and capital ownership can become far more equal. That sounds like Catch-22, yet one lesson elites would be wise to take from the Industrial Revolution is that their own privilege is only sustainable if they are ready to share. Emaciating the broad population will not only deprive the capitalist of consumers, but will sooner or later, lead to violent overthrow.*[21]

Notes

1. Hulsroj, P. and Aliberti, M., *Essays on the Optional Society—and a Letter Concerning Inclusion* (ExTuto Publishing, 2021).
2. '*Even so, the fact remains that freedom is not absolute. It is contextual and relational*' (Hulsroj and Aliberti, 2021, p. IX).
3. Piketty, T. and Saez, E., 'A theory of optimal inheritance taxation', *Econometrica*, **81**(5) (2013).
4. https://www.theguardian.com/commentisfree/2017/jul/24/utopian-thinking-fund-welfare-state-inheritance-tax
5. Fullerton, J., *Regenerative Capitalism—How Universal Principles and Patterns Will Shape our New Economy* (Capital Institute, 2015).
6. Fullerton (2015), p. 77.
7. Asaf, E., Carvalho, I., Leke, A., Malatesta, F. and Tellechea, J. T., 'The secrets of outperforming family-owned businesses: How they create value—and how you can become one', representing views from McKinsey's Private Equity & Principal Investor's Practice and its Family-Owned Business Special Initiative, November 2023.
8. Hulsroj and Aliberti (2021), p. 6.
9. This discussion is based on an article published by the author with Stefano Mariani in the *South China Morning Post*: Marcovici, P. and Mariani, S., 'How reviving Hong Kong's inheritance tax could help restore equality and social mobility', *South China Morning Post*, 4 May 2018 and on an article by the author in a publication of the Society of Trust and Estate Practitioners: Marcovici, P., 'Time for a shake-up', *STEP Journal*, July 2018.
10. See https://www.imf.org/en/News/Articles/2015/09/28/04/53/sp061715
11. Among these is an excellent article by Andrew Halkyard, then Associate Professor in the Faculty of Law at the University of Hong Kong, entitled 'Hong Kong estate duty: A blueprint for reform', *Hong Kong Law Journal*, **30**(1), 47 (2000).
12. Marcovici, P., 'Why Hong Kong should develop a tax treaty network', *Tax Notes International*, **3**(Jan), 95 (1991).
13. Part of the following discussion is based on an article that the author wrote with Samantha Morgan and Jefferson VanderWolk: Morgan, S., Marcovici, P. and VanderWolk, J., 'A taxing reality', *STEP Journal*, January 2022.

14. https://ec.europa.eu/commission/presscorner/detail/en/IP_21_7028
15. See the OECD's Model Legislation Related to Country-by-Country Reporting and the Guidance on the Implementation of Country-by-Country Reporting: BEPS Action 13, Updated December 2019, para. 5.8 on p. 19.
16. https://gabriel-zucman.eu/files/report-g20.pdf
17. *A Blueprint for a Coordinated Minimum Effective Taxation Standard for Ultra-High-Net-Worth Individuals*, June 2024. https://gabriel-zucman.eu/files/report-g20.pdf
18. Pp. 6 and 7.
19. Soong, S., 'France backs calls for the global taxation of the wealthy', *Tax Notes International*, April 2024, p. 595.
20. Agyemang, E., 'Should governments tax the great boomer wealth transfer', *Financial Times*, 15 April 2024.
21. Hulsroj and Aliberti (2021), p. 128.

CHAPTER 5

Any Amount of Wealth Is Enough to Destroy a Family—Some Thoughts About the Psychology of Wealth

It is human nature to think that if we had the wealth, we would be happy. But does being wealthy really bring happiness? Clearly, there is a need for a certain level of wealth to meet one's needs, but how much is ever enough? Research has shown that after a certain point, having more does not continually add to one's happiness, and from my experience, it is simply all too often that wealth is destructive of families and relationships.

I believe that it takes work to not only be happy with what you have, but to ensure that the next generation and others in any family are positively rather than negatively impacted by any wealth that might be shared. How succession plans are developed and implemented can have a dramatic effect.

Wealth is created in any number of ways. An entrepreneur can work hard to create a profitable business. Professionals can accumulate wealth through their work, and by investing their savings. Employees can come into wealth through bonuses and stock plans. Liquidity events on the sale or listing of businesses and otherwise can arise. Luck may play a big role, as may family, political and other connections. The creation of wealth can be fast and easy, or a long and slow road, or somewhere in between.

Wealth also comes through inheritance, gifts, divorce and in many other ways.

How and when one arrives at wealth can have a big impact on the psychology of the wealth owner and on how the wealth involved will be grown, protected and shared. Someone who inherits may never feel the wealth is really theirs or that their input in the wealth creation or preservation process was of any value. The successful entrepreneur who received help from a parent or in-law may not feel they did it themselves and may thereby view wealth in a very different way than a wealth creator who started with nothing and did it all on their own. In families, it is often the case that while thought is given to creating wealth, not enough thought is given to how the wealth will be transferred and, importantly, the effect of a gift or inheritance on the individual receiving it.

In their *Theories of Change*, each of the family examples—the Apples, the Birds and the Cranes—need to understand the importance of the psychological issues that can come up for their families and how these, if not considered and attended to, can become derailers that affect what the families are hoping to achieve as their ultimate impact goals. As an example, if among these is the goal of having a family that is 'happy and healthy', this is severely compromised if there are mental health challenges that go unaddressed.

For families wanting to encourage the younger generation to become entrepreneurs of the future, as may be the case for the Birds and Cranes in particular, understanding the *fear* that the younger generation often has, given the accomplishments of the founders of the family business and others, is an example of what needs to be navigated. This fear, fuelled by insecurity and accompanied by paralysis, is all too often taken advantage of in wealth and business-owning families by outsiders to the family who initially advise on, and soon virtually kidnap, family business and investment interests.

How wealth is derived and the psychology involved also affects perspectives on how much is ever enough.

Is it possible to classify someone as 'rich' when the term is so subjective? For the vast majority, having 'enough' is something that never really happens, particularly given consumption and expectations—both of which are moving targets. Someone who is just starting out, and who has virtually nothing, hopes for salary increases and opportunities. If your savings are in the thousands or less and your income just about covers your spending, it is easy to see someone who owns their own home and drives a nice car as being 'rich', but is that homeowner really feeling rich if their savings do not cover more than a few years of their current lifestyle? Are they looking out of the window of the home coveted by someone with less than them, gazing at a larger home that their neighbour owns, and thinking about how nice it would be to live there? Is the neighbour living in the larger home distracted from enjoying it by dreaming about owning a private plane or some other possession of one of their wealthier acquaintances that they think they would like to have?

> *Even though I'm constantly negotiating this issue with patients in position of elite power, I always forget that people of wealth seldom view themselves as such. This is partially because notions of wealth are relative constructs and partially because we've been acculturated to attribute negative moral associations to people of wealth that include their being mean, selfish, entitled, greedy, narcissistic, dishonest, and not worthy of redemption.*[1]

I have worked with many, many families with wealth in the double digits of millions who definitely do not feel 'rich'—yet, for the vast majority, being a 'millionaire' is something only for dreams. Families may own various homes, but this comes with the costs associated with running properties that are not producing any income. The cars, clothes, jewellery, schools, insurance, entertainment, travel and other things enjoyed by those who can afford them come at a cost, and maintaining a lifestyle can get more and more expensive as wealth grows and consumption and expectations expand. As a result, there is little question that even the 'rich' worry about money, and whether what they have will run out. The choices out there in relation to spending seem almost limitless ... there is always a house, car, boat or other thing that is a bit nicer or bigger than the one we have, and which costs a bit more than we can afford. And as Peter Hulsroj, the co-author of *Essays on the Optional Society*, pointed out to me, wealth becomes a competitive scoreboard once every conceivable consumption issue is taken care of. So, is there ever really enough?

The question of how much we need is a difficult one, but it is highly relevant to the issues that come up in relation to transfers of wealth and how to best deal with the issue of succession. Even more important are the many psychological issues involved within and outside the family that come into the picture. The cast of characters can be a big one and, from a psychological perspective, the issues can be complex and ever-changing.

Looking at the typical players involved is a good starting point to understand the potential problems and, hopefully, avoid them. Much of asset protection and succession planning is based on ensuring that all the relevant *'what ifs?'* have been asked and addressed. Thinking about the possible actions and reactions of the different people in and out of a family who are interested in the family's wealth is a good starting point for some of these *'what ifs?'* that are particular to the family involved.

The Wealth Creator

Family wealth almost always has at its origin an entrepreneur who created the wealth. This can be someone who started with nothing, and who built a business or career that changed the financial picture for the family. This can also be someone who started with substantial amounts from inheritance or otherwise, but who were themselves successful in wealth creation—perhaps through shrewd investments, excellent stewardship of a family business or through the creation of new businesses for the family.

Still, the origin of most family businesses is a hard-working entrepreneur who started with nothing. Grandfather may have emerged from poverty with the drive to build, and in his lifetime achieved amazing results, allowing the possibility of long-term financial security for his immediate family and descendants. But has grandfather so dedicated himself to his business that he lacks the other elements often needed for a balanced life, such as close friendships, family relationships, outside interests and more? How does the move from poverty to comfort affect the wealth owner? Many never feel that they are really 'safe'—and to protect their family and their wealth, grandfather may be surprisingly frugal, never able to accept that success has come to such an extent that there will be no return to the difficulties of the past. But how does this conflict with the expectations of a spouse or a child, or one of the in-laws marrying into what they perceive to be a 'wealthy' family? And can these conflicts become destructive?

A wealth creator who started with nothing may also not be good at saying no to his children, spoiling them and destroying their dreams with too much. And what happens if the wealth creator worked for years and years, living on little, and suddenly the business is sold and wealth comes fast and high—is the change to the wealth creator's life positive?

It is easy to point out to the wealth creator the value of developing balance in their life, spending time on things other than their business and wealth, enjoying their family and developing outside interests that support a happy retirement. It is much harder to expect that the typical wealth creator will change. As a result, in working with wealth creators on the many issues that arise in asset protection and succession, it is important to try to understand things from their perspective, and to help them understand how their decisions (or lack of decisions) will affect their business, their families and themself.

The super successful wealth creator is often at the centre of a complex set of family and business relationships, his or her success influencing a number of emotions among family, friends, colleagues and others—emotions that the wealth creator himself may not understand or appreciate exist. Is the son or daughter of someone who is a larger-than-life financial success condemned to never be able to feel the sense of accomplishment that can be so important to the question of 'happiness'? Can the wealth creator properly work on transition issues that will ensure success of the family business as it moves to the next generation? Maybe there *are* steps the wealth creator can take to increase the chances that wealth and success will not be destructive of either their business or family relationships.

At one extreme, a wealth creator may get everything right. During their lifetime and career, the wealth creator might move from a singular focus on making money and building their business to spending more time with family, developing philanthropic and other interests, and thinking about how best to deal with asset protection and succession planning. Here, there is no one right answer for every family—but where the wealth owner involved puts enough time and thought into the ongoing process of putting in place what might work best in their circumstances, the chance of getting it right is certainly there.

Getting it right also means that the wealth creator understands that wealth is transitory and that it is not wealth that should be the glue that keeps a family together. If the wealth is gone, is the family also gone? Or do what the family represents, and the relationships involved, survive and thrive whatever happens to family wealth?

The spending habits of the successful wealth creator are often interesting to observe. These can range from wealth owners who remain frugal and criticize spouses and children who 'overspend' to wealth owners who themselves overspend, resulting in unrealistic expectations for those who may succeed them; lives destroyed at discovering that there is little left over, contrary to what they had expected and quietly planned for. To me, it is crucial for the wealth creator to understand how important it is to communicate clearly within a family and to understand how much of what our children learn comes from example. And for those whose achievements are enormous, how can they ensure that the achievements of their children, spouses and other relatives are not diminished by the wealth creator's own success?

Wealth creators are not always mothers and fathers who affect their spouses, children and grandchildren with their succession and related decisions. Increasingly we see wealth creators who are young, and sometimes very young, and whose wealth has a tremendous impact on their relationships with siblings and fairly young parents who never achieved the success one of their children has achieved. Does a successful young person have an obligation to 'share the wealth' with siblings or parents? How can family relationships best be preserved when there is outsized financial success by one family member?

Psychologically, the wealth creator is a difficult one to deal with, and the issues change as the wealth creator ages and family dynamics change. The introduction of spouses, mistresses, paramours, second families and more adds to the complexity—and to the challenge of ensuring that wealth is not destructive of the family involved.

And it is not only the wealth creator who faces mental health challenges. As outlined below, there is a wide cast of characters in and around wealth and business owners, and all are affected by the dynamics of wealth. And of course, those who 'have' are not immune from the mental health challenges all families face.

> ... *I've discovered that while we've been acculturated to believe otherwise, celebrity identities and the power inherent in them are not enough to protect the human beings who live underneath them from the problems all human beings face. In fact, the power, property and prestige that come with these identities actually complicate and cause different forms of pathology. We think power and fame are keys that provide liberation from life's challenges, but my experience and research show they do not. Yes, at the edges of life they can provide physical protection and comfort, but at the core of existence, a place we call the self, they can create a fragility that causes destruction and despair.*[2]

The Wealth Creator's Spouse

There is little in the world that is black and white, and this certainly applies to the spouses of wealth creators. Maybe the spouse is a second or third spouse, or a first love or arranged marriage that has lasted years. The spouse may have previously been a mistress or paramour, or may themselves have come from a family with meaningful wealth and/or position. Or the wealth creator's spouse may be a wealth creator themselves, involved in their own business or career. Often the spouse is an integral part of the wealth creator's business and success, working hand in hand with the wealth creator.

Family dynamics and the whole issue of asset protection and succession will be affected by the wealth creator's spouse, and where the spouse survives the wealth creator, his or her role can be ever more important in dealing with the question of whether wealth will destroy the family involved.

Relationships with the younger generation can vary ... it is not every mother or father that is loved and respected by their children, and too often for good reason. And where the marriage is a second, third or further marriage, relationships can be particularly strained, largely because money becomes a central issue.

Are things any different where spouses are of the same sex? In my experience, not at all—expectations and questions of fairness are the same, and often enough, children also come into the picture. Yet, dynamics and the legal position can be very different, as can perceptions of siblings and others on what their fair share is in the event of a succession event occurring.

I have worked with many wealth creators who, at some stage of their life, end up marrying a younger (and sometimes much younger) second, third or further spouse. Almost inevitably, issues in and around the question of money arise. If, say, Dad, has three children in their forties and fifties and remarries a younger woman, perhaps younger than his youngest child, financial issues invariably come into the mix. Is the new spouse a gold-digger? Of course! There is *never* a question of whether or not the new young spouse is a gold-digger. The new spouse *is* a gold-digger. The only open issue is the *extent* to which money came into the picture for the new spouse ... and if she is not particularly attracted to the money, there is little assurance that she will not become a gold-digger at some point in the future.

This may sound like a very cynical view of relationships, love and marriage. But the reality is that attraction involves a 'full package' ... looks, personality, fitness, intelligence, prospects, coming from a 'good' family *and* wealth. So, in planning, my approach is always to expect the worst, and if things turn out for the best, all the better, but it is important to plan for what can and does all too often happen ... a huge difference of views on money between the children and, in particular, a second or third (or further) spouse.

When Dad marries someone younger than his youngest child, it is rarely the case that this does not raise a question in the minds of the children regarding what this is going to end up costing them in terms of their interest in their father's assets. Where there are more children of the second or further marriage, the risks to the first set of children are even greater. From a legal perspective, marriage, cohabitation, divorce, adoption and having children all have potential ramifications. But there are also considerable psychological issues, which are often less easy to manage.

The children may well not say anything to their father about their real concerns ... how will the new wife their father has chosen affect their financial interests? This unspoken concern may end up poisoning the relationship between the children and their stepmother, and also affect their relationship with their father, as the children show lukewarm (at best) support for the person their father has chosen to spend his life with.

Could all this bad feeling be addressed, at least in part, through some advance planning and greater communication within the family? What if Dad, before marrying, makes irrevocable arrangements to make clear what his children will end up getting, either now or on his passing? And if, as part of the plan, Dad puts in place binding agreements with his new wife, that she accepts, clarifying what she will end up getting if the marriage lasts and she survives her new husband, will this help ensure that the new relationship will work for all concerned? Could it be that once the question of money is off the table, the children will be more open to focusing on the potential happiness of their father and the reality that the new spouse may lighten the burden they would otherwise be under to take care of their father in his old age?

Or will Dad neglect the work necessary to minimize the risk of disputes, allowing even family photo albums carrying memories of his children's upbringing to pass to a new young wife who just throws them away when her elderly husband dies? Will a lack of foresight result in his relationship with his new wife moving into one where he increasingly depends on her care and she tightens the screws, focusing on the money she wants in exchange?

The broad range of spouses can include a spouse of a wealth creator who him- or herself has meaningful assets, and perhaps their own family legacy that comes with those assets. I worked with a family where a woman in the older generation came from a wealthy and well-known family. Her father had employed the man who eventually became her husband and provided him with the capital he needed to eventually start his own business. The wife used her own resources to support the growth of the business, and while she was not directly involved in the further wealth creation, spending her time raising a number of children, it was pretty clear that her own family legacy and wealth was highly relevant to the success that her husband enjoyed. As the wealth of the family grew, so did the reputation and legacy of the husband. Increasingly, both within and outside the family, there was little recognition of the contribution of the spouse and her own family's legacy to the wealth created. This led to considerable differences of opinion in relation to the succession and asset-protection plan ultimately adopted by the family, and to the unhappiness of the ageing spouse who was increasingly feeling left out of the process.

Understanding the dynamics of wealth and respecting the history of the family involved can be an important step in the succession process. And like all areas of asset protection and succession planning, the issues are not only of concern to those with millions or billions, but to all of us.

Ageing Relatives—Alive ... and Well?

The ageing wealth owner is fast becoming a disaster area in wealth planning. This can be a grandparent or great-grandparent, a mother or mother-in-law, a father or father-in-law, or anyone else in the family. We are now living well into our eighties and nineties, with increasing numbers of people living well into their 100s. Accompanying this change in demographics are significant issues for families in relation to how wealth moves from one generation to the next, and when.

One simple question that ageing populations give rise to is when the younger generation should begin to benefit from assets that are intended to pass from one generation to the next. In the case of Brooke Astor, a well-known New York socialite whose son ended up in prison for having, among other things, helped himself to some of his mother's assets, her approach did not work. Brooke Astor lived to well over 100, delaying her son's inheritance until he was in his eighties. It is one thing to pass wealth to children on death when one lives until the early seventies, and the children are in their mid to late forties, but if we add thirty years of life to the mix, is it really right to make children wait for their inheritance for that long?

As we move into a time of ageing populations, it is a responsibility of the older generation to make their plans clear, and to consider the possibility of finalizing their thinking on succession several decades before their death. If the children are in their forties or fifties, should this not be a time when at least some of the assets that are to ultimately pass to them are actually divided and transferred? Isn't this safer than holding onto assets until dementia sets in and household staff and others can interfere with the succession process, converting assets to their own benefit? I have been disturbed by reports of doctors and nurses caring for the aged becoming beneficiaries of their patients' estates, and have seen multiple cases of trusted advisors, bankers, lawyers and others, worming their way into the succession process, taking advantage of their elderly clients. It is not only spouses and in-laws who are gold-diggers that need to be protected against.

As people age, there is a real risk of their becoming increasingly concerned that the 'money' is what keeps their family interested in them. Members of the older generation are often afraid to let go of their wealth, thinking that their wealth is the main reason for their children and grandchildren to visit—a sad way for a successful wealth owner to feel, but a reality of how many do. I am a believer that a good succession plan is one that is adopted early in life, and which at the right time is discussed openly and sensitively within the family so that intentions are clear, reducing the risk of bad feelings and disputes when it is difficult or late to adjust things. At the right time, the succession plan should be fixed, with changes only being possible if a majority of family stakeholders agree.

As people age, there is also the increase of varying forms of dementia. Memories fail, and as they do, paranoia creeps in. We forget where our glasses are, and this develops into thinking that someone stole our glasses. Sometimes this paranoia presents itself openly, with the older generation accusing household help or even family members of stealing. Often, the paranoia is internalized and translates itself into the ageing wealth owner delaying any gifts of assets or openness on the estate-planning process. Hanging on to the assets and keeping secretive is a way of keeping control and power, and for someone challenged by the ageing process, retaining control over something may seem critical.

There are many psychological issues that come into the mix when it comes to succession. Controlling your wealth until the very, *very* end may feel right, but all too often it means that there is no well-thought-out succession plan. Assets disappear for lack of anyone knowing where they are, possessions are stolen by those who know that they will not get caught, and individual siblings may press their own agendas with ageing parents, resulting in long-term damaged relationships and potential for destructive family disputes. Anger with children may result in assets passing to grandchildren much earlier than they should, and with negative effects on the ability of the children to play their roles as parents.

The Second Spouse

Second marriages or other domestic relationships affect everyone in the family, both emotionally and financially. Sometimes the second marriage is encouraged by family members after the death of a spouse. In other cases, the second marriage may have caused a messy break-up of a first marriage, and children and the former spouse will view the second spouse as an enemy from every perspective. Relationships can be very complex, including second and third domestic relationships that happen while the first marriage is still intact. In some religions and cultures, this is accepted, in others it is not. But in all cases, issues arise, both emotional and financial.

The overall responsibility, in my view, is with the wealth owner. It is he or she, when embarking on a second or subsequent marriage, who should consider the impact on their family and wealth and proactively address these issues to seek to protect the family from destroying itself and the wealth involved. Those 'lucky' wealth owners who live through their second marriage with no legal or other challenges may well be leaving a legacy of problems, with the legal actions regarding their assets happening after they pass away.

In later chapters, the 'tools' of wealth management will be a topic, and how these tools, such as trusts, can be used to address family needs will also be described. But to really make these tools work, the wealth owner has to think about the *'what ifs?'* in the context of what they know about their second spouse and of their first family. And if there are children and other stakeholders that the second marriage brings into the picture, the need for careful thought and planning also comes into the mix in that respect.

The reality is that the second or subsequent spouse will themselves benefit hugely from an open approach to financial issues. The more things are made clear at the outset of a relationship, the less room there is for uncertainty, and the more possible it is to anticipate that the relationship that develops will be less about money and more about what is important to really make the relationship work for all involved.

If the wealth owner fails to take early action in and around a second marriage, as sensitive as it may be, their own family should step in and encourage dialogue. Waiting for Mum or Dad to take action may leave things too late, and rightly or wrongly, it is not uncommon to see virtually all the family wealth go to a second spouse when there is little upfront planning and discussion within the family. Timing can be everything, and from every perspective.

The First Mistress or Paramour

My eldest son was born at the Adventist Hospital in Hong Kong. I was standing in front of the glass window to the nursery looking for my son (I have to admit that all babies look pretty much the same at that stage) when I noticed a client of mine also looking through the glass. He introduced me to the mother of his new child, who was sitting in a wheelchair, having just given birth. This was not his wife.

Living and working in Hong Kong, I developed a sense that mistresses are an Asian concept—having run across so many wealth owners with complex multiple relationships. I moved to Switzerland in the mid-1990s and began working with wealth owners from around the world, and was poignantly reminded that mistresses are not an Asian concept, but a *global* concept.

In some countries, co-habitation can give rise to meaningful legal rights to assets and income. In all cases, out-of-marriage liaisons can disturb the succession process and, most importantly, family relationships.

And it is certainly not only about mistresses, but also the paramour, the male version of a mistress (with the terms 'mistress' and 'paramour' both being highly inappropriate in many cases). Out-of-marriage affairs can range from the most insignificant to meaningful, lifelong relationships and second families.

From the psychological perspective, all are affected—the mistress or paramour, the wealth owner involved with them, the wealth owner's spouse and family. Not everyone may know of each other, and this confidentiality may in and of itself be an objective of effective asset protection and succession planning. Approaches using the tools of wealth planning can help to prevent what so often happens—long-term out-of-marriage relationships coming to the surface after the death of the wealth owner.

For the mistress or paramour, there may well be plenty of non-financial reasons for the attraction. But can we really say that there are many cases where the money involved is not at least a factor? And maybe an important one? The wealth owner probably knows that their money is relevant, and may even think that the position is clear, with their paying the rent and providing gifts from time to time. But will the paramour stick to this price as he becomes less secure of his attraction as the years go by? Will a close relationship move from excitement and affection to blackmail?

There is one golden rule about mistresses and paramours. Never give them a lump sum of money. Within months, the mistress or paramour is back asking for more, having lost the money gambling or through some shady investment.

It is the wealth owner who is in control of decisions on how to financially deal with the situation of a mistress or paramour, or multiples thereof. Not thinking about things is often a mistake. Like with families, openness with the paramour or mistress about the financial aspects of the relationship, and good use of the tools of wealth planning, can help. For example, a wealth owner can use a variety of structures to provide an annual allowance to the paramour, but only on the condition that he remains quiet about the relationship and does not make any other claims. If the paramour is cooperative, he receives the allowance. If he is not, he loses it all. Not a guarantee that there will be no trouble, but something that may help.

In my work, I was generally taking the side of the family—either looking at things from the perspective of the wealth owner or from the perspective of other family members. I often ran across situations of mistresses or paramours being egged on in relation to their financial expectations by outsiders—their own family and friends, and sometimes more sinister 'handlers' with economic interests in the outcome.

The mistress or paramour will often have very different views on what is owed to them than the wealth owner has. But in some relationships, the mistress or paramour may have pretty valid reasons to think they deserve the share of the wealth they are seeking.

Within wealth-owning families, the issue of a mistress or paramour with whom a parent or spouse is involved can be traumatic, and certainly not only from a financial perspective. A mistress or paramour will often come to realize that they had better get hold of some assets while wealth is still in the hands of the wealth owner—creating issues as the wealth owner ages, and as the relationship moves—as it so often does—from excitement to extortion.

And like everything else having to do with families, it is not always black and white. It is sometimes the mistress or paramour who needs protection, and who is the one dedicating themselves to a relationship which might not provide them with the long-term financial security they deserve, particularly when they are the ones who are of real meaning to the wealth owner over the years. It again falls to the wealth owner to ensure that the right things are done at the right time.

The Second Mistress or Paramour ... and the First Is Not Thrilled

The reality is that the 'value' of mistresses and paramours is at least sometimes their youth and the excitement of something new. The move to a new relationship will almost certainly raise many issues for both the new and the old playmate.

When the first mistress or paramour finds out about the new player, this is often a trigger for their wanting to ensure their financial and family status. What was previously a private relationship that the broader family was not aware of may come out into the open, with financial and emotional consequences.

The second mistress may well be looking to establish herself by making herself known to the first—again creating havoc. For the wealth owner involved in these relationships, initial excitement may well turn into a nightmare. Making things clear on what the financial deal is and the consequences of causing trouble can help keep things under wraps and is certainly worth the effort. It is easy to say that the best way to avoid difficulties is to stay away from toxic relationships—but this may be naïve given the realities in the lives of all too many wealth owners.

For both the new and old companion, financial issues are part of the relationship. It is the responsibility of the wealth owner to accept this reality, and to plan their affairs accordingly.

The Children in the Second Family

Each participant in a wealth-owning family has their own perspective on wealth and their entitlements in the succession process. But most important when thinking about children is how the succession process may affect their lives. There is no question whatsoever that growing up without wealth but with the right family support is much better than growing up in an environment of uncertainty as to how your mother or father feel about you, and confusion on whether financial 'messages' are messages about the way a parent feels about a child.

Having a mother or father who is the 'second' spouse or playmate brings its own complications, given the emotions of the second spouse and his or her views about the first, and the children of the first, and the common financial preference of the children of the first relationship. Where family businesses are involved, the issues become even more difficult to manage, particularly where the wealth owner envisions their children, from whichever relationship, working together in harmony. This can work, but often doesn't, and the question that arises is whether there is anything the wealth owner can do early on to reduce the risk of disaster, both personal and financial.

But it is not only the wealth owner who impacts the wellbeing of the children of the second or third (or further) family. The second parent, who may not be a wealth owner him or herself, will have a tremendous impact, as will step-siblings, grandparents and others. Is bad feeling inevitable, or are there steps that can be taken to minimize the risks? And if you are the 'victim' of a wealth-owning family, are there steps you can take to protect yourself from destruction? Sometimes being destructive (or protective of your own interests, as might be your perspective) is the key, and understanding your rights and how they can be enforced (through persuasion or legal means) can be critical. This, of course, is something that all beneficiaries of wealth need to understand—wealth can destroy relationships, but early and clear action, based on understanding what is really going on, can be critical.

There are many practical and legal approaches that can help secure the financial position of members of a wealth-owning family. But in the end, the most important thing is to avoid wealth being destructive of one's life, and all too often the frustration of not getting what you think you deserve can become an obsession. The more each individual can focus on themselves and building their own independence, both emotional and financial, the better off they will be.

The Sons

Much has been changing, but there still often remains a reality that expectations and arrangements involving male children *are* different. This sometimes results from cultural differences, such as in traditional Chinese families where the older son, and sons generally, are favoured in financial support and inheritance. This also results from a broader reliance on the older son as the one who has the responsibility to carry forward the family legacy, including family wealth and businesses.

Religion can also come into it, and *Sharia* law, applying to Muslims, generally hugely favours the male line, with sometimes dramatic consequences. As an example, the estate of a father who is a Sunni Muslim in Lebanon leaving only daughters would go in large part to the deceased's brother or his deceased brother's sons—this regardless of whether the deceased was estranged from his brother or nephews and regardless of the deceased father having wanted his daughters to be the only beneficiaries of his estate. It is also the case that in virtually all cases where *Sharia* law applies, sons will receive twice the share that daughters receive.

Even where cultural and religious elements do not come into it, males are often, though clearly not always, the main breadwinners, with women far more often being the ones to have to take a temporary or permanent break from their careers to raise a family. Does this mean that a son should inherit more than a daughter, the daughter being less likely need support from her parents given the ability to rely on her husband? Should a son inherit less because of his earning capabilities, with a daughter getting more because of the possibility that she may not be able to earn anything throughout the period of parenting she may undertake?

How do sons feel when they benefit more than their sisters, for whatever reason—cultural, religious or otherwise? I have seen many relationships among siblings destroyed because of differences in treatment by their parents, and the destruction all the greater where the recipients are of a different world than their parents. The father or mother may come from a different generation, tied to religious and cultural traditions and obligations, with the younger generation much less so, if at all. If a son is then favoured over his sister, does he have an obligation to make things fair once the assets come to him? In the traditional Chinese family, the older son had the obligation to look after his sisters and younger male siblings. If the children are thoroughly westernized, will the older son, having received the bulk of his parent's assets, do the 'right thing'? If he doesn't know how his sister feels about having received less, what will the effect of this be on their relationship? What if he does know how she feels, but likes the idea of having received more? If the son shares with his sister, is it enough, in her eyes, if the amount is not equal? And even if it is, does the son begin to affect their relationship by making his sister feel that she 'owes' him for his generosity?

There are often reasons not to treat children equally in gifts and inheritances, and certainly culture and religion are important elements in ensuring that wealth and the approach to its distribution within a family are not destructive. Where the religious or cultural elements are solidly believed in by all involved, the problems are less likely to arise than they do in families without clear rules to guide them. But in my experience, distributing wealth unequally among children without adequate preparation and discussion within the family is one of the most destructive things a parent can do.

But is there value in an approach that puts the older son in charge of the family business and family affairs? Professor Joseph Fan of the Chinese University of Hong Kong[3] has lectured and written on the failed performance of companies whose ownership passes to trusts rather than to a responsible family member, such as an older son—the traditionally favoured approach in Chinese families. Meanwhile, Professor Roger King of the Business School at the Hong Kong University of Science and Technology has undertaken studies showing that the eldest son is the *least* able, psychologically, to ensure success. Professor King's research suggests that second and subsequent sons are more entrepreneurial than their careful older siblings.[4]

For me, governance is the key, whatever approach is taken in succession, and whatever tool is used to achieve the future running of a family business or of family wealth. Having a trust in place that is designed to protect the interests of the family does not mean that a business will fail if the trust contains the right governance checks and balances. Using structures that make it clear who owns assets among the younger generation, perhaps equally, but also putting the right incentives in place for those leading the business to feel that they are adequately rewarded for their efforts can be as effective (if not more so) as the traditional focus on the eldest son.

There is no one answer that fits all circumstances, but the issue of succession is one that requires considerable attention if assets, businesses and relationships are to be preserved and enhanced.

The Daughters

The female line in a family can face a number of challenges, cultural, religious or otherwise. And fortunately, there are now family businesses around the world headed by women who have sometimes had to overcome considerable hurdles to reach positions of leadership.

Daughters, however, often still have to take career breaks to take care of their children, whether for a short period or otherwise, and daughters may have particular financial needs. One that is of utmost importance is the need for lifetime financial independence, if the wealth of her family allows for this. If parents have wealth that might transit from one generation to the next, something to consider for both sons and daughters is to not have the value involved be available to the next generation all at once.

A wealth-owning client of mine had a considerable estate he was planning the transition of. Planning for the next generation seemed straightforward to him; his children all in their early adulthood, well on the way to establishing their own young families. Perhaps a situation where the decision on how and when to distribute would be easy—just dividing the assets equally and having them shared among the younger generation. But one of his daughters had married into a mega-wealthy family ... not millionaires, but multi-billionaires.

Did this mean that the one daughter, as opposed to her other siblings, should not receive anything, not being in need? Or would being fair and protecting sibling relationships require an even distribution among the children? I asked about the daughter's spending habits, and how she was relating to the family she had married into. I asked whether she was spending within or above her means, and whether she was over-spending, trying to keep up with her husband and in-laws, proving her status as herself coming from a wealthy family and not needing her husband's family's money. Not surprisingly, my client excitedly confirmed my suspicions. His daughter had been quickly going through the funds he had provided to all of his children as an interim distribution of his wealth.

While his other children were prudently investing what had been advanced to them, the daughter who had married into billions was using her own money to contribute to a lifestyle of private jets, couture clothing and more. What I advised was that my client and his wife consider an estate plan that would *not* have his daughter receive her full inheritance on their deaths, but rather, through the use of the 'tools' of wealth and estate planning, she be provided with something more than just an inheritance—financial independence from her husband or anyone else for her entire life.

By holding back the full inheritance and having it made available in parts over her lifetime, whatever happened, the daughter of my client would avoid having to depend on her husband, and there would also be a level of control over her spending. She simply would not have the ability to 'spend it all' in a few years, something not difficult to do notwithstanding that she was likely to inherit in the range of US$15 to US$20 million. Living amongst billionaires, and paying for her own clothes, jewellery, travel and more to show her wealth, would have otherwise meant that she would have gone through her inheritance in only a few short years. Through some careful planning this simply could not happen.

Divorces are all too common, and while we may lament this state of affairs, much, much worse are those who are confined to a dysfunctional and dangerous relationship for economic reasons. Providing any child (or anyone else) with financial independence is an important gift. The ability to walk out at any time can be critical.

But what of the other siblings in the case of my client? They were being prudent with what their parents had given them. Should we have arranged for different treatment of the daughter who had married into wealth from those who were doing it all on their own? I am not a believer in differences being made among children except in the most extreme cases. As a result, I advocated a long-term approach being taken on the same basis for all of the children involved. This required some careful thinking and the design of an approach that would permit the next generation reasonable access to what they needed for the right reasons—education of the younger generation and the ability to deal with healthcare and other costs, and the ability to invest. But to me, the equal treatment of the younger generation is a key element towards helping to keep the younger generation together and avoiding having wealth destroy the family.

Are these issues only issues for the super wealthy? Or is it even more important to protect what may be left to the younger generation when the amounts involved are relatively small, but the needs of the younger generation and the effect of even modest financial help great?

In one of the fictional families described earlier, the Apples, there are three adult children, only one of whom is financially independent of her parents. The family have some savings, but the figures are modest. But would it really help to consider uneven distributions that favour children who still depend on help from their parents? Would this not encourage bad feeling and be a punishment for the child who is independent? And what if things change in the future, with the child now less in need being in need while financial circumstances change for the others? Keeping things as even as possible is the safer bet.

In-Laws—A Broad Spectrum

What about children's spouses, and particularly those from modest backgrounds. Are they 'gold-diggers' that need to be protected against? Did my new daughter-in-law marry my son for money? Is it safer for my son to marry a woman from a wealthy family?

In my years of work for wealth-owning families, I met many who engineered marriages among their children to families seen as their peers in terms of levels of wealth, thinking that this was a way to avoid the 'gold-diggers'. Is this a safer bet?

In my experience, the level of wealth of the spouse of a child from a wealthy family has little relationship to the threats to wealth that divorce gives rise to. And the reality is that the question of whether a son or daughter-in-law is a gold-digger is an irrelevant question to ask. Your son- or daughter-in-law *is* a gold-digger. It is just a question of degree. And if they are not hugely gold-diggers today, they may well become so in future, as relationships and their own financial circumstances change.

All relationships involve money, at least to some extent. We are attracted to our partners because they have good personalities; they have a wide circle of friends; they are 'buff', keeping themselves in shape and looking good; there is physical and emotional attraction;

they have a good career and prospects for the future; they come from a wealthy family and can provide; they have the toys that make life more fun ... The degree to which money comes into it may differ from relationship to relationship but thinking that there is *no* element of money coming into it at all is often wrong. The wealthiest of potential spouses for your children will be thinking about what money your children might inherit or generate themselves. And if the issue is not at the forefront at the outset of the relationship, it can well move to the forefront later, when the financial position of the other party changes or when there is a rocky time in the relationship and a desire to 'punish' comes into the picture.

Best is to *hope for the best, but plan for the worst*, and to accept that every such relationship involves money, at least to some extent.

Whether a spouse comes from wealth or not, having some understanding of how things work in the event of a breakdown in the relationship is very important for the younger generation. Pre- and post-nuptial agreements are only part of the picture. How one spends, and from where money is accessed, can have a big effect on who gets what in the event of a breakdown of the marriage. Whose money is used to pay for homes, education of children and more is also an issue to be considered early on. Money can run out, and if the safety net is represented by the savings or inheritance of one of the spouses, what happens to that if the marriage breaks down?

It is often much easier to sort things out upfront when the intended spouse of one of your children is *not* coming from wealth. It may sound mean, but it is much easier to come to clear financial arrangements with someone from a modest background than with someone who sees themselves as financially ahead of the family they are marrying into. Which means even more care is needed if your child is marrying into a family of wealth, to avoid your child, and your wealth, becoming victim to what could happen.

Should spouses be excluded from family discussions in or out of 'family retreats' in the case of a wealthy family? How much should they know about family wealth? More on this later in relation to pre- and post-nuptial agreements, and the destruction of wealth that divorce can give rise to, but it is important to remember that the wife or husband of your child will be raising your grandchildren and will be involved in protecting their interests. Total exclusion from the family is not the answer, but neither is unlimited trust. In fact, *trust no one*.

Where the in-law is from a wealthy family, this is not any answer to the many questions that have to be asked as part of the *'what-ifs?'* an effective asset protection and succession plan needs to address. In fact, the wealth of your son or daughter's partner may be the basis on which your child overspends ... trying to prove their own independence. Reliance on the wealth of their partner can result in your child losing the important financial independence that your wealth should be able to offer.

And wealthy families often get there for a reason—they are not stupid and have money as their focus. Upfront, the man or woman your child may be planning a future with may themselves be carefully planning their own financial protection, allowing your child to be the spender, while they are the saver. When a divorce is looming, wealth can be the basis of investments in the best lawyers, experienced in ensuring the destruction of the wealth and wellbeing of the victims of attack. Your child marrying into wealth means *more* prudence, not less, in a world of danger and destruction of wealth and relationships.

There are also plenty of psychological issues that come into the mix. How sad for a successful mother and father to have worked hard to provide a solid start for their children to have one of their children feel 'poor' given the wealth they have married into. How sad to have a son or daughter, successful in their profession or business, be undervalued given the success of their father-in-law or mother-in law. We need to find ways to ensure that our children do not measure their success by how much money they have in the bank, or what they are able to consume or earn. It is too easy to fall into the trap of measuring your success by the wrong things, and it is here that parents can do much to help their children avoid money being destructive of their lives and relationships.

From white to black, there are many shades of grey. And sons-in-law, and daughters-in-law, will fall on every point of this broad spectrum. It is safest to take the view that they are all gold-diggers, and none are to be trusted ... not because they are or will be gold-diggers or they are not trustworthy, but given that without the right protections in place, wealth and relationships will be at risk. The right planning means hoping for the best and planning for the worst. Checks and balances and ensuring that wealth goes to who you really want it to go to is key. But it is also important to avoid having any plan for the worst stand in the way of achieving the best—or becoming a self-fulfilling prophecy!

I have seen many situations of families where sons-in-law and daughters-in-law have played a critical role in not only protecting family wealth, but in hugely growing family wealth. I have also seen families where, for cultural and other reasons, hugely talented in-laws (and their children) have been wastefully excluded from family businesses.

I was approached by a Chinese family divided between Hong Kong and Singapore a few years ago, and was asked whether I could contribute to the family's thinking on the next steps of their estate plan. A well-known family, the plan, at its early stage, was to document the historical ways of the family: only sons bearing the family name could enter the family business—daughters would be given some liquidity, a small fraction of what would have been an equal share of the family business, and their children, not bearing the family name in most cases, would be permanently excluded from the possibility of entering the family business. Does this make sense? I indicated that I would certainly not be the one to decide for the family, but given my involvement that I would at least want to put on the table the possibility of the family moving to a more 'modern' and circular approach to succession, avoiding 'waste' and allowing for the possibility of talented daughters, sons-in-law and the children of daughters, whether bearing the family name in whole or in part, being able to participate in the family business. I was not invited back for a second meeting.

I have also seen situations where family wealth, due to the premature death of an only child, fell into the hands of a son-in-law who then used his in-laws' assets to establish himself in his second marriage and family, favouring his new family over the grandchildren of the wealth creators. The wealth-owning parents had left their assets to their daughter, leaving it to her to decide how to plan for the future. The daughter, sadly, died young, without any planning, resulting in most of the wealth passing to the control of her young husband. Perhaps safer would have been for the older generation to have made clearer provision for their grandchildren, protecting against what ended up happening.

Checks and balances; trusting no one; assuming the worst. In-laws step up to the plate more often when things are kept in check, as with anyone else. Making things clear and fair, and, most importantly, understanding the succession plan and the '*what-ifs?*' is the key to protecting wealth and relationships.

The Grandchildren

Should we just leave our wealth to our children, and leave it to them to work out what is best for their own children? It is compelling to do this, and there is sense in accepting that only your children will be in a position to monitor how your grandchildren develop and what their real needs are. But the tax laws and other challenges that can threaten wealth dictate that one should plan not only for grandchildren, but for further generations.

Inheritance taxes apply in many countries, and with the focus on wealth and income inequality, their application may increase rather than decrease in future. In many cases, skipping a generation in the estate plan allows for inheritance taxes to also skip a generation, resulting in enormous wealth preservation. If I leave US$1 million to my son, and he does not spend the capital during his lifetime, he will leave the US$1 million to my grandchildren. If there is a 40% inheritance tax that my son is subject to, the grandchildren get US$600,000. If I had left the capital to my grandchildren directly, and perhaps only the income to my son, my grandchildren would get the full US$1 million. Different countries treat these things in different ways, but the principle of considering longer-term transfers to younger generations can be important.

From the perspective of asset protection, including protection against divorce and other claims, skipping a generation may also be valuable. For example, in the case of divorce, courts increasingly look to the assets and income available to a spouse—and regardless of whether these are in a trust or other structure. If I leave my assets to my son in a trust, but my son benefits from that trust while married, it may well be that what is in the trust can be considered to be subject to division in a divorce. This could mean that an important family business falls at least in part unfairly into the hands of a potentially undeserving spouse. Could more protection be achieved by leaving the business to future generations, with only income interests, or other assets, being available to those marrying and potentially divorcing?

It is often also a good idea to consider reserving a portion of wealth for grandchildren and further generations as a way of ensuring that at least some portion of family wealth is protected against many risks, including bad investment decisions by the children, legal claims against them and more. But should a grandparent determine the age at which a grandchild comes into significant wealth? There may be circumstances where this is appropriate, but to me, it is better to carve out wealth for future generations but leave decisions on when grandchildren should receive—other than money for their education and health—to their parents, who may want to ensure that their own children do not get too much too soon. Is it right for a grandparent to generously provide for grandchildren, but for this money to then go to the grandchild when he is 22, perhaps at a time when his parents believe he would benefit from focusing on completing his education and building a career? Could coming into money too soon compromise the parenting that is ongoing? Grandparents can be generous—but it is often the better bet to leave most decisions on when grandchildren should benefit to the children to decide.

The Siblings

Not easy, but worthwhile to try for, is having a set of siblings who together support the succession process and encourage dialogue with their parents on the subject. In a world where it is difficult to trust, a set of siblings who can really rely on each other is a tremendous gift.

Sadly, it is often the case that siblings do not get along, and that they have their own psychological issues associated with the wealth that may eventually come to them. When siblings marry, their spouses come into the mix, and almost inevitably change the balance among siblings. One in-law may be a success on their own; another may be dependent on the family wealth of the family they have married into. One in-law may contribute to the family business; another may be taking advantage of the good nature of his mother-in-law and father-in-law. And are the in-laws involved in encouraging their spouses to 'grab' assets from their parents, fuelling bad feeling among siblings?

There is work that families can do early on to help encourage siblings to communicate better and openly discuss issues that, when covered up, can simmer into disputes. But it is also critical to realize that trying to keep the children 'together' is not always the best way to go. Using the tools of wealth planning, planning for the worst and hoping for the best, is often the best way to go. This means thinking carefully about whether trusts, companies or other structures require the younger generation to stay together, and if they do, whether there are solid approaches on means to resolve the disputes that are pretty inevitable to arise. How can a disgruntled sibling be bought out; and their children, wanting again to be part of the family business, buy in? How can assets be protected from those in and out of the family who may be destructive of not only family wealth but of family relationships?

The Friends

Having wealth affects not only relationships within families, but also friendships, business relationships and otherwise. Here too the amount of wealth doesn't matter—having more than others (or being perceived to have more than others) affects all relationships, and care and preparation is often needed.

In the work I do with families, I try to emphasize to the younger generation the need to keep a low profile, and the advantages of being discreet about wealth. How to deal with friends and business contacts seeking financial help—whether through loans or investments—is also a topic worth spending time on when families meet to discuss their wealth and to consider what they can do to preserve both relationships and money. With friends, it is sometimes best to simply have the philosophy of *never* lending them money—if they really need help, just make a gift, as getting paid back is a rarity. Lending money is a good way to lose friends. And in business and business ventures, everyone needs to be vigilant—scams abound, and the best way to deal with friends and contacts promoting investment and business ventures is with a high degree of professionalism. All members of wealth-owning families should learn from the need to ensure that any investment is well considered, well documented and based on the reality that it is very easy to invest, but not always easy to get your money back.

Even the wealthiest and canniest of families get dragged into scams, some of remarkable complexity and which in hindsight carried all the warning signs that should have been heeded. An investment approach promoted by someone with little understanding themselves of the investment involved; hoped-for returns that simply do not reflect the realities of the investment world; complexities that even professional advisors do not understand. I have seen so many scams over the years that I believe every wealth-owning family needs to discuss with all generations how these work and the reality that many are implemented through the unwitting involvement of friends and business contacts of wealth owners, who themselves may not realize that a scam is underway.

So, as is the case with everyone else, when it comes to friends and business contacts, *trust no one*. Not because your friends and colleagues cannot be trusted, but because, with the right scepticism, wealth, friendships and relationships can be preserved.

The Eighth Culture

I came across the phenomenon of '*third culture kids*' from a friend of mine, Lesley Lewis, a psychologist who has focused some of her work on this area. On reading about the topic, I learned that third culture kids are usually children of one or more expatriate parents. The child, in their development years, grows up in a culture other than that of their parents. So, a 'third culture kid' includes an adult whose formative years were spent in this kind of circumstance—say a child of Americans who grows up on an army base in the Philippines.

Generally, 'first' culture refers to the culture of the country from which the parents originate; the 'second' culture is where the family resides and the 'third' culture is the group of individuals—say the expats in a particular place—who have their own cultural ties different from either the culture of the parents' origin or the place where the family is actually residing.

Of course, this gets even more complicated, with some referring to a 'fourth culture', where, for example, each of the parents may be themselves from different cultures—Mum from Sweden and Dad from the United States.

Much has been written about the psychological challenges associated with being a third culture kid. While there are also plenty of advantages to being a third culture kid, there can be identity confusion in terms of where the individual actually belongs. There are further possible challenges. A sense of fragmentation between multiple identities that can result in a lack of cohesive self-concept. Rootlessness and restlessness come from frequent moves. Social and emotional challenges can include difficulties in forming deep connections and a feeling of isolation and misunderstanding by friends not having had the same experiences. Repeated goodbyes to friends and places lead to grief and loss. Feelings of fatigue from needing to constantly adapt to new environments and a feeling of being a cultural chameleon are also symptoms, together with many others.

Given that the 'fourth culture' has been taken, in a sense, by those who may have parents from different cultures, I feel that it is easy to come up with fifth, sixth and further possible cultures one can be confronted with. And as the number four is often not seen as a lucky number, I have appropriated the number eight for something that I have observed—*the culture of those of wealth*, itself a culture that also has the potential to contribute to the destabilization of mental health. So, for me, there is the 'eighth culture'—the wealthy.

This has a number of psychological issues for wealth-owning families, but also impacts how wealth owners should be thinking about their family ecosystem and the reality that the survival of the family and its business interests over generations requires a focus on community and planet.

The culture of the wealthy and the psychological dynamics involved are unique. The wealthy have their own social networks—exclusive schools, clubs and otherwise. There is also an intense pressure to succeed and maintain status—meaning high expectations and pressure from a very young age. Gated communities, bodyguards and increasing detachment and seclusion increasingly limit the member of a wealth-owning family's exposure to diverse socioeconomic environments, compromising their understanding of different life experiences. Fear and paranoia lead to more focus on security and greater detachment from society at large. As inequality and other societal imbalances increase, the *need* for detachment and greater focus on security becomes more real and the psychological harms greater.

This unique eighth culture, with the appearance of being fun—given the trappings of wealth involved—carries many psychological challenges. Deep isolation, loneliness and trust issues—given questions of whether relationships are real or driven by financial motives. Identity and self-worth are a problem for those having difficulty separating their identity from that of a family of achievement, reputation and success. High expectations can lead to anxiety and depression, fuelled by fear of failure. Privilege can lead to a feeling of entitlement and disconnection from broader society—hindering the development of empathy and understanding. And a lack of financial necessity can lead to struggles in finding meaning and direction in life.

The psychological challenges have consequences not only for the wealth-owning family. Our societies themselves face challenges as a result. The exclusive clubs and schools of the wealthy reinforce inequality and limit social mobility. Perceptions of elitism and disconnect from broader society are reinforced. The political and economic influence of wealth owners, overly focused on their own interests, can lead to policies that further entrench inequality. And there may be broader cultural impacts that are unhealthy—such as the reality of the over-emphasis on material success in our societies.

These are areas wealth owners and those advising them need to think about. And families need to focus on *holistic sustainability*—understanding and accepting that sustainability of the family and of its wealth and business interests relies on the sustainability of the external world—planet, community and more. Holistic continuity planning for a wealth-owning family cannot neglect the need for continuity of more than just the family and its wealth. And the mental health of members of the wealth-owning family can depend on maintaining connection—not just to the other wealth-owning members of the 'eighth culture'.

> *... although our world creates a privileging of celebrity, wealth, and power, we don't appreciate the degree to which those features isolate the human beings who live within that identity. It's much easier to see the isolation of people who exist in positions of powerlessness in our society than to see it in human beings we've been trained by our families, our communities, our capitalistic marketing machine, and even our religions to adore and aspire to become—or to resent, envy, and disdain.*[5]
>
> *What and whom these people possess, the accolades they receive, the dizzying levels of success they achieve—these do not produce the peace of mind, the connection, or the happiness they thought they would. Their power, while producing a certain type of freedom, enslaves them in other ways.*[6]
>
> *To be happy and contented in life, we need not relinquish our wealth and power, nor downgrade our dreams and aspirations. We must, however, break through the hard and cold veneer of life's gilt and establish warm and nurturing relationships with ourselves, key people in our lives, and the communities in which we live.*[7]

Wealth provides many advantages, but also comes with unique mental health challenges. A connected society is in everyone's best interests.

***

News about the difficulties of well-known families and the failure of their asset protection and succession plans seems to be growing in frequency and drama. The problems we hear about cross geographies and cultures. It is simply untrue that families from one part of the world or of a particular religion are truly different from any others. The notion that we all love each other and do not fight and involve lawyers the way others do is just that—a notion that is sometimes a misleading dream of the older generation, thinking that everything will just work out. The children may well show up holding hands at dinner at their parents' home every Friday evening, but sadly the children also show up in the offices of their lawyers ready to do battle as soon as their parents are dead or incapacitated—and sometimes before.

The stories we read about, while usually concerning the very wealthy and very famous, are sadly the same stories that plague *every* family, regardless of the level of wealth—because any amount of wealth is enough to destroy a family.

Notes

1. Hokemeyer, P., *Fragile Power—Why Having Everything Is Never Enough—Lessons from Treating the Wealthy and Famous* (Hazelden Publishing, 2019), Loc 2799.
2. Hokemeyer (2019), Loc 145.
3. Fan, J., *Chinese Business and Succession Planning* (Connect, CUHK Business School, Chinese University of Hong Kong, 2012), Vol. 4.
4. Williamson, L., 'You need these 4 attributes to successfully take over a family business', *Hong Kong Tatler*, 2 March 2018 and *Perspectives from ISB*, 23 March 2018. Roger King is the founder of the Roger King Center for Asian Family Business and Family Office at the Hong Kong University of Science and Technology Business School (HKUST Business School).
5. Hokemeyer (2019), Loc 242.
6. Hokemeyer (2019), Loc 333.
7. Hokemeyer (2019), Loc 534.

CHAPTER 6

The Derailers—Addressing the Many *'What-ifs?'*

Wealth-owning families face any number of *derailers*—events internal and external to the family that can disrupt the family's journey to its impact goal. As addressed in the previous chapter, mental health is an important area that families need to focus on. Mental health challenges are, of course, themselves derailers—family members suffering mental health challenges are not going to be at the top of their game in forwarding the family and its business and investment interests.

But there are many other potential derailers other than just mental health. These derailers reflect *needs* that families have—areas of planning and circumstance that need to be addressed. Some of these needs affect all families, and relate to issues like succession and asset transfers, something that everyone has to face at some point.

Other needs may be specific to a particular family, such as a need relating to a disabled family member requiring special care or some other issue specific to the family, such as a second marriage, or concerns about particular assets in which a family has an interest.

A third category of needs is driven by the tax and other laws that apply to the family—either by virtue of where the family maintains residential or citizenship connections or by virtue of where they invest. Religion can also come into the picture in this third category, with *Sharia* law being an example. For Muslims, religious law governs many aspects of inheritance as well as other areas of economic life, and these rules are part of the laws of most, if not all, Muslim countries.

Set out below are some examples of the different kinds of needs wealth owners have, and some first indications of how they can be addressed. It is very important to keep in mind that it is never the case that a family has only one need—albeit a particular issue, whether relating to taxation or a special dynamic within the family, drives the planning process. Successful succession and asset-protection planning requires that a holistic view of needs be undertaken, and that these needs are all addressed as part of the approach to be adopted by the family. And as needs change, whether due to changes within the family or in the external world, the approaches taken need to adapt.

Knowing Where the Assets Are—And Not Having a Plan Is a Plan

A fundamental and seemingly straightforward need of every wealth owner is to understand the basics of succession in relation to their assets and hopes for how their assets will pass to others in the event of death or disability.

The first step in succession planning is to understand that having no succession plan *is* a succession plan. If I die, something will happen to my assets, and this notwithstanding that I may not have actually thought about my succession and planned it. The laws that apply where I live and where my assets are located will come into the picture, and in most countries, the succession of those who die without having made a will or taken other steps in planning will set out who will be entitled to the assets of the deceased. In most countries, the assets of someone dying without a will go in set shares to a surviving spouse, children and, depending on the circumstances, to more distant family members. So, a very first step for any wealth owner is to understand what happens if there is no planning and to make sure that the default plan is one that the wealth owner is comfortable with and understands.

But there are many issues with not thinking the succession plan through. One fundamental need of any wealth owner is simply to ensure that the assets one has will really go where one wants them to go, and here a first step is to ask the question of whether the right people know about the assets and where they are.

When I ask most wealth owners what they have, the answer is not always as straightforward as one might expect. A typical wealth owner, if they tell me the truth, will describe a number of bank accounts, not all of which their families may know about; safe deposit boxes in different banks, and sometimes different countries, with jewellery and other valuables—in some cases, *jewellery from my mother that she didn't want my wife to have ... she wanted the jewellery to go to my daughters, so my wife doesn't know about the safety deposit box.*

The list goes on to include shares of companies that the wealth owner has invested in; amounts owed by friends and business colleagues the wealth owner may have lent money to; maybe interests in companies in countries with foreign ownership restrictions, such as Indonesia, where the shares are in the name of an Indonesian friend or business associate *who knows that if I die the shares should go to my children* ... and more assets, that only come to mind later in the process of trying to get a grip on what the wealth owner has.

A number of years ago I was working with a wealth owner who was a particularly well-organized person. He had good records and lists of assets, and a solid recollection of the many small and larger businesses and investments he had interests in. When I suggested to him that part of the succession planning process would require identifying what he actually owned, and how such ownership was documented, what he thought would be an easy process ended up taking more than two years to complete. The wealth owner kept remembering investments he had made and assets he had that he then had to search for documentation on. Ownership records on offshore companies, real estate investments and many other items had to be reconstructed, as not everything turned out to be as well documented as he thought. Keys to safe deposit boxes had to be found, and arrangements made for ensuring that the right people would have access to the safe deposit boxes at the right time. Some of the companies he had set up over the years had their records maintained by lawyers who had retired, and quite a bit of work had to be done to track things down.

If it is so difficult for a well-organized wealth owner to quickly identify their own assets and ownership structures, what happens when a wealth owner dies, and his spouse or children (or others) have to work out what they had, where those assets are and what they are worth? If the safe deposit box containing valuable jewellery is in a country like Canada, the United Kingdom or the United States, even if the wealth owner is not a resident or citizen of the relevant country, tax exposures can arise given that valuable assets are actually physically located in Canada, the United Kingdom or the United States, countries the wealth owner may have believed would be safer locations in which to keep valuables than the wealth owner's own country of residence in Latin America or Asia. Taxation based on the location of physical assets arises in some countries but not others. Yes for art collections in the United Kingdom, no for the same art collection located in Switzerland when owned by a foreigner. This information is highly relevant to the decision of where to keep valuable items.

And what of personal possessions, such as art, jewellery and other valuable collectibles? Is death a time when doctors, nurses, household staff and others have an opportunity to help themselves to items meant to go to others? Will the friend in Indonesia in whose name the shares are registered—given foreign ownership restrictions—do the right thing and acknowledge that they own interests for the benefit of the family or will they 'forget' to say anything about it and even if asked, claim that they owned the assets themselves?

When people die or become disabled, their assets all too often just disappear, and there are many circumstances where what one has worked hard to keep for the next generation or for others simply falls into the wrong hands.

It saddens me to watch the many different versions of *Storage Wars*, a television reality series that focuses on storage units that have been forgotten or abandoned, with contents auctioned blindly when rental payments have not been kept up. I cannot help thinking about the owner of the goods that someone has bought at auction and is sifting through, the owner of which may have died or become disabled before having been able to arrange for how what they own should pass to the next generation. The big 'win' in the reality programme is when one of the storage units includes something of real value ... but who is the winner? Is it the person the real owner of the assets wanted to benefit, or some stranger who bid on a storage unit's contents without even knowing what was inside?

At every level of wealth, it is very important for the wealth owner to ensure that those who are meant to benefit from the assets know about the assets and where they are. A good succession plan is well thought out, and ideally those who will be inheriting assets are part of the succession process and are in a position to make sure they actually get what they were supposed to get.

I have run into a number of cases where trusts and foundations established by wealth owners were not disclosed to family members, something quite common in times when wealth owners in Europe and elsewhere were led to believe that good planning involved hiding their assets from tax authorities and others. In too many situations, advisors ranging from lawyers to trustees to protectors and others ended up helping themselves to all or part of the assets involved. Where families finally discovered the structures their deceased parent had created, it was often too late to recover the full value involved.

While the wealth owner is alive, things often go pretty much according to plan, with advisors seeming to do the right thing. But after death, the question arises as to who will actually make sure that the trusted intermediary will actually do what they are supposed to. And where individuals are involved, what if they become disabled or pass away? Is a successor in place and, if so, is the successor trustworthy?

In one case I was involved with, an American lawyer had made use of the entire trust fund after the death of his client, and by the time the family found evidence of the existence of the trust and took action, the lawyer involved was in his late eighties and claimed he had Alzheimer's and no recollection of anything to do with the trust.

What rights the children had in relation to being the beneficiaries of trusts, and the responsibilities of trustees, and other such things are discussed in the next chapter. But the example brings out some important learnings for any wealth owner. Where secrecy is the over-riding objective, there is a much higher degree of risk that the right oversight is missing from the structure.

Fortunately, today, fewer wealth owners are falling into the trap of tax-undeclared money—given global transparency and increased tax enforcement—but for those who might, for any reason, opt for approaches that focus on secrecy, it is important to not lose sight of the many other needs a wealth-owning family has. An over-riding need is for a succession structure that ensures the right people, such as the wealth owner's children, come into the assets, and advisors and intermediaries have someone, or more than one person, keeping an eye on them. If those meant to benefit do not know anything about the asset-holding structures that are in place, they are simply unable to enforce their rights.

I am a great believer that a safe succession structure requires that those who are to benefit have at least some idea of who to call and where to get the information they need about what may be coming to them. It may not always be appropriate, given ages or otherwise, for the younger generation to know specifics on amounts or other details regarding what they may come into, but knowing what they should be looking for and what to do on the passing of their parents is critical. This is something the wealth owner has to anticipate, failing which there needs to be more than just one person who has the obligation to follow up and do the necessary.

For a wealth owner, not having a plan is a plan, and if there is no clarity on who gets what, there is much in the way of confusion and unhappiness that can result. Mother and father may have retired, and now spend time with their son and daughter, each of whom have their own families and homes in different places. Mother leaves some of her jewellery in a safe in her daughter's home for mother's use when she visits; father leaves one of his important antique wristwatches in a safe in the home of the son. When mother passes away, to whom does the jewellery belong? What of the watch when father passes away? If in their wills (or maybe there are no wills) the specific items were not mentioned, who will get the assets? What if the son argues '*Dad gave me the watch, that is why it is in my safe*'. Does the watch then fall outside of the estate on death, not being an asset divided between the son and the daughter, if that is what the will provides in relation to assets, as it was gifted to the son earlier? Will the lack of clarity create a division between the son and the daughter, giving rise to wealth being destructive of family relationships?

Wealth owners need to make things clear and also need to understand that the risk of the wrong people coming into their assets is much greater, the less clarity there is about what they have and the steps that need to be taken on their passing.

A colleague of mine had been advising a Latin American family where the very significant family business involved was ultimately owned by a Panamanian holding company. Now out of favour in most jurisdictions—given moves to transparency—the company had issued 'bearer' shares, shares which are not registered in the name of any particular shareholder, but rather where the share certificates themselves represent the ownership of the company. Like currency, whoever has the shares owns the company and, indirectly, all of its assets. The owner of the business had a mistress and maintained an apartment he shared with her. His children worked with him in his business, and when he died, they assumed that the business had become theirs, together with the other assets that passed to them on the death of their father.

The children were in the process of restructuring the business when they were asked by their bankers, as a formality, to prove their ownership of the company. The children hunted through their father's papers, searching for evidence of their ownership. Learning that the holding company had issued bearer shares, they conducted a search for them. After some time, their father's mistress was contacted as the search extended to the apartment the father had shared with her. It was only then that the mistress revealed that she had the bearer shares, claiming that they had been given to her well before the death of the father—meaning that the shares had not passed to the children together with the other assets of their father that went to them on his death. The children ultimately prevailed in lengthy litigation that proved the father's intent to have the shares pass to his children, but the lawyers involved did very well financially out of the dispute, and not every similar case ends as happily for the younger generation.

It is useful and important for wealth owners to keep an inventory of their assets, and regularly review and update both the inventory and the approaches in place in relation to what is to happen in the event of death or disability.

Regular stress tests should be conducted to ensure that everyone knows what will happen if there is an unexpected event that gives rise to death or disability. Advisors should be in place in a way that provides for effective oversight, perhaps with one unrelated advisor keeping an eye on another, and with clear instructions in place to family members and others about who should do what in the event of death or disability. And most important is the need for good communication within the family, in age-appropriate ways, about the succession process. This can ensure that those who may come into assets are aware of what is planned, something important not just for tracking down the assets, but to avoid misunderstandings and allow the succession process to be a collaborative one that has the chance of preventing wealth becoming destructive of family assets and relationships.

Succession, Wills (Including 'Living Wills') and Probate

The reality is that we will all die one day. Death and preparing for the possibility of disability represent more needs that apply to all wealth owners.

Succession, wills and what happens on death are subject to the laws that apply to the estate of someone who passes away. Similarly, in the event of disability, what happens to assets and their management is subject to the laws that may have application. For a typical wealth owner, what law applies is not always clear, particularly where the wealth owner may be a citizen of one or more countries, resident in another and have assets in a number of other countries. Conflicts of law may arise, and the law governing how assets are to be dealt with may be far from clear.

There are some general principles that wealth owners should be aware of regarding the succession process. A first general principle is that where there is no will that governs the estate, something still happens to assets on death, but this is determined not by what the wealth owner intended, but by the applicable law. The applicable law will likely be the law of the jurisdiction where the wealth owner was domiciled, resident or a national of at death, but this may be affected by other factors, including the location and nature of the assets on death and the law applying there. The law that governs in the place the assets are located may well provide for a different approach to succession than the law of the domicile of the wealth owner.

In most countries, where one dies without a will, the assets, on death, go to specified family members—perhaps a surviving spouse and parents, and if there are children, often in shares to the surviving spouse and children. If there are no close family members, then assets go to more distant relatives in specific shares, and sometimes simply to the relevant government once there are no relatives surviving.

For an estate governed by Islamic law, at least four different issues become relevant. First, not only the spouse and children will be forced heirs, but also any surviving parents. Second, if the spouse is not a Muslim, such spouse will not receive a forced heirship entitlement. Third, if a child is adopted or illegitimate, that child will receive no share of their father's estate. And fourth, Islamic law does not provide for a *per stirpes* approach to succession, with each branch of a family receiving a share. Instead, the Islamic rule of degree applies, meaning that if the deceased had two sons, one of which predeceased leaving a grandson, the whole of the estate passes to the surviving son, and nothing at all to the orphaned grandson.

A change of religion from, to or within Islam can result in the inadvertent disinheritance of family members. Further, conversion away from Islam can result in the individual undergoing conversion themselves, losing inheritance rights. In jurisdictions with split systems, such as Bahrain and Lebanon, a change from the Sunni to Shia schools of Islam (or vice versa) may affect what forced heirs get, for example, in the case of a testator who has only daughters surviving him.

The most important thing is to understand who is going to get what, given your circumstances and planning (or lack thereof). And then it is key to ask yourself the critical question: who is going to make sure that all goes as it should, preventing assets being stolen by employees or others who have access to them?

If there is one, the will usually determines where the assets go, but for wealth owners having assets in multiple jurisdictions, having more than one will may be something to consider. If I have a will drawn up in my country of domicile and die with assets in another country, it is important to understand the procedures in that other country that will be necessary to cause the assets to pass from having been in my name into the name of those I want to benefit from the assets. In some cases, easier and quicker than 'proving' a will from another country might be to have a separate will for assets in a particular country. If there are multiple wills, ensuring that the first will in my country of domicile does not conflict with the foreign will becomes important. At a minimum, my home country will should make reference to any other wills that I might have. But this is not always the case, given that there may be reasons to retain confidentiality about the assets located in the other country.

Something the laws of many countries (but not all) provide for is that when one marries, previous wills become invalid; when one divorces, gifts to spouses specified in an earlier will are treated as if the spouse had predeceased. This may be a good thing, but there can sometimes be surprising results, meaning that the wealth owner needs to keep an eye on these things and be in a position to ask advisors the right questions. There are many examples of individuals who had set up careful estate plans dividing their assets on death among their children and their spouse. The spouse passes away, and the widow or widower develops a new relationship that leads to remarriage. As the original will would commonly say that if the spouse predeceases, the children receive the entire estate, the surviving spouse may well think that all is as it should be when they remarry—the expectation being that the new spouse, who may have their own wealth or to whom specific gifts through trusts or otherwise may be made, would not benefit under the will. What many wealth owners do not realize is that the new marriage may result in the carefully drafted will being considered to have been revoked, meaning that if the wealth owner dies without making a new will, the new spouse would now receive—in addition to what the wealth owner may otherwise transfer to her in trust or otherwise—a substantial share of his estate on his intestacy.

Even where one has a will that is valid, a number of issues can arise. One relates to whether the will meets the requirements of forced heirship rules that may have application to the estate of the deceased. In most common law countries, like the United States, Canada, the United Kingdom and others, there are no forced heirship rules (subject to some important exceptions such as Louisiana in relation to some heirs, Scotland for moveable assets and Singapore for its Muslim citizens).

As a result, if a wealth owner decides to leave all of his assets to one particular beneficiary, whether within or outside of the family, this is allowed. If dependent family members get nothing or very little, they may be entitled to apply for financial aid from the estate, but they have no particular right to any particular percentage of the assets involved. In other countries, particularly civil law countries, like France, Germany, Switzerland, Indonesia, Taiwan and Japan, 'forced heirship' rules apply, meaning that specific family members are considered to be entitled to specific portions of the estate of someone who dies, with only a limited part of the estate being able to be freely transferred as the wealth owner wishes. *Sharia* law, applying to those living under Islamic law, similarly provides for a forced heirship approach.

Needless to say, forced heirship rules and how they apply vary from legal system to legal system, with, in some cases, there being an ability for family members to give up their forced heirship rights contractually. But this is not always the case, and in some forced heirship systems an ability to contractually give up one's rights is not possible. Under some forced heirship systems, gifts can be given freely during life; in others, gifts may be invalidated so as to protect the forced heirs. In Islamic inheritance law, gifts made in a person's final (terminal) illness may be clawed back and become part of the estate's assets for division. And what constitutes a final illness may vary jurisdiction to jurisdiction. For today's wealth owner, great complexity can arise where one lives in a country with forced heirship but owns assets in other countries that do not have such rules, or vice versa, where one lives in a country that does not have forced heirship rules but assets may be owned in a country that does. There are some special rules that apply country by country in relation to the estates of foreigners, allowing them to opt out of forced heirship; there are also some multilateral agreements among countries that affect the issue of cross-border succession. All of these can be highly relevant to effective estate planning.

Trusts and other 'tools' of wealth planning can sometimes help ensure that the wishes of wealth owners are achieved, notwithstanding the complexities of forced heirship regimes. This is discussed in the next chapter, but most important for the wealth owner is to really understand the laws that apply to their succession. A wealth owner should always be considering the *what ifs?*, including the question of *what if I die?*, and the effect of forced heirship and other rules on how assets will pass to the next generation.

When someone dies, also relevant is the question of how assets actually move from one person's name to another's, whether or not there is a valid will in place. Where someone dies owning assets, this is not something that occurs automatically. In most countries procedures have to be undertaken to establish who has rights to the relevant assets, whether under a will or otherwise, and this procedure is often referred to as 'probate'—the official proving of a will and the entitlements of beneficiaries thereunder, or in the event of an intestacy.

These procedures have a number of negatives for many wealth-owning families. First, the procedures are not necessarily quick and, depending on the circumstances, a family could find themselves in financially difficult circumstances given the delay between the death of the wealth owner and when they actually get hold of the assets. Probate procedures can also be expensive, with some countries even providing for lawyers who work on the probate to not be paid on the basis of the time they spend, but rather on a percentage of the value of the estate. And probate is usually a public procedure, meaning that information about assets and who gets what is not a private matter.

The problems of probate point to a need for wealth owners to address these issues, and some of the uses of the 'tools' of wealth planning are to avoid probate in respect of assets, allowing immediate access to assets to those who are meant to benefit, and without the costs or delays (or public disclosures) that probate attracts. But even where a wealth owner has a trust, insurance or other structure hold specific assets, a will is usually still needed, as it is almost inevitable that there will be other assets the wealth owner owns at death that will need to pass from his ownership to the ownership of those he wishes to benefit.

Of course, it is not only death that makes taking care of one's assets impossible; a variety of disabilities can affect the ability of a wealth owner to look after their affairs. Discussed elsewhere in this book are changing demographics and the effect of living longer on wealth owners and their needs, but part of good succession planning is to consider who will be able to make decisions if you are unable to make them. Stress testing the succession plan also means considering what happens if you become disabled and unable to communicate; or if dementia or other disorders make it impossible for you to make decisions about your healthcare or financial situation. In the absence of clarity on these issues, decisions may fall to those in or out of the family who, under the relevant law, are able to apply for the ability to make decisions in your place—but is this always the right person to do this? Has the wealth owner considered that the nasty spouse they were about to divorce may be the one who ends up with the power to make decisions not only on their assets, but also over whether or not they remain on life support?

'Living wills' are one way to deal with these issues, and where the laws of a country so permit, one can document wishes as to who can make decisions if you cannot. Usually, the term 'living will' refers to the question of who can make medical decisions for someone who lacks the capacity to do so. But country by country there are approaches that can be taken to include in this planning powers over investment and other decisions. Some of the other tools of wealth planning, such as trusts and foundations, can also be used to set out who should be in a position to handle things in the event of disability.

But like with succession generally, it is usually not enough to just name one or more people to look after your affairs in times that you are unable to. On an ongoing basis, having discussions with those involved, and making sure the right 'checks and balances' are in place, can be key. Just appointing one person to look after your financial affairs may be risky, with the person having more power than they should, and with little oversight. Perhaps decisions should be made by a committee, with governance and succession procedures that the committee must apply. Making sure that whoever is going to make decisions understands the decisions you would like to see made is also critical. A living will is, like any element of succession planning and asset protection, something that needs ongoing review, reflecting changes in relation to assets, the individuals to be involved in making decisions and otherwise.

A couple without children appointed me under their living wills, together with another advisor, to make decisions regarding medical care in the event of their disability, once the other in the couple was not around or able to step in. They did this without having said much to me about what their wishes were, and I made sure, as an advisor, to ask for a meeting to discuss their thoughts on medical interventions and related matters, something that—given my responsibilities—I will do on an ongoing basis. Interestingly, one of the couple told me that it would be her wish that in almost any circumstance of serious illness she would want me to make the decision to '*pull the plug*' ... her husband had the opposite wish, that under pretty much no circumstances should such a decision be made.

Without clear ongoing communication and discussion, an advisor will not be able to make decisions that reflect what the wealth owner would have really wanted. A good advisor will insist on getting the information he needs—and a responsible wealth owner will make sure their advisors are kept up-to-date on what the wealth owner hopes for and will put mechanisms in place to help ensure that the right decisions are made.

Divorces (and Relationships Generally)

Another need relevant to virtually every wealth-owning family relates to the financial and other issues that relationships give rise to, including what happens upon divorce.

I was giving a talk to a group of wealth-owning families, and made a statement that I believe in. I said *divorce is one of the world's biggest destroyers of wealth*. I had invited a friend of mine to join me for the talk, Sharon Ser, one of the top divorce lawyers in Hong Kong. Sharon, not a wallflower, jumped from her seat and shouted out *Philip is wrong! Divorce is not the biggest destroyer of wealth in the world. Divorce is the biggest CREATOR of wealth in the world.*

Sharon, of course, often acts for the person claiming assets in the event of a divorce and is proud of her record of getting the most out of hapless wealth owners (and their children) whose marriages are ending. While she certainly has helped many wealth owners protect themselves against claims where they are lucky enough to have her on their side, her disagreement with my comment helps emphasize the risk to wealth that divorce gives rise to. With up to 50% of marriages in many parts of the world ending up in divorce, wealth owners need to understand the odds and ensure that divorces they suffer, or that their children suffer, will not end up destroying family wealth and businesses.

Divorce laws and entitlements of spouses differ greatly country by country. In some countries the financial entitlements only arise where there is a real marriage, while in others co-habitation arrangements may also have meaningful financial consequences. A first step, therefore, is to try to figure out what laws will actually apply to a divorce, not always an easy matter. In the case of wealth-owning families, it is not uncommon for a couple to have married in one country, lived in several others, and to be maintaining homes in more than one place. Often, in the case of a divorce, there can be forum shopping in the sense that a spouse looking to achieve a particular financial result can try to get the courts of one or another country to take jurisdiction over a divorce. It is also often the case that whoever goes to court first might well find that their choice of court will govern the divorce.

English law has emerged as an increasingly problematic jurisdiction for wealthy spouses or ex-spouses. Even where a divorce has been completed in another country with a spouse having received a modest award, there may be an option for the poorer spouse to then move to England and petition for a 'top-up' award against the wealthier ex-spouse. Enforcement may be an issue, but this is an increasing danger to wealth owners with property interests in the United Kingdom or in jurisdictions that are likely to enforce English judgements.

Something that I believe wealth-owning families, and particularly the younger generation, need is an understanding about how these rules work, and how the steps they take in relation to a divorce can make a dramatic difference.

The Christian wife of a Muslim man may get nothing on death or in the event of divorce in certain *Sharia* law countries, given that they are not Muslim; the same wife taking action in London, where the couple may have a house or flat, could end up with half her husband's assets. I sometimes tell friends of mine in Hong Kong who come from wealth-owning families and who are considering divorce and fretting over the financial consequences to not go home and tell their husbands or wives that they are thinking of divorce; rather, they should say '*I love you dearly ... but we need to move to Switzerland for business*'. Hong Kong often follows the UK approach of 50/50 divisions of marital assets—and without an automatic exclusion of inherited assets. If the divorce takes place in Switzerland rather than Hong Kong, the wife may get a fraction of what she would get under Hong Kong law, particularly in relation to those inherited assets.

A mistress in Hong Kong will get virtually nothing, as there is no formal marriage; a mistress in California or Vancouver may get a massive settlement, as co-habitation, and not just marriage, results in financial rights on a break-up of the relationship. Wealth owners need to understand how these things work, and in every family, education about the risks of divorce and relationships is a necessary part of effective asset protection.

There are planning approaches that can be undertaken to protect assets in the case of divorce, and particularly opportunities for the older generation to do things that will make it difficult for the spouses of their children to make claims against assets deriving from the older generation. But not all works, and it is interesting to see how many cases there are of families who have lost control of substantial businesses and wealth through a lack of attention to the risks involved.

Even discretionary trusts, discussed later, are often 'looked through' when there are divorce claims—the focus being on what are 'marital assets'. In a simple example, mother may put the family business and assets in a trust of which her children are discretionary beneficiaries, thinking that this will protect the assets from a divorce claim in the younger generation. Over time, distributions from the trust are occasionally made to the younger generation, the relevant letter of wishes providing for discretionary allocation of a portion of the trust to one of the children. On divorce and, depending on the country the laws of which apply, the spouse of the son or daughter will easily be able to say that the relevant portion of the trust, albeit discretionary, is a 'marital asset' as the funds were used in the marriage and remained available to the spouse against whom claims are being made. And the idea of the child not disclosing the trust or other assets as a way of protecting assets is not an option, as in most countries, a spouse, on divorce, has to disclose all assets, including trust interests, and a failure to make such disclosure accurately might not only result in criminal and other penalties, but also enrage a judge who discovers the truth and who is then likely to be far from sympathetic.

But what if mother, in the example, puts the family business in a trust that the younger generation *cannot* access directly, and a smaller amount of wealth in another trust the younger generation does receive distributions from? Might this reduce the risk of the family business being seen as a 'marital asset' that might become part of a divorce claim?

Do wealth owners need to understand this in order to ask their advisors the right questions? Do wealth owners need planning even if they trust their children? For me, the answers are yes and yes—advisors may not always look at things in the holistic ways that wealth owners need them to—and therefore the responsibility is back to the wealth owner to ask the right questions, and to seek the right advisors. And as to trusting your children, it is certainly often the case (but not always) that you can ... but, sadly, it is less often the case that you can trust their spouses or near-spouses. And your children need to understand that how they use the money and other assets you make available to them will have an impact on whether their spouse can get hold of them in the event of a divorce.

Pre-nuptial and post-nuptial agreements play an increasing role in the protection of wealth in the case of a break-up of a marriage or other relationship. Not always a perfect fix, the laws of an increasing number of countries do pay attention to agreements entered into before a marriage (pre-nuptial) or after a marriage (post-nuptial) relating to the economics associated with a dissolution of the marriage. But there are many issues to consider in these arrangements, and good advice is usually needed considering the many different ways in which countries view such agreements. A general given is that for an agreement to work, the spouse signing the agreement needs to have had independent advice and full disclosure of the assets of the person they are about to marry or live with, factors that make it important to proceed carefully and in the right way.

In relation to the younger generation, I believe it is critical to discuss pre-nuptial agreements and their usefulness very, very early on in the process of discussing family finances and succession within a family. If Mum and Dad put off discussing pre-nuptial agreements until their son or daughter arrives home holding hands with *the* one, and on meeting him or her the parents then tell their son or daughter about pre-nuptial agreements and their necessity—'*uhm, son, can we speak in the kitchen?*'—the younger generation will often perceive the discussion as a negative judgement of the specific person they have brought home for their parents to meet. Much more effective is to have the discussion about pre-nuptial agreements well before the younger generation introduces the man or woman of their dreams, and to make pre-nuptial arrangements a family requirement that is communicated to potential spouses as part of the overall family governance approach, and not something subjective and specifically related to them.

Relevant not only to divorce is the fact that a number of countries (and, in the case of the United States, this is a state-by-state issue) have 'community property' rules that basically allocate assets to a spouse, in the absence of a pre- or post-nuptial agreement to the contrary, prior to any dissolution of the marriage or other relationship. It is one thing to find that on divorce a spouse is entitled to a portion of marital assets, but it is often a surprise for wealth owners to discover that assets they thought they independently owned are actually not owned only by them, regardless of whether their marriage dissolves.

A typical fact pattern involves a family business that grows over the years as children become involved. Over time, the parents may decide to transfer all or part of the business to their children, and some of the children may move to different countries, continuing to work in the family business, and expanding its global reach. If a child moves to a jurisdiction where community property rules apply, such as would be the case in California, a spouse may become an owner of part of the business (or at least part of its value) without the family being aware of this. Say the family business grows in value during the time one of the children lives in California, working on expanding the business in the United States. The child, at some stage, may decide to transfer the business into a trust or other structure for the benefit of his children—but under community property rules he cannot. The child may have good reasons for wanting the family business to be in a trust for his children and not for the benefit of his spouse—maybe the spouse has children of a previous marriage living with their other parent, or who are independent and who, in any event, have nothing to do with his family business, which had been established by his own parents or grandparents.

The spouse will be considered to own half of the growth in the value of the business that was achieved during the time the couple lived in California, meaning that a transfer of the business by the child whose family established the business requires the consent of that spouse—consent the spouse may very well refuse to give without a significant financial settlement.

Community property rules may be sensible as a way of protecting a spouse or other partner co-habiting with a wealth owner. But is it right that community property rules can break up a family business and sometimes require that it be sold in order to comply with laws the family may not have even been aware of? The child may be planning to leave more than enough to his spouse after his passing or disability, to provide generously for her, keeping her in the lifestyle to which she had become accustomed. But the child may not want to provide a share of the family business, and to risk it then going to people outside his immediate family, such as children of his wife's first marriage or otherwise.

Such wealth protection objectives can become impossible to meet in an example such as this one. While living in California, and, say, tripling the value of the business, the wealth-owning child and his wife were living in 'community of property'. As a result, half of the value created during their time of residence in California already legally belongs to the child's wife. Even in the absence of a divorce, the wife is a co-owner of assets registered in the name of her husband, and the only way he could legally transfer the assets to a trust in favour of his natural children and restrict his wife's interests to lifetime distributions to maintain her lifestyle, would be with her written consent.

Could wealth planning help in these circumstances? Maybe. If the parents of the wealth-owning child do not transfer the business to the child, but rather put it in a trust for future generations, separating the business from other assets the child would have access to, this might well work. Trusts are expanded on in the next chapter in the context of how they can be one of the *tunnels and bridges* used to get around typical derailers and help the family achieve its impact goal.

In the case of divorce, it is easy to say that the rights of the spouse or other party are there because they need to be protected. And this is often the case, and why laws are in place to provide this protection.

But for a wealth-owning family, and particularly where wealth is at the higher level, it is critical to understand how laws designed to protect a spouse can be abused to provide a spouse with rights to family businesses and wealth that by no stretch of the imagination they should have access to. And with lawyers charging on contingency, is it fair that family wealth falls into the hands of those who fuel the flames of marital disputes? It is even increasingly common to see litigation funded by investors in litigation, making it ever more important for wealth and business-owning families to undertake protective continuity planning.

Second Families

It is not unusual to run across wealth owners on their second, third or subsequent marriages or similar relationships, often involving children from more than one spouse, and a set of complex emotional and legal issues. When a wealth-owning parent remarries or establishes a new or additional long-term relationship, there are many financial and psychological consequences, and it is rare to find families that actually manage to avoid all of the potential pitfalls.

The issue of second families does not affect every family, but is an example of a derailer that can be specific to a particular family, requiring special consideration.

One of the biggest issues that often arises in relation to new marriages and relationships is the consequences of the break-up of earlier relationships. While second (and further) marriages often arise after the passing of a spouse, and the widow or widower beginning a new relationship, there are many cases where the earlier spouse is being effectively 'replaced' by another.

One of the first and very clear lessons to be learned from the bad experiences of others is the vengeful way in which marriages can break up when a second relationship is looming. I have worked with several families where, in earlier and happier times, spouses were brought into family business and related meetings, provided with full details on family and business assets, and, as a result, equipped with information and materials that helped them to make the divorce process both difficult and expensive.

While it sounds mean to think of the worst, meaning that a relationship will break up, in today's world it is only prudent to help families consider minimizing the potential risks that come with spouses being too involved in what might rightfully be viewed as an inappropriate area. In-laws can and do have very important roles in wealth-owning families, and in many cases contribute hugely to the continuity of family businesses and otherwise. But where relationships are at an early (and more fragile) stage, it is worth giving some thought and discussion to what a spouse should know and participate in.

The risks, in my experience, are even greater in the case of second, third and further relationships, with these relationships all too often linked to economic motivations, as the 'older model' is being traded in for the younger. Letting the new spouse know too much, and letting them be too involved, can not only be dangerous in terms of what may happen if that relationship breaks up, but can be particularly destructive of family relationships given how the wealth owner's children will feel about the new partner of their parent, particularly when the other parent is still alive.

Second and further marriages often cause more issues within families than the wealth owner establishing the new relationship thinks. The wealth owner often ends up in a difficult situation that jeopardizes not only the wellbeing of his children, but the chances of success in his new relationship. As a believer that money comes into the picture in every relationship (because everyone is a gold-digger, at least to some extent), recognizing this is a first step towards finding approaches to help the process not be a destructive one.

A very common pattern is where a wealth owner has a close relationship with his children, and his marriage comes to an end—either on divorce or the death of the spouse. The close relationship between the wealth owner and his children is challenged when the wealth owner begins establishing new relationships, and particularly as a new relationship moves to a second marriage or co-habitation. Money inevitably becomes an issue. Often the wealth owner doesn't really want or need to marry again, but the new companion is the one putting the pressure on to formalize the new relationship.

While there are many cases where children would want to see their widowed parent happy in a new relationship, unless the financial situation is clear, it is difficult for any new spouse to be accepted, particularly where the new spouse may be younger than the children of the wealth owner and where they may have a clearer perception of the financial objectives of the new spouse than their parent has. The wealth-owning parent likely has a different view of their new spouse and faces difficult initial conflicts between their new spouse and the children of the previous marriage.

If financial issues are not clearly dealt with at the outset, there is huge potential for unhappiness, uncertainty and danger. The relationship between the new spouse and the children will be strained, and this may cause both the new spouse and the children to focus on money more than they should. Over time, the new spouse inevitably exercises more and more influence over the wealth owner, asking for gifts and insisting on provisions for the future that take up bigger and bigger shares of family wealth. Family businesses may be at risk. Tensions increase, and families and relationships are destroyed.

The approach that I advocate is to ensure that financial arrangements and understandings in and around a new marriage or cohabitation relationship are made clear at the very outset. Depending on how this is done and when, it may be possible to engineer an approach that not only keeps everyone reasonably happy, but which provides a foundation for strong and supportive long-term relationships between all involved. Ideally, the discussions take place before the marriage, and the new spouse goes into the relationship with clarity on what he or she should expect should the new marriage come to an end on divorce or death. For the wealth owner, having the discussion upfront and agreeing the arrangements may be unromantic and challenging, but it is a good way to make sure that the issue of money is dealt with effectively and in a way that hopefully avoids a lifetime of effort by the new spouse to worm his or her way into getting more. Quite common here would be a pre-nuptial agreement that might provide relatively modest amounts if the marriage lasts only a short time and increasing amounts otherwise, but the key here is for clarity upfront.

And the safest approach to benefit the children and protect their interests is to consider making arrangements for them clear as well, with at least some assets being transferred—if not to them at the time of the new marriage, into trusts or other structures that are designed to ensure that there are *no circumstances* where the wealth owner, coming under pressure from their new spouse, could compromise what has been ensured will go to the children. In other words, this does not necessarily mean that the children get a large amount right away or that the wealth owner is no longer able to make investment and other decisions. What it does mean is that the wealth owner makes an irrevocable commitment to what the children will eventually get, and what part of the assets should remain in the control and discretion of the wealth owner.

While this approach means that the wealth owner is giving up at least a portion, and perhaps a large portion, of their wealth (if not their administration of it), the upside is great. If the new spouse knows what he or she will be getting out of the deal upfront, money is off the table, and the new marriage can progress with a focus on the wellbeing of the couple and their long-term happiness. And as to the children of the wealth owner, knowing what they will be getting and that their new step-parent has no ability to affect this in future, even if their parent becomes increasingly dependent on the new spouse, makes the chance of the relationship between the children and the new spouse developing in a positive way all the better. Reflecting on circular economy principles as discussed in an earlier chapter, finding ways to improve relationships can help avoid the possibility of the family 'wasting' resources—resources that can include a new spouse who has the potential to help, not hurt, the family along the road to its impact goal.

While I cannot say that these steps will always address the bad feelings that can arise within families where there are second, third, fourth and further marriages, I do believe that the approach can much reduce the unspoken concerns of the younger generation and avoid some of the bad feelings that can grow between children and their step-parent and parent. As to the new spouse, I like to believe that clarity on what he or she will ultimately get will help move money 'off the table' in the relationship—hopefully, with the economics clear, the new spouse will not be spending time 'working' the wealth owner as he or she ages, trying to get more and more than was initially planned—a scenario which is all too often the case. And the upfront discussion of money allows the new spouse to evaluate whether they want to go ahead with the marriage on the terms on offer. If all works out, the wealth owner's children understand the arrangements and weigh in on the marriage, and perhaps can celebrate that their parent has someone to spend their later years with and who, potentially, could help with the support of a parent they care deeply about.

There are many, many other issues that accompany the 'second family' situation, and disability is one of them. If a wealth owner becomes incapacitated (including falling into dementia in old age), who will call the shots on his or her assets? In the case of an ageing wealth owner who enters a new marriage, the new young spouse may be the one the law will put in charge. In the absence of the advance planning that I advocate, will this be a comfortable situation for the wealth owner's children or for the incapacitated parent? Could this fuel costly and destructive disputes?

In second and subsequent family situations, also relevant is who gets personal effects—family photos, heirlooms and other items. Should a new spouse get family albums that have childhood photos of stepchildren and a previous spouse? What if the albums are in the home the deceased wealth owner shares with his new spouse? Is the home (and its contents) going under the control of the spouse creating potential friction? Asking all of the relevant '*what ifs?*' is crucial to an effective asset and succession plan, particularly when there is a new family.

Financial and psychological issues can be even more severe where the second family involves children—whether step-children, given that the new spouse is also divorced or widowed, or a new set of natural children. Should all the children be treated equally, or are the children of the first marriage to be favoured? There are no magic answers, as each family situation is different. For me, the crucial thing is for decisions to be made and reviewed on an ongoing basis, and ideally for the real wishes of the wealth owner to be implemented—not approaches that are developed over time based on who in the family puts the greater pressure on the wealth owner. And all too often, because little in the way of thinking takes place, the wealth owner dies or becomes disabled before they have put a well-thought-out plan in place, leaving it to the law of the relevant jurisdictions to work out who gets what.

Second and further families include relationships with mistresses and paramours, a topic discussed earlier, and which also brings into the picture the question of illegitimate children. There are many surprises that can emerge where there are illegitimate children. Some trusts exclude them from benefit; others include them. Does the wealth owner know what his trust provides? Is it what he intends? And under the laws of some places in the world, California being an example, an illegitimate child is actually entitled to get what his legitimate siblings get. A wealth owner may leave everything to his two legitimate children and nothing to an illegitimate child, but this may only lead to costly and destructive litigation that the illegitimate child, if well advised, may undertake.

Multi-jurisdictional Families

The world is getting smaller, and it is increasingly common to find wealth-owning families whose members are living in different countries, holding a variety of citizenships and coming under the tax and other laws of the varied countries to which they are connected. It is very hard to predict where one's children will ultimately study, live and work—and as a result, understanding the issues that multi-jurisdictional families face is another need that all wealth-owning families have.

A parent living in Singapore and holding Singaporean citizenship may have a daughter who is a US citizen and/or resident. Rather than fearing complexity, the cross-border world is one that allows for a number of tax and other benefits if carefully navigated. Because a US person can generally receive assets tax-free (albeit with reporting requirements depending on the source of the assets and the amounts involved), there are many tax advantages that careful planning can result in when there are US taxpayers in the younger generation. And when some of the children live in yet another country, while this adds complexity, it may also add opportunity. One example is that income accumulated in certain foreign trusts can give rise to punitive tax rates when distributed to a US beneficiary; capitalizing that income and first distributing it to a Canadian resident family member might allow for tax-free distributions from the relevant trust to both the Canadian resident and, subsequently, to the US beneficiaries if properly handled. While the only thing to be sure of is that the tax and other rules constantly change, part of what a wealth owner needs is the ability to take advantage of a multi-jurisdictional family, and the benefits that diversification of residence and citizenship locations can provide.

The issues are not only tax related, and as discussed elsewhere in this book, places of residence and citizenship can affect everything from the ability of creditors to have access to assets, exposure to political risk and many other things.

Of course, it is impossible to find any advisor who has all the answers, particularly if multiple countries are involved. An effective advisor, however, is one who is able to raise the right questions, helping to navigate complexity and recognizing that a multi-jurisdictional family may be able to find opportunity in their exposure to different legal and tax systems.

Changing Demographics

Lifespans are increasing. Medical care is improving, and individuals are in a much better position than they used to be to understand the lifestyle and other choices that impact them. But when one lives to eighty, ninety or 100 and more, this has an impact on the succession process, and brings with it a number of issues that need consideration by all wealth-owning families.

The traditional approach to succession has been and continues to be to arrange for a will, supplemented by other tools, such as trusts and insurance arrangements, all of which are oriented to passing wealth on at the death of the wealth owner. The wealth might move to a surviving spouse who lives for a further number of years, and on the second death, moves to the 'younger' generation. But with many living much longer than they used to, is this traditional approach really the right one, and is it safe?

One of the first important considerations is whether it makes sense for 'children' to be inheriting at the age of sixty or seventy, as may be the case if their parents live to ninety or 100. And if the younger generation predecease their parents, the planning done for grandchildren and further generations may not have adequately reflected the input of the parents of the beneficiaries, the generation below the aged wealth owner.

It may well be that the older generation would prefer to hold on to what they have for good reason and to not benefit their children—this is fine, and a personal choice, but it is a good thing to make the approach clear to your children so that they know they should not be waiting a lifetime for something to come to them. The difficult family situation of Brooke Astor, discussed earlier, provides a good example of the problems that can happen. By the time Brooke Astor, a wealthy philanthropist, died, she was well over 100 years old. Her son, who was over eighty at the time of her death, had taken advantage of her growing dementia, making use of his mother's assets and encouraging her to change her will when she did not have the mental capacity to do so. While the son, who was imprisoned for his actions, was clearly a wrong-doer, perhaps the problems of the family could have been reduced had there been greater dialogue between Brooke Astor and her son regarding her intentions in relation to her assets, and perhaps the need for her son to do more to make his own way. And had Brooke Astor gifted to her son, early on, part of the inheritance she did provide, might this have not only benefited her son, but encouraged him to take better care of his mother in her last years?

But if we give part of our assets to our children long before our death, will there be enough left to ensure a comfortable retirement, and provision for every eventuality? Can I trust my children to take care of me in my old age? Given that my philosophy is not to trust anyone, perhaps it is dangerous to give too much away to children or a younger spouse early on, as you never know what can happen. Even if your child can be trusted, which I optimistically assume to be the case, what if he dies without provision to protect you, resulting in the child's wealth passing to a spouse who then remarries and creates a new family? Living a long life is a good thing. But succession plans need to adapt to new realities. One family I know involved a wealth owner who remarried, and established a trust that provided for his new, younger wife to be protected financially on his death by receiving the trust income for her life, with the balance of trust assets, on the death of his wife, going to his children. A fair and appropriate approach, but what happens if the younger wife, after the death of the wealth owner, is still alive and well at ninety-eight, and the wealth owner's children, in their late seventies and who could use some money, have still not inherited given that the arrangement does not benefit them until their stepmother passes away?

Using trusts and other structures, it is possible for a wealth owner to protect themselves, at least in part, from some of the issues that living longer give rise to. I can establish a trust that sets aside a portion of assets determined to be sufficient to cover my needs and more for my entire life, howsoever long I may live. The balance of assets might also be held in trust, with set conditions and times for access by my children, but with thought given to protecting against more coming out of the trust than my children should have, meaning that if a child predeceases, for example, the remaining assets will not immediately, or not fully, go to a surviving spouse, but perhaps revert to be held for the older generation and eventually grandchildren or others who are intended to benefit.

Planning in view of the possibility of living much longer than was the case in the past is also important as a means of addressing some of the real issues aging wealth owners face. It is sadly common to see the elderly suffering from forms of dementia, first not remembering where they left their possessions, and soon developing a form of paranoia, suspecting staff and family of stealing their possessions. Money becomes something to hang on to, with a sense developing that it is the tie that keeps the younger generation coming to visit.

I encourage the families I work with to discuss these dynamics openly at an early stage of their planning, and to clarify the approach that works best for succession in the context of their own family. For me, the objective should be to ensure that the last 20 years of a long life are as free as they can be from ongoing discussions about money and succession. There is always a need for review of the succession plan, and reflection of inevitable change in the regulatory world and within the family, but the more succession plans are discussed and agreed within the family very early on, the more likely that wealth will not become destructive.

Family Conflict Resolution

Most of the older generations I have worked with over the years wear rose-coloured glasses and believe that their children (and presumably grandchildren and further generations) will all love each other and get along famously, working together and looking after each other. Sadly, and this crosses all cultures I have run into, it is far from always the case that the younger generation get along, let alone look after each other's interests.

Developing mechanisms for the resolution of family conflict is clearly a need that all families have.

Where there is a family business, it is more often the case that governance approaches are put in place to deal with disputes that can arise. But too often, where the assets do not involve an active business, little if any attention is paid to how to resolve a potential dispute.

Whatever the vehicle used for the succession of assets from one generation to the next, be it a trust, company, partnership or otherwise, thought needs to be given to whether it is really important for the assets to remain together. Permitting a division of assets in specified circumstances can often avoid many problems.

It is a nice thing for families to invest together, and there can be significant benefits to them doing so, but if the relevant stakeholders cannot get along, is trying to keep them together going to do more harm than good? Given that splitting things up does not necessarily mean that each family member has immediate access to all the assets (e.g., where trusts are used), allowing family members to go their own way might be better than encouraging bad feeling and, possibly, costly litigation. But even before contemplating any sort of division of assets should be the establishment of procedures for how disputes might be resolved, and by whom. And, like virtually everything else in relation to succession, the more the dispute resolution approach is discussed and agreed among family members, the more likely it will be respected by them and work.

Business Succession and Family Constitutions

While not all families are involved in active businesses, the succession issues business- families have to deal with are highly relevant to all families and bring to light areas of need that all families need to address. And family constitutions, which are increasingly used as part of the succession process, are not only relevant to families that have businesses that pass from one generation to the next.

Much more information and education on effective business succession is available to the wealth owner than is available on the many other issues wealth-owning families face. Business schools around the world provide training to the younger generation, and many advisors focus on the issues in and around family business governance and structures.

What I find, however, is that the education available to wealth-owning families tends to be focused on education of those who will succeed in the management of a family business. Insufficient education is available to those family members who may not become managers of the family business, but who need coaching on how to become an effective *owner and steward* of a family business. And related to this is that for families that do not have a family business, but rather a portfolio of investment assets, there is again a lack of effective and thoughtful training and education available. But where assets are investment assets rather than ownership interests in a business, many of the issues involved are the same, given that real success comes from an approach that is akin to owning a business—being equipped with what it takes to ask the right questions of those managing the business or the assets, and understanding the rights and responsibilities of an owner. Succession in family businesses and family investment assets requires real preparation of the younger generation (and of spouses who may become successors), as well as ensuring that the right governance approaches are in place.

A key starting point in looking at family businesses and succession is to recognize that when the founder of the business is alive and well and running the business, there is less need for governance and structure than is the case as the business passes through the generations. The founder of the business knows almost everything that is going on and has a tight rein on things. The founder is entrepreneurial and driven, and in control of the business. As the business moves to the second, third and further generations, whether or not the same level of entrepreneurial drive exists as it did during the founder's time will be an issue. Certainly, the control of the founder is no longer there, and these factors make the need for family governance critical—the use of structures and approaches designed to allow a business to thrive as it navigates generational change.

One family that I worked with a number of years ago provides a good example to highlight some of the many issues that business-owning families face. Interestingly, as is sometimes the case, it was not the older generation of the family that had involved me and other advisors in their planning process, but rather members of the younger generation who realized that unless their parents would undertake more in the way of sophisticated planning, the business of the family, and the family itself, would be at risk. Three members of the younger generation, in their forties and fifties, took the lead to try to sort things out for their family, something they ended up doing very successfully.

The business in issue was one that had been established by a single individual, the grandfather of the generation that had approached me. Grandfather started a manufacturing business, and successfully built it up. Grandfather had five sons, but died at a very early age, just before reaching fifty. At the time of his death, only one of his five sons was over twenty years old, and that oldest son took over his father's business. As his four brothers reached an appropriate age, they joined the family business, and the five brothers eventually worked extraordinarily well together, building the manufacturing business into a global conglomerate, with operations in several countries and diversifying into a number of areas, ranging from banking to retail businesses and property development.

Trusting each other, the five brothers did not pay much attention to how the family business was owned, and given the political and other dynamics of their home country, went to some lengths to ensure that not all their business or personal assets were in one single structure or in the ownership of any one of the brothers. As the global business developed, particular businesses were owned by one brother, other businesses by another; there were bank accounts in Switzerland and elsewhere in the name of one of the brothers, and certain properties in the name of another. But the assets involved were considered to be the assets of all five, treated by them as part of one family business.

All five brothers themselves had children and many, but not all of them, were active in the family business. In some cases, spouses of the children were employed by the business. The children, being in their forties and fifties, themselves had children, making it clear that the question of business and asset succession was going to become more and more difficult, with the growing population of family members, particularly in the younger generation.

The wake-up call for the family came when the oldest brother of the five passed away. After his death, his children sought to clarify what they were about to inherit, and they put forward the legally valid position that they (and their surviving mother) were entitled to the assets that had been legally owned by their father. The four surviving brothers disagreed, and pointed out that while the five brothers had owned the business and other assets of the family in an unorganized way, the family always treated the assets as the assets of the family as a whole, and not as the assets of any one family member, despite how the assets were legally owned. Fortunately, the four brothers were able to convince their nieces and nephews that the family and the family business would benefit from a structured succession approach. The first step for the family was to develop a family constitution.

Family constitutions are increasingly used by families, not only those with a family business, to set out a framework for the more detailed planning that will subsequently take place. One of the biggest benefits of a family constitution is not the constitution itself, but the *process* of family engagement and discussion that implementing a family constitution results in. What a family constitution covers can vary significantly, but can include many items that are important for business-owning families to consider. And family constitutions, and the areas they cover, are very relevant to families who may only own passive assets, and not actually be in businesses that are to pass from one generation to the next.

In most cases, while family members sign the relevant family constitution, it is not a legally binding document. Rather, the constitution is then used as the basis for creating binding documents that can include partnership and shareholder agreements, trust or foundation structures and other arrangements that do provide legal rights and responsibilities.

A few of the many items a well-thought-out family constitution might contain:

- *Background on the family and family business*: While the family may know its history well, thinking about how the family business started, the values of the founder of the business and the family origins, can be a useful starting point for the constitution and for the family discussions that putting the constitution in place will require.
- *Mission and vision*: Drawing on the history of the family business, the objectives of the family can be laid out, covering what the family hopes to achieve for the benefit of the family, the family business, employees and the communities in which the family lives and operates. This, of course, will be a relevant part of the overall impact goal of the family, as would be a focus in the use by the family of the *Theory of Change* as a planning methodology.
- *Family governance*: While related to the governance of businesses and assets, apart from the structures used to own assets, families can consider how the family itself will be involved in its own governance. Typically, a family council or similar body will be established, and procedures set out for who in the family will populate the council, how decisions will be made and how family council members can be appointed and replaced.

Often the family council is elected by a family assembly, and issues relating to assembly meetings, votes and other matters will be covered as part of the governance approach. A key issue for families is the question of the extent to which spouses participate in family meetings and overall governance. If this is not made clear, difficulties can arise later, as the discussion of the issue of whether spouses should attend family meetings can become personal in the sense that the discussion becomes about a particular spouse, affecting family relationships and otherwise. If Dad remarries, should he be able to bring along his new, young wife to a family meeting despite the children and grandchildren being disturbed about the divorce, and Dad's choice of new partner? Should a son or daughter-in-law be excluded from participating despite being successfully involved in and contributing to the family business, and clearly being responsible for raising the next generation of family members?

- *Who are family members?* Apart from spouses, upfront consideration of how the family views stepchildren, adopted children and others is important, and ideally the issues are discussed before specific questions arise about specific family members, a potentially emotional and divisive issue.
- *Family assets and who really owns them:* A critical issue for families to consider is the extent to which members of the younger generation are meant to be owners of assets or custodians of assets for further generations. Often, when I ask the younger generation about this, they think they are the owners of the assets they inherit, and that they are free to do with those assets what they want. When I ask the older generation, they are often much more oriented to viewing their children as stewards of family assets and the family business—taking over their management, helping to preserve and grow the business for the benefit of further generations of the family. If assets pass to the younger generation before the question of stewardship versus ownership is addressed, it is often too late to ensure that the values and expectations of the older generation will be respected. Can your daughter sell the Picasso that your father left to you and which you hoped would stay in the family? Or should she enjoy it and live within her means, leaving the painting to the next generation to also enjoy?

- *Family values*: While family values are something that has to be part of the upbringing of children, setting out the values of the family in writing is often a good way of cementing the approach to business and wealth that the family is committed to. In the media and elsewhere, wealth owners are looked at as the 'rich' and there is a caricature of the wealth owner living a lavish lifestyle, splashing money around, and with the younger generation in the families involved living a spoiled and pampered life, getting all the material things they want and spending apace. There are certainly many who fit the caricature, but in my experience, there are many, many more wealth owners who take responsibility for the wealth and businesses they own, and who understand that material possessions and a lavish lifestyle do not bring happiness and harmony to them or their families. I work with a number of families at the more extreme levels of wealth who live surprisingly modest lifestyles, and happily so, and whose children are brought up to understand that an upper-middle-class comfortable lifestyle may be more appropriate and fulfilling than a life of private jets and yachts. Discussing family values and reflecting them in the family constitution is part of the process of helping the family to agree on the principles they wish to live by.
- *Family education*: There are many elements of education that are important for wealth-owning families to consider, including the background that might be needed for those family members who want to join the family business. The constitution can also lay out how the family will support educational costs, and not only for university and otherwise, but for specialized programmes offered by business schools and others which are designed to prepare the younger generation for their responsibilities as wealth and business owners. In a number of families (and also in the education programmes offered by many universities to business-owning families) there is not enough emphasis on training not only those who will be involved in managing a family business, but also those who will become owners of a family business. How to read a balance sheet, be an effective board member, ask the right questions of executives running a business, are all some of the many skills that need to be learned by those who will be effective owners of a family business. Having a development framework for family members can be important.

- *Employment policies*: Should every member of the family (and maybe their spouses) have a right to work in the family business? Addressing the employment policies associated with family members working in the family business is a key area for a family to address, recognizing that the question of who is right to work in a family business will give rise to much in the way of potential unhappiness. Successful family businesses have clear guidelines as to the expectations regarding the backgrounds of those family members who want to work in the family business, including educational requirements and, often, minimum levels of experience working outside of the family business. The issue of employment of family members can be so difficult for family businesses that have passed several generations, that some families adopt the policy of having *no* family members managing their businesses, using only professional managers who are not family members. Instead, the focus of the family is on preparing the younger generation to be effective owners of the family business, and on governance structures to deal with issues in and around ownership of the family business.
- *Expenses and use of family assets*: The constitution should also consider the extent to which some expenses of the family may be communalized, and related to this is the extent to which communally owned assets, such as a family house, boat or otherwise, will be used and paid for. Can family members use a ski chalet owned by the family freely? Can they offer it to their friends? What are the financial arrangements? If none of these things are considered and discussed, there is much room for dispute as one family member makes more use than another of a family asset and incurs expenses that the overall family is responsible for.
- *Social responsibility and philanthropy*: The family constitution is a good place to set out the family's views on responsible investing and philanthropy, and family values in relation to the family business, and its importance to non-family stakeholders, such as employees and the communities in which they live and work.
- *Entrepreneurial children, competition, and the role of a family 'bank'*[1]: Where there is a family business, families often focus on the many issues they need to consider in ensuring that the younger

generation are well prepared to be involved in the business. What many families are less well prepared for are the challenges that having a particularly entrepreneurial child can raise, and how to encourage and develop the entrepreneurial objectives of the younger generation. I worked with a family where one of the children, supported by his father both emotionally and financially, started an online business in the same area as the 'bricks and mortar' family business. Over the years, online activities became very important for the future growth of the family business, and the fact that a close family member was competing with the family business became both problematic for the business and divisive for the family, as siblings and others adopted the view that their brother had built a valuable business using family resources, contacts and more. Eventually the problem was addressed through a buyout of the son's online business, and bringing him back into the family business, but the example shows the need to address whether the younger generation can compete with the family business, and also who should own new businesses that the younger generation may develop on their own, but with financial support from the family. A family 'bank' might be a good approach to consider as a means of providing financing to the younger generation for a venture they want to undertake on their own. This does not require the establishment of a formal bank, but would involve setting out how decisions will be made on whether or not to fund a venture someone in the family wants to undertake and, if so, on what terms. This can be by way of a loan, where the entrepreneur owns the new business they establish, but repays the family, with interest, for the help. But what if the business fails? And if the loan is unsecured and the business succeeds, should the return to the family be more than just a low interest rate? Perhaps more fair would be that the family obtains a minority stake in the new business or investment. Having a 'family bank' approach allows for a structured approach to making decisions about supporting family members in their efforts to establish new businesses outside the framework of the original family business and what is meant to be kept together. Less critical than the actual formula used is to ensure that the issues are discussed, and that there is a perception of fairness to the approach that the family buys into.

Perhaps the family can invest in a business a child wants to get involved in by lending 80% of the funds needed, and investing the other 20% as equity. If the business succeeds, the family owns 20% and the child 80%, and the child repays the debt. If the business fails, the family loses the 20% equity investment and while the loan is not repaid, the amount involved comes out of the future share of family wealth the child would have ultimately received.

- *Compensating family members involved in the family business:* A thorny issue that business-owning families face, and which the family constitution should discuss, is how family members will be rewarded for the work they do in a family business. How should a daughter be rewarded if she takes on the leadership of a family business that she inherits 50/50 with her brother, a successful doctor who—while supportive of his sister—is not directly involved in the business? I usually advise families to consider treating their children equally, so would support the idea of the 50/50 share split in relation to the family business, and for the daughter running the business, her being compensated as she would be if she were working outside the family business in a similar role. This might require discussions with compensation specialists, and agreements on bonus and phantom stock arrangements to reflect the success she achieves. But this does not always work. In one family I was advising, the reaction to my proposed approach of the older son, who had begun to take things over from his father, was that if he did not directly own a meaningful stake of the company disproportionate to his siblings not leading the business, he would leave. His view was that he did not want to work for his siblings, and as an entrepreneur, wanted an entrepreneur's return for his efforts. So, there are no magic answers on how to make this work, but it is best to have discussions and arrangements broadly in place upfront, and here developing the language to be used in a family constitution can be helpful in directing the attention of the family to this important area. I received on this topic some helpful comments from the head of an important family office serving a family leading a globally recognized consumer product business. While he asked that I do not mention his name in this book, he did share that one of the most important derailers, in his view, is oriented to the often quoted statistic that only

3% of family businesses survive beyond the third generation. Whether or not true, he wrote to me, the failure rate is extraordinarily high and the problem relates to the speed with which a sense of entitlement embeds itself within wealthy families – they lose the hunger that created their wealth in the first place and which is very much required to maintain and enhance it over generations. Successful families (fifth and sixth generations and beyond) find ways to retain and foster the hunger. They do this by removing any sense of entitlement to the family's wealth and this by establishing a system where the rewards are shared between those (few) who are actively contributing to the continued wealth of the family rather than just drawing on it.

- *Family mentors*: Through the family constitution or otherwise, considering formally appointing mentors to the younger generation can be most useful whether a family business is involved or not. The work that parents do in guiding their children can be enhanced by others, in or out of the family, being involved as mentors as children move into family business management or ownership roles. Where the dynamics of the family permits, uncles, aunts and others can be a part of this. Having a formal approach to mentorships can be important and beneficial.
- *Expectations regarding pre-nuptial agreements and trust arrangements*: Divorces in the younger generation can have a dramatically negative impact on a family business and family assets generally. Among the planning approaches wealth-owning families can take are well-structured discretionary trusts and, where they are respected under the relevant law, pre-nuptial and post-nuptial agreements. Having the family constitution lay out expectations regarding such arrangements and their being a condition to inheritance is important. Where pre-nuptial planning strategies are agreed upfront within a family, the discussion is unrelated to any particular potential spouse, avoiding the bad feeling that can otherwise result. When the need for pre-nuptial agreements is provided for in a family constitution, and a member of a family is able to explain to a potential spouse that the pre-nuptial arrangement is a pre-requisite for their being able to participate in the family business and wealth, the pre-nuptial arrangement is an easier one to discuss and put in place.

- *Pruning the family tree*: Families that manage to keep their businesses intact over the generations tend to be families that accept that it is almost inevitable that not everyone in the younger generation will see things the same way. Allowing for the likelihood that there will be family members who will not want to participate in and support the family business, and having clear procedures for how to buy out their interests and at what price, has been a key way successful families have managed to keep businesses in family hands over the generations. While I like to see clear exit procedures, I also like to anticipate the ability of a *return* to the family business, with procedures that allow members of further generations of a family branch that may have sold out to buy their way back in. Valuations and procedures on this front can be tricky but are well worth thinking about. And as discussed in the context of circular economy principles affecting owners of family businesses and wealth, a *revolving door* is perhaps a better way of ensuring that human resources within the family are not wasted. The idea here is that rather than exits, family members are encouraged to know that while they can always distance themselves from the family and its business and investment interests, the structure keeps the door open to their return, and to the possibility that their children and grandchildren may want to be closely involved with the family and its activities.
- *Harvesting the family business*: I have run across business owners, usually the founders, who sometimes say that they want the business to stay in the family 'forever'. Well, forever is a very long time, and it is clear that a business that is valuable today may not be particularly valuable in the future. Technologies change, economies change and businesses change. Effective succession of a family business is often reflected by flexibility in what the family business is seen to be. Governance arrangements that are put in place should provide for procedures to determine when and how elements of the family business can be 'harvested'—sold when it makes strategic sense to sell the business, likely with a view to reinvesting the proceeds in new businesses that form the constantly evolving 'family business'. Businesses and families are dynamic, and the constitution,

and background family thinking and discussions, should best accommodate this. I like to think of the family business and investments collectively as the *engine* that is a key element of the family ecosystem. The engine may be a family business or more than one family business; the engine may include or only be made up of passive investments; the engine can and will adapt to changes in the family and in the external world. Rather than focusing family members on being able to contribute to the family business specifically, the focus becomes on resilience and flexibility and the ability to play key roles in ensuring that the engine runs smoothly.

- *Family retreats*: Connected to the family constitution are usually arrangements for regular, perhaps annual or more frequent, family meetings, involving the 'family assembly' or other body, or a more informal get-together of the family to allow the family not only to review its business and wealth, but to work on connecting the family and keeping it connected. As families grow, and businesses move to subsequent generations, more work is needed to keep a family together, and the family retreat becomes a key element of this. Families that hold successful retreats put much thought into their agenda, and many have some sessions that only family members attend, and others where advisors, such as lawyers and trustees, also participate. There are many things that an effective family retreat can achieve, and for families whose assets are simpler than those families seeking to preserve significant family businesses, family retreats are still an important thing to consider, to help communicate the succession and asset-protection plan with family members, and to keep them up-to-date on where things are and what to do if the wealth owner dies or becomes disabled.
- *The family legacy and individual legacies*: The family constitution will often start out with a discussion of the family history and, combined with its focus on the family business and on the family's thinking on philanthropy and social impact, will represent the family legacy. It is often useful to consider, in the preparation of a family constitution and in discussions with family members, what 'legacy' really means, and the need for all family members to have the ability to achieve their goals

and to be proud of doing so. Success should not be measured by the past business success of the business founder, and for each generation, consideration should be given to what 'legacy' really means. The founder of the business sometimes views his or her legacy as the business itself, not always a healthy thing, as this may make it difficult for the founder to let go and transition the business to the younger generation. In some cases, the founder may find himself lost on retiring, staying at the helm of the business until the very last moment, and, through his dominance, not adequately preparing the younger generation and professional managers for the roles that they will have to assume once the founder is no longer around. A founder who feels his legacy is the family business may also be less flexible about 'harvesting' the business— selling it at the right strategic time to allow the family business to evolve into businesses of the future. Here the family constitution and the surrounding discussions can seek to encourage a leading role in the family's philanthropic and related work, and in areas—including the mentoring and coaching of the younger generation—that help make the concept of legacy a broader one than just the family business the founder established. For family members who did not found the business, having the constitution and family assets permit them to develop their own legacies can be important. For the younger generation, it is hard to compete with past success in their family, particularly if the success that the family celebrates is linked to money and not much more. Having the ability to establish their own businesses, art collections and charitable endeavours can afford the younger generation the opportunity to create their own legacies, with success measured in any number of important ways, including contribution to family reputation, contribution to the community and otherwise.

- *Investment policies:* Investment policy statements (IPS) can play a significant role in governance, especially when the family is not actively involved in investment management or when decision-making powers are delegated to a few individuals or external parties. The IPS also becomes essential when there is a need to uphold specific ethical or moral values or investment principles.[2]

Even where a family does not use a family constitution, just thinking about and discussing the issues a typical family constitution covers can be a useful thing.

Doing Good—Philanthropy and Families

Another need of all families relates to philanthropy, and other means of helping others.

Many wealth owners, at one point or another, consider what they can do to help the world, and philanthropy is often the way they achieve this. Related, but different, is a focus on ensuring that investments have a positive impact on society, and an increasing number of investors focus not only on the investment return, but also on the impact their investments have on all stakeholders—employees, communities and more. Blended-value investing, which focuses on bringing value not only to the investor but also to others, is increasingly an area of interest for wealth owners.[3]

But doing good is not always easy, and philanthropy, and impact investing, are by no means areas where a wealth owner can just assume that everything will work out right. Sad stories in the area of philanthropy abound, just as they do in relation to the many families destroyed by wealth.

A friend of mine, the head of a trust company in Asia, told me of her involvement, after the fact, with a foundation that had been established by a woman with significant funds she had inherited from her husband. The couple had been childless, and the woman had suffered from cancer, which eventually took her life. Before her passing she arranged for her trusted advisor, an Austrian lawyer, to establish a foundation that he would run, and which would receive her assets on her death. The foundation was established to contribute to cancer research. After the death of the woman involved, her assets moved to the foundation and to the control of her Austrian lawyer. The foundation was eventually depleted of all its assets, none of which ever went to cancer research or for any use other than meeting the costs of the Austrian lawyer himself. The foundation funded many luxurious trips the Austrian lawyer and his wife took. While the lawyer occasionally visited cancer research facilities, he never used any of the funds for anything other than his own personal expenditures.

The lesson is not that philanthropy cannot be achieved, or that foundations or Austrian lawyers are bad. Rather, the lesson is that no one should be trusted—not because they are not trustworthy, but because there should always be 'checks and balances' in place that limit the ability of someone in a trusted position to abuse the trust that was placed in them. The wealth owner whose funds went into the foundation had choices when she created the foundation, and among these choices were to take approaches that would ensure that her trusted Austrian lawyer would not have power to abuse his position the way he did. And that at a minimum, there would be a third party with the job of ensuring that the foundation did what it was meant to do.

Philanthropy has the potential to be a binding force for families and can also be an important way to establish family legacy, apart from a family business or family wealth. It is sometimes difficult to get the younger generation to work together on a family business or family investments. Where the focus is on helping others, getting family members together can be easier to achieve, particularly if work on this is done early on, involving children in philanthropy and its importance when they are young.

I sometimes encourage families to consider setting aside a small amount of money for the younger generation to use as part of learning how to be responsible wealth owners. At a family retreat, it can be fun to get the younger generation together—say children between ten and fifteen years old—letting them know that a sum of money has been allocated to them that they are responsible for investing. Discussions then take place on investments and how they work, but in a way that the younger generation can relate to. Why does McDonald's do better when there are difficult economies and people have to save money? Why are restaurant chains focusing on healthy food showing success? I will ask a group of children about PlayStations as against the Nintendo Wii, or more current new products. Inevitably, imaginations are captured, and with the help of investment specialists we can discuss companies that the younger generation can relate to, helping them come to choices on how to invest the money that has been allocated for the purpose.

A year later, when the family gets together again, we look at the investment performance. Why has Sony increased in value? Why has McDonald's struggled? We look at how much money the investment strategy earned, and now the group has to work together to figure out how to give the profits away. We bring in speakers from various charities—someone can speak about UNICEF and the needs of children in different parts of the world; the World Wide Fund for Nature and its efforts to save endangered animals; the Make-a-Wish Foundation, and examples of children whose lives they have enhanced. The younger generation learn that there are many, many in need, and limited resources that can be made available to help, and together the younger generation in the family decide how to give the money away.

All too often, there is strife among the siblings in wealth-owning families, but the difficulties do not, at least yet, extend to their children—cousins who have an opportunity to learn how to work together as a family. A focus on the outside world rather than on wealth they will be keeping themselves is a great way to learn responsibility and how to cooperate, and also to learn about investing and many other important skills that will serve them in future.

Philanthropy can also be a key part of family legacy, itself a difficult and important topic for many wealth-owning families. Mum may have established a successful business, but as she ages, is she obsessed with the business becoming her and her family's legacy? Maybe the business is a great one, but one that at some point should be sold to achieve the best result for the family and the business itself. Will Mum be lost once the business is sold? If the business passes to the next generation, and one of the sons runs it, is the business his legacy or that of his mother, or that of the family? Will the son have a sense of fulfilment even if he manages not only to be an effective steward of the business but also to grow it substantially? For Mum, getting involved in philanthropy in a serious way can be a means to establish a family legacy that is apart from the family business, and one which she can continue to build and be proud of regardless of whether the family business is sold, or whether she hands over the business to her children or to others to run. And for a son taking charge of a family business that he did not create, his own philanthropic endeavours can become his personal legacy and represent achievements of his own.

The philanthropic endeavours of families can also be effective training grounds for family business roles that family members may be encouraged to take. A fifth-generation member of a well-known business-owning family shared with me that membership on the board of his family's foundation provides great preparation and exposure to younger family members on their way to the family's business boards as the approaches taken to sharing board materials, going through financials and otherwise are very similar. And the foundation board roles provide exposure of the skills of family members that may not have otherwise come to light.

But like other areas of family wealth and businesses, it is not always the case that having family members work together will be successful. There have been many families where philanthropic projects the younger generation have been forced to work on together have been the cause of strife and litigation. And the philanthropic passion of the older generation may not be the passion of the younger. Dad may want to support schools in the village in China where his own father grew up—how relevant will this be to Dad's children, who may have grown up in the United States or elsewhere, detached from the community Dad's philanthropic venture focuses on?

An interesting approach to philanthropy was taken by the Sainsbury family in England, where a common platform was established to support the philanthropic efforts of the younger generation. Children in the family were given resources to establish their own charitable structures, focusing on their own passions, but opportunities to work together with their siblings and other family members arise through their sharing of legal, tax, accounting, implementation and other resources key to making philanthropic ideas become a reality. The Sainsbury approach shows a way of keeping the younger generation together; doing good in a professional way while encouraging the individual initiatives of the younger generation.[4]

Like all elements of wealth ownership, philanthropy is not easy and takes work and commitment. There are many philanthropic endeavours that languish, with the younger generation neglecting the opportunity to focus on what can be achieved, leaving funds that could be made available to make a difference sitting passively. There are also many abuses in the world of philanthropy and perhaps too many examples of families trying to do things on their own. Sometimes it is much, much more effective to cooperate with others in philanthropic efforts and use advisors who have experience and who know the right questions to ask.

A group of advisors that I work with mentioned to me one of their clients who wanted to establish a health clinic in Peru as part of their charitable endeavour. The advisors, hired by the family, travelled to the relevant community and found that there was a public clinic pretty much across the street from the clinic that was to be established by their clients. When they asked the family why they were setting up a 'competing' clinic so close by, they were told that the family found the public clinic inadequate. The advisors explored the management of the public clinic, and ended up recommending that more good would be achieved if the family contributed to the public clinic, and helped it up its game—something that was ultimately done for the good of the community involved in Peru, and which facilitated an easier and more effective approach to doing good.

Tax also comes into the charitable world, and tax laws around the world are not yet where they need to be to reflect the reality that our world is getting smaller and smaller. In many countries, tax deductions are provided where there is charitable giving, but those deductions properly focus on giving to real charities, and controls are established to ensure that this is the case. All too often, though, tax laws require that charities be based in the same country as the donor to be easily approved, meaning that a wealth owner resident in one country may find it difficult to give to a charity in the country of origin of, say, their parents. Cross-border giving is a complex area, and while solutions are emerging, careful navigation of tax laws is necessary to ensure that tax deductions are maximized, permitting more to go to the charitable destination the family has in mind. The King Baudouin Foundation in Belgium is one of the players working on encouraging cross-border giving and lobbying for change in tax laws to facilitate the reality that need is not only in the country in which wealth owners may reside.[5]

On the tax front, there are also some interesting bigger-picture issues for wealth-owning families to consider. Where the wealth owner lives in a country with a significant inheritance tax, leaving money to children may come at a significant tax cost. US$100,000 left to a child may leave the child with, say, US$60,000 to give to charity if a 40% inheritance tax applies. But if donations to charity are exempt from inheritance tax, as they often are, instead of leaving the US$100,000 to her daughter, Mum can ask her daughter to administer a charitable fund Mum sets up with the US$100,000—now making considerably more available for the charitable endeavour.

Where there is a family business, more in the way of tax efficiencies can be achieved. If the wealth owner lives in a low or no-tax country, giving money away may not achieve much in the way of tax deductions. But if the same wealth owner owns a business that operates in various countries and which includes subsidiaries in higher-tax countries, maybe having one of the companies in a higher-tax country make the charitable contribution will allow for a significant tax deduction, again allowing more funds to be available to do good. Maybe paying tax is also a form of doing good, but it is a less direct way of orienting funds to where they need to go.

Thomas Piketty is a French economist and major advocate of high inheritance taxes to address, among other things, wealth and income inequality. I agree with the notion that those with wealth have a responsibility to make the world a fairer place. But I am more comfortable with the wealth owner having the ability to drive the philanthropic process themselves ... giving money away directly rather than giving the money to governments in the form of higher taxes, hoping that the governments will be efficient in their use of higher tax collections. I am not a believer that governments will always get it right ...

Creative tax thinking in the charity area can be a beneficial thing to do. Another example of tax-efficient giving would be a family that invests internationally, and reviews what taxes are 'left on the table'. The family may be one that gives meaningful amounts without tax benefit being obtained, possibly because the family is resident in a country with low or no taxation, such as would be the case for a family based in a number of countries in the Middle East. Tax may not form part of their thinking, but if they review their global investment portfolio, there may be withholding taxes on, say, dividends from high-tax countries that are incurred on a regular basis. Withholding taxes on dividends, in the absence of tax treaties having application, can be high—in Canada, withholding taxes are imposed at the rate of 25% of dividends; in the United States at the rate of 30% and in Switzerland at the rate of 35%. What if the family involved creates a structure, such as a partnership, which allocates dividend flows to charities? If properly structured, withholding taxes can be eliminated given charitable exemptions from the withholding tax, meaning that the amount available to be given to charity will be substantially increased.

Blended-value and impact investing are not charity, but involve focusing on investments that are not only responsible investments, but also provide returns that go beyond investment returns to the wealth-owning family. All stakeholders, from employees to communities in which a business operates, can be beneficiaries of well-thought-out investments, and more and more thinking is being done in this area. It is not always easy to measure returns beyond investment returns, but work is being done on this, and there are many working on it, including Jed Emerson in the United States, citied earlier as one of the leading thinkers on blended value.[6]

Blended value can also relate to venture philanthropy that benefits a business—not new thinking, but thinking that has, to some extent, been lost. There was a time in Chinese traditional family businesses, for example, when the business worried about the education, health and further care of its workers. A factory would be built in a new community, and as part of the project, the business would establish homes for workers, schools and hospitals, and would take care of the workers in their retirement. Has the world moved too far in terms of businesses focusing only on short-term profits and lining the pockets of managers and shareholders, leaving it to the vagaries of governments to look after their workers and communities? Did the US healthcare system prior to the Obama presidency show success in caring for all stakeholders? Is the US education system, with its costly private universities that limit access for those without resources, the best way to encourage upward mobility?

Wealth-owning families can, should and do think about these things, and also about how doing good can also be good for their businesses in the long term.

Privacy and Confidentiality

It is sad to see how moves to tax transparency, driven by abuses of bank secrecy and otherwise, are compromising the human right to privacy and the ability of wealth-owning families to keep their affairs confidential even when they may have good reasons to do so. It is a pity that countries that were once the champions of privacy have abused their positions, permitting the misuse of bank secrecy and other regimes to facilitate tax evasion and shield the identities of, among others, corrupt politicians and other criminals and thus endangering legitimate wishes for privacy.

The world now lacks a real champion of the human right to privacy, and this leaves the wealth-owning family to its own devices to find the right investment and asset ownership structures that allow for full tax and other legal compliance while retaining the privacy and confidentiality that wealth owners need and deserve.

Privacy is a need that all families share, and apart from the question of tax-related reporting obligations comes the question of whether and to what extent families themselves affect the ability of a family to maintain privacy in relation to family assets and approaches to asset protection and succession.

Privacy is a human right, and for all wealth-owning families, can be essential to the family's safety and security. This is certainly the case where families are connected to countries with significant political risk, or where corruption, crime, and other dangers are rife. But even where the countries to which a family is connected are developed and relatively 'safe', privacy remains an important and legitimate need. Is it ever safe for a wealth-owning family to have detailed information about their wealth available to the public and for access to be provided on the location of homes and other personal details?

As covered earlier, the tax landscape has been fast changing, and automatic exchange of information and other initiatives are transforming the ability of governments to have information on the income and assets of wealth owners connected to their countries. Tax compliance for today's families is critical, and as a result, your government being aware of your income and assets should not be a problem. If it is, a family should be considering what steps to take to ensure that they can maintain privacy while being compliant. This might involve use of ownership structures for assets and businesses that legally avoid reporting or taking advantage of mobility and the ability of some or all of the family to relocate, and to be based in countries where governments can be trusted to not misuse the information they have. And while there are many initiatives developing that contemplate public ownership registers, there are, fortunately, a number of reasonable voices cautioning against information being made available to other than those who need to know. Tax authorities knowing about one's assets and income is one thing—the press or other 'interested parties' having the ability to access information is not only unsafe, it is simply not right.

So, for wealth-owning families, having a privacy 'audit' is increasingly an important need. Understanding who has what information on the family and its assets, and what the family can do to legally ensure that information only goes where it is necessary to go is essential.

Apart from the world of taxation and related reporting requirements, there are many other issues relevant to privacy that families need to consider and address. This includes the development of policies within a family about the use of social media and also how family members act in public, including in relation to their consumption and other habits. Educating the younger generation about keeping a low profile and the dangers of information falling into the wrong hands is important, and in an increasingly complex and challenging world, a critical part of helping families to avoid wealth being a destructive force.

Investments, Liquidity and the Diversification of Ownership Structures

Another clear need every wealth-owning family has is to have the right structures in place to permit investments to be made, something that requires thought and reflection on a number of issues.

Tax efficiency is clearly important, and understanding the tax systems relevant to an investment is key. Getting into the investment may be easy, but care needs to be taken to work out the eventual exit, and the possible tax costs that may arise.

The first step is always to look at the tax system relevant to the wealth owner personally, and how this affects taxes arising at every step of the investment process, as well as on realization of the investment or on transfer of the investment on death or by way of gift to family members or others. Tax exposures in the country or countries where the investment structure may itself be located will also be relevant and, of course, taxes in the country in which the investment is made. Finding the right investment approach requires looking at the rules in all relevant jurisdictions, and the starting point is almost always the home country of the investor. Access to tax treaties, maintaining the ability to take advantage of tax exemptions, foreign tax credits and similar things all come into the mix.

With increasing tax transparency, rules are rapidly developing in relation to information exchange, much of which is now automatic. Intermediaries such as banks and trustees have the responsibility to exchange information, making countries aware of whom the beneficial owners of assets are. Other forms of exchange of information are extending to information that includes how profits are allocated between jurisdictions, allowing each to capture what their rules consider to be that country's fair share of taxation.

While wealth owners need to become comfortable with the notion that governments will know what they are doing, a key need of families is to have a clear understanding of which governments get what information. In a world where not every country has tax and legal systems that can be trusted, knowing where one's financial details are going is vital. Something that I often suggest to families is that they determine how the investment and asset holding structures they use will impact information disclosure, noting that keeping assets in separate baskets can sometimes help manage the risks associated with more information flowing than actually needs to flow.

Most wealth owners understand very well the need to diversify investments in order to reduce risk; fewer understand the value of diversifying ownership structures. The reality is that information disclosure and risk can also be managed through a diversification of ownership structures. A simple example can be made in relation to protecting assets from divorce claims in the younger generation. As mentioned earlier, in many legal systems, a spouse may have a claim over assets that are considered to be 'marital assets'—assets available to the married couple and used by them. A wealth owner who has all their assets in a single trust, for example, may allow children to benefit from the trust either before or after the wealth owner's death. Use of the assets by children can well expose the entire trust to being considered a 'marital asset'. Safer might well be to have a separate trust or other structure be the vehicle from which children receive funds, allowing larger amounts to be set aside for further generations and for other purposes in structures that are more likely to protect against marital and other claims.

For wealth owners investing in a variety of asset classes and in investments in different countries, having specially designed approaches for each asset class and investment destination can make sense, and bring efficiency (and speed) to the investment process. And of increasing importance is having a quick way to deal with the burden of compliance, and the many questions that have to be answered when bank accounts are opened or where funds are being dedicated to specific collective or individual investments.

Liquidity is a related need, and the structures adopted by families can affect how quickly assets can be mobilized for whatever purpose they are needed. Having funds tied up in complex structures that do not provide ready access may not be ideal if the investment objectives of the family suggest a need for quick decisions and ready access to funds.

Important in thinking about diversification of asset ownership structures is the question of whether it is also important to diversify who in the family owns the wealth of the family. This will depend on the circumstances, but diversifying ultimate ownership is also often a prudent thing to consider. If a wealth owner is sued for any reason, assets not owned by the wealth owner may be protected. If the wealth owner separated himself from ownership early on, by way of a gift or other transfer to the younger generation or to a properly established trust or insurance structure, perhaps real ownership diversification and asset protection can be achieved.

It is interesting that global tax approaches, such as that relating to the global minimum tax described in an earlier chapter, are also potential drivers of diversified ownership. For a family trust with the level of revenues that would trigger coverage by the global minimum tax rules, having the assets involved held in multiple trusts (a diversification of ownership) might well provide a legal way out of being in scope.

Tax-advantaged Investing

Dealing with tax is only one of many needs that families have and is an example of a need that is affected by countries of residence, citizenship and investment. An understanding of a family's tax position and the effect on tax exposures of where residence and citizenship are maintained and how investments are structured and located is critical. And in an increasingly transparent world, and one in which it is difficult to achieve meaningful and safe investment returns, tax-advantaged investing is becoming more and more important.

There are many facets to what tax-advantaged investing means, but in the simplest terms, to invest on a tax-advantaged basis involves focusing on the *after-tax* and not the pre-tax return on an investment. It is very easy to get into an investment, but often not enough attention is paid to the question of how one will exit from the investment, and what the tax consequences of this might be.

In measuring risk and return, the tax result will be highly relevant. Uncertainty as to how a country may tax investments is part of the evaluation of risk. Today, a number of emerging markets, including India and China, have been focusing on taxing the returns of foreign investors, and have been enforcing tax approaches that were not previously thought to apply. This uncertainty in tax treatment is clearly a risk factor that a well-advised wealth owner should be taking into account in working out what investments to make.

A good general example that can be made to highlight what tax-advantaged investing involves relates to investments that may be made into real estate. In the context of the United States, a non-US investor who is considering buying real estate can do this in any number of ways. They can buy the property in their individual name, they can set up a US company to own the property, they can use a non-US company to own the property or use a number of other structures including trusts, foundations or partnerships, and can even combine ownership approaches, perhaps having a non-US company that owns a US company make the investment. Financing of the purchase and how this is effected can also be one of the planning opportunities the investor has. All of these choices can dramatically impact the after-tax return, and relevant here will be not only how the United States taxes income generated from the real estate and any gains on a future sale, but also how the investor's home country will treat the investment.

So, where does the wealth owner begin in developing a tax-advantaged investing approach to a contemplated investment, say a real estate project as in the example set out above?

The first step is to understand the home-country tax position. If the wealth owner lives in a country that taxes on the basis of residence, and this tax is imposed on a worldwide basis, then a relevant question will be whether there is a credit or exemption for any foreign taxes that may arise given that the investment is being made in another country. Most countries that tax on a worldwide basis will provide such credit for foreign tax arising on a real estate investment, but obtaining the credit may require that the investor owns the real estate investment directly. In other words, if the investor owns a company that owns another company that owns the real estate, will the home country provide a tax credit on a dividend the wealth owner receives from proceeds of the investment if the actual tax paid to the country in which the real estate is located was paid by a holding company that is two tiers down the ownership chain?

Rather than tax credits, some countries provide exemptions for the foreign income involved, and while tax treaties can be important, in relation to real estate a treaty will usually confirm that the country in which the real estate is located (the United States in the example) has a first right to tax, with the country of residence of the investor having to provide a tax credit or other relief against possible double taxation.

Other differences in how the home country may tax the foreign investment will also be relevant, however, including whether there are CFC rules that would affect corporate ownership of the real estate, and whether there are other rules, at the home-country level, that dictate one form of ownership over another.

From the home-country perspective, the simplest scenario will be where the wealth owner lives in a country that does not impose tax, or which does not tax foreign income at all. In this case, the only focus in tax-advantaged investing will be the country of investment (the United States in the example). Focusing only on the rules of the United States, it might be easiest to have the individual own the property directly. But in the United States, in the case of foreigners owning US assets, such as real estate, exposure to US estate tax can arise, with significant potential tax on the value of the US assets owned by the individual at the date of death.

The US estate tax, which applies to the worldwide assets of US citizens and domiciliaries on death, only applies to US assets in respect of foreigners, but is a potentially expensive tax in that it does not focus on profits from an investment, but on the entire value of the investment itself. And while US citizens and domiciliaries enjoy large exemptions, meaning that only reasonably wealthy families actually pay the tax, for non-US persons not eligible for additional treaty benefits, the exemption available is limited to US$60,000 of US assets (a relatively small figure). With rates of inheritance tax that can, at the federal level, reach as high as 40% of the value of the investment (2024 rates), the 'after-tax' cost of the investment, taking into account estate tax alone, can be huge.

So clearly, for the investor, if the real estate to be purchased will be held for the longer term, the risk of estate tax arising because of the death of the investor has to come into the mix. Given the high rates of tax involved, avoiding, in a legal way, exposure to estate tax can be a key element of tax-advantaged investing. And this, in relation to the United States, is an issue not only for real estate, but also in respect of other US 'situs' assets, such as classic car collections kept physically in the United States, jewellery in safe deposit boxes in the United States and, most importantly, shares of US companies, including portfolio holdings of publicly listed US companies. With regard to the latter, estate tax treaties between countries can sometimes protect against US estate tax, but there are many circumstances where such treaties do not apply. And where investors own US shares in their portfolios, asset managers have been slow to remind the investors of their exposure to estate tax, a matter that will come under increasing focus and enforcement as the world moves to tax transparency and the United States is able to take action against banks and others who are involved in managing the assets of global wealth owners and who fail to encourage tax compliance.

So, avoiding estate tax in relation to the real estate investment may be an important objective for the wealth owner in the example. One possibility might be to consider leveraging the investment—and thereby ensuring that on death the value of the property is reduced by the mortgage outstanding on the property. This is a simple technique that many wealth owners use, and not just in relation to US real estate investments. Another possibility would be to not own the real estate directly, but through a non-US company. On death, the wealth owner would not die owning US real estate, which attracts US estate tax, but rather would die owning the shares of, say, a British Virgin Islands company that owns US real estate. In this case, as the British Virgin Islands does not tax on the death of an owner of British Virgin Islands company shares, no tax should arise. But, for this to work, the British Virgin Islands company has to be 'real' in the sense that it is not a sham. It is not enough to just 'wrap' the real estate in corporate ownership—the company needs to be respected as the real owner, and proper governance is therefore important—full and proper documentation at the corporate level of how the company obtained its funding, minutes of board and shareholder meetings showing the reality of the company, and much more. Ensuring the proper substance of the company is key to achieving the legal avoidance of US estate tax that is sought.

But in the context of the United States, corporate ownership, by a British Virgin Islands or other offshore company, may carry with it some negatives. If the real estate being invested in is income-producing, the British Virgin Islands company may be considered to have established a branch in the United States, attracting exposure to a 30% withholding tax on net profits (the 'branch tax'), even if those net profits are not remitted outside the United States. And unlike an individual owner of the property, who when selling the property at a profit is able to take advantage of substantially lower capital gains taxes that apply to individuals, a company pays the highest possible rates of capital gains taxes. So, these exposures also come into the mix in working out the best approach to use for the investment. Perhaps other structures, involving intermediate US holding companies that the British Virgin Islands company owns, the possible use of trusts or partnerships instead of corporate structures (given that they retain the possibility of individual tax rates) and otherwise, may need to be considered.

There is no question that, at the time the investment is made, it is easiest and cheapest to just invest and worry about tax issues later. The reality, however, is that once the real estate has been purchased, it becomes more costly to restructure ownership later. And the tax costs of not having considered the after-tax return and how this can be maximized can easily wipe out any gains, and possibly more, particularly if inheritance-type taxes come into the picture.

A simpler example of tax-advantaged investing involves focusing on withholding and capital gains taxes on portfolio investments, and the possible tax savings that can be achieved through reliance on a tax treaty. If I invest in a publicly listed company that is a US or Swiss company, and I am not a US resident for tax purposes (and not a US citizen), I can sell the shares at a profit with no tax, as neither Switzerland nor the United States tax capital gains on a sale of shares owned by foreigners. However, if I invest in companies that produce part of their return through dividends, I need to be mindful that both the United States and Switzerland (like many other countries) tax dividends paid to foreign shareholders by way of a withholding tax—in the case of the United States at a rate of 30% and in the case of Switzerland at a rate of 35% (at the time of writing). Similarly, if I invest in an interest-producing investment in Switzerland, I may be subject to a 35% withholding tax on the interest I receive, such as on a corporate bond. This withholding tax can have a significant impact on my after-tax return, even if I am living in a jurisdiction, say Hong Kong, that does not itself tax me on my foreign income.

If I use an intermediate company to own the investment, say in the British Virgin Islands or elsewhere, the withholding tax is a certainty, as the British Virgin Islands does not have any favourable tax treaties with the United States or Switzerland, the countries of investment in my example. If I am, however, a resident of Hong Kong, a tax treaty between Hong Kong and Switzerland can provide substantial tax savings. No equivalent treaty with the United States is in place, meaning that unlike my Swiss dividend and interest returns, which under the treaty could decline from 35% to 15% in the case of dividends and 0% in the case of interest, the withholding tax in the United States would remain at its 30% level, where it applies. Given the significant tax savings and enhancement of my after-tax return, it is critical for me to understand the after-tax position of investments in either the United States or Switzerland in order to make an informed choice as to which of the two countries to invest in. Looking at the after-tax return has to be added to the elements that make up the overall investment decision, including industry sector, currencies and other factors.

Importantly, coming out of the opaque world of hidden money, many asset managers do not pay attention to tax-advantaged investing, particularly where the wealth owner is a cross-border investor. To achieve the most tax-efficient means of investing, it is critical to take into account home-country tax exposures, tax exposures in the country in which investment structures are located and tax issues in the country of investment. This process is not one that many are able to manage effectively, and it is up to the wealth owner to raise the right questions in relation to investments to make sure that the after-tax return is what it can and should be.

Linked to an understanding of tax-advantaged investing is the ability of an asset manager to report investments and performance in a way that facilitates tax filings in relevant countries, including the home country of the investor. A major failing of many wealth managers is their inability to either provide a true tax-advantaged investing service, lacking the understanding of the three levels of tax that are often involved (the home country, the country in which an investment vehicle is located and the country of investment) and, linked to this, lacking the ability to handle the compliance involved, including tax reporting and applying for relevant withholding and other tax refunds. Global custodians holding shares for wealth owners offer a commodity business, at low margins, and do not generally do the work that has the potential to significantly add to returns.

Wealth management is a knowledge business, but sadly run by many who are more focused on their own interests than on the need to invest in and manage knowledge for the benefit of their clients. A wealth owner has little choice but to get a handle on what is relevant to their own situation and be in a position to ask the right questions that will lead them to the right advisors. And for the wealth manager who gets it right, the opportunity to excel and attract clients is significant.

Asset Protection and Preservation

The term 'asset protection' is a very broad one and covers many areas of need of all wealth-owning families. Dealing with tax efficiencies, protecting against the risks of divorce in the younger generation and many other areas already discussed involve asset protection. But another more specific area relates to creditor protection—keeping assets safe in the case of litigation and claims from potential creditors.

There are moral issues in and around the area of asset protection. Should a doctor who makes a mistake be able to protect some of his assets from claims by a patient who has been wronged? Should an owner of a chemical factory be able to shelter assets from claims if the chemicals end up polluting a river and affect the health of those living close by? Should a ship owner be able to protect himself against claims associated with an environmental disaster created by leakage from an oil tanker?

The world is increasingly litigious. In the United States and elsewhere, lawyers can work on contingency, meaning that they do not get paid unless they win. Litigation-funding firms are investing in legal disputes. Ambulance chasers advertise freely and widely, soliciting clients and encouraging them to *sue, sue, sue*. Directors of public companies are increasingly at risk of lawsuits from investors and others. How can and should a prudent wealth owner seek to protect himself?

There are a variety of ways that wealth owners can use structures, including trusts, insurance policies and other approaches, to help limit the risk that litigation will reach all assets. The main thing about asset-protection trusts and other structures is that they only really work if, after the structure is established, the founder remains solvent despite the transfers of assets that have been effected. What this generally means is that the asset-protection structure needs to be set up before and not after legal claims arise. As an example: a wealth owner has assets with a value of US$2,000,000, including investments in real estate, liquid assets in banks and otherwise. The wealth owner also owes money under mortgages and business loans that have been taken out, and debts total US$800,000. The wealth owner's net worth is therefore US$1,200,000, being the total of the assets owned, less the amounts that are owed. If the wealth owner makes a transfer to an asset-protection structure of less than US$1,200,000, after the transfer, the wealth owner remains solvent; if the transfer is more than US$1,200,000, the wealth owner has become insolvent through the transfer, and the asset-protection structure can easily be challenged as a fraud on creditors. More importantly, if the wealth owner in the example has not done any planning and has discovered that there is a possible claim against him, it may well be too late to avoid any transfers being considered to be fraudulent and subject to challenge. In other words, if the asset-protection structure is set up *after* there is reason for a claim to arise, it is much easier for the structure to be challenged by a claimant.

There is much more to effective asset protection, and this includes ensuring that the structure used, whether a trust or otherwise, is truly irrevocable and legally distances the wealth owner from the assets that have been transferred. Ideally, the wealth owner cannot himself benefit from the assets in the future, though a variety of approaches can allow ongoing influence over the assets involved and the possibility of the assets being used for his benefit at some point. But again, in simple terms, if a wealth owner has truly given assets away while solvent and before there are any claims, such as by way of an irrevocable gift to a trust that only his children can benefit from, the assets are no longer his, and in the event of a future claim, they may well be protected.

There are also practical issues that a well-thought-out asset-protection structure will take advantage of. If assets are located outside the country in which claims may arise, this in and of itself may make it more difficult for a future creditor to access them. Further protection may be afforded by laws in the country in which the asset-protection structure is located, such as rules that require that any claims be made within particularly short timeframes if a creditor is arguing that a transfer has been fraudulent. Some jurisdictions, like the Cook Islands, actively promote the asset-protection benefits of trusts created under their laws by making it difficult for foreign claimants to take action and by not enforcing a judgement that may be obtained in another country against the wealth owner involved, even in the case of bankruptcy. High burdens of proof for claimants apply, and as a result, the Cook Islands, and some other jurisdictions, have created an industry offering asset protection to those involved in high-risk professions or businesses.

While the notion of aggressive asset protection may well have a dark moral side, asset protection as a general matter is a need all wealth owners have. When dealing with succession planning, it is always good to also have an eye to asset protection, not only at the level of the wealth owner, but also at the level of the wealth owner's children and other successors, a much easier task. Again, a simple example: a wealth owner may have funds they plan to leave to their son, a surgeon practising in the United States. The wealth owner has grandchildren, but feels that it is easiest and best to just leave their assets to their son, and have him take care of how he would like to pass the assets on to his children. Once the wealth owner has passed away, the assets come into the ownership of the son. If a lawsuit arises and a valid claim is made against the son for malpractice, the assets will certainly be at risk, and any benefit to the grandchildren will be lost. If the wealth owner, instead, leaves part of their assets to their son, and another part to a structure, perhaps a trust, for the benefit of only the grandchildren, then the assets at risk in the event of a claim against the son will only be the assets the son actually has. Even if the trust set up for the grandchildren leaves it to the son to decide at what ages the grandchildren might benefit, so long as the assets clearly cannot fall into the son's ownership, asset protection has been achieved.

It is certainly easier not to think about all the possible risks to wealth that can arise, and just leave things to the younger generation to sort out. But in a complex world, this is not always the best way to go.

Art, Jewellery, Classic Cars and Other Valuable Special Assets

Almost all wealth-owning families have the need to address the specifics of the assets they have, and which will form part of what moves from one generation to the next.

Particular thought needs to be given by wealth owners to how assets such as jewellery, art and similar items are dealt with as part of an effective succession and asset-protection plan. There are many reasons why assets such as these need special attention, and among them is the reality that values, the location of assets and other issues can all be particularly problematic. This area represents a need of wealth-owning families that differs from one family to the next, the succession and asset-protection process having to adapt to the particular assets of an individual family.

When there is a liquid portfolio of assets under management, there is usually custody with a bank, and when there is a need for assets to pass to the next generation, while planning is needed, at least there is usually not a huge amount of difficulty finding the assets or knowing their value. But when Mum has an important collection of jewellery she is passionate about, her children (or spouse) may or may not know which of her pieces have what value, or even where they are. On death or disability, pieces may be stolen or lost, and often are.

Also problematic is where valuable items are physically located. In a number of countries, inheritance taxes arise if valuable moveable items, such as cars, art or jewellery, are located in the country involved. A wealth-owning family may live in a country that has no inheritance taxes, but if they keep valuables in the United Kingdom, the United States, Canada and many other countries, inheritance taxes can arise based on the fact that the assets involved are physically in a country that imposes an inheritance tax. Varying exemptions arise, but for valuable assets, the problem can be a very real one. Careful planning is important, and this sometimes involves ensuring that the asset is not in individual ownership, but rather held through some sort of structure, such as a properly established and administered company set up in a country that itself does not impose a tax on death.

If Mum, who is not a US citizen or domiciliary, owns valuable jewellery kept in a safety deposit box in the United States, estate tax will arise if on Mum's death the value of all her US assets exceeds US$60,000 (with some variations of the relevant amount depending on applicable estate tax treaties). Mum can avoid this tax by either keeping her jewellery in a safe box in a country that does not impose inheritance tax on the moveable assets of foreigners, such as would be the case in Switzerland, or by having the jewellery owned by a properly administered company formed outside the United States, perhaps in the British Virgin Islands or elsewhere, such that on her death the jewellery is not owned by her, but rather by the company, meaning that the assets passing on death are the shares of the company, a British Virgin Islands rather than US asset. US estate tax is thereby avoided. With a tax as high as 40% of the value of the assets involved at the federal level (state taxes, where they apply, can add to this), a meaningful amount of tax is involved.

Not thinking carefully through where valuables are kept can result in expensive mistakes, and for wealth-owning families that have homes in various places, the ownership of the homes may well have been well structured, with good advice obtained at the time of acquisition. But once the family begins furnishing the property, and bringing their artwork, jewellery and other collectibles into the homes, less thought may be given to the consequences (tax and otherwise) of this in the event of the passing of the wealth owner.

A number of other tax issues arise in relation to valuable items such as art and jewellery. Value-added taxes can be high, and when art (as an example) is brought into a country that charges such taxes on imports, this can be a significant cost. Lots of planning comes into addressing value-added taxes, including the type of entity that is used to own the art. There are also sometimes surprising other taxes that arise, including 'use' taxes in some US states. These excise taxes are similar to value-added taxes, and can be a problem when, for example, art is brought to a home a family may maintain in a state that imposes such taxes.

As with everything, there is much more to be considered than just tax. The distribution of family heirlooms, regardless of value, on the death of a wealth owner can be an extraordinarily emotional and divisive issue. If a parent has not made it clear who gets what when they pass away, how the children work it out may be a difficult process. Even worse is where the actual ownership of a family heirloom is not clear. Mum and Dad may have retired, and now spend time visiting their grandchildren, with regular visits to the homes of each child. Over time, they may leave family heirlooms and collectibles at the homes of their children—jewellery, art, whatever. On death, questions may arise as to whether the parent gave the item to the child in whose home the asset has been left. One child may think they own the item, the other may think the item should be considered part of all the assets their parent left to all children to divide. Something of relatively little value may become the cause of bad feelings and disputes.

It is much safer for wealth owners to consider, early on, how best to deal with special assets, taking into account tax and other issues and considering carefully what might happen if the wealth owner dies or becomes disabled. If whoever is intended to come into the ownership of the assets involved is unaware of their existence, value or location, real problems may well arise, including theft of the assets by staff or others, sales at significant undervalues and confusion as to the intention of the wealth owner in relation to how those meant to succeed to the ownership of the assets are meant to divide things up. It is certainly easier to just leave the problem to the younger generation to sort out, but this is not always a great thing to do if the objective is to help preserve values and family relationships.

I have had many clients with important family heirlooms that they have specific ideas about in terms of who should end up with them. Mother may have inherited jewellery from her own mother, and her intention may well be that only her granddaughters will get the jewellery—often thinking '*certainly not any of my daughters-in-law*'. Mother may then die prematurely, and under the approach taken by her in her estate planning, or under the relevant law if she has not done any planning, the jewellery comes into the ownership of her surviving husband. After a time, he falls into the clutches of a pretty young thing who ends up with all the jewellery on his death (if not well before), leaving out not only the daughters-in-law from benefit (who likely would have treasured the jewellery, protecting it for their own daughters), but everyone else in the family, including the granddaughters.

Political Risk

Political risk is an example of a need that is driven by the laws that impact a family, something that can arise through the residential or citizenship connections of the family, or by virtue of where investments owned by the family are maintained.

A first-generation Canadian, my parents had moved to Canada from Europe, escaping the destruction of the Second World War and the asset confiscations and other trials they had endured. Growing up in Canada, I saw political risk as a very distant and historical danger. In my legal studies, and in my initial work as a lawyer in New York, political risk was not something that formed part of what I was exposed to.

When I moved to Hong Kong in the early 1980s, I became aware of the underlying political risk that was a concern to wealth owners in Hong Kong and elsewhere in the region. In the run-up to 1997, the year in which Hong Kong was handed back to China by the United Kingdom, political risk came to the forefront in the thinking of wealth owners in Hong Kong and the international business community. One of the most capitalist places in the world, Hong Kong, was going to become part of one of the most communist places in the world, China. It was at this time that I began to become very involved in the asset-protection planning of those exposed to political risk.

But what is 'political risk'? In fact, there are many risks that a wealth owner is subject to that can fall under the heading of 'political' risk, including changes in the tax landscape—perhaps in part as a result of an increasing focus on income and wealth inequality. In the context of Hong Kong in the run-up to 1997, however, the main political risk that most people focused on was the question of whether private ownership of assets would be respected by China, which in the 1980s did not have much concept of such ownership in its own communist system.

Under international law, a country is viewed as being legally able to expropriate assets located within its borders. This reflects the sovereignty of countries, and the general principle that a country can make its own rules regarding who owns what. Expropriation of domestic assets is therefore something a country can validly do. As a general principle of international law, however, if the assets are owned by nationals of another country, compensation must be paid. The extent to which this general principle can be enforced, however, may be limited and will very much depend on times and circumstances.

So, in the context of Hong Kong, the general legal position under international law supported the main fear of wealth owners in the run-up to the handover of Hong Kong to China—as that as Chinese nationals, a wealth owner could find themselves subject to rules forbidding private ownership of assets, effectively resulting in confiscation. If the assets were not owned by foreigners, there would be no rights of compensation. Even where foreign ownership existed (say the ownership of Hong Kong assets through a non-Hong Kong company, or direct ownership by a wealth owner with foreign citizenship), it was by no means clear that compensation would be paid or whether such compensation would be fair if paid.

Because of the fear of confiscation, many international businesses restructured themselves, often using a corporate 'inversion'. The Jardine Matheson group, the Hong Kong and Shanghai Banking Corporation (now known as HSBC) and many others undertook this form of planning (interestingly, HSBC considered, but decided against, a return to Hong Kong as a corporate base given regulatory and tax advantages; political risk, however, likely remained a barrier to this).

Historically, many Hong Kong-based businesses began as Hong Kong companies. As the business expanded, global subsidiaries would appear beneath a Hong Kong holding company, and eventually complex global structures developed with Hong Kong parent companies owning many subsidiaries and affiliates both in Hong Kong and outside. For public companies, the Hong Kong parent company would be the listed vehicle; for private companies, the Hong Kong parent company would be a holding vehicle owned by the wealth-owning family.

If China were to expropriate or confiscate assets in Hong Kong, the fear was that the Hong Kong holding companies would themselves be taken over and that the new government would then control all the global subsidiaries and other assets involved, the expropriation or confiscation thereby extending beyond Hong Kong borders.

Through corporate 'inversions', this risk was, supposedly, addressed. In the case of the Hong Kong and Shanghai Banking Corporation, the new holding company of HSBC became a UK company, with the Hong Kong operations of the bank becoming a subsidiary, theoretically limiting the risk of an expropriation or confiscation in Hong Kong to only the Hong Kong operations. In the case of the Jardine Matheson group and many others, the new holding company became a Bermuda company with, again, all the foreign operations of the group owned through that holding company rather than suffering the risk of being owned by a Hong Kong parent company.

Corporate inversions are, however, only part of effective political risk-minimization planning. Given that a country is, under international law, effectively allowed to confiscate the assets of its own nationals, if the individual owner of a corporate group established outside the risk country (again, say Hong Kong) is himself living in Hong Kong, could the government not confiscate the shares of the overseas holding company the wealth owner has an interest in? While the foreign country in which the holding company is based may not recognize a confiscation, the answer is generally yes, meaning that for real protection, the ownership of companies outside the risk country should be set up in a way that reduces risks. Ideally, after the corporate inversion, the wealth owner transfers his interest in the foreign holding company to a structure that cuts off his ownership, thereby making it difficult for a confiscation to be achieved. In simple terms, the wealth owner no longer owns the foreign holding company, and now its shareholder is an appropriately formulated trust, foundation, insurance policy or other structure outside the risk country, which is designed to cut off the ownership of assets by someone living in a country that may be subject to a confiscation order.

Planning of this kind can be very sophisticated, but achievable, and surprisingly—in a world where political risk features—very little attention is actually paid to this area by wealth owners, despite the fact that they often invest or live in troubled countries.[7]

There is also another level of political risk that is even less well considered than the risk of asset confiscation. In some countries, like the United States, there are rules that allow action to be taken against 'enemies' of the country. This action can include freezing or vesting orders that can either tie up the assets of an 'enemy' or actually allow the US government to take them away. When the US-supported Shah of Iran fell, the United States froze the assets of Iran and of Iranian citizens in the United States. Wealthy Iranians who had put assets in the United States with American banks, thinking that this was a way to increase the safety of their assets, found their assets frozen and were forced to go through difficult and costly litigation to recover them. During the Noriega crisis, when the United States was seeking to arrest Manuel Noriega, the drug-dealing leader of Panama, President George Bush (the older, smarter one) threatened to freeze the assets of Panama and Panamanians if Noriega was not handed over. At the time, I had several clients in the shipping industry, many of whom used Panamanian companies to not only own their ships, but also own their personal real estate in the United States. I had a number of frantic calls from clients asking if their home in California or their apartment in Manhattan, owned by a Panamanian company, might be frozen if the crisis continued. The answer was yes.

The younger President George Bush (the less clever one), at the time of the Iraqi crisis, used his powers to vest, or take away, the US assets of Iraq and Saddam Hussein and his family.

Today, sanctions come and go over perceived 'enemies' of the United States and other countries, affecting a wealth owner's access to assets. While these sanctions may often be appropriate, caught in the net can be assets of innocent wealth owners seeking to protect their wealth from an unstable or immoral government.

The ability of a country to freeze or vest assets belonging to 'enemies' is another level of political risk. In my example of the concerns of Hong Kong wealth owners in the run-up to 1997, the year of the handover of Hong Kong to China, had China actually confiscated privately owned assets in Hong Kong, what would the consequence have been of a confiscation of the Citibank building on Garden Road or of any other US-owned assets? Could the United States have retaliated by seizing a Chinese-owned airplane landing in Los Angeles? Could the United States have frozen the US assets of Hong Kong families and businesses? The answer is 'possibly', and from a planning perspective, using approaches designed to cut off ownership by family members who may be in states subject to freezing or vesting orders is another element of good political risk planning.

But what of assets located in a country that itself may be troubled? One approach that can sometimes be taken is to leverage the assets involved—borrowing on the security of the assets, effectively passing the risk of expropriation or other actions to the lender. Usually this is not overly practical, however, as in situations of political unrest lenders are aware of the risk and insist on personal guarantees and other security. Other steps can, however, be taken in a similar vein, such as avoiding cash accumulations at the corporate level, and otherwise. Political risk insurance is also an option, and this is sometimes available privately or in combination with public variations of such insurance, the latter largely designed to encourage investment in developing countries. Adopting investment structures that allow access to such protection, where it exists, can be important as publicly available political risk insurance may be restricted to policy owners from particular countries or who make use of particular investment approaches.

Investment-protection agreements, and their use, also suffer from insufficient attention. Investment-protection agreements are usually bilateral agreements between countries (although there are increasingly multilateral agreements that come into play), and what they provide for are clear rules that require compensation in the event of a confiscation or under-compensated expropriation. Most importantly, this is combined with clarity on dispute resolution, with independent arbitration being provided for. While one may have uncertainty as to whether a treaty of this kind would be respected, it is worth considering that certain countries, such as the United States, may be in a particularly strong position to enforce such agreements, given the American assets most countries own, including US treasury bills and other financial instruments. So, if I am not an American, and am investing in a country with political risk, should I do so using a British Virgin Islands or other offshore company, given that the entity is tax-free? Or should I ask whether the British Virgin Islands has an investment-protection agreement with the country in which I am investing? And not surprisingly, many of the 'pure' offshore tax havens, like the British Virgin Islands, have very few, if any, investment-protection agreements. But if I use a US company, say a Limited Liability Company (LLC), to make the investment, I may well be able to avoid any US tax arising, given the 'flow-through' treatment of an LLC, while accessing the US investment-protection agreement with the country I am investing in. Singapore, and many other 'midshore' (as opposed to offshore) tax havens can also provide benefits of this kind. There will be a need for substance if an intermediate investment company is being used and many other considerations to ensure that the relevant investment-protection agreement can work, but the role of such agreements in political risk minimization must not be underestimated. Citizenship of ultimate beneficial owners, among others, can also become relevant under these agreements and be part of an overall political risk-minimization plan.

It is generally easy to make an investment, but all too often not enough attention is paid to the risks of the investment, and how one will eventually exit. The time to think about this is in advance, as it is cheaper and easier to address tax, political risk and other issues when setting things up for the acquisition, rather than later in the process.

Also relevant in any investment is the governing law and applicable forum of the contracts used. When capital levies were imposed in Cyprus, bonds of Cypriot banks lost their value ... but those bonds that were issued under UK law and non-Cypriot forum rather than under Cypriot law and jurisdiction fared much better, with those holders being favoured. Ensuring that a foreign court with a solid and dependable judicial system and applicable laws will deal with any potential political risk event can be critical to managing things.

Capital levies imposed by Cyprus, a clear form of part-confiscation, were actually branded 'taxes' by many. In my thinking, a tax is something you know about in advance, and which can form part of a decision on whether and where to invest. It is a clear form of political risk where a country imposes an unexpected tax without warning, and it is interesting that the notion of capital levies is one that has received favourable attention from commentators focused on ways of addressing debt levels of countries and perceived growing inequality of income and wealth. Thomas Piketty, in his writings, refers to capital levies as a means of collecting revenues from those who should pay, and his suggestion of this form of 'tax' (again, nothing more than a part-confiscation of assets) was picked up by commentators that included the IMF (which then backed down on the reference to capital levies as an appropriate fiscal tool) and the German Bundesbank.

Tax changes, however, are a clear form of political risk, and it is unfortunate to see countries not appreciating that constant changes in the tax laws affect how investors evaluate the risk of investing in the country involved. As an investor, I want to be able to know upfront how much tax an exit from the investment will result in. India and many other countries have, of late, created great uncertainty among foreign investors given changing interpretations and enforcement of tax laws. Even the United Kingdom, given constant changes to how foreigners are taxed in respect of their UK real estate interests, is clearly a country of political risk for wealth owners who need certainty in order to plan their affairs.

Addressing political risk will be an increasing need of wealth-owning families. The current focus on income and wealth inequality, increasing populism in the political sphere and the difficult financial position of many countries is increasing risk, and not only in parts of the world one normally thinks of as unstable.

Security and Kidnapping Risks

Depending on the countries to which a family is connected, as well as other factors, security and kidnapping risks may be of particular relevance. Safety and security are, of course, issues relevant to all families, but geography and circumstances will certainly have an impact on the priority with which the area needs to be considered.

A very wealthy family invited me to their family home for a meeting. Living about ninety minutes from the airport I travelled to, I was picked up by the family chauffeur in a lovely comfortable car. I settled myself into the back seat, opened my briefcase and removed papers, getting ready to do some work during the journey. I chatted with my driver, and soon became so engrossed in our conversation that I put all my papers away and spent the entire journey learning about the security world.

My driver was actually not only the family chauffeur, but also the head of security for the family. A retired member of the UK security forces, my driver explained to me that he was a member of a small group of specialists, most with similar backgrounds, working for families at the higher end of the wealth spectrum. We had a wide-ranging discussion, and among the many things he shared with me was the fact that kidnapping is not something that only takes place in developing countries, but is actually an ongoing problem in many more unexpected places in the world, including the United Kingdom, Japan and elsewhere. He explained that one of the biggest challenges for those involved with ensuring the security of the families they serve is where kidnappers are not professionally organized, his view being that at least with 'professional' kidnappers, there is an ability to go through an almost accepted routine in the event of a kidnap. First, he explained, is to require 'proof of life'—evidence that the person you are negotiating the return of is actually still alive. Second, demands for ransoms are often way out of proportion to what will actually be accepted, and there is a process of negotiation that precedes coming to the right figure. And in many, many cases, at least according to the person I was having the discussion with, the authorities are either not involved or are very much on the sidelines in the process, the decision on whether to bring the authorities into the picture very much depending on the country involved. In some, it is the authorities who are themselves potentially linked to the kidnappers.

Our discussion covered many areas, including the important training security consultants can provide to family members about how they should act, and how they can stay out of trouble. In the case of one family that I worked with a number of years ago, they brought security specialists into a family retreat—a meeting of the family designed to review financial, succession and other matters. The security specialists led a discussion on security, and how family members could avoid danger—and for the relevant family, this included coverage of danger in England, where some of the children were studying, dangers in Pakistan, where the family owned businesses and spent time, and in other locations to which the family had ties. In Pakistan, the family was warned to take different routes from their home to their places of business, staying away from routine journeys that could be monitored and be part of a kidnap plan; the younger generation studying in England were warned about keeping a low profile—how to dress, how to interact with others and how to deal with problems if they arise. For many families, reviewing issues in and around personal safety and security to seek to avoid anything happening is most worthwhile.

Over the years, a question I have often asked myself is what happens when there is a kidnapping and a family does not have a pre-existing understanding of what to do and who to call. And what if the person kidnapped is the matriarch or patriarch, who her or himself knows where the available funds are and otherwise is in a position to make decisions. If an unprepared spouse or child is contacted by a kidnapper and told '*if you want to see your husband alive, we want $5 million by tomorrow, and if you call the police, he will die ...*', what does the recipient of the call do? Will the threat regarding what happens if the authorities are contacted be acted upon? How will the $5 million be obtained if the wealth owner is himself the one kidnapped?

What I encourage families to consider is to hire security consultants as part of their overall review of asset protection and succession. With the right expertise upfront, the family is better equipped to know how to avoid problems and, importantly, how to react and who to call if there are problems. And sometimes related to this is ensuring that there are funds available, perhaps in trust or otherwise, that can be accessed if needed in relation to a ransom request. Kidnapping insurance is another option, though one that some families evidence concern about, given the disclosure of information that obtaining the insurance can require.

Do I Need Separate Structures for All These Things?

Wealth-owning families face many potential derailers, and my summary of some of these reflects only a portion of the needs families have given the special issues that arise in particular families, and the needs driven by the nature of their businesses and investments, where they live and invest, and much more. But does this mean that the family needs separate planning and structures to address each of their needs? The answer is that how assets are held, and succession and asset protection is planned, should ideally be holistic, with each structure reflecting all the needs of the family.

The same trust that is used to achieve a tax benefit for the family should be the trust that achieves political risk and asset protection, and which provides for the governance that is set out in the family constitution, if there is one in place. Interestingly, when a structure is designed to address more than one objective, the structure becomes a stronger one from many perspectives. In a number of jurisdictions, tax laws may allow for a challenge to favourable tax results where an ownership structure has been specifically designed to obtain tax benefits. Where a structure is set up with the sole purpose of protecting the assets from creditors, this may make it easier for the structure to be challenged in the event of claims being made. Where the structure can be shown to have been set up for many valid reasons, this may well help the structure achieve the asset protection and tax benefits sought.

This said, as part of good planning in today's world, I am a believer in some diversification of ownership structures and approaches.

If I go to a good investment advisor, there is one thing pretty much every advisor will say: The investment world is an uncertain one, and diversification in investments is key to long-term safety and growth of assets. In the case of the structures families use to own their assets, there is actually little thought given to diversification. In some families, all assets are simply owned by Dad, and the expectation is that Dad will do the right thing and eventually pass the assets to Mum if he predeceases, and to the next generation otherwise. But what if Dad is sued—the entirety of the assets are then at risk. What if Mum predeceases, and Dad ends up in the clutches of a new, gold-digging spouse? Would Mum have wanted her share of the family assets to end up going to the new spouse's children from her previous marriage rather than to her own children? If all the assets of the family are in one single trust, and distributions are made, tax authorities in a number of countries have the right to see everything that is in the trust.

Where assets are divided in different, well-thought-through ownership structures, the benefits of ownership diversification can be achieved, something that in my experience is not sufficiently discussed and considered.

Notes

1. As mentioned in an earlier note, the notion of a 'family bank' was introduced in Chapter 7 of the first edition of *Family Wealth: Keeping it in the Family* and reprised in the second edition published by the publishers of this book. Hughes, J. (Jay) E. Jr., *Family Wealth: Keeping It in the Family – How Family Members and Their Advisers Preserve Human, Intellectual, and Financial Assets for Generations* (2nd Revised and Expanded Edition) (Wiley, 2010). Jay reminded me that the idea of a family bank was one developed by Jay's father and which Jay then used in his further research and writing.
2. Stefan Liniger, the co-founder of a Swiss trust company, Conduct, reminded me about the importance of the investment policy statement. I have used his words, for the most part, in addressing how the IPS can usefully form part of a family constitution.
3. Jed Emerson is respected as the originator of the concept of 'blended-value' investing (see https://www.blendedvalue.org/blog). Among Emerson's books on this and related topics is Bugg-Levine, A. and Emerson, J., *Impact Investing: Transforming How We Make Money While Making a Difference* (Wiley, 2011).
4. See https://www.sfct.org.uk/#:~:text=About%20SFCT,supermarkets%20(J%20Sainsbury%20plc)
5. See https://kbs-frb.be/en/transnational-giving-europe
6. As mentioned, Jed Emerson has written several books on blended value, impact investing and otherwise, all very much worth a read. His more recent book is Emerson, J., *The Purpose of Capital: Elements of Impact, Financial Flows and Natural Being* (Blended Value Group Press, 2018).
7. A recent article on the subject of political risk minimization that I collaborated on with Hussein Haeri, KC and Iraj Ispahani appeared in the May 2024 Newsletter of the Hong Kong branch of the Society of Trust and Estate Practitioners. A version of that article is Haeri, H., Ispahani, I. and Marcovici, P., *A Brave New World? Political Risk Minimisation for Wealth and Business Owners* http://philipmarcovici.com/wp-content/uploads/2023/10/White-Paper-Political-Risk-Minimisation-October-2023-1-1.pdf

CHAPTER 7

Bridges and Tunnels—Using the Tools of Wealth Planning to Navigate the Derailers

If, while reading this book, you suddenly hear a rush of water and find that a pipe in your home has burst, you will call a plumber. The plumber arrives at your home not with just one tool, say a wrench, but with an entire toolbox containing screwdrivers, wrenches, hammers, pliers and many others. In succession and asset-protection planning, there is also a toolbox, and there is no one tool that addresses the needs of every family. It is often the case that many of the tools of wealth planning are used for the same wealth-owning family, and some of the tools might be mixed together to bring the best result.

This chapter discusses only some of the many wealth planning tools that are commonly used. Effective planning requires that the family understand the tools that are in place in relation to their wealth, at least such as to allow them to be in a position to ask the right questions of their advisors and other service providers.

I refer to these tools as *tunnels and bridges,* linking their use to the *Theory of Change* and the idea that good planning starts with knowing the destination—what are we trying to achieve? And once the destination is clear, we work back to where we are and develop the roadmap to the destination. In order to get there, it will be key to identify the *tunnels and bridges* that can overcome the derailers—the many things, internal and external to the family, that can negatively impact the family's ability to get to where it wants to go.

Wills

The laws of most countries provide for some form of will, or testament, that can be used by a wealth owner to set out how their assets will pass in the event of their death. Wills can, in a number of cases, also be used to determine the laws that apply to an estate. The European Union Succession Regulation is a good example of this.

If a wealth owner dies without a will, something will still happen to their assets, but here the succession will be determined by the relevant law, which may or may not be the law of the deceased's residence, domicile or nationality, particularly if some of the assets are located outside of that country.

Wills are useful, as no matter what additional approaches are taken in the succession plan, it is pretty inevitable that there will remain assets in the personal ownership of the wealth owner at the time of their death.

For a will to be valid, care must be taken that the formalities for executing a will are properly followed pursuant to the law that is relevant. Many countries require that wills have at least two witnesses who are in each other's presence at the time of execution. This said, a will that is not witnessed is, in a number of countries, valid if it is a 'holographic' will—a will that is handwritten and not typed.

If the wealth owner has an interest in assets outside of his home country, consideration might be given to having a further will that is drafted under the law of the country where the assets are located. But here care needs to be taken to ensure that the two wills—that of the home country and that of the country where the investment is located—fit together, something often achieved by having each will reference the other, and having the home-country will cover all assets other than those covered by the second will, which specifically covers the asset(s) in the country of the investment.

Where a home-country will covers assets outside the home jurisdiction, after the will is proven to be the deceased's last will, usually under a procedure known as probate, the will can then be proven as valid in other countries in which the deceased may have owned assets. These procedures can take time and be costly, and it is for this reason that some of the other tools of wealth planning can come into the picture, such as trusts, foundations, insurance policies and others. In most cases, wills provide for immediate distribution of assets, and for the appointment of an executor, the person responsible to follow through and ensure that the instructions contained in the will are followed. An executor has a high level of responsibility, and this includes, in many cases, responsibility to ensure that taxes which are due are properly paid, sometimes including past income taxes the deceased may have failed to pay. Being an executor is something that should not be taken lightly, and when drafting a will and choosing an executor, understanding the personal liability that an executor has is important for the wealth owner—who may not have in mind that the executor will, to protect himself, declare to tax authorities any taxes that the wealth owner had decided to illegally evade.

But as with any involvement of advisors, friends or family members who may be appointed to look after things if the wealth owner is unable to, there is a need to consider whether there is appropriate oversight in place in relation to the executor, and an ability for the family to ensure that the executor is not abusing their position.

At the time of writing my earlier book, *The Destructive Power of Family Wealth*, a dispute was in progress in relation to the will of Leona Helmsley, the widow of New York real estate tycoon, Harry Helmsley. The New York State Attorney General argued, on behalf of charities benefiting under Leona Helmsley's will, that the fees charged by four executors (two of her grandchildren from her first marriage, and her lawyer and a business advisor) were out of line—a reported US$100 million, representing an hourly rate of US$6437 for their work, which the executors argued was extraordinarily complex. Since that time, the courts ruled and confirmed that the compensation of the executors could stand despite the objections of the New York Attorney General's office, which had found the compensation exorbitant and wanted to see it reduced by 90%. In confirming the appropriateness of the US$100 million fee, the court indicated that hourly rates could not properly reflect the efforts and challenges involved.

As mentioned earlier in this book, there is no client better than a dead client. For Leona Helmsley, widely reported as being a particularly unpleasant individual, her executors seem to have been given more power than they should have been in relation to their ability to charge—and this is only one element of the 'checks and balances' that any appointment of an executor under a will should be subject to.

In the case of younger wealth owners, particularly those with children, there are questions they should be considering in the use of wills given that in the event of death, the beneficiaries may be of a very young age. At what age is it appropriate for the younger generation to receive a significant amount? Is it helpful for an 18-year-old to come into millions? And if there are even younger children in the picture, who will look after the money until they come of age? A will can provide for a trust to be created to protect vulnerable beneficiaries, and often the trustee will be the person appointed as the executor. Particular care in choosing an executor and providing for succession in the role is needed if the will creates a trust. And if there is no one appointed to the role, or if there is no will, perhaps the relevant court will appoint close family members to take charge of assets. In the context of your family, is this what you want? Is it safe to rely on those who would come into this position of power? What if a trusted godparent or sibling who has the role of 'looking after' the children of someone dying young gets into personal financial difficulty? Will they be tempted to abuse their position?

As with all the tools of wealth planning, checks and balances are key. It is possible to consider having more than one executor, and depending on the family, there are ways to ensure that there is at least one person in the family who knows what the deceased wealth owner had in mind and can keep an eye on things being done as intended, and as the will provides. And as with all wealth planning, wills need regular review as assets change, the regulatory world changes and families change.

Marriage, under the laws of many, but not all, countries invalidates wills—not remembering this when starting a new life, and perhaps remarrying, can result in startlingly different results than expected. If I leave my assets to my children under my will, and then remarry, if I die without a new will, depending on the relevant law, my new wife may get far more in the way of a share of my assets than I would have wanted given the short time of our marriage.

In a typical will, the person making the will sets out specific assets they want to go to specific beneficiaries. This allows for clarity on who gets what family heirlooms, and can be an important element of planning that avoids the misunderstandings a lack of clarity of intention can result in. Remaining assets are then often divided into particular shares, and wills are fairly flexible in the detail that can be provided. In addition to directly benefiting family members, a will can also direct that certain assets pass to other wealth planning structures, such as a trust that may already be in place or which may be created by the will itself.

Trusts

Trusts can be very confusing tools in the wealth planning toolbox, given their flexibility and the many different kinds of trusts that can be established. But this variety and flexibility make trusts a very useful succession and asset-protection tool.

Trusts are creatures of the common law, first developed in England and adopted by most common law countries, such as Canada, the United States, Hong Kong and the many offshore centres whose laws track English law, for historical or other reasons. Adding to the confusion associated with trusts is that civil law countries, like Switzerland, Liechtenstein and others, seeking to compete with jurisdictions offering trusts, have developed laws that allow trusts to be established in their countries, despite the lack of a common law legal system.

Common law countries have generally been clear about the tax treatment of trusts. While the relevant rules are, like all tax rules, constantly changing, countries like the United Kingdom, Canada, the United States and many others have long had tax and related reporting rules covering most uses of trusts. More recently, civil law countries have joined in clarifying the tax treatment of trusts, with civil law countries such as Denmark, Italy, France and Switzerland being examples of countries which have done this. Often the tax clarity treats trusts as transparent for tax purposes, but in many cases, trusts that are well thought out can provide meaningful tax benefits. Sometimes, such as in relation to France, the use of trusts might be tax inefficient given the heavy-handed treatment accorded to them by the tax authorities.

An increased focus on trusts by tax authorities has led some to believe that trust use is on the decline, and some trust companies have even been sold by their bank owners because of a misguided notion that the main reason families use trusts is to hide the money and illegally evade tax. The reality, however, is that trusts provide many important benefits in the succession and asset-protection process, and that even where no tax benefits are achieved, the trust may be at the centre of a well-thought-out succession and asset-protection plan. And well-planned trusts can provide many legal and appropriate means of managing tax exposures, particularly in complex situations.

A trust is a relationship, not a legal entity. When I set up a company, that company is itself a legal person, and I can open a bank account, for example, in the name of the company. When I establish a trust, I am the settlor, or founder of the trust, and I transfer assets to a trustee, which can be an individual or a trust company. When I transfer my assets, I am taking advantage of something that the common law provides for (and which civil law generally does not), which is to reflect the divisibility of the ownership of an asset between its *legal* ownership and its *beneficial* ownership. If I own a pen, I am both its legal owner and its beneficial owner. This means that I can sell the pen or give it away, and I can also benefit from the pen, using it to write and consuming the ink it contains. If I transfer the pen to a trustee and provide that the trustee should hold the pen for my benefit during my lifetime and for the benefit of my children after my death, I am dividing the legal and beneficial ownership. The trustee becomes the legal owner of the pen, with the ability to sell or gift the pen—subject to what the trust arrangement provides. But the trustee is not allowed to benefit from the pen, as the trustee is not the beneficial owner. The beneficial owners of the pen, in my example, include me during my lifetime, and then my children. If the trustee benefits from the pen, the beneficial owners can sue and win unless the trust document allows the trustee to benefit, such as in relation to the fees the trustee charges, and which it can take from the trust assets to pay themselves.

The division of legal and beneficial ownership is very useful in succession and asset-protection planning, and in relation to tax planning, as when I set up the trust, I separate myself from the legal ownership of the asset. But more on this a bit later.

Once legal ownership passes to the trustee, it is the trustee who owns the asset. Sometimes confusing is the fact that a trust is not a legal entity. This means that it is not the trust that owns the asset, but rather the trustee. I may have called the trust 'The Pen Trust', but there really is no such legal entity. If the trustee wants to open a bank account, the trustee cannot do so in the name of The Pen Trust, as there is no legal person with that name in existence. Rather, the bank account has to be opened in the name of the trustee, who can, but does not have to, reference The Pen Trust, having the account be in the name of the trustee as trustee of The Pen Trust.

The fact that no legal entity is created means that the liabilities of a trustee are high. While trust documentation is often designed by trustees to limit their liability, trustees are themselves the owners of the assets, and if there are lawsuits associated with them, the trustee will be in the firing line. Trustees also have a high level of responsibility to the beneficiaries of a trust, owing their primary responsibilities to them.

Technically, trusts, other than trusts involving land, do not need to be in writing. As a practical matter, the trusts used by wealth owners are always in writing and can take a number of different forms in terms of how they are documented. Most common is a trust deed, a document that sets out the name of the creator of the trust, the settlor and also the name of the trustee. An alternative is a declaration of trust—this is a document that reflects the declaration of a trust by a trustee, signed only by the trustee, and which does not necessarily name the settlor. It is less common to use a declaration of trust today given the many reporting requirements associated with the use of trusts and the need to document those connected to it, but the declaration of trust is part of the flexibility associated with how trusts can be created and documented.

The parties to a trust include the settlor and the trustee, both already mentioned. But it is worth pointing out that the flexibility of trusts makes it possible for persons other than the settlor to also contribute assets to the trust. I can have a friend establish The Pen Trust by contributing US$5 to the trustee and signing the trust deed as settlor. The trustee then accepts the settlement monies, and in the relevant documentation, provision is made for the trustee having the power to accept other assets from other people. I can then contribute my valuable pen to the trustee to hold pursuant to the terms of The Pen Trust. I do not have to sign the trust deed, and my name may not appear as settlor. Broadly, what has occurred is that there is a nominee settlor, my friend who contributed the US$5 to establish the trust. I, however, am the 'economic settlor', albeit not named. The tax laws of most countries understand the possibility of this approach, and focus on the economic settlor and the assets the economic settlor contributes to the trust.

In addition to the settlor and the trustee, the other parties to the trust are the beneficiaries. The trustee, as mentioned, owes its primary duties to the beneficiaries, and this can sometimes be of concern to a settlor who thought that they could call the shots.

Once the assets are transferred, unless the trust arrangement provides otherwise, the settlor will find that the trustee's focus is on its obligations to the beneficiaries—a good thing in the protection of trust assets, but an important thing for a control freak settlor to understand before the trust is established.

There is also an optional additional party that many trust arrangements include, and that is a 'protector' or 'guardian', whose functions are usually provided for in the trust deed and provide a check on the trustee. It is common for the protector to have the ability to remove and replace the trustee, and to provide input on certain actions of the trustee, such as a decision to make distributions.

There are many kinds of trusts, and much to be said about the rights of beneficiaries, the liabilities of trustees, trust documentation and otherwise. Many resources are available to wealth owners and their advisors who seek to learn more about trusts, but I will focus on four characteristics of trusts that can be fundamental to understanding how trusts can and do work to address many of the needs of wealth-owning families: *revocable, irrevocable, fixed* and *discretionary*. Understanding these terms and how they work can go a long way in helping one to understand trusts and how they can be used.

When a settlor creates a trust, a first choice that the settlor has is whether to have the trust be revocable or irrevocable. In the case of a revocable trust, the settlor has a legal right to revoke (or cancel) the trust, with the right to require the trustee to return the trust assets to the settlor. The opposite is an irrevocable trust, where the settlor does *not* retain the legal right to get the assets back. In the latter case, the settlor may be a potential beneficiary and still have an ability to benefit, but there would be no legal right to cancel the trust and force the trustee to return the trust assets.

If I ask a typical client whether they prefer a trust that they can cancel and require the return of assets from, as against a trust where the trustee may or may not have to give the assets back if there is a change of mind, most clients will say they absolutely want a revocable trust. Not so fast. What if the wealth owner owns a chemical factory, and is concerned that future risks may arise from legal claims related to pollution associated with seepage of chemicals or otherwise? If the trust is revocable, and the wealth owner has a right to get the assets that he transferred to the trustee back, it will not be at all difficult for a claimant to access the trust assets in the event of a successful lawsuit. But if the trust were established on an irrevocable basis, with no legal right for the settlor to get the assets back, the position would be very different—particularly if, at the time the trust was settled, there were no legal claims against the settlor in the offing, and the settlor remained solvent after settling the trust.

Another choice that the settlor has is to have the trust provide for fixed beneficial interests or for the trust to be discretionary. For example, I can settle a trust and require that the trustee, when each of my children reaches the age of twenty-one, divide the trust assets and give half to each. In the case of a fixed interest of this kind, if the trustee does not give my son half the trust assets when he reaches the age of twenty-one, my son can sue the trustee and succeed in recovering his share of the trust assets. The alternative to a fixed trust is a discretionary trust, where the trustee can decide who to give the assets to in the trustee's 'discretion'. In this kind of arrangement, the trust deed, which provides for the discretion the trustee has, is often accompanied by a non-binding record of the settlor's wishes, either in a letter of wishes from the settlor, in a memorandum the trustee makes of the settlor's wishes, or otherwise.

I can therefore create the trust and provide that the trustee has discretion regarding when and if any beneficiary will benefit and then supplement this with a letter of wishes setting out my thinking. In my letter of wishes, I can confirm that the trustee has full discretion and that the expression of wishes is non-binding, but I can ask that the trustee, in exercising its discretion, consider distributing the trust assets to each of my children, in equal shares, when they reach the age of twenty-one. In this case, if the trustee does not exercise its discretion in favour of my son when he reaches the age of twenty-one, my son cannot generally force the trustee to hand over the assets, as the trustee has no fixed obligation to do so, having discretion as to whether to follow the letter of wishes.

If I ask trust settlors whether they want a trust under which their children can sue if the trustee does not hand assets over at a designated age as against a trust where the trustee only pays out 'if they feel like it', most will think that what they want is a fixed trust, where their child can sue to get the assets at the relevant time. Again, not so fast. What if my son marries the sleazy girl down the street and around the time of his coming of age to receive trust assets, the marriage is in difficulty and divorce claims may arise? The assets may well be much safer against a divorce claim if my son does not have a legal right to the trust assets—the same in relation to a claim for medical malpractice if my son is a doctor and in relation to other potential claims.

Tax laws, of course, differ from country to country, and how trust interests and transactions are taxed depends on the law that applies. There are, however, some general approaches to the taxation of trusts that track, in a logical way, the legal and economic difference between a revocable and an irrevocable trust and a fixed and a discretionary trust.

If I own an asset that today has a very low value and live in a country that has both a tax on gifts and a tax that arises on my death, if I believe the asset will increase in value over time, will my family benefit more from my creation of a revocable trust or from an irrevocable trust? Generally, a transfer of the asset to a revocable trust will not attract a tax, as my right to revoke means that I have not made a completed gift—I have the right to get the asset back so, in effect, I still own the asset. While it may seem like good news that there is no tax on the transfer of the asset to the trust, my continued ownership of the asset may well mean that I am not only taxable on income generated by the asset (despite its being held in trust), but that when I die, and the asset is worth much more, inheritance tax will then apply. Once I die, I lose my ability to revoke, and the transfer becomes complete. If, on the other hand, I transfer the asset to an irrevocable trust, the gift is complete and gift tax will apply, but on the value of the asset today, which is much lower than the value it will have in the longer term. By the time I die, the asset may be worth much more, but no inheritance tax will apply as I gave the asset away a long time ago.

If the trust in my example is a fixed trust, then the ownership of the asset, from a tax perspective, is often attributed to the beneficiary or beneficiaries with the fixed right to the asset. This might mean that income from the asset is taxable to them and that if they pass away, an inheritance tax will arise. If the trust is discretionary, and the beneficiary has no direct legal interest in the asset, there may well be no income tax to the beneficiary on income on the asset, and no inheritance tax if the beneficiary dies. In some countries, tax is avoided unless and until there is a distribution to a beneficiary, and even then tax may be reduced or avoided. In other countries, rules may attribute the income to someone involved in the trust, perhaps the settlor, in order to provide for an ongoing tax charge. But the principles of revocable, irrevocable, fixed and discretionary often go a long way to helping one understand how trust interests are taxed, and the planning that can take place, particularly where families are divided between countries.

Trusts can be beneficial when revocable and fixed, but often trusts that are irrevocable and discretionary are particularly useful. But if I have no right to revoke the trust as settlor and the beneficiaries (which can include me, the settlor) have no fixed legal right, does it not mean that we have to trust the trustee? How can I advise this when my advice is, always, *don't trust anyone*?

This is where the 'checks and balances' necessary in relation to all succession and asset-protection planning come into the picture. I can start off the process by limiting the trustee's discretion in the trust to choosing among a class of possible beneficiaries, rather than leaving this open ended. For example, I can have the trust deed provide that while the trustee has discretion as to who might benefit from the trust, I can limit this to choices the trustee has among a set class of potential beneficiaries, such as members of my immediate family—perhaps me, my wife, my children, my grandchildren and further issue. In this way, the trustee, in exercising their discretion, cannot make a distribution to a member of his own family, if the trustee is an individual. But is this enough protection?

What if I pass away and my trustee, an individual, has discretion to make a distribution to anyone within my family? I may have provided, in a non-binding letter of wishes, that my wish was for the trustee to divide the trust assets between my two children at a particular age. My trustee, wanting to get their hands on the valuable pen that I may have settled into the trust, can see that they have discretion to choose among a class of beneficiaries that includes my wife. The trustee starts up an affair with my widow and distributes the pen to her as a beneficiary of the trust, and uses it to draw flowers on her arm. Is this what I intended when settling the trust?

An important control over a trustee of a trust is a protector, an optional party to a trust. If, in the trust in my example, I required the trustee, before an exercise of discretion in favour of any beneficiary, to first give thirty days' written notice to the protector, combined with a power to the protector to remove and replace the trustee, a decision of the trustee to benefit my wife would require the trustee to first notify the protector of his intention to do so. The protector, knowing that I had wished the benefit to go to my children, can point this out to the trustee who, if he fails to do the right thing and benefit my children, can be removed and replaced.

There are many important issues to consider in deciding on an appropriate protector, or committee of protectors, and particularly on how and who replaces them. In many standard trust deeds, it is the protector who can appoint their replacements... but is this safe from the wealth-owning family's perspective? Subject to the tax and other issues that need to be navigated, I like having the family itself have the ability to appoint or approve successor protectors, but the most important thing is that the family really understand their structure, and ask all the right *'what if?'* questions to ensure that the right checks and balances are in place. And a big danger is when the advisor to the family, perhaps the trustee or the protector, is the one providing recommendations that are blindly followed—there is a conflict of interest that is inevitable here, as many trustees would, of course, prefer to not have a protector keeping an eye on them and their fees or, at a minimum, would prefer to themselves appoint and control the protector. And in relation to protectors, they may have incentives to not want family members to be able to remove them.

On trustee fees, it is interesting to consider a dispute that arose involving trustee fees relating to a trust created on the death of artist Robert Rauschenberg. A Florida court decided that a US$24.6 million award to three individuals acting as trustees was appropriate compensation.

Robert Rauschenberg had left his estate to a revocable trust, the sole beneficiary of which was the Rauschenberg Foundation. The trustees managed the trust assets for several years while the assets were being transferred to the foundation. The trustees initially claimed US$60 million for administering the trust; the Rauschenberg Foundation claimed they were owed no more than US$375,000 for their work.

Ultimately, the trustees were awarded fees based on the value of the trust, which was substantial. While they did not receive the amount they initially claimed (US$60 million), the fees were still extraordinary given the relatively few years of work involved.

The lesson for wealth owners is that with trusts or any other arrangements, making it clear upfront what trustees or others involved can charge is critical. And also critical is to have oversight, through a protector or otherwise, allowing for someone to have the power to remove and replace a trustee who—for any reason—may work other than in the best interests of the beneficiaries and contrary to what the creator of the trust would have wished.

In relation to trusts, the question of jurisdiction, or the laws under which the trust should be established, often comes up. While there are sometimes good reasons to form a trust under the laws of one jurisdiction or another, such as to take advantage of strong laws that protect assets against creditors, or to address forced heirship rules or otherwise, generally I am fairly relaxed on the issue of jurisdiction, at least among the numerous countries with good trust laws, an effective judiciary and clarity that trust assets will not be taxed on the basis of where the trustee is located. More important than jurisdiction from my perspective is the choice of trustee.

Trustees can range from individuals to corporate trustees, and among the latter are trust companies that are owned by banks and 'independent' trust companies that are not linked to banks. Increasingly useful for some families are private trust companies (PTCs), trust companies established to be the trustees of only trusts for a particular family or group of families. It is tempting for a family to opt for having a PTC be the trustee of trusts they establish, given the sense of control this provides. But for a trust to achieve its objectives, the trust has to be real, meaning that the trustee has to properly exercise its functions as a trustee. Where PTCs are used, it is critical to ensure that they actually perform their trustee roles as required, and that the governance of the PTC is effective and able to evolve over the time the relevant trust remains in place.

Many considerations come into deciding on an appropriate trustee, but one of the most important questions is whether the trustee is capable of really doing the job of a trustee and is willing to do so. A competent trustee needs to know what the trust assets are, given the trustee's responsibility to look after them for the benefit of the beneficiaries; a trustee needs to know the family in order to be there if there is death or disability in the older generation; a trustee needs to monitor tax and legal developments that will affect the trust, and the parties to the trust in terms of tax, reporting and other obligations. This all seems obvious, but a reality is that there are many, many trustees who have been far more focused on the trust fees they receive and on volume business than on really doing even the basics of what a real trustee must do. It is also a reality that wealth owners, not knowing the right questions to ask, choose trustees for the wrong reasons—often based on cost and without adequate consideration of whether the trustee is really able to perform the functions the family really needs, both now and when the creator of the trust is no longer able or alive.

Individuals can be effective trustees, but there are issues given the succession that is necessary to provide for, since individuals are not around for more than a lifetime. Trust taxation may also be affected by where the trustee resides, and an individual may move from one country to another. And from a liability perspective, if my trustee steals from the trust, my children, as beneficiaries, can sue, but what if the trustee now claims to have dementia and is broke? Not to say that individuals cannot be good trustees, but asking the '*what-ifs?*' can help ensure that the right checks and balances are in place to protect against what can go wrong.

There is much, much more that can be said about trusts, and wealth-owning families need to consider the benefits (and dangers) of trusts to determine whether a trust makes sense in their planning and, if so, how the trust should best be established. But the complexities of trusts arising from their flexibility and the many ways they can be established, and ever-changing tax and other laws, lead many wealth owners to think that it may be best to just leave their assets to their children, and let their children work out whether or not to establish trusts given their own circumstances. Just leaving it to the kids, however, may not be the best choice.

If mother lives in Hong Kong and has $10 million she plans to give to her son, also a resident of Hong Kong, should mother use a trust to make the transfer? Hong Kong does not have a gift or estate tax, meaning that if she gives her son the money, no tax will arise. So why not give him the money directly rather than thinking about using a trust and having to think through all the complexities? The son receives the $10 million—no tax—but is everything well protected?

The son becomes a plastic surgeon, and in his first operation he puts the ear where the nose is and the nose where the ear is. The son gets sued, and it is pretty clear that the $10 million will disappear. The son marries the sleazy girl from down the street, and well before anything to do with a breakdown of the marriage, she comes up with a hare-brained business idea and asks for some of the son's money to get her 'business' started. He finds it hard to say no, and some of the money disappears.

The son, like many in Asia, decides to move to mainland China to take advantage of China's developing economy. At a certain point, he will be considered to be fully subject not only to worldwide taxation in China, resulting in his being taxed on earnings on the money received from his mother (which, in the case of Hong Kong, would have only been taxation on Hong Kong and not foreign-sourced income), but also in due course to currency and foreign investment controls.

If the son decides to move to Canada he will freeze to death, and also be subject to worldwide taxation, meaning that tax will arise on the income he earns on investing the money received from his mother, regardless of the source of the income. Depending on the province in which he lives, tax rates can approach and even exceed 50% (a not insignificant figure) and if the son dies, and wants to leave assets to his children, a deemed disposition on death will trigger more in the way of taxation, with capital gains taxes arising on any gains in value of assets owned, despite the fact that the assets are not actually sold.

A move to the United States and to many other countries would also result in worldwide taxation, and to potential exposure to inheritance and other taxes depending on the level of assets at death and other factors.

But what if mother, instead of giving her son the $10 million, transfers the money to a trust in respect of which her son is a discretionary beneficiary? Mother can retain the right to revoke the trust, keeping things simple and in her control, and many of the risks to wealth that would otherwise arise would be well managed.

A claim by a creditor against the son would, in many cases, not succeed in reaching the trust assets—given that the son was not the one to transfer the assets to the trustee and is not accorded any legal right to the assets, being only a discretionary beneficiary. On this front, the retention of a power to revoke the trust in mother's favour will also be helpful, and a similar analysis would apply in the event of a divorce by the son.

If the son's new wife has a clever business idea and pressures the son into providing her with funds, he can simply refer his wife to the trustee who is in control of the trust assets and of any decision regarding distributions. Given the responsibilities a trustee has in relation to investment decisions and otherwise, it is unlikely the trustee would invest in the wife's business in the absence of good reasons to do so, allowing the son a face-saving way out of handing over any of the money.

If there is a change of residence to China, the assets remain outside China's tax and foreign exchange control net, by simply not being owned by a resident of China. In certain circumstances, even a distribution from the trust to the son when resident in China may be tax-free or tax-advantaged.

A move to Canada will still result in the son freezing to death, but the assets and income in the trust will be free of Canadian tax and deemed disposition rules, meaning that investment income can accumulate on a tax-free basis. Both during and after mother's life, if income is properly capitalized within the trust, distributions to the son, when resident in Canada, can be achieved on a tax-free basis, despite the distributions being fully reported to the Canadian tax authorities, as they would need to be under Canadian law.

A move to the United States or to other countries could also take place without the trust income and assets coming into the income and estate tax net; with distributions, in the case of the United States, being tax-free during mother's life, given her right to revoke the trust (making the trust a 'grantor' trust under US tax law) and limiting taxation after her death to income of the trust that arises after her passing to the extent distributions take place. While complex, the US tax position can be managed in a number of favourable ways, providing significantly more in the way of tax benefits than would arise if there were a direct gift of the assets from mother to son.

In fact, around the world, trusts established by foreigners benefiting residents on a discretionary basis are not only favourable from a tax perspective, but also minimize reporting and other challenges to wealth owners.

So, what if mother gives the money to her son, and he is the one to then set up the trust? The tax, reporting and asset-protection profile of the trust is then completely different, with countries like Canada and the United States taxing the son on the income of the trust given that he was its settlor. In the case of creditor and other claims, the trust will be less protective, as the person being claimed against was the person who transferred the assets into trust.

Trusts are not always the answer, but all wealth owners should consider the possible benefits that a mobile younger generation can achieve where a trust is in place. And unlike a will, which generally distributes assets on death, a trust allows assets to be held by a third party who can consider the right time to make distributions, and how best to achieve things in a way that is favourable to the family.

However, not every country treats trust interests in a tax-advantaged way—so care and planning on an ongoing basis is necessary.

As with any succession and asset-protection plan, trusts should be subject to regular 'stress tests'—reviews where the right *'what-if?'* questions are asked and problems addressed. What if I pass away early, and my children are young—who will guide the trustee on making the right decisions in relation to how much my children should receive and when? What if the people I know at the trust company are all gone… who will keep an eye on the trustee and have the ability to replace the trustee if this is needed? What if my wife remarries and her new husband is a gold-digger interested in the funds in the trust? Are the right controls there to ensure that I have made arrangements to protect my wife financially while being sure that there will be money left to take care of my children after her death, rather than going to her new husband?

Foundations

Foundations and trusts are increasingly interchangeable wealth planning tools. Foundations, unlike trusts, derive from the civil law, and traditionally were established under the laws of civil law countries, like Liechtenstein, Panama and others. However, common law countries, such as the Bahamas and Jersey, now allow foundations to be established under their laws. Similarly, civil law countries, such as Liechtenstein and Switzerland, provide for trusts to be administered in their countries and, in some cases, to be established under domestic trust legislation. These developments basically reflect the reality that jurisdictions compete for business and look for ways to encourage wealth-owning families to establish structures under their laws.

Foundations, traditionally, were established in a very simple way, and historically all too often with privacy at the core. Assuming no one would find out about their existence, many traditional foundations in Liechtenstein and elsewhere were basic in their approach, providing for the creator (or founder) of the foundation to retain 'founder's rights', basically allowing for a right of revocation and other rights against foundation assets, with a list of fixed beneficiaries entitled to the assets and income in particular circumstances or at particular times. Often the founder would him- or herself be the 'first' beneficiary, with 'second' beneficiaries being the spouse and children after the passing of the first beneficiary. Basically, these foundations were akin to revocable, fixed trusts, and provided little in the way of asset protection and tax minimization given the legal right to assets that the founder and beneficiaries had.

Foundations can, however, feature similar flexibility to trusts, and it is possible to establish a foundation that is irrevocable and discretionary, with the approach taking a variety of forms. But foundations are different from trusts in a number of ways, and it is important for the wealth-owning family to understand some of these differences.

Foundations, unlike trusts, are legal entities. This means that if I set up a foundation, the foundation itself can own a bank account and own assets in its own name. This differs from a trust, where the legal owner of the assets becomes the trustee. Among other things, this has an impact on responsibility. In the case of a trust, a trustee, being the owner of the assets, has unlimited liability in the sense that the assets are the responsibility of the trustee. In the case of a risky asset, such as a leaky oil tanker delivering its cargo to the United States, a trustee will be very hesitant to take on legal ownership of the tanker given the potential liabilities involved. In the case of ownership by a foundation, being a separate entity, there is limited liability, meaning that claims, in a very general sense, can only be made against the assets of the foundation itself. This is a simplistic description, in that there are many exceptions that apply, including limitations of liability that a trust document may provide, and liabilities that often 'pierce' the separate entity veil of a foundation. A foundation board, which makes the kind of decisions a trustee makes, may also incur liabilities, but in very general terms, the liability of a trustee is quite a bit more significant than that of a service provider involved with foundations. This is a reason that foundations are often cheaper to establish than trusts.

Being creatures of the civil law, foundation documents are often much simpler than trust documents. As the civil law involved sets out the rights and obligations of the various parties, the documentation of an individual foundation is often short and to the point when compared to the lengthy documents that trusts require, largely to ensure that trustees have the power they need to properly administer the trust assets. But unlike trusts, foundations do not generally have the same degree of responsibility to beneficiaries as is the case for trusts. In the case of a foundation, the founder is generally the main person the foundation owes its responsibilities to; in the case of the trust, it is the beneficiaries to whom the trustee owes its primary duties. These differences do not suggest that a foundation is better than a trust, or that a trust is better than a foundation. Rather, the differences mean that the wealth-owning family needs to ask the right questions, and understand the structure they have in place and what the responsibilities of those involved actually are.

Traditionally, an advantage of foundations over trusts is that foundations can, if the family so wishes, last 'for ever'. In the case of trusts, common law provided for the rule against perpetuities—the concept being that the ownership of assets cannot be kept in trust for ever. Different trust jurisdictions featured different rules on how long a trust could last, but today, more and more jurisdictions have eliminated the rule against perpetuities, allowing trusts to also last for ever, if that is the way in which they are set up.

Control is another area of historical difference between trusts and foundations, with foundations, as separate entities, not having the risk of failing if the founder retains too much in the way of power. In the case of a trust, a trust can fail if the settlor retains too much control—in effect, there is no trust as the settlor has not given up his ownership of the assets. This said, in a number of trust jurisdictions, laws have been adapted to permit more and more control to a settlor, again, to at least some extent, making trusts and foundations increasingly interchangeable instruments.

To add to the possible confusion, the term 'foundation' means different things in different circumstances. Under the laws of some countries, a foundation can only be established if benefits go primarily to charity; in other countries, the term 'foundation' can be mixed up with trust use. For example, it is not uncommon to find a trust established that is called 'The X Family Foundation'—technically a trust, but in its name referred to as a foundation.

As with trusts, key for any wealth-owning family is to really understand the structure they have in place and to ensure that it not only achieves what it is they hope to achieve, but that the right people are involved, with appropriate oversight not only during the lifetime of the wealth owner, but after the wealth owner's death or disability. In the case of a foundation, like in the case of a trust, the ability to make changes to those in charge and to ensure that there is appropriate governance in place is critical.

Partnerships

Partnerships are an increasingly valuable tool for wealth owners to use, and a variety of partnership structures can be used to address the planning needs of wealth-owning families. In basic terms, a partnership is not a distinct legal entity, but rather an arrangement to conduct business. But there are many ways that partnerships can be set up, and lots of variations on approaches under the laws of the many different countries where partnerships can be established.

While partners are generally responsible for the liabilities of the partnership, this can be managed by having the partners of the partnership be LLCs, or by using a 'limited' partnership that allows for limited liability of individual partners.

Like trusts, partnerships can be very flexible tools, and this allows them to be used by wealth-owning families to address a number of needs. Partnerships can also be mixed with trusts and other wealth planning 'tools'.

Perhaps examples of how partnerships can be used can provide the best flavour of how attractive they can be as succession and asset-protection planning vehicles. Mother has established a business that has a value of $5 million. Mother lives in a country that has both a tax on gifts she makes, as well as a tax on the value of her assets that pass on death. Mother is running the business, but has children who are involved in the business, and to whom she eventually envisions leaving the business. The business is going very well, and mother anticipates that by the time she passes away, the business is likely to be far more valuable than it is today.

If mother holds on to her interest in the business, and it passes to her children on her death, inheritance taxes will be imposed on the value of the business at that time. If the business has gone up in value to, say, $50 million, the tax that arises will be based on that value. Thinking about this might encourage mother to consider transferring her interest in the business to her children now. This would attract a gift tax, but at the current value of the business, in the example $5 million. On the death of mother, there would be no further tax, because she would already have disposed of the asset involved.

While an early transfer of the business to the children could be attractive from a tax perspective, it would mean that the children own the business and control it, something mother may not be entirely comfortable with. Perhaps a family partnership can provide a better result.

Mother can transfer her business to a family partnership and obtain in return an interest in the partnership that provides her with a priority right to receive, on sale of the business, the current value of the business, being $5 million, and to receive a fixed amount of profits while the business remains in the partnership. Mother's partnership interests can also carry all the voting rights in relation to the business to be conducted, keeping control with mother, while 'freezing' the value of her interest in the business. Mother can then give or sell partnership interests to her children, which, for the moment, would not provide any voting rights (or limit such rights).

In very broad terms, today the value of the partnership interests mother is transferring to her children is virtually nil, as all the value of the business as it stands today is with the partnership interest she retains. A gift of the partnership interests may therefore result in no or little gift tax. As the value of the business grows, the value of the partnership interest that mother holds is 'frozen' in that it remains the $5 million mother would receive were the business to be sold. If, when mother passes away, the business is worth $50 million, inheritance taxes might only apply to mother's interest in the partnership, the value of which is frozen at the $5 million figure. The children already own their partnership interests, which reflect the remaining value of the business, $45 million, and there is therefore no tax to pay on this, and the children, through their inheritance of their mother's voting interests, now own the voting control of the business.

There are many variations on this theme that can be achieved through the flexibility of partnerships, and while in a number of countries there are specific tax rules and valuation principles associated with retention of voting control and other elements, the broad tax advantages can be achieved while also permitting the family to reflect the ownership approaches that are appropriate in the circumstances.

While similar benefits can be achieved through structures involving other than partnerships, variations of partnership approaches are commonly used to provide efficient ways to hold real estate. If a husband and wife are planning to purchase a holiday home in France, for example, despite not being residents of France, they would be subject to a variety of taxes, including wealth taxes (depending on the value of their property) as well as inheritance taxes that arise on death. If the property is put in the name of their children from the outset, inheritance taxes may be avoided, but control of the property falls into the hands of the children, which may not be ideal for a number of reasons. By having the family hold the property through a partnership, if there are two children, there are now four owners, and the value of each family member's interests may be below the threshold for wealth tax to apply. Further, ownership of controlling interests, through a partnership approach, can ensure the parents that they control decisions on use and sale of the property. On death, only the value of the parents' interests, now limited through the value already owned by the children, would be subject to inheritance tax.

Tax-wise, partnerships, unlike companies, are generally 'flow-through' vehicles, meaning that it is not the partnership itself that is taxed, but rather the partners of the partnership. This can provide a number of advantages, including access to lower capital gains tax rates applicable to individuals rather than corporations, as in the case of the United States. Using the United States as an example, the flow-through nature of partnerships means that if a partnership is set up and is owned by non-US partners, there is generally no tax if the partnership does not earn US-sourced income. And under US laws, there are LLCs that can be established and which can qualify for partnership treatment, meaning that the vehicle can be a hybrid between a company and a partnership.

Tax is not the only reason partnerships are often used in family succession and asset-protection structures. Partnerships can be hugely flexible in terms of governance and economic arrangements that are put in place, and can even have 'trust-like' elements to them, opening the door to even more possible planning uses. For example, mother can be the general partner of a partnership that provides for mother, as general partner, to have a fixed interest in the value of the partnership, say again $5 million. Mother can have her two children hold partnership interests with a fixed value of $1 million each. As the general partner, mother can retain the ability, in her discretion, to allocate additional value to the limited partners (her children) or to new limited partners. If the partnership has a value of $10 million, $7 million is, in effect, 'owned' by mother and her two children; the remaining $3 million is held in a manner that is similar to a discretionary trust or foundation, but which, depending on the country whose tax laws apply, attracts different (possibly better) reporting and tax consequences.

Like with trusts and foundations, the flexibility of partnerships makes it very important for the wealth-owning family to really understand what they are getting into, and to ask the *'what-ifs?'* that can help ensure the assets remain in the ownership and control that the wealth-owning family expects and plans for.

Companies: Offshore, Onshore and Midshore

Companies are common vehicles used to own assets and businesses, and there are many choices in how and where companies can be established.

Very commonly used have been tax-haven, or 'offshore' companies. These are companies that are established in one of many offshore financial centres competing for business from investors and wealth owners looking for simple, tax-neutral approaches to asset ownership. Jurisdictions that come into the picture here range from the British Virgin Islands to the Bahamas and many others, all generally offering relative simplicity and low cost in the corporate formation process, and no tax exposures at all, particularly where no activity takes place in the offshore centre itself.

This tax-free treatment, however, is only in the country in which the company is set up. The first question in relation to tax exposures is always the home country of the wealth owner himself—despite the fact that the company may not be taxed in its country of incorporation, the home country may have tax rules that impact things in a substantial way. These rules, as discussed earlier, can include taxing the company as if it were resident in the country of the wealth owner, if the company is considered to be managed and controlled by the wealth owner in his country of residence. Anti-deferral rules, such as CFC rules, can cause immediate taxation of the income of the offshore company, and a number of other tax rules can come into the picture, including the home country simply ignoring the existence of the offshore company if it lacks substance and is considered to be a 'sham'.

Having a company own an asset rather than owning the asset directly can bring a number of advantages; however in some circumstances there may be clear disadvantages. Advice is usually needed.

If, for example, I own a valuable classic car that I physically keep in the United States, and I am not a US citizen, resident or domiciliary, I may nevertheless be exposed to US estate tax on my death given that on my death, there is a moveable asset that I own, the car, physically in the United States. If, on the other hand, the car were owned by a non-US company, say a company in the British Virgin Islands, when I die it is not the asset in the United States that I own and which passes to my family (the car), but rather it is the shares of the British Virgin Islands company that pass. Providing the company is 'real', in the sense of my having respected it in all relevant transactions and appropriately documented things, I die owning shares of a non-US company, thereby avoiding US estate tax exposure—and in the British Virgin Islands, no tax on my death arises. If my home country also has no tax that arises on death, tax exposures do not arise.

Some countries have rules that seek to limit the ability of wealth owners to 'envelope' assets in companies, and an example of this is the United Kingdom, where using a foreign company to own domestic residential real estate not only does not provide protection against inheritance tax, but comes at additional tax costs.

Increased tax transparency and an overall focus by countries on collecting what they view to be their fair share of tax revenues is putting pressure on traditional offshore companies, which are generally established in locations where there is minimal substance in terms of employees, business activities or otherwise. Various approaches can be used by countries to attack the use of offshore companies, including ignoring the existence of the company if it lacks substance, treating it as resident in the home country or elsewhere if the company is in reality 'managed and controlled' from the home country (something that is a common taxing approach in countries including Canada, Switzerland, the United Kingdom, Hong Kong, Singapore and others) or focusing on 'transfer pricing' rules to insist on income earned by the offshore company being reallocated to taxable entities more involved in generating the relevant profits. Moves to a more global approach to taxation, such as the global minimum tax initiative discussed earlier in this book, will have further negative impacts on the desirability of offshore companies.

While it is more than likely that a good number of traditional offshore centres will continue to not only survive, but thrive, offshore centres are under challenge, and a good part of tax planning is moving both onshore and midshore. Reporting and taxpaying are often simpler where the wealth owner uses onshore planning. The

United Kingdom is an example, with relatively low tax rates for UK companies, and the United States another, with reporting and tax-paying being much simpler where US structures are used for US taxpayers. But there are still many cases where wealth owners benefit from using companies outside their home country, and this not only from a tax perspective, but for confidentiality, asset protection and other reasons.

Increasingly, midshore locations are attractive places for companies to be established. There is no real definition of what it means to be 'midshore', but generally the term would describe locations for companies (and other structures) that are not traditional tax havens, but rather substantial financial centres whose tax and other laws provide incentives to establish structures there, and from where business and investment activities can be coordinated. Falling into this category would clearly be places like Hong Kong and Singapore, where territorial tax systems and low tax rates combine with solid tax treaty networks and sophisticated infrastructures supporting the needs of investors and businesses. Also falling within this category are traditional onshore centres like the United States, Switzerland and others, that offer a number of attractions to foreign investors making use of their financial and corporate centres.

Where companies are used, wealth owners need, as with all of the 'tools' of wealth planning, to pay attention to governance, and understand what happens in the event of death or disability. In the case of a company, the shareholders are the owners of the company, and if the wealth owner is a shareholder and dies, those shares will pass, perhaps under their will. If the shares of the company are held in a trust or foundation, the trust or foundation will govern what happens to the ownership of the shares on death.

Shareholder agreements are a common and necessary tool setting out the rights and obligations of the shareholders of a company, and even where ownership is only within one family, such agreements are often necessary to avoid difficulties associated with exits from the business by family members, restricting transfers to people outside the family, dealing with capital raising and many other issues. Like partnerships, companies—depending on where they are established—can also be quite flexible, and different share classes can permit voting rights to be retained by the older generation, while value is accorded to the younger.

Estate 'freezes', as described earlier in relation to partnerships, can also be achieved with companies. For example, father can transfer a business to a company in exchange for redeemable preference shares that have voting rights; father can have a fixed right to the current value of his business, and perhaps a fixed return of, say, 5% on that value. The common shares that reflect growth in the value of the company can go to the children, and these shares, worth nothing at the outset, would represent the future growth in value of the business, the shares of father being 'frozen' in value at the figure set as the redemption value of the shares, being the current value of the business.

Some families, at the more sophisticated end of planning, even use publicly listed companies as part of their family asset-holding structures. This is something that comes up where a family is in a third, fourth or further generation, and where multiple shareholders create complexity in terms of permitting sales of shares and transparency on financial performance and other matters. By having the company that may hold a family business, for example, be publicly listed, family members can enter and exit the business, and obtain transparency on financial results. Through special classes of shares and otherwise, control can be retained to the family.

Investment funds are another similar vehicle that families can use, and these can also have elements of public listings in them. Like in the case of companies, the availability of favourable tax treaties and investment protection agreements is a factor in the choice of location for such funds.

The Family 'Bank'

The family 'bank'[1] is another wealth planning tool, and was discussed in the previous chapter in my review of family constitutions. The family 'bank' is more of a concept on how financial support for family members and their endeavours is accounted for, rather than about the establishment of an actual bank.

Fairness is a key objective that wealth owners should have if they seek to avoid wealth being destructive of relationships. Where Mum or Dad provide funds to a child, whether to help them in establishing a business or to buy a home or otherwise, the question of fairness arises if there are other children who do not receive the same support. The family 'bank' is a way of dealing with this.

It is the case that some families do consider establishing an actual bank, sometimes for political risk protection, given that banks have capital requirements, making it difficult for a home country to insist on the repatriation of funds where a family has the funds invested as the capital of a licensed bank in a foreign country. But this is not the type of family 'bank' that I advocate all wealth-owning families consider creating in a notional way, perhaps as part of family trust arrangements or otherwise.

The objective of the family 'bank' is to ensure a feeling of fairness in relation to the endeavours of the younger generation that are supported by family assets. The family bank can, for example, clarify what element of the support provided is a loan to the family member and what element is something else—perhaps a gift or an investment. A loan needs to be repaid at some point, possibly from the share of family assets that family member will eventually inherit. A gift does not have to be repaid. An investment by the family means that the family takes risks—if it is an investment into a business the child is establishing, and the business does well, the family benefits; if the business fails, the family takes a loss.

Key to success of the family bank concept is to develop fair approaches that are accepted by family members, and which can adapt to the needs of the family. The family bank can also be used as an approach to deal with unequal consumption by the younger generation, whether for special advanced education or for help buying a home or otherwise.

The more discussion that takes place within families on how the younger generation will be supported, the better, and parents who take into account the thinking of their children are more likely to avoid wealth being a destructive element within the family.

Insurance Products

A variety of insurance products are part of the wealth planning toolbox, and insurance products are increasingly used by wealth-owning families to address not only tax minimization and management objectives, but asset protection and more.

There are many different kinds of insurance, including traditional insurance on a home against fire, earthquakes and other threats, and coverage of loss of possessions and potential liabilities of all kinds. For significant wealth owners, insurance needs in this area can be complex, and can in some cases involve forms of 'self-insurance', including the use of 'captive' insurance companies that are wholly or partially owned by the family itself. In some cases, tax and other benefits can be achieved through such arrangements, but the more common wealth planning uses of insurance come in the area of life insurance and life annuities.

In the case of insurance, like in the case of trusts or foundations, there are different parties involved. If I set up a trust, I am the settlor, and the person I transfer my assets to is the trustee. In the case of insurance, if I am establishing a life insurance policy, and pay the relevant premiums and have the right to designate the beneficiaries, among other things, I am the policy owner. I pay the premiums to the insurance company, another party to the insurance arrangement. The life policy will designate one or more lives assured. This can be a life policy that I own which pays out on my death—in this case, I am both the policy owner and the life assured. I can also buy a life policy over the life of my wife, or over our lives jointly; in this case, either my wife or the both of us are the lives assured. When I establish the policy, I specify who will benefit from the policy upon the death of the life assured—and perhaps it is my children who I name as the beneficiaries.

In the tax area, insurance can provide interesting consequences, and this, of course, depends on the tax laws that apply to the wealth-owning family, and to the insurance structure itself. The first step in any tax analysis is to understand what happens when a premium is paid to the insurance company by the policy owner. Unlike a trust or foundation that is established, the transfer is not normally viewed as a gift, attracting a donation or similar tax if one applies in the country of the wealth owner. In fact, the policy owner is actually buying something—the policy providing the insurance coverage—and this is not generally a taxable event. In some countries a small excise or other tax may apply to the premium payment, but this is not a tax on a donation or on income. Reporting requirements for the policy owner may also be very different from those that might apply where a trust or foundation is established.

Once the insurance company receives the premiums, a further question will be the extent to which the insurance company itself pays tax, given that the amount the insurance company will eventually pay out to my family will be affected by the inside build-up of the policy, represented by the premiums paid, returns on the investment by the insurance company of the premiums, less the charges imposed by the insurance company and any taxes that apply. In a number of cases, insurance companies are established in countries where only the fees charged by the insurance company are taxable, and not the investment returns that form part of the inside build-up of the policy—this can be attractive, as it means that more money can be available for an eventual payout to my children. But do I as the policy owner get taxed on the inside build-up? Does the life assured?

In many countries, if the policy is a genuine life insurance policy, the owner of the policy is not taxed on the inside build-up within the policy. And in the case of the life assured, there are almost never any tax issues that arise, as the life assured only provides the measurement of time during which the policy will remain in place; being a life assured does not necessarily involve any policy ownership or other interests.

What does it mean to be 'genuine' life insurance? Generally, this revolves around the concept of mortality risk. In a traditional life insurance arrangement, I may agree to pay the insurance company a premium of $5000 each year. Under the policy, if I die before the age of seventy-five, the insurance company pays my family $50,000. If I die after paying two years of premiums, I win the bet—I may be dead, but I only paid $10,000, two years of premiums, to have the beneficiaries of my life policy receive $50,000. The insurance company lost the bet—it took 'mortality risk', believing that I would live long enough to more than cover the eventual payout, but was wrong. Because of the mortality risk that the insurance company assumes, it is common for insurers, before putting the policy in place, to review the health of the life assured, and at a certain age, life insurance may not even be available, or may be prohibitively expensive, because of the mortality risk involved.

What if I have a portfolio of assets worth $1 million, and instead of paying an annual premium to the insurance company, I agree on a single premium—I transfer the investment portfolio to the insurance company as the one premium for the life policy. And perhaps, as can be done, the insurance company places the portfolio in a unit-linked policy, where the investment portfolio is owned by the insurance company, but managed by the same asset manager that I used before I purchased the policy. Most importantly, how much will the insurance company pay the beneficiaries of the policy in the event of my death? If the policy is nothing more than an insurance 'wrapper', perhaps the deal is that the insurance company will only pay out the investment portfolio, returns on the investment since the policy was established, less the charges of the insurance company. If I die soon after the policy is established, does the insurance company suffer any mortality risk? In my example, the answer is no.

In many countries, if there is insufficient mortality risk, the policy is not respected as being a life insurance policy, meaning that the policy owner is still considered to own the assets that are in the policy. This results in the policy owner being taxed on the inside build-up of the policy on a current basis—the investment returns on the portfolio I transferred to the insurance company as a single premium would be taxed to me each year, as if I still owned the portfolio. But frequently, if there is sufficient mortality risk, the policy owner is not taxed on the inside build-up, a big tax advantage, particularly if the insurance company is located in a country that does not tax the insurance company on that build-up. How much in the way of mortality risk is needed for this favourable tax treatment? In some countries this is clearly set out in the relevant tax rules. In other countries, the rules are less clear, and input from tax professionals is needed to be sure that the tax results are as expected.

Still on tax, there are other tax issues that life insurance involves. If I am the policy owner, what happens on my death? The ownership of the policy may transfer and, depending on whether or not I am the life assured, the beneficiaries may receive a payout. In some countries, such as the United States, the policy owner is considered to have something of value when he dies, and the transfer of the ownership of the policy will result in the potential of estate taxes applying. For this reason, it is relatively common for large life policies to be owned by trusts designed to avoid estate taxes applying, and minimizing any gift taxes associated with premium payments.

The death benefit of life insurance policies is often tax-free. In some countries taxes do apply to the beneficiaries, but sometimes at lower rates than on other receipts.

Life policies can also be structured to permit the policy owner access to funds during their lifetime, through borrowings on the security of the policy or otherwise. Here too tax issues arise, and in a number of countries, limited borrowings can permit tax-free access to funds held in the insurance structure.

Apart from life insurance, a variety of annuity products can also provide interesting tax and other benefits. In some countries, like the United States, annuity products can be designed to provide retirement benefits, as is the case for deferred variable annuities. In very simple terms, tax laws facilitate the use of approaches that permit someone to place money in a deferred variable annuity, avoid taxation during the period during which the insurance company invests the premiums, and then be taxed only on receiving retirement benefits from the fund. The approach provides the tax advantages associated with tax deferral, or a delay in taxation until such time as the proceeds are paid out. The advantage here is that 100% of income in a particular year can be fully reinvested, without any deduction for tax, meaning that there will be more money that accumulates than would be the case were tax paid each year.

The tax benefits of a retirement product along the lines of a deferred variable annuity can be even more interesting where the approach is used for someone who is not initially a US taxpayer, but who moves to the United States on a temporary basis. If, for example, an individual is living outside the United States and is not a US citizen, a move to the United States on a temporary basis would result in the individual being taxable in the United States on worldwide income during his period of residence in the United States. If immediately before a move to the United States the individual transfers an investment portfolio to a trust or foundation, US tax rules would require tax to be paid on the earnings of the trust, even if the trust is outside the United States. A variety of reporting requirements would also be triggered. If, on the other hand, the individual, before a move to the United States, purchases a deferred variable annuity, if all is properly handled, there would be no US taxpaying or reporting requirements associated with the purchase of the annuity given that this takes place before US residence is established, and no taxation during the period of residence in the United States given that there is full tax deferral on the inside build-up within the annuity. If the individual leaves the United States before retirement and the triggering of annuity payments, no tax arises.

Of course, strategies such as this one always require careful review of the tax and reporting rules at the relevant time, and tax laws are always changing. But creative cross-border use of insurance and annuity strategies is part of the wealth planning toolbox.

Insurance products are not only about tax. There are many other potential benefits to wealth-owning families, including clarity about how assets pass on death and, also, asset-protection and other benefits. On the asset-protection front, once assets are in a well-structured life policy, if properly planned, the assets in the policy can be protected against spousal and creditor claims. From a political risk perspective, ownership of the assets is now with the insurance company rather than with the wealth owner, and if the insurance company is in a more secure country than that of the residence of the wealth owner, political risk protection may be meaningful. And increasingly, insurance approaches are available that facilitate not only the holding in policies of liquid assets, but also the shares of family businesses and other assets.

Insurance is an area where the costs associated with the policy may not be anywhere as transparent as they should be. While things are changing from a regulatory perspective, requiring the provision of a much higher degree of clarity to the wealth owner on the actual costs of insurance, it is very important for the wealth-owning family to really understand who is getting what where an insurance policy is being put in place. Not only are commissions sometimes much higher than one would expect, but hidden costs and kickbacks are part of what is seen as fairly standard. Conflicts of interest are also common, and this is an area discussed in the next chapter in relation to not just insurance.

Derivatives and More

There are many other 'tools' in the wealth planning toolbox, and addressing the real needs of wealth owners requires identifying the right tools and using them in the right way to achieve objectives that will help families navigate an increasingly complex world. Derivative products, in simple terms, involve contracts that provide for benefits that track underlying securities—providing a return that mimics the return that a security would otherwise provide.

A number of years ago, I was involved in helping a family deal with an inheritance tax issue arising in a country whose laws imposed an inheritance tax where ownership of a company exceeded a certain percentage, say 5%. The wealth owner owned slightly more than this percentage of a publicly listed company that had been a family business, and that he did not want to sell shares of. Seeking to achieve avoidance, in a legal way, of the inheritance tax, the wealth owner sold enough shares to a bank in order to come below the 5% ownership threshold, but entered into a derivative contract with the bank under which payment to the bank was made from the proceeds of sale to obtain a derivative providing the same economic returns as the shares that had been disposed of and a right for the holder of the derivative, after a set number of years (designed to take place after the death of the wealth owner), to reacquire the shares that had been disposed of. In simple terms, while economically the family was in the same position that they would have been had no shares been sold, the use of the derivative allowed for inheritance taxes to be minimized.

Tunnels and bridges—the tools of wealth planning—can be used by families to help address the derailers (things that come up and which can prevent the family from reaching its impact goal). Once a family has agreed their destination, it is good practice to work back, figure out where things stand at present and develop a strategic roadmap that leads to the destination. The tools of wealth planning, such as an effective trust or foundation, may become a key *tunnel or bridge* that helps the family navigate the derailers and get to where they are going.

Note

1. As mentioned in earlier notes, the notion of a 'family bank' was introduced in Chapter 7 of the first edition of *Family Wealth: Keeping it in the Family* and reprised in the second edition published by the publishers of this book. Hughes, J. (Jay) E. Jr., *Family Wealth: Keeping It in the Family – How Family Members and Their Advisers Preserve Human, Intellectual, and Financial Assets for Generations* (2nd Revised and Expanded Edition) (Wiley, 2010). Jay reminded me that the idea of a family bank was one developed by Jay's father and which Jay then used in his further research and writing.

CHAPTER 8

Advisors—We Need Them but Need to Control Them

Advisors are almost always necessary, but it is important to understand their role, and to manage them in an appropriate way. And an effective advisor is one who has the interests of their clients at the forefront, and positions themself as a true trusted advisor.

For a country developing its tax policies, as would be the case for Dagland, advisors may be both internal and external to government. In both cases, while expertise is needed given how technical tax laws are, critical is for advisors to be controlled by those in charge of developing policy and keeping things kept systemically simple—which is both necessary and possible if a country really wants to move towards a tax system that is regenerative, transparent and simple.

> So we have a situation where people who don't understand tax rules vote for politicians who don't understand tax rules who then come up with more tax rules. No wonder it's a mess.
>
> Politicians can't write the rules themselves, so they get accountants to help. But it's in the interest of both the accountants and the government to keep everything complicated. The accountants keep their fees (and their loopholes) and the politicians get to keep their donations from special interest groups and to keep raising taxes without the electorate understanding what they're doing.

> *And politicians inevitably write their laws in response to short-term issues and media stories, often with a patch or a tweak, but never stepping back and saying, 'What should the big picture look like?'*[1]

For the wealth owner, it is not just a question of negotiating fees, but of really understanding how bankers, lawyers and accountants work and charge, and, importantly, the hidden ways they can profit from their clients' wealth—and from disputes that arise in the family.

Letting an advisor 'kidnap' the succession process is very dangerous, and all too common in a complex world where 'leaving it to the experts' seems to be the way to go. It is, after all, the wealth of the family involved—not the wealth of the advisor—but there are many situations of advisors becoming the 'gatekeepers' to the family's wealth, using wealth that is not that of the advisor to benefit themselves in a number of ways. This chapter focuses on advisors—who they are, how to choose them and how they charge.

It is important to understand that for many advisors there is no client better than a dead client. A client of a private bank, trust company or law firm may, depending on the mechanisms in place in relation to succession, become extraordinarily valuable once dead, given the limited ability of surviving family members to provide an appropriate check on fee charging and discretionary decision-making. Dead clients cannot question fees or fire advisors—so it is critical to ensure that the right checks and balances are in place in relation to structures that may have been established during the lifetime of the wealth owner.

Even the most honest and reliable individual or organization can abuse their position if there is a lack of oversight. A good rule of thumb is to simply operate on the basis of *trusting no one* in developing the right succession plan. This is not to say that no one, whether in or out of the family, can be trusted. Rather, if too much trust is accorded to anyone, there is a risk that such trust may be abused. It is critical for appropriate family members, such as the spouse and children of the wealth owner, to be prepared to take on an oversight role in relation to advisors, and to help manage the transition that can otherwise risk having the advisors end up being the ones in control. A good advisor is one who proactively helps their client understand the need to have the right oversight. There is no better way to sell your services than by *not selling*, but rather by telling the truth.

The more the wealth owner understands their real needs, and the roles of advisors, the more the right controls can be put in place. To really understand their own affairs, a wealth owner does not need to know all the answers—in fact, the world is so complex that there is no one who has all the answers. But the more the wealth owner is able to ask the right questions and to admit to not understanding elements of the structures in place in relation to their family's wealth ownership and succession plans, the closer they can get to meeting their responsibilities to their family.

This book is also for advisors to wealth-owning families, and particularly for those at an early stage of their careers. My view is that the more an advisor is able to align their interests with the interests of their clients, the more successful they will be and the more rewarding their career will be, not only financially, but in terms of allowing the advisor to enjoy the knowledge that they are really helping the client families they serve. Transparency on fees is one part of being a real trusted advisor, and in the education and development of those in the financial services industry, much more needs to be done to develop a sense of ethics and high standards that focus more on long-term relationships than on short-term revenues.

Where and when should the wealth owner start the process of understanding their succession structure? The answer is that it is never too early to begin the process, and for the younger generation or others with an expectation of inheriting or otherwise receiving benefits, the more they understand, the more the family will be protected.

Lawyers and Accountants

Things on the legal, tax and accounting front are increasingly complex and ever-changing, and there is little chance for any wealth owner to be able to navigate safely without the help of the right advisors.

The first key step is to find the right advisors, and one of the biggest dangers is running across a lawyer or accountant who does not acknowledge what they do *not* know. It is not at all uncommon to find wealth owners who have turned to their business lawyers or accountants for help in succession and asset-protection planning, only to find that the advisor(s) took on the job without having the experience or knowledge needed to do it properly. A superbly competent commercial lawyer may well *not* have the experience and knowledge needed to put together a will or trust, but may turn their hand to it, making a mess of things for the family involved. A good, trusted advisor will acknowledge where they need help, and most effective for the family is for their long-standing commercial lawyer or accountant to stay in the picture, liaising with specialists who can provide the input the family really needs.

Tax has been a driver of much of the planning that wealth-owning families undertake, and another failing is over-reliance on a tax specialist who may not be best placed to provide the holistic input that a family really needs. A US, UK or other tax specialist may well provide solid advice on tax-minimization approaches relevant to their country of expertise, but they may not have the human and other skills needed to help the wealth-owning family develop a holistic succession plan. Something I have seen many times in my career is trust and other structures that have been implemented by tax advisors whose sole focus was addressing a particular tax issue. The wealth-owning family, not knowing the right questions to ask, only later discover, to their detriment, that the structure in place failed to serve them on many other fronts, including in relation to asset protection, good succession planning for the younger generation, and even the tax laws of other countries relevant to the situation of the family and their investments.

Among the many examples I have seen of such failed planning included many trust structures established for Hong Kong-connected wealth owners during a time in which Hong Kong had an estate duty, a tax on death that no longer applies. Complicated trust structures were used to avoid the tax, and often the wealth owner did not fully understand the limited power retained once the assets were put in trust. An over-focus by advisors on the estate duty elements of the structures often resulted in insufficient attention being paid to other issues, such as when family members and others would have access to assets, and tax issues relevant to their own countries of citizenship or residence. Despite Hong Kong having eliminated estate duty, many historical structures remain in place, with the succession of assets within families following approaches that were not designed around thinking about what would be best for the family, but rather around avoiding a tax that no longer exists.

Another very common failing in planning is the over-emphasis on US taxation that international families sometimes fall into, in part from fear of the heavy-handed enforcement of US tax laws and from the approach of some US advisors who fail to consider that the tax and other laws of other countries are also of relevance to the families they serve. Non-US families buying real estate in the United States, or who have children who live in the United States or who hold US citizenship, sometimes find themselves victims of expensive and complex structures that may well address US tax issues, but which fail to take into account even more important needs relevant in their home country, both tax and non-tax. A revocable trust, for example, can be a very good approach for a foreign wealth owner to take with a view to benefiting a US citizen child in a tax-effective way given the US 'grantor trust' rules that would allow tax-free benefit to the US child on the death of the non-US grantor. But what if the creator of the trust is sued or gets divorced? And what of the tax issues in the creator's home country? Having the right to revoke the trust may not be the ideal.

One of the worst problems I have run across are approaches that have been adopted by families who have been misled by advisors—whether lawyers, bankers or others—about the protections afforded by bank secrecy. Despite the many changes that have taken place to encourage tax transparency, there remain advisors who mislead families into thinking that hiding their assets and income is a way to go.

Countless wealth owners were told by their bankers, lawyers, accountants and other advisors that no one would find out about their hidden structures and accounts. With growing transparency, families have been discovering that they not only have more in the way of tax to pay than they would have had they complied with the tax laws relevant to them, but that they now suffer criminal and civil penalties and other costs that compliance could have avoided.

In some cases, families, thinking that hiding the money was the best solution, neglected to do the work necessary to plan for their succession in the right way. I worry that increased enforcement of tax laws is resulting in some families putting all or part of their wealth in assets that are outside of the banking system, where tax compliance is increasingly having to be demonstrated, and through approaches where the assets involved—be they cryptocurrency, art, diamonds or gold—are not maintained in structures that properly protect the assets through the succession process. Is it worth breaking the law and risking your assets as a means of paying less tax? I recently learned of one wealth-owning family going through a name change as a means of supposedly evading tax liabilities—an approach which is not only illegal, but one that gives rise to many risks associated with the succession process.

The more the wealth owner is able to understand their real needs, the more they can help ask the right questions and assemble a team of advisors who can work together efficiently and look at things holistically.

A first step for the wealth owner is to understand that no accountant or lawyer will be an expert on everything, and particularly not when matters cross borders, which they almost always do. But too many of the lawyers and accountants that families work with pretend to know what they do not, a real problem given the complexities that need to be navigated. An effective advisor is one who knows what they know, and knows what they don't. For the wealth owner, it is ideal if a trusted advisor can coordinate input from the various advisors who may need to be involved to address a complex situation. Tax laws may come into the picture, as may trust rules and the impact of both in more than one country. This alone may require a team approach.

The results, the costs and the whole process will depend on how the project is managed, and how well the initial work is executed and then updated and adjusted to adapt to changes in the law, the family and their assets—changes which are inevitable.

Large global law and accounting firms can be an answer given that, at least theoretically, they should have the experience and capability to handle multi-jurisdictional and disciplinary issues. But they have their limitations, and it is important for the wealth owner to understand how some of these firms work (and charge). I spent my legal career in a large global law firm, and while I am a big believer in what they can achieve for clients, I am also a believer that results can be achieved in as cost-effective a way by smaller, single-jurisdiction professional firms providing that the advisor the family is working with understands their own limitations, and knows the right questions to ask, and to whom.

The reality is that professional services are extraordinarily expensive, something that is lamentable, but which is a product of an increasingly complex world, the high cost of running a professional firm and what are sometimes unjust income expectations of the professionals involved.

Personally, when I use a lawyer or accountant, I like to first ensure that I am using the right person for the right job—I want to know that the lawyer or accountant I am working with has experience and knowledge in the area that I need help with. Given that many professionals charge based on the time they spend, I certainly do not want to pay for the time my advisor takes to learn an area they are unfamiliar with. I am much better off with an advisor who charges a higher hourly rate, but who has done the same or similar work many, many times before. Also important to me is to develop a reasonable budget for the work I anticipate needing to have done. Open-ended arrangements can only lead to unhappy surprises, and the way lawyers and accountants are often incentivized in their own firms is to involve many more junior people in the job, and maximize the revenue generated.

I may see a partner of a law firm who is super experienced and knowledgeable, and who 'sells' me on his ability to handle what I need to have done. They agree to take me on as a client and to move forward. When I leave the office of the lawyer, the partner calls in two members of his junior team, briefs them on my matter, and asks them to write a memo. The junior lawyers are themselves under financial incentives that require them to bill as many hours as possible—in some law firms, bonuses are not paid before lawyers bill 1800 and often more hours a year. With a month's holiday a year, this works out to more than eight billable hours a day, assuming a five-day week. And it is absolutely common for the successful young lawyer to be billing 2000 or 2200 plus hours a year. How can this really work, if during the working day the lawyer is also going to the washroom, eating lunch, reading up on legal developments, attending internal management and other meetings, going to the dentist or doing whatever else they need to do? There are many cases of abuse and overbilling, but even where time recording is honest, does this really work out to the benefit of the client?

The young lawyers run off to the library, research things in areas they are not familiar with, look at previous work and draft a memorandum for the partner to review. He reads it, spends hours correcting it, finally gives up, tears it in two and dictates a letter to me, his client, that is to the point, and reflects his knowledge and maybe a bit of the results of the research his young lawyers spent hours and hours putting together. The result may be good, but the bill I get reflects a massive number of billable hours that I should not be paying for.

Clarity on a budget in advance of work done is the right way to keep a check on how lawyers and accountants work, and where possible, a fixed cost for a fixed outcome is the way to go. But this does not always work, as there will be circumstances where a budget or fixed fee will not be appropriate, as what needs to be done may include negotiations or other steps that are not easy to predict at the outset. Here, huge transparency on how the lawyer or accountant will work, and who will be involved, is key, as well as getting very regular updates on work done, costs and progress.

I remember a client once telling me that his preferred choice of lawyer was to find a hardworking, busy and experienced sole practitioner, very familiar with the area of law that was involved. The lawyer would then not have the ability to involve young lawyers in the project, creating the 'leverage' that larger firms use to enhance profits, with partners of the firm earning from not only their own time spent, but from the time spent by their juniors. I am not sure that this is necessarily the right solution in every case—to me the key is transparency on costs and the anticipated outcome, and not being afraid to discuss money at every stage of the process.

Over the years I have had many clients who asked for discounts, and most law and accounting firms will offer these. But more important than a discount on hourly rates is to have an agreed fee for an agreed deliverable. I do not really care how high the hourly rate is if the outcome is delivered at the right price. If I pay US$200 an hour to a lawyer who will spend fifty hours on the job, learning the law, involving colleagues with even less knowledge, is this better than using a lawyer who charges US$1000 an hour, but who only spends five hours adapting something they recently did to my circumstances, and who addresses my needs based on their solid experience?

Managing the advisors is important, and while it can be boring work for the wealth-owning family, the reality is that outcomes will be better and cheaper the more they understand their own situation, and are able to ask the right questions. There is now much in the way of information available from many sources, without cost, on virtually any issue one faces. Doing a bit of advance reading and narrowing the question to the lawyer or accountant can both help manage costs and focus the response to what it needs to be. And where the wealth owner does not want to do this themselves, using an intermediary—whether from a family office the family maintains or perhaps from a private bank or otherwise—can make a big difference. Someone who is an experienced consumer of legal and accounting services can be of big help to wealth-owning families.

And for the private banker or other intermediary, equipping yourself to be able to help families work with legal and tax advisors efficiently helps make *you* the trusted advisor—you don't need all the answers to be able to play this critical role, but you do need to know how to ask the right questions, and to leverage your contacts and experience to the benefit of your clients.

If I plan to move to a certain country and invest there, I will hunt around for an advisor from that country who looks like they know what they are doing. I will let them know my plans, and hopefully the advice I get will be the advice I need and at a price that is reasonable. If I am already working with a private bank or other organization that operates in a number of countries, maybe that private bank has resources—in the form of wealth planners or others—who work with clients of the bank who have similar needs to mine. If this is the case, they will, given their constant work on the issues, know who the main advisors are with experience in the area; they will know the right questions I should be asking; they should know the right price I should be paying for advice—and may even have better negotiating power than me to get the right advice at the right price, given that they are important clients of the advisors involved, referring work regularly given their involvement with similarly placed families. Making use of intermediaries in the right way can be of real value to the wealth owner, and within private banks and other organizations providing services to wealth owners, understanding what clients really need, and how to help them by making effective use of networks of internal and external experts, can be key to success.

Private Banking and the Wealth Management Industry

I became exposed to the wealth management industry many years ago when I began working with families in Hong Kong in the early 1980s. The handover of Hong Kong to China was being negotiated in the run-up to 1997, and wealth owners in Hong Kong were beginning to focus on political risk. Families and businesses began to restructure, and many wealth owners began diversifying their investment, residence and citizenship destinations to the United States, Canada, Australia, Europe and elsewhere. Providing advice to affected families, I began working with private banks, trust companies and others in the industry, but learned very quickly that many private banks and others servicing wealth owners were simply not meeting the real needs of their clients. My work with the wealth management industry intensified after my move in the mid-1990s to Switzerland and my close to fifteen years in Zurich providing legal and tax advice to both global wealth owners and their advisors.

Private banking and wealth management is big global business. Private banks generally make their money from managing the liquid assets of their clients, charging a percentage of assets under management (AUM). But what wealth-owning families need is much, much more than help with the management of their assets. And for private banks and others, I think it is important to understand that asset management is increasingly a commodity, and one where pricing challenges will increase significantly. The reality is that markets are ones that all asset managers are dealing with, and while it may be possible to outperform the competition from one year to the next, broadly, when markets go up, portfolios do well, and when they go down, they do not. Index funds and automated 'robo-advice' are permitting dramatic cost savings, making what many financial advisors charge for commodity services unsustainable in even the medium term.

Typically, a client of a private bank would have assets managed by the private bank. If the wealth owner has US$5 million in liquid assets, the bank would seek to provide discretionary asset management services, charging, say, 1% of the assets involved as their fee. The bank would thereby earn US$50,000 a year from the family involved, but the assets would simply be managed in the same way the bank manages the assets of other clients of the bank with similar risk profiles, meaning that not much is actually tailored to the individual family involved.

Today, around the world, there are increasing regulations that require asset managers to provide transparency on charges to their clients, but there continue to be many circumstances of hidden charges that asset managers, such as private banks, impose on their clients. In my example, the private bank earns 1% on the AUM involved; but is the client aware that the bank may have made arrangements to receive 'retrocessions' or kickbacks from investment funds in which they may invest the client money they have under discretionary management? Relatively recent court decisions in Switzerland require banks to refund retrocessions they historically received in a number of circumstances, but unsurprisingly the industry is pretty quiet about the rights their clients may have to obtain refunds of amounts their advisors secretly received.

Hidden commissions and other benefits are by no means confined to Swiss private banking, and it is fortunate that regulation is increasingly protecting wealth owners from abuses that have been rife in the industry. But are wealth owners reading the small print in the documents private banks and other asset managers provide them? Are they signing away their rights and consenting to practices that they would object to if they read the documents in front of them more carefully? I believe that it is critical to really understand how your asset manager charges, and for a successful private bank or other advisor to provide *genuine* transparency on fees. And in relation to fees of private banks, I have seen big disparities between the sometimes lower costs imposed by North American and European financial institutions and advisors versus those in Asia. Families often think things are cheaper in Asia—the reality is that pricing practices of the past, now more regulated elsewhere, continue in other places.

But how many financial services providers really align themselves with the interests of their clients? How often are fees charged for asset management more than once through a fee being charged to the client for a service, and then the investment made into a product offered by the same bank or other asset manager, with further fees arising that are not disclosed to the client or even to the relationship manager of the bank involved, helping to keep actual costs murky to the client family?

For wealth owners, there is no choice but to be very critical in review of how banks charge, and to consider—where one has negotiating power given the level of assets involved—*not* signing the standard documents that banks put in front of you, but rather setting out your own terms, mandating your advisors to work in a way that makes sense for the wealth-owning family itself. Even where the amount of wealth involved is not enough to dictate your terms to the banks you work with, my suggestion is to agree in writing the actual service you expect to receive, and to make it clear what your expectations are. You may well have signed all the standard documents that your bank has required, the small print of which is generally all looking to protect the interests of the bank, not yours. But this does not mean that you cannot separately have a letter of agreement with the bank that lays out in detail exactly what services the bank will be providing, and how these will be delivered.

Private banks often offer a range of services other than asset management, but where they make their money is still from AUM and the charges imposed on them. But, as mentioned above, I believe that asset management is increasingly a commodity, and that pricing is and will continue to be under serious pressure in the years to come. The reality is that all asset managers are dealing with the same markets. Markets go up, and markets go down, and it is therefore not easy for an asset manager to consistently outperform their peers. As the world becomes more and more complex, those asset managers who can outperform their peers tend to be those who are very specialized, perhaps operating through a hedge fund or otherwise. So, for a private bank, can they really sustain the charges that they currently impose on the asset management they perform, given that technology increasingly allows for investment performance that can match or exceed the performance of typical private banks at a much lower cost? It is interesting to compare the results of investing in indexes with the traditional stock-picking of discretionary asset managers, and also compare the costs involved.

Warren Buffett, famously, wrote in relation to advice to his heirs:

> *My money, I should add, is where my mouth is: What I advise here is essentially identical to certain instructions I've laid out in my will. One bequest provides that cash will be delivered to a trustee for my wife's benefit. (I have to use cash for individual bequests, because all of my Berkshire shares will be fully distributed to certain philanthropic organizations over the ten years following the closing of my estate.) My advice to the trustee could not be more simple: Put 10% of the cash in short-term government bonds and 90% in a very low-cost S&P 500 index fund. (I suggest Vanguard's.) I believe the trust's long-term results from this policy will be superior to those attained by most investors—whether pension funds, institutions or individuals—who employ high-fee managers.*[2]

But there is much more than just asset management that an effective private bank can and should provide. A wealth-owning family needs a trusted advisor who is not only able to take charge of asset management in relation to liquid assets, but also able to help the family in relation to investments in real estate, art and anything else the family is interested in. There may also be a family business in the picture, and certainly asset protection, succession planning and tax minimization will be topics of interest to the family. But if the private bank is focused on income it earns on AUM, will it really be able to help the family in all the other areas of need?

There are many private banks today that offer a variety of services to families. Asset management is usually the cornerstone, but the bank may have, in addition to the *relationship manager* the family deals with, specialists such as *wealth planners*, a trust company with *trust officers* and a variety of others who can help address the needs of wealth-owning families. These resources, if properly used, can be of enormous help to a family, and can be much more valuable than the asset management the bank may provide. But in many private banks, how wealth planners and trust company representatives charge and what their role should be is far from clear. In a number of cases, there is confusion about whether these functions are *profit centres* or *cost centres*, and the reality is that when the CEO or other manager looks at the figures, it is all too tempting to think that where the bank really makes its money is based on AUM and nothing more, with the high salaries of good wealth planners being a cost to be cut rather than a function to be focused on and built.

In times when private banks abused bank secrecy, and basically said to the wealth owners they worked with '*we don't need to care about the tax or other laws of your home country—no one will find out about the assets we hold for you—let's go for lunch*', the services and charges of the bank involved were not something the clients really focused on. If a client of a private bank was evading a tax imposed at 40% or more of the income that they earned, and was also evading inheritance and other taxes that could absorb a large percentage of the assets, the client did not really focus on the 1% or higher charge the bank was imposing on assets under management, or the retrocessions and other kickbacks the bank was receiving, or on the high transaction costs the bank added to the bill, together with charging the client for the nice lunch they took the client to.

And where assets were just hidden from view, the banks involved did not need to invest in really understanding the tax and legal systems of their clients, or in software permitting them to provide clients with the tax reports the clients need to fill in their tax returns. And rather than investing for clients in a way that legally minimizes taxation through tax-advantaged investing reflecting the specific tax rules of their clients, banks invested for all their clients in exactly the same way, a cheap and easy way of doing business. Many of the clients of private banks historically had *hold mail* arrangements—the money being hidden from home-country authorities, the client did not want to have any mail come from the bank to their home. Instead, bank statements would be held by the bank, and on an annual visit to the bank the relationship manager would point to three large boxes of unopened bank statements and ask '*Do you want to go through all these?*' Many clients would not, and the banker and the client would go to lunch, leaving the bank statements unopened, with little review of bank charges, performance on asset management or otherwise—the client happy with the savings enjoyed through the illegal evasion of tax, the high charges of the bank and the poor performance on investments being worth it.

But in a world of transparency and tax compliance, there is a huge shift that some private banks have been struggling to cope with. It is no longer possible for a private bank to arrogantly serve clients from around the world—to be effective, a private bank needs to understand the *real* needs of their clients, and this requires knowledge of the home-country tax and legal system, the ability to provide tax reporting and tax-advantaged investing, and the licensing of the private bank enabling them to legally provide services to clients from the country involved. Even the largest of private banks cannot therefore really service clients from all over the world on their own—there is a need for specialization. And clients who are fully compliant with their tax obligations are much more focused on the costs they incur in using a private bank, and on investment performance. In relation to costs, it is key to see that the client is actually receiving value, meaning that sustaining high fees on AUM will be increasingly difficult for a successful private bank.

An effective private bank needs to understand the real needs of their clients, and to align themselves with the interests of their clients. But all too often the wealth management function in banks has fallen into the leadership of investment bankers who tend to think in a very short-term and transactional way. More interested in the earnings of the bank in the next quarter than in what is in the best interests of their clients, the boss focuses on AUM, where the bank earns most of its income, and the incentives are on increasing AUM, rewarding those bankers who manage to bring new money into the bank to manage.

I have often debated with the CEOs of private banks the question of whether a private bank needs more *hunters*, most CEOs arguing that what they need are effective salespeople—bankers who can *hunt* for new clients, bringing AUM to the bank. I argue, usually unsuccessfully, that private banking is not a business for hunters, but rather a business for *farmers*—those who get to know the family they work with, meet the in-laws, develop long-term relationships that lead to growth not only in AUM, but in the relationship and the long-term retention of the family as a client of the bank.

What clients of private banks really need is a trusted family advisor, and continuity in relationships that avoids the family having to re-educate relationship managers given the turnover in staffing suffered (or encouraged) by the industry today. If I meet a relationship manager of a private bank and discuss with them holistic issues affecting my family, I will be hoping the relationship manager will remain with the private bank for the longer term, and ideally after my own passing or disability, enabling them, with their colleagues, to look after my affairs for the benefit of my family. But compensation systems within private banks, and how staff are managed generally, work against this alignment of interests, and increasingly relationship managers in private banks move all too frequently from one bank to the next.

The first question to an experienced relationship manager exploring the possibility of changing banks they work for is not what their name is, but rather how much in the way of AUM they might be able to bring with them when moving banks. The turnover in the industry, combined with the idea that clients belong to the relationship manager rather than the bank, fuels a disincentive to relationship managers institutionalizing clients. Even where a private bank has excellent wealth planners and trust officers able to help in providing holistic input to a family, the relationship manager may decide against introducing a client to their colleagues for fear that the client may *like* the wealth planner or trust officer. If the relationship manager then leaves the bank, they will have more difficulty dragging the client with them to a new bank, hence the disincentive of institutionalizing the client.

The wealth management industry is a huge business in chaos. Change is happening on many fronts, with the business models of the past falling away as tax and related transparency becomes the norm. Banks have and will continue to bear enormous compliance-related costs, in part due to the abuses of the past. Enormous fines have been paid to the United States and to other countries in and around abuses of tax and other laws, and these will continue for some time to come. Some banks are pulling out of elements of the wealth management industry as a result, and others are closing down operations in traditional wealth management centres, such as Switzerland. Smaller private banks are finding it difficult to survive, and new entrants to wealth management are likely to come from the technology sector, where new thinking and approaches may be better placed to serve wealth-owning families.

I worry that families will be facing increasing risks of fraud and otherwise as those in the industry suffer decreasing security for their own futures.

Independent Asset Managers, Multi- and Single-Family Offices

The failings of private banks have led to the creation of independent asset managers (IAMs) and multi- and single-family offices, and variations on a theme. Pricing abuse, high turnover of relationship managers, misalignment of focus and poor service generally have resulted in many families fleeing the private bank, turning to individuals who sometimes were previously with a private bank to ask from them what they do not get from banks.

The typical IAM was a successful relationship manager with a private bank who develops good relationships with their clients, but who sees the inability to provide what clients really need within the environment of a private bank that focuses more on short-term profits than on long-term relationships. The relationship manager resigns from the bank and convinces some of their better clients to continue working with them, with the relationship manager now working independently, providing the client with asset management and related services, while leaving the portfolio of assets with either their former bank or with another bank, which now acts only as a custodian of the assets.

In very basic terms, the exit of the banker from a bank and the conversion of the bank from being an asset manager into being nothing more than a custodian of assets results in a meaningful loss of income to the bank, with the example of a 1% fee on AUM now going down to 20 or 30 basis points (and often much less) for the custody the bank continues to provide. The IAM charges the client the 70 basis point difference, meaning that the client is still paying an overall 1%, but now has an IAM more committed to providing the continuity of relationship that the client really wants, and which the private bank failed to deliver.

I believe that family offices, both the single-family office and the multi-family office, are also products of the failings of the wealth management industry to serve the real needs of families.

Defining the term 'family office' is not easy, and there are many versions of family offices that bear little resemblance to each other. Today, private banks, law firms, accounting firms, trust companies and others market 'family office' services, further confusing the term.

The reality is that every wealth-owning family has a family office, whether they know it or not, and that it is difficult to find any two family offices that are the same. Someone, in every family, is taking care of things that a typical family office would deal with. A family involved in a family business may have the chief financial officer, or whoever is handling the books for the business, also keep an eye on personal investments, perhaps liaising with asset managers, and also paying bills on real estate and otherwise managing private assets the family holds. In effect, the individual involved is the family office, but not being well structured, the function may or may not be managed in a way that is best for the family.

The family office, or part of it, may also be handled by one or more people in the family—perhaps one of the children looks after a property in a particular country, while the wealth owner's spouse handles private bank accounts and the underlying investments. Typically, the 'family office' is a disorganized collection of functions that may be partially handled within the family, partially handled by staff of the family business and partially handled by external advisors, including lawyers, accountants, trustees and private banks, but with no overall coordination and supervision, resulting in a more expensive and less effective structure than the family could put in place.

The more formal family office is where a family sets up a 'single' family office—a function put in place just for their family. Here, there is no one model that families adopt, or which is the 'right' one. A senior accountant with the family business coming to retirement might be appointed as the head of the family office function, coordinating the external advisors providing support to the family in relation to assets and succession and asset-protection structures. This would be the start of a simple family office, the idea being to have someone keeping an eye on things in a coordinated way.

Family offices can be very sophisticated, even where the family office is representing the interests of only one family. Some family offices bring in their own asset managers, replacing external asset managers, or acting in the role of determining asset allocation and supervising external asset managers. In some cases, the family office can include the trust function, with private trust companies administered for the benefit of the family involved. Looking after the 'toys', which can include cars, airplanes, boats, holiday homes and more, can also occupy the time of family offices.

For many families, the cost of a family office and the distraction of running it makes the idea of a multi-family office of interest. Here the services involved are being provided not just to a single family, but to many families. As the multi-family office grows, it begins to look more and more like a private bank—albeit without the custody of financial assets. Some of the failings of private banks can develop as the focus moves away from alignment with the interests of a single family to the interests of those working at or owning the multi-family office. But if there is a real focus on aligning interests, then the multi-family office can be an effective way for the wealth owner to get what they need.

Interesting to observe is that the IAM and multi- and single-family offices usually come into the picture when the wealth-owning family gets fed up with the poor service they get from their traditional private bank. And while the private bank ends up being nothing more than a custodian, the IAM or family office begins to focus on negotiating even these fees on behalf of the wealth owner, putting more pressure on the private banks.

Can any of the private banks get it right? I believe they can, and must. And given the continuity and financial resources they can bring to the table, families can be *better* served by private banks than by IAMs or multi-family offices.

Conflicts of Interest—Everyone Has Them!

Typical private banks have many conflicts of interest, and one of the challenges the industry faces is that clients have increasingly become aware of these. If I have an account with a private bank, they have an interest not only in managing my money, but in directing me to investments in products they have a financial interest in. These may include internal investment products where the bank earns further fees, or third-party products where the bank gets some form of benefit, whether a retrocession or otherwise. Transactions may give rise to revenue for the bank, and this may create an incentive to 'churn' the account. If I use a trust company that is owned by a bank, does the trust company have an incentive to keep AUM with the bank as a means of enhancing overall revenue? For some banks, the trust function has traditionally been a cost centre, specifically for the purposes of expanding AUM.

But if I turn to an IAM or independent trust company, or to an independent lawyer or accountant, am I assured of freedom from conflicts of interest? In my view, the answer is *always* no. *Everybody* has conflicts of interest of some kind, and for the wealth owner, the best thing is to accept that this is the case, and to be aware of what the conflicts of interest are, so that these can be managed.

The lawyer or accountant I work with may or may not be getting a financial benefit by introducing me to an asset manager or other specialist. In the end, it doesn't really matter so long as I know and understand what the benefit they may be receiving is. Most lawyers will not accept financial benefits given the ethical issues involved, but some will. Even where there are no financial benefits in the picture, is there a conflict of interest when a lawyer refers me to a trust company that in turn hires that lawyer on a regular basis? Is the lawyer referring me to the trust company that is best placed to meet my needs, or is he referring me to a trust company that will give him more business because of the referral?

There are many other conflicts of interest that wealth owners need to be aware of, and these include the growing regulatory and other burdens that are placed on advisors to wealth-owning families. Banks are increasingly required to document their clients for anti-money laundering purposes, and need to understand the origin of assets and, increasingly, the tax compliance of those owning the assets involved. With obligations to file suspicious activity reports without tipping off the wealth owners involved, 'trusted' advisors—which can include, in many countries, lawyers, accountants, real estate agents and others—could well have their own interests ahead of those of their clients, something that the wealth owner certainly needs to be aware of.

Tax authorities globally are increasingly putting responsibilities on tax and other advisors to monitor abuses of tax systems, requiring reporting and other steps where certain strategies or structures are implemented. Automatic exchange of information, through the US FATCA system and the OECD's CRS, requires a broad range of intermediaries—including trustees, insurance companies and banks—to confirm the tax residences of their clients and to provide relevant tax authorities with information that includes not only income and gains, but bank balances and more. The growing compliance burdens are certainly increasing costs, which will be passed on to wealth-owning families, but are also discouraging some from continuing to provide services to sectors of wealth owners. Americans are an example, with a number of banks outside the United States having restricted the services they provide to families with US residential or citizenship connections.

Given the risks to financial intermediaries of getting it wrong, there is a shift to hyper-compliance—some intermediaries going overboard in terms of intrusive questions and documentation, something well-advised wealth owners can try to manage and resist. Also increasingly problematic will be that information exchange will include significant information that has no taxing impact, but which may well give rise to complex discussions with tax authorities and others. I may live in a country where there is a tax on interest income, but no wealth tax—does the relevant tax authority need information, which they will now get, about my bank balance? I may be the protector of a trust that benefits a family in another country, but as a 'controlling person', information on the trust income and assets may be sent to my country of residence. Will I have difficulties explaining to my tax authority that the assets and income should not be taxable to me? Will these discussions require explanations and documentation that will hugely increase costs to the family with an interest in the trust? Will my country of residence trigger information finding its way to other countries, which may use the information not only for tax enforcement, but perhaps corruptly against the interests of the family with an interest in the trust assets?

There is no replacement for the wealth owner and his or her family really understanding how advisors work. The wealth owner needs them—but needs to manage them, and to prepare the family for the work they need to do to keep eyes open, and to make sure that they get what they pay for, and know what they are paying and why. And with growing transparency and information exchange, key is to know who will be getting what information, and to ensure that intermediaries comply in a sensible fashion.

And for advisors, understanding what clients really need, and aligning interests with the interests of clients, is key to being the trusted family advisor—an advisor who is not measured by how markets perform and who is a commodity, but an advisor who is valued for telling the truth, and always having the client's interests at heart.

Notes

1. The Rebel Accountant, *Taxtopia* (Octopus Publishing, 2024), pp. 271 and 272.
2. Berkshire Hathaway Inc., Letter to Shareholders (2013), p. 20. www.berkshirehathaway.com/letters/2013ltr.pdf

CHAPTER

Getting It Right

It is possible to get it right. For countries, families, banks, trustees and others involved in and affected by issues in and around taxation, asset management and protection, and succession planning. And wealth can and should be something that is a positive thing for wealth-owning families and the societies they live in.

But getting it right and avoiding having wealth destroy a family does take thought and effort on an ongoing basis, given that things are always changing, both in the external world and within families.

Stress Tests and Understanding That No Plan Is a Plan

It's never too early to begin to think about the succession process and to work out what would happen to your assets if you were to become disabled or to pass away prematurely. A 'stress test' basically means asking the *'what-ifs?'*: *What happens to my assets if I pass away, and is whatever plan I have in place appropriate to my current circumstances and what I would like to see happening? Most importantly, will what I have put in place in terms of planning be destructive for my family and wealth?*

If you were to pass away suddenly, what happens to your assets? This will, of course, depend on what structures may be in place to deal with the transition of wealth, including trusts and other vehicles. If there are wills that have been validly executed, these will also come into the picture, and the laws relevant to where assets are located will also be key. But who will make sure that the right things are done, and that assets are actually tracked down and properly looked after and transferred? Is there an inventory of assets that has been kept up-to-date, and do family members or others who are meant to benefit know where they should go to get information about what to do if something happens to the wealth owner? In my experience, it is actually pretty rare for things to be smooth, and stress-testing succession may well mean thinking through exactly what will happen in the event of death, and making sure that what is intended is what will really take place. Part of the stress-testing is also to review whether what has been put in place will not create problems in terms of those who may have expected to benefit not benefiting, or for other reasons. And if excluding or limiting the benefit of family members or others is actually intended, would it be better to clarify this before the death of the wealth owner or not?

Wealth owners often worry about the cost of putting the right succession plan in place and of regular health checks on the plan. But the cost of getting it wrong is almost always multiples of what it would have cost to get it right. And the costs of getting it wrong are not only financial costs.

There are no black and white answers to what is the right way to deal with all of the intricacies of succession, but the key is to review what is in place on an ongoing basis. Given changes in assets, in family dynamics and the external legal and tax environment, reviewing things on an annual basis makes sense, at every level of wealth.

The approach of stress-testing the structures and approaches in place is not limited to considering what happens on death, but also what would happen in the event of incapacity, divorce and a number of other sudden or not so sudden things that can affect the assets within the family.

The stress test becomes a *continuity audit* designed to help families reach their impact goals.

Knowing What You Have and Where the Assets Are

It is terribly common for assets to get lost and stolen as wealth owners age and during the process of succession. Asking yourself how family members or others are meant to track assets down in the event of your passing or incapacity is important, as is to ensure that those who will be dealing with your assets actually know their value and what intentions are in relation to them in the event of death. Where there are valuables kept at home or in safety deposit boxes or elsewhere, will the right people find them and do the right thing with the assets? The best protection is to make sure that those who are intended to benefit know what they should be looking for, but this is not always possible or appropriate given the ages or positions of those involved. Here, using trusts or foundations may be the best approach, but the general guidance is to make sure to think about these things—not doing so is almost sure to be problematic.

Advisors, the 'Family Office' and Who Will Be Doing What

Every wealth-owning family has, in effect, a 'family office'—one or more people who handle things in and around the assets of the wealth owner. Often, the wealth owner is closely involved while they are around, but is attention paid to who will take over this function in the event of death or incapacity?

There may be excellent tax and succession advice that has been obtained, but are the lawyers and accountants who were involved at the outset now in the picture on an ongoing basis? Very often, the legal or tax advisor is transactional, in the sense that they may have been involved in drafting a will or setting up a trust, but as the years go by their files are out-of-date or lost as they retire or move on to other careers or firms. How to pick up the trail may be very difficult after the passing or disability of the wealth owner. Even the most sophisticated of families, and ones who have professionally run family offices, may not have everything set as it should be. Spending a day going through exactly what would happen in the event of death or incapacity, and thinking this through, is something that wealth owners should be doing regularly, as it is pretty inevitable that not everything is arranged as it should be, given constant changes in assets, in family circumstances and in the regulatory and tax world.

Communication and Avoiding Surprises

I may be idealistic, but I am a believer that much in the way of bad feeling and risk in relation to succession planning can be avoided through ongoing communication and openness within families regarding how the succession process will proceed. As children get older, getting their input on the succession process is valuable, and the more those who are to receive assets know about what they are meant to get and where the assets are, the safer the succession process can be.

In complex situations involving second and subsequent marriages and otherwise, avoiding surprises is part of effective planning. The destruction of relationships, litigation that follows the death or disability of the wealth owner and associated problems are more likely to occur if there are surprises that emerge when the wealth owner is gone. When everyone knows what to expect, and has been given every opportunity to provide input into the process, there is much less danger of bad feeling and disputes later on. Hoping no one will find out about your mistress is less effective than having a clear financial arrangement with your mistress that discourages her from causing problems when you are not around.

Most effective in communication is to set up family retreats, ideally annually, covering age-appropriate issues and allowing for good discussion within families about the assets of the family and how transitions are meant to take place. Medical and dental check-ups are something we should all undertake regularly, and ideally comprehensively. As we age, medical check-ups become even more important. In the case of succession and asset protection, looking at things comprehensively and regularly, and involving those who will benefit from our assets, is exceptionally important.

How Far Do We Go to Minimize Tax and to Protect Assets from Claims of Creditors, Spouses and Others?

As a tax lawyer, my job has been to work with wealth owners and to help them legally plan their affairs such as to minimize tax exposures. But how far should one go to pay the least amount of tax possible? Is it an ethical obligation of wealth owners to pay headline rates of tax to help address wealth and income inequality and to not take steps to reduce tax exposures? Where is the line between legal tax planning and illegal tax evasion... and what of tax avoidance, something that used to be considered legal and appropriate, but which is increasingly condemned by tax authorities and others?

These are issues families need to consider and which often require good advice and input from professionals who are able to help wealth owners understand the risks and where the moving line of what is legal and what is not actually is. I am a strong believer that wealth owners have a responsibility to society to pay their taxes and to help in addressing inequality. I am not, however, a believer that tax systems and governments always have it right or that tax systems are always fair in how they work. Wealth owners have choices on where and how they invest, where they live and hold citizenship, and when and how to transfer assets to family members and others who they wish to benefit with their wealth. Whatever the view of the wealth owner on how ambitious to be in their tax planning, the key is to make informed decisions, and to understand the choices that one has.

I have seen many, many wealth owners who have created much in the way of unhappiness by trying too hard to pay less tax; this through assets that were lost by being so well hidden from tax authorities that they ended up being hidden from those intended to benefit from them. I have seen assets that have fallen into the hands of corrupt governments, lawyers, accountants, bankers and others, and have also seen families miserable at being forced to stay away from their country of origin to avoid being taxed there. Is it worth living alone in a tax haven, away from family, friends and one's culture and heritage, in order to pay less tax? Can you take it with you when you die?

I have worked with many wealth owners who have delighted in having more wealth available to do good in the world and to expand their businesses, benefiting their communities, employees and others, through careful, proper tax planning, and through adopting a lifestyle that allows them to spend time in a variety of countries, but with taxable residence being maintained in countries with fair and reasonable tax systems. So, getting it right is a balance—an informed and well-considered decision on what matters and how to both enjoy life and family, and legally minimize tax exposures.

I do not fully subscribe to Thomas Piketty's view that governments are best positioned to decide on how much to take away from wealth-owning families through taxation and to redistribute that wealth. I am much more of a believer that wealth owners are better placed than governments to ensure that money made available to help others is properly and effectively applied. But governments have their function and tax cannot become fully voluntary. There are no absolutes—wealth owners need to make informed decisions, and also need to get more involved in how the world addresses the needs of those who need help, something that too many wealth owners have ignored. And laws have to be respected, including tax laws.

And is it right and ethical to protect assets from a claim of creditors, or from a claim from a spouse on divorce? Should a wealth owner consider all his sons- and daughters-in-law to be gold-diggers, as I have suggested they are? Again, there is, to me, no clear right and wrong here. The wealth owner should simply make sure they understand how things work and how they can go wrong, and then make informed decisions on how best to try to have things work out the way they want them to work out.

And I stick by my view that one should hope for the best, but certainly plan for the worst.

Women and Wealth

There are ways for wealth owners and their advisors to tailor some of their planning to women, focusing on some of their special needs and on some continuing realities. Whether in marriages or otherwise, women, like men, need to know and understand things having to do with money to protect themselves and their families.

When it comes to mechanical things, men often pretend to know more than they do, and women sometimes less than they do. Changing the lightbulb, installing a computer or television set, putting up a picture—it seems that women often leave this to men, who pretend they know what they are doing before they finally call an electrician or plumber to fix the mess they have made in trying to do it themselves. When it comes to money, this should not be the case.

In a marriage or other relationship, a woman should be asking herself whether she knows exactly what would happen if her partner died or became disabled, or if the marriage otherwise came to an end. I have come across many situations of women who have no idea how much money their husband actually had, and where the money was. In a divorce or on death of the husband, there is a mess to sort out, and the possibility of the widow or divorced wife being left in very difficult financial circumstances.

A woman does not need to know how to fix a computer (and neither does a man), but she does need to know who to call if her computer stops working. And in the case of money and the ownership of assets, a spouse has every right to know who owns what and who to call and what to do if things go wrong.

There is one very important reality about women and wealth. Chances are that they will end up with the money, one way or another—so they better know where it is and how to deal with it. Women live longer than men, and in a marriage it is likely that they will outlive their husband. And if the marriage fails, which many do, the wife will and should end up with something—so everyone needs to be prepared.

For wealth owners, educating their children to understand what they need to know about wealth and marriage, and the risks that are inevitable, is very important. Not only daughters need to know how to protect themselves, and how to make sure that they are financially independent in their relationships, allowing them to be better spouses and better parents as a result.

What Mum and Dad Meant

Most of the unhappiness and disputes I have seen in families in and around succession have to do with arguments about what 'Mum and Dad meant'. Dissatisfied with who among the children gets what, the disgruntled child says that Dad actually meant to leave that asset to them, or to have had a business run by the children in a certain way. I am a great believer in ensuring that Mum and Dad make it clear what they mean long before Mum and Dad are not around. Family retreats and discussions in and around the succession process can go a long way towards achieving this, and in wills, trusts and other succession instruments, accompanying these with clear expressions of wishes can also be a good and important thing to avoid future disputes. Assuming that your children and other heirs know what you mean is not safe. Putting things in writing and explaining your thinking while you are around, and inviting discussion, is a better way of avoiding disputes.

I have seen many wealth owners who sign wills and trust documents that are put in front of them by their legal and tax advisors, which contain little more than the basics on who gets what. Standard form documents are not the way to ensure that intentions will be met. Accompanying this with explanation can go a long way to avoiding disputes, and I sometimes suggest that wealth owners also consider recording themselves to outline how they would like to see things go. With easy technology to do this today, why not have a video recording of what the wealth owner would like to see happen with their assets, including their businesses, and how they would like to see the next generation carry things forward?

The Reality of Emotions, Psychology, Ageing and Communicating with Money

I acknowledge that I am idealistic in my thinking that communication within families, early on, can go far to address many potential circumstances of unhappiness and disputes. But I am convinced that communication is critical to avoiding problems. I also believe that in today's world of wealth owners living longer and longer, the ideal is to consider making at least some transfers of wealth to the younger generation earlier, to avoid children waiting to inherit until the death of a parent. Is it really right that a child should only inherit at the age of eighty, when their Mum or Dad dies at 100?

I am also idealistic in suggesting that children be treated equally, to the extent possible, and that money not be used as a means of communicating within families. I acknowledge that there are many realities that come into it, including specific family issues, such as children who are unable to deal with wealth safely. Is it good to give money to my children early if they are too young to deal with what they get and may squander my hard-earned resources? Is it right to treat my children equally when one of my children has really not turned out well and has significant problems with substance abuse or otherwise? Will my children take care of me in my old age if I take advantage of opportunities to save on taxes by making early distributions?

But some of the limitations on wealth owners doing the right thing are more psychological than real. Am I afraid that my children will not visit if I don't use my money as the way to keep them interested in me? Am I thinking about treating my children unequally in my succession plan as a way of communicating my disappointment with one of my children? There is a role, for many families, for psychologists and other health professionals to be part of the succession process and to help navigate the complexities that wealth-owning families face. A part of the 'stress tests' of the succession process should be questions about the psychology of money, and its effect on every generation.

Is it easier to just give it all away to charity? Frankly, no ... this still causes many issues for families. Nothing is easy, and the work that families need to do is ongoing.

Can Private Banks, Trustees and Other Advisors Get It Right?

The key to success in the relationship between wealth owners and the service providers they use is for the interests of the two to be aligned, and for there to be real openness on issues such as fees and conflicts and more.

As mentioned in the last chapter, I have not been impressed with the wealth management industry and its leadership. I have also been very unimpressed with regulators in many financial centres seeking to maintain and build the wealth management sector of their economy. Wealth management is big business, but a changing and chaotic one, where the players of today may well not be the players of tomorrow. We are already seeing disruption in the industry, and clearly Silicon Valley and the Googles, Apples, Amazons and Alibabas are going to be an increasing part of the future of banking and wealth management.

Getting it right, and aligning with the interests of wealth owners, means that there needs to be an understanding that families are about the long term and about relationships. I am critical of investment bankers running private banks, but am open to the possibility that an investment banker can learn that long-term relationships can have value, and that it is not only a large transactional fee in this quarter that brings value to a bank.

A few ideas on strategy for private banks follow, but for all involved in the process of helping wealth owners, there is enormous opportunity given the needs that wealth-owning families have. It is surprising how misunderstood these needs are by law and accounting firms, with only relatively few having organized themselves to meet the holistic needs of wealth-owning families. Some law and accounting firms have actively stayed away from working with other than companies, thinking that serving wealth owners means routine will and trust work, not understanding that working for the owners of businesses means exposure to comprehensive tax, legal and other issues that only the most sophisticated of advisors can handle. For the wealth-owning family, finding the right advisors can be tricky, but the first step is to understand what you really need.

The typical private bank, today, focuses on asset management, which is where they think they make their money. In developing strategy, there are a few things to consider.

Asset Management Is a Commodity, and Pricing Will Be Increasingly Under Challenge

Markets are what they are, and it is difficult to outperform a competitor, given that everyone is dealing with the same markets. With technology, it is possible to obtain information increasingly easily, and with a variety of index and other products, it is easy for a client of a private bank to replicate performance at a substantially cheaper price.

Does your client really need pages and pages of 'market thinking' from you, expensively produced, when similar information is coming to them from the many private banks chasing them for business? Do they need this information when they can get it on their own from elsewhere, and where the information may be more trustworthy? Do you actually need to manage money for your clients, or would they benefit more from an honest, low-cost approach to your helping them review their total asset and investment portfolio, helping them in consolidated reporting, understanding their asset class and geographical asset allocation and helping to guide them to lower-cost, lower-risk ways of managing and investing their assets?

Understanding What Your Clients Really Need

The needs of wealth-owning families are considerable, and vary depending on where they live, where they invest and on issues particular to their family. Can you really provide services that address a family's real needs without specializing in families from particular countries or who invest in particular assets in particular places? How do you go about really understanding and getting to know the families you work with, particularly if your relationship managers are not trained to do much more than sell the asset management services you think you make your money from?

Continuity and Encouraging Your People to Institutionalize Clients

If it is true that wealth owners are looking for trusted advisors who will be there for the long term, is your bank equipped to bring people onboard who will remain with the bank for their entire career? Or are compensation approaches designed to reward short-term profits, encouraging those working with clients to 'sell' rather than develop relationships? And if rewards are short term, will your staff have an incentive to institutionalize clients by introducing them to specialists in other areas than their own, such as wealth planning, trust services and otherwise? Are those working with clients incentivized to move to other banks to get promotions, or are compensation systems designed to retain staff for their entire career?

Private Banking Is a Knowledge Business—Is Your Bank Being Run Accordingly?

The needs of wealth owners are increasingly complex, and the regulatory burden on banks, trustees and others in the wealth management industry are constantly increasing. Is your bank equipped to operate as a knowledge business, where there is a focus on capturing and sharing knowledge at all levels?

In my work with private banks, I rarely ran across any that focused on knowledge as being their main asset. In the consulting world, firms like McKinsey and others make knowledge the *core* of what they offer, and put huge effort into developing approaches to knowledge management and sharing that allow them to be learning organizations—companies that learn from every client engagement, and ensure that knowledge is shared internally and used externally to improve the output provided to clients and to help educate both clients and potential clients, attracting more business. If a private banker works with a client from a particular country, and in the course of setting up a succession and asset plan for the client, is exposed to legal and tax advisors from that country who help put something of value in place, how is that knowledge and experience captured and shared with others in the bank who may serve similarly placed clients? Are the advisors involved invited to help in the training of bank personnel, and to help the bank develop products and services that are relevant to clients from the same country? Or does the next banker working on a similar project start from scratch, with no base of knowledge to draw on?

Complexity and Compliance Are Your Friends

For many private banks, increased complexity and compliance has encouraged exits from some markets. The United States is a good example, with a number of private banks no longer providing services to Americans because of the aggressive enforcement of US tax, securities and other laws by the authorities, in part as a reaction to the historical abuses of banking secrecy by the private banking sector. The perception that working with US clients is too complex and that compliance with reporting and other requirements too burdensome does not factor in that dealing with complexity is what clients need help with. The United States is the largest wealth management market in the world—for a private bank to exit a market of that size because of complexity shows a lack of strategy and foresight, given that complexity will inevitably grow in dealing with other markets, whether involving clients from emerging economies such as China or clients from developed countries such as the United Kingdom or elsewhere.

The more complex things are, the more wealth-owning families need help. The simple reality is that private banking of the past, when bankers would say '*we don't care about the tax or other laws of your country, because we have bank secrecy—let's go out for a nice lunch*', can no longer exist. In fact, such an approach to client needs was never appropriate or helpful, but too many in the industry long for the days of easy answers.

Should a Private Bank Own a Trust Company?

In the United States, it is very common for trustees to be individuals—often lawyers in law firms offering estate planning and related services. While corporate trust companies exist, they are less ubiquitous than in the international arena, where the vast majority of trusts are administered by companies. A few years ago, virtually every bank offering private banking services had their own trust companies, but with increased tax and reporting requirements affecting trustees, and more of an understanding of risk, a number of banks have been selling or closing down their trust operations.

There are really no right or wrong answers to the question of whether a private bank should own a trust company, and there are strategies banks can take to stay close to clients, despite not being in the trust business. I do generally like the idea of a private bank owning a trust company, but this assumes that the bank involved is aware of the critical need that trusteeships have of serious expertise and commitment, and a real focus on understanding, managing and pricing risk. The upside for banks and clients is that a bank-owned trust company can offer a holistic and long-term solution for families; for the private bank, it is a 'sticky' service that automatically connects multiple generations of the family to the bank.

A good indicator of the value of a trust or other fiduciary operation is research conducted by the Boston Consulting Group, which shows that the average private banking client keeps an account with a private bank for six or seven years, while where a trust is in place, the relationship will remain for an average of twenty years.[1]

Understanding the Value of Relationships and Aligning Interests

Owning the client relationship is where the value is in private banking. High relationship manager turnover, loss of confidence arising from over-selling of products and a focus on short-term revenue and many other missteps have forced wealth owners into the arms of

IAMs, multi-family offices and other providers better able to cherish and build on long-term relationships. Private banks often become nothing more than asset custodians, a low-margin and commoditized business that is difficult to compete in given the dominance of large players who have made massive investments in technology and the like, permitting them to offer solid, global custody.

There are many ways to understand the value of relationships and to align interests. One is to reflect on the statistic mentioned earlier regarding the length of time the average client of a private bank remains with the bank when they have a bank account only as opposed to maintaining a fiduciary relationship, such as a trust. If a private bank earns US$75,000 a year from a family that maintains a bank account with the private bank, the value of the client can be calculated by developing a present value of the client—projecting the expected revenue from the client for the six or seven years the client is likely to stay. Say this figure is US$400,000—if the client, instead of just having a bank account with the bank, were converted into a client that also maintains a trust with the bank, on average, the client is likely to stay with the bank for twenty years. This will pretty much triple the value of the client to the bank in present terms, a value that is too seldom measured in typical private banks.

In fact, I believe that the Boston Consulting Group's suggestion of the enhanced value of a client where a fiduciary structure is in place *underestimates* the value. The reason for this belief is that where there is a trust in place, the trustee gets to know not only the wealth owner settling the trust, but the beneficiaries—usually the children and spouse—and other family members, all of which not only helps create a stickier client relationship, but leads to new clients and more funds under management. And most importantly, the client family is getting what they really need—a long-term trusted advisor who really knows the family, and is providing services that are holistic, focused on much more than just asset management.

Keeping the Relationship Manager (and Others) There for Their Entire Careers

A key driver of success is aligning the interests of the wealth manager, employees and clients. There are many ways of doing this, and among them is to recognize that wealth management is a business of long-term relationships, and one that requires an approach to clients which reflects that working with a wealth owner requires an understanding that the wealth owner is part of a family, and that client needs will include, by necessity, issues in and around succession and asset protection. There will be wealth managers who do nothing but manage money, but if this is the case, they had better have something to offer that stands out if I am right that asset management is a commodity, and one that will—with technology and greater access to information—face severe pricing challenges.

If long-term relationships and families is what it is all about, then having client-facing staff who are with the private bank for their entire career becomes a key success factor. How can this be achieved? There was a time when a traditional private bank truly offered long-term relationship management. But this has become, in all too many cases, a thing of the past. Private banks are constantly restructuring and chopping and changing their strategy, rewarding 'hunters' bringing in new clients rather than 'farmers' developing existing clients. Relationship managers and others are encouraged to think short term and to move from one bank to the next in order to progress their careers. Private banks are increasingly publicly listed, or otherwise faced with having to produce short-term financial results.

I know of families who years ago met their relationship managers when they were at the start of their career. The relationship manager would get to know the family when they were in their late twenties or thirties, and would visit the children at boarding school (the orphanages of the wealthy), attend weddings and funerals, and work closely with experts within and outside the bank in areas from tax and trust planning, to personal security and otherwise. When the relationship manager approached retirement age, the relationship would be seamlessly passed on to a more junior colleague.

In my ideal world, a private bank today would create incentives that are long term, and ensure that successful relationship managers build their careers with one bank, aligning interests and having every incentive to institutionalize clients. An example might involve reducing upfront salaries, and increasing compensation that is long term, and one element of this could be to reward the relationship manager for the added value to a bank of the client establishing a fiduciary relationship within the bank, possibly through a trust or otherwise. If the relationship manager has been with a bank for two or three years, and it is clear that they are honest, hardworking and otherwise make the grade, the view should be that they will stay with the bank for the long term. If this is not the view, then they should be exited from the bank. Once they make it past this initial threshold, they should—from many perspectives—be provided with job security, and an assurance that if they continue to perform well, aligning with the interests of the bank and of the families the bank serves, they will be with the bank for their entire career, and beyond.

If the banker, for example, has a client with a bank account and a certain amount of money under management, the client has, as mentioned earlier, a value to the bank given the fees the bank earns, and the expected number of years those fees will be paid depending on how long the client is likely to stay with the bank. If the relationship manager introduces the client to the trust company owned by the bank, and now the client family has a fiduciary relationship, the expected number of years the client family will be with the bank triples. This enhanced value of the client to the bank is a measurable figure, and part of this value can be shared by the bank with the relationship manager.

But rather than a one-off bonus to the banker, as many banks currently provide, the relationship manager, in my model, would receive compensation over the full period during which the client family is expected to maintain the relationship. Twenty years is the estimate of the Boston Consulting Group where there is a trust in place. The compensation to the relationship manager may not be immediate, but is being paid to encourage the relationship manager to 'farm' the client family—to keep them close to the bank and to develop relationships with the younger generation and others.

The idea is to provide the relationship manager with a financial incentive to stay close to their clients, with the commission for having increased the value of the client family to the bank only continuing to be paid so long as the family remains with the bank. And if the relationship manager retires before the full twenty years pass, the commission would continue, providing that the relationship manager keeps links, in their retirement, with both the family and the bank, and is focused on ensuring the success of the succession process within the bank, helping in the handover of day-to-day activities to the next generation of relationship manager. In retirement, the relationship manager continues to earn income from the hopefully many families he or she has managed to help connect to the bank, and stays close to the families and the bank beyond retirement, helping to align the interests of all involved.

This approach is not limited to trusts and other fiduciary structures, but reflects a different way of working and thinking, and one where building and maintaining relationships rather than short-term transactional profits are rewarded.

How Wealth Planning and Trust Services Fit with Asset Management

Many banks struggle with how and whether to offer wealth planning, trust services or both. Misguided CEOs look at where the bank earns its money and think that asset management is the key. Given the need to invest in knowledge and compliance in order to safely provide either of wealth planning and trust services, a number of banks are exiting those businesses, ceasing to provide clients with services beyond asset management. To me, this is a mistake, and while it is not at all necessary to have both these functions internal to a bank, I am a great believer in the need to provide holistic services in order to 'own' the client relationship and provide clients with value that goes far beyond the fees the client pays to the private bank.

Banks that do have trust or wealth planning services (or both) struggle with whether these functions should be cost centres or profit centres. For me, it does not matter whether a trust company or wealth planning service is a cost or profit centre—what does matter is whether the client, as a whole, is paying a fee that ensures that the bank overall is earning a reasonable profit. What this means is that having a trust company owned by a bank that ignores the value of the client to the bank in other areas is simply not a good way to operate. And on the fees a client pays, looking at this in terms of what the bank earns in total is a better way to go than to have internal units competing with each other. This is not only in the client's interest, and I am a strict believer that it is only those who put the client's interest first who will succeed for the long term.

Leveraging Networks—Share Your Ability as an Educated Consumer of Legal, Tax and Other Services Wealth Owners Need

While very large, global private banks are able to internally provide trust, wealth planning and other services to complement the various areas of asset management they cover, smaller organizations may not be able to maintain the expertise necessary to cover in any comprehensive way the needs of the families they seek to work with. This does not mean that the smaller organization cannot compete. Even the largest of banks cannot provide all the services that families need, and wealth planners and trustees within banks themselves need to rely on outside experts, such as lawyers and accountants and others specialized in the many areas that wealth-owning families may need expertise on.

Managing and maintaining external networks of experts is a valuable thing for effective private banks and others in the wealth management space to do. As a knowledge business, ensuring that there is an effective flow of information from those with expertise to the bank is key, as is sharing that knowledge internally. Developments on the tax and legal front affecting wealth owners, issues in and around security and kidnapping, dealing with special assets such as artwork and otherwise, and many other topics are routine areas of need for wealth-owning families.

An effective private bank leverages its networks of experts, helping to bring them together with families, and helping families manage how they consume legal or other services. When I as a tax lawyer was asked questions directly by a wealth-owning family, often the family—not being experienced consumers of legal services—would ask the wrong questions, or ask questions that were much wider than they really needed to ask. This would have an impact on the cost of providing a response, and also on the usefulness of the response. In the case of a private bank, there is every opportunity to help clients in their use of specialists in every area, helping to identify the right advisors for the right questions, helping to narrow the questions asked and to manage costs and the process.

High Net Worth, Ultra High Net Worth, Rich, etc

As soon as a private banker hands me a business card that reads '*Head, Ultra High Net Worth Unit*', or something along those lines, I know I am dealing with a private bank that does not understand its business.

Terms like 'high net worth' or 'rich' are subjective terms, and have no room in communication between a private bank and its clients. It is insulting to a wealth owner to not be in the group of clients who are most valued by the private bank, and for those who are in the group that is ostensibly most valued (maybe these are the ultra, ultra, ultra, ultra high net worth clients), do they really want brochures that advertise this? Perhaps there is a bit of a *nouveau riche* angle here, but to me a smart private bank simply makes *every* client feel that they are getting top service because they *are* getting top service—for what they pay. And it is this latter point that is key.

Frankly, I think that segmentation of clients is important, but the approach should simply be a matter of discipline—banks and other service providers need to match the service provided to the wealth-owning family to what the family pays. The approach should be designed to ensure that the family is receiving value for money and real assistance, but in a way that makes economic sense for the bank.

In fact, the large volume of affluent families makes it sensible for a private bank or other wealth manager to orient certain products and services to such families, delivering input efficiently, allowing for pricing to be competitive while profitable. For the wealthier families with more in the way of complex needs, services may need to be more bespoke, but again, discipline in how services are delivered is key.

What I often see are expensive resources within private banks, such as wealth planners, spending too much time reinventing the wheel with clients who are not paying enough for the time being spent, and this largely through poor knowledge management and a reality that staff end up spending more time with clients they find fun than the ones who might be in a position to pay for more in the way of service. And with all the private banks chasing the much smaller pool of 'billionaires', is enough attention paid to the reality that this community is over-banked and generally can often negotiate their way to much lower fees than may be economically viable for the service provider?

Putting Together Strategy, Marketing, Compliance and Training

I spent some years establishing and then running a company that was involved in knowledge management and training. Among the services we provided were training services for private banks and trust companies. I had long been involved in helping private banks and others in the area of strategy, and have always been a believer in the need to link strategy with training, and also to the marketing and compliance functions.

I am bemused by the lack of focus by the leaders of private banks on training, with CEOs more often than not relegating training to relatively low-level personnel to handle, and treating training as a 'check-the-box' item on the agenda, very quickly reduced when the budget is reviewed for areas that can be cut. As a knowledge business, a private bank or other provider of input to wealth owners needs to understand the ongoing need for training, and also what exactly it is that people need to be trained on.

An over-focus on selling skills, and pushing bank products, is far from the key to success. A best-of-class approach, to me, would be for the training function to be closely tied to the strategy of the bank, meaning that the first step in the process is to develop and adopt a clear strategy. This might, among others, result in a focus on particular markets and particular segments of wealth owners, and on particular approaches to asset management.

A decision on strategy then leads to the need for the involvement of the compliance function—understanding how to legally work with clients from the markets of interest that have been identified, and how to ensure that products and services which are adapted or developed for such clients can be marketed and serviced in a compliant way. Business issues will come up at this stage, including in relation to pricing, an important thing being for banks to understand and price risk—charging the right price for the services that are provided, and holding back from providing services that are just too risky for the bank to engage in.

The training function should be part of the strategy and compliance process, the objective being to train staff of the private bank to implement the strategy of the bank, and to do so in a compliant way. Marketing comes clearly into the picture as well, as key to delivering on strategy is for marketing personnel to design their marketing approach to help achieve strategic objectives.

Clients often have latent needs—needs that they do not know they have. The most effective marketing is often oriented towards education, and to raising the awareness of the family of their needs, and how the private bank is able to meet those needs through provision of its products and services.

Joining up strategy, compliance, marketing and training is critical to success and efficiency, but few in the industry really get this.

Recruiting and Training Rather than Poaching, and Focusing on Skills, Not Perceived 'Ability' to Work with the Wealthy

It was perversely amusing to observe the actions of private banks not so many years ago in Singapore and elsewhere, during a time of difficulty in finding good relationship managers. A perceived shortage of talent in private banking led private banks to look for client relationship managers from outside the private banking industry—and often they turned to the luxury retail business for their new recruits. While private banking is a luxury business in many ways, and perhaps has, as a business, much to learn from how luxury brands are managed and developed, the reality is that a pretty young thing, male or female, working for a luxury jeweller or car dealership, does not generally have the skills needed to be the trusted family advisor in the context of true wealth management.

Where a private bank is simply looking for someone to sell its products, maybe the approach makes sense, but to me, how private banks recruit (and from where) tells me much about their lack of strategy and long-term focus on aligning the needs of clients with those of the bank. I believe that private banks should try harder to develop their own talent, recruiting from business schools and elsewhere, looking for recruits from different countries, with the language skills needed to navigate a global client base. A focus on training and retention should be part of the process, creating long-term careers that encourage bankers to think of what is best for the bank and its clients, rather than their own short-term objectives. With a good chunk of current recruiting focusing on poaching bankers with a book of business from an existing bank, the current merry-go-round of relationship managers moving from one bank to another is simply not in anyone's interests—not in the interests of clients, not in the interests of the private banks, and not in the interests of the individual bankers involved.

Do Wealth Owners Need a Bank, a Family Office, an Independent Asset Manager or a Lawyer or Accountant to Handle Things?

From the perspective of the wealth-owning family, what they need is help in many areas, and what help they need will depend on where they live, invest and do business. What they need will also very much depend on the individual family circumstances and dynamics. For the wealth manager, the question is whether to seek to address the needs of clients holistically, or just focus on what the wealth manager may be best at—this could be asset allocation and discretionary asset management, or knowledge about the succession process or some other area of specialty.

Of importance to every family is to find trusted advisors—people who can help with expertise in one or more areas of relevance, but ideally people with their own networks of specialists able to help wealth owners, and who can be brought in as needed to address particular areas of need. This trusted advisor role can be played by a lawyer, accountant, asset manager or other intermediary, and from a business perspective, it makes sense for private banks and others in the industry to consider the need to train staff to not only sell products, but also move to 'owning' the client relationship—something of enormous long-term value to the bank, and which aligns with what is best for wealth-owning clients—trusting relationships that can transition from one generation to the next.[2]

Education Is the Key

For the wealth-owning family, it is critically important to think about the family's succession and asset-protection strategies and to periodically review whether what is in place really meets the changing circumstances of the family. But to do this well, and to properly keep an eye on advisors, all members of wealth-owning families, at the right age, need to be brought into an ongoing programme of learning, leading to responsibility as wealth owners. Whether or not a son or daughter will be involved in managing a family business, they need to be prepared for whatever role they will ultimately have, even if this role is limited to being an owner of the business together with other siblings who may be involved in the management of the business. And where there is no business, just having the ownership of a portfolio of assets requires preparation.

Learning is an ongoing process, and opportunities to learn from other families and their successes and failures can also be instructive. Many private banks run training programmes for wealth owners, sometimes orienting things to the younger generation and sometimes towards the family more generally. These courses can be useful, if only to allow interaction with other families, but it is good to prepare those in the family attending for the reality that part of the objective of the bank in organizing these programmes is to sell their bank. It is unlikely that the training will say much about how to review pricing and how charges are imposed and might best be negotiated, and quite likely that the training will be oriented towards the products and services of the bank rather than the specific needs of the family.

Banks that understand the principle of *selling by not selling*—telling the truth, and really helping families navigate the complexities of wealth ownership generally—do a better job of generating business from the education programmes they run, but all too often those in charge do not really get it.

There are many education options for families outside the world of private banks and the programmes they run for their clients.

A number of top business schools worldwide offer education to wealth and business-owning families, and these programmes can often be customized to address specific issues within individual families, something that can be particularly useful.

Your children need to be prepared… to resist the thousands of investment scams out there, to understand how to navigate difficult divorces and the ever-changing regulatory world, and to work well (and safely) with the advisors they will need to help guide them.

***

When I work with families, I often insist on not only meeting with and discussing matters with the older generation, the wealth-owning matriarch and/or patriarch, but also with each member of the younger generation—individually and in private. It is here that I learn about concerns and mistrust among siblings, and various unspoken issues in the family. It is with this feedback that I am better able to get a sense of the needs of the family, all of which have to be taken into account holistically in the succession and asset-protection plan to be adopted.

Too often the matriarch or patriarch is over-emphasizing one issue or the other—perhaps focusing on tax minimization or the risks of divorce in the younger generation, the complexity of which makes it all the easier for advisors to keep the family in a mysterious fog about how the family's own assets are owned, administered and, most importantly, to be passed on to subsequent generations.

Is there an adequate succession and asset-protection plan in place? Have all the right '*what ifs?*' been addressed? Does the next generation know what they should be doing to ensure the safety and security of family assets going forward?

It is possible for families to get it right. And it is very important that they do.

Notes

1. I do not have a published citation for this statistic from the Boston Consulting Group, but it comes from my work with BCG in a joint project with that firm's Zurich office a number of years ago. At the time, I obtained permission to reference the statistic in my teaching and writing.

2. An excellent paper by James (Jay) E. Hughes Jr. on what a *personne de confiance* is, as opposed to a *personne d'affaires,* is only one of many outstanding resources at www.jehjf.org. See the paper at https://jehjf.org/a-reflection-on-the-nature-and-practice-of-the-role-of-the-personne-de-confiance-in-a-system-of-family-governance-historically-and-today/. Jay Hughes has been cited earlier as the author of *Family Wealth: Keeping it in the Family* and the co-author of each of *The Cycle of the Gift* and *Family Trusts.* As one of the most thoughtful family business advisors in the world, Jay's paper expresses perfectly what it takes to be a trusted advisor to wealth and business-owning families.

CHAPTER 10

The Apple, Bird and Crane Families—and Dagland—Their *Theories of Change* and the Process to Get There

In this last chapter of the book, I set out how the *Theory of Change* can be used as a methodology by families seeking to navigate a world of complexity affecting their succession and asset-protection plans. I also outline how a country, like our fictional Dagland, might use the *Theory of Change* to become an example of a society that treasures the value to the country of wealth and business owners and unleashes the transformative power of family wealth to address urgent societal needs, including wealth and income inequality and other priorities.

Beginning with families and their approach, our three example families have a number of shared needs and can start their use of the *Theory of Change* in a similar way. But as we get into some of the complexities of the individual families and their ultimate impact goals, the strategic roadmap to the ultimate destination will itself, by necessity, be more complex. However, for all three families, the methodology will be virtually identical.

The Families

A reminder of the fictional families mentioned earlier.

The Apple family is made up of Reginald Apple and Martha Apple and their three children, Brenda, Susan and David. Reginald and Martha did not start out with much in the way of wealth, but through careful savings they now own a home free of a mortgage, have a comfortable lifestyle, and have put aside somewhere in the range of US$500,000 in savings. Now in their early 60s, Reginald and Martha want to make sure that their own retirement needs are met and that, to the extent possible, they can help their children in their lives as much as they can. Both Reginald and Martha are employed and working full-time, though they do anticipate moving to part-time work in the coming years.

The Apple children range in ages from twenty-eight to thirty-three and while all three are unmarried, Brenda, the eldest, is in a long-term relationship with Alex that is looking to become more serious.

All of the Apple children are working, but only Susan, who is thirty, is earning enough on her own to cover her living expenses. Reginald and Martha provide supplemental allowances to each of Brenda and David to help them cover their housing expenses, something they have had to do since Brenda and David left home a year or two after graduation from university.

The Bird family is more of a business-owning family and Alfred Bird is a third-generation Bird—at least in his estimation. Alfred's father, George, claims that Alfred is actual G-2 (second generation) given that it was George, in George's view, who saved the family business from certain collapse.

The family business, a chain of fifteen retail hardware stores, had its origin with the first Bird Hardware operation established by Alfred's late grandfather, Alexander.

Alfred is sixty-five and George is ninety-one. Alfred has three children, Emily, Doug and Frederick, and seven grandchildren. Alfred recently divorced his wife, Sheila, and has since developed a relationship with Sophie, who is younger than Emily, Doug and Frederick.

George is widowed and has just started a relationship with Giselle, fifty, whom he met on a cruise he took two years ago with some friends.

The matriarch of the Crane family is Sara Crane, a uniquely gifted and widely respected entrepreneur. Now seventy-five, Sara, three years ago, sold the tech company that she had established and eventually built into a globally recognized brand. The family wealth is now well over US$4 billion and is invested in a broad range of private equity and portfolio holdings.

Sara's husband, Sid, died five years ago, and Sara's three children, Ed, Sam and Syd (a name similar to her father's but with a different spelling) are all in their thirties and early forties and married.

For the examples and our discussion, we can keep open the countries of residence and citizenship of these families. While this will, of course, be extremely relevant, the principles of the *Theories of*

Change would be broadly the same, with actions taken to get to the impact goal that would take into account the realities of where the family (and individual family members) live and where business and related activities take place.

Holistic Continuity and Legacy Planning

Before exploring the *Theory of Change* and how it can be used for the three families in their planning, it is useful to recognize that what all three families want to undertake is an approach that can align relational, operational and financial strategies with a view to helping each family ensure that their families and their business and investment interests can achieve success and prosperity and this, ideally, across generations. In my experience, while it is pretty obvious that each family needs to focus on continuity and legacy, many wealth and business-owning families are derailed (and distracted) by internal and external events. These can include some of the things outlined in earlier chapters of this book, including ever-changing tax laws, political risk, internal family dynamics and otherwise.

Some well-advised families undertake continuity 'audits'—reviews of their planning approaches designed to confirm whether what is needed to achieve continuity is in place. Formal or informal audits of this kind are a healthy practice for families.

For all three families in our examples, holistic continuity and legacy planning is what is needed. This will include a number of elements, and these will be something we bring into the *Theories of Change* and resulting strategic roadmaps for each family.

Each family will need to consider:

- Alignment of the strategic vision for the family, aligning family values with business and investment goals.
- Ensuring a balance of focus between 'family' and 'business/investment' interests.
- How to ensure that there is good dialogue in the family that supports mutual understanding and collaboration, combined with a focus on developing the younger generations for their roles in helping the family achieve its goals.
- Effective succession and asset-protection planning that focuses on supporting smooth transitions and decision-making.
- Balancing future financial needs of the family and its business and investment interests with current needs and expectations.

- Focusing on resilience—of both the family and its business and investment interests. This will require consideration of potential derailers and other disruptions that can occur.
- Philanthropy and social responsibility will need to be embedded. Each family does not exist on its own and is part of a wider, interconnected, ecosystem. Societal needs are needs that families which seek continuity must confront and address.
- The personal growth of each individual family member, and their individual *self-actualization*, are key to the success of the family as a whole and the family's collective business and investment interests. This brings in the need for support for personal growth and wellbeing, physical and mental, for family members as well as professional and related development that family members may need.
- Compliance on the legal, tax and regulatory front is necessary, but ensuring that tax and other exposures are legally managed in the right way can be critical.

If the three families undertake their *Theory of Change* and what is involved, the possibility of achieving strong family relationships and a reduction of conflicts can be an outcome. Where there are shared goals and clear communication, the chances of avoiding conflicts are much improved. A long-term focus and clarity can enhance the resilience of the family business and investments and provide approaches to asset protection that can support not only current generations but also future ones. And a focus on community will not only help enhance the reputation of the family, but help the family itself achieve sustainability given the family's reliance on community to achieve its impact goal.

The First Step—Starting at the End—And Choosing a Date!

The first step in a *Theory of Change* is to focus on the impact goal. That means that for all three families in our examples, a visioning exercise needs to be undertaken. No question that over time the impact goal may change, and be adapted to changing circumstances, whether from within the family or external to the family.

For the Apples, the Birds and the Cranes, the timeframe to be focused on may well be different. As mentioned earlier, for the Apples, an appropriate date to set for developing the family's impact goal might be to project forward to when the parents, Reginald and

Martha, will be in their 90s, so thirty years from now. That might be a time that reflects well the planning goals of the family—Reginald and Martha would like to ensure that, among other things, they are financially secure during their later years and retirement, and that all is set for a smooth and beneficial transition to the next generation.

For the Bird family, planning might be somewhat more long term. The family business has been in the family for three generations, and maybe the family might choose a future date of fifty or sixty years from now for considering the family's impact goal.

In the case of the Crane family, an even longer-term approach might be appropriate. Some wealth and business-owning families consider things over decades; others think in centuries.

The timeframes chosen by the Apples, the Birds and the Cranes can and should be adjusted and tested over time. As steps are taken to put the plan in motion, the families and their business and investment interests will evolve. The theory of change can adapt, and the vision for the future will always change.

Developing the 'Impact Goal'—What Is Our Destination?

For the Apples, a key impact goal is to ensure that when Reginald and Martha are in their nineties, they can look back to having enjoyed a comfortable retirement and with their planning completed and all in place to ensure their own health and happiness and that of their three children. In relation to family assets, the key for the family is to ensure that they are available to support the impact goal and, ideally, objectives of the family beyond.

For the Birds and the Cranes, their fifty-year vision for the family and their business and investment interests would be to have a happy and healthy family that is supported by employees, partners, community and planet, and with an investment and business 'engine' that runs on 'autopilot', with prepared family members steering the way forward.

Each family is part of an ecosystem that includes family members, friends, employees, communities and planet. Each family has its family interests and also its business and investment interests. In developing their impact goals, the Apple, Bird and Crane families benefit from thinking about what a healthy ecosystem for their family would look like years forward, helping them to identify the steps necessary for the family to undertake to get there.

It is a very worthwhile exercise for families to consider their impact goals—their agreed vision of what 'success' looks like, both on the family front and in relation to investment and business interests. Ideally, this visioning is detailed and regularly revisited. And with clarity on the direction the family is heading, knowing what needs to be done today to get there is easier to identify and manage. The overall *Theory of Change* exercise helps the family to develop a strategic roadmap and action plan that they can implement, with the help of internal and external advisors as needed.

For the Apples, success in planning will mean that the impact goal is reached in the lifetimes of Reginald and Martha. In their nineties, Reginald and Martha will look back on a comfortable retirement. Planning is in place to allow for succession to the survivor of the couple, keeping the home available to whichever of them lives longer. On the passing of both parents, the home goes to the next generation, in equal shares, but under arrangements that seek to equalize benefits to the three children, Brenda, Susan and David.

As Reginald and Martha have helped out their children financially from time to time, and in particular Brenda and David, the impact goal might include reference to a transparent and unanimously accepted approach to equalizing benefits to the next generation. In simple terms, help provided during the lifetimes of Reginald and Martha is recorded, and amounts that may have been provided are treated as loans that are repaid on the passing of both parents, resulting in equal treatment of their children.

It is inevitable in families that some of the younger generation may need more in the way of financial support than their siblings. But the unequal treatment that can result can be a derailer that disturbs family relationships. Ensuring a mechanism that is transparent and results in adjustments designed to bring equality can be important and can be implemented in a variety of ways. In the case of Reginald and Martha, they might consider having their wills leave everything to the survivor of the two in the event of either of them passing away, and then leave the assets that remain to be divided equally among the next generation. But in relation to what the next generation might receive, there can be an adjustment for recorded advances made during the lifetimes of Reginald and Martha. Given that only Susan, one of the three Apple children, is earning enough to cover her living expenses, support through allowances from their parents is likely to continue for Brenda and David, possibly for some time.

In the impact goals of the Apple family, the three Apple children, treated equally, would be in a position to benefit from their parents, and to do so in a way that would contribute to the welfare of the family. This will likely involve some attention to pre-nuptial and other arrangements associated with marriages and other relationships the younger generation enter into.

The impact goals for the Birds and the Cranes, as mentioned, would be set fifty years forward for the purpose of immediate planning. At that time, a healthy and happy family would also be envisioned, but here linked to a business and investment engine designed to support the family and its ecosystem for generations forward.

For the Birds and the Cranes, visioning a future ecosystem for the families and their income and investment interests might be shown in diagrams, with the first being along these lines.[1]

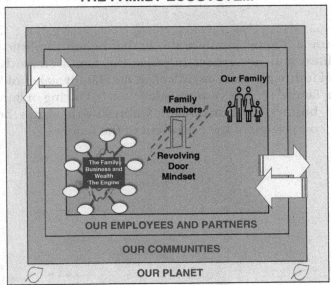

This first diagram sets out the overall family ecosystem. In the diagram, there are several elements the families might consider as they design their ideal future. The diagram sets out the 'family' and the 'engine' and between them a 'revolving door'. Surrounding these elements are employees and partners, communities and planet—all elements critical to the family, its engine and the ability of the family to achieve its impact goals.

The two elements that are critical are 'family' and the 'engine'. In relation to family, this requires attention and work to ensure that the intentions of the family are realized—putting things in place

that ensure a 'happy' family and one that benefits holistically from the business and investment interests the family stewards for the benefit of future generations, as well as non-family stakeholders. The focus on 'family' requires *extreme balance*—a balancing of family interests with business and investment interests—the latter being the 'engine' component of the ecosystem of the family.

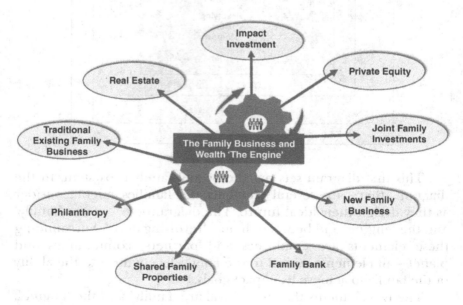

The 'engine' can be a specific family business or a portfolio of businesses; it can be purely financial and/or include a portfolio of business interests; and the 'engine' can include components such as the family bank, a concept discussed earlier in this book as an approach to financing investments that the younger generation, among others, may wish to make.

Neither the family nor the engine can survive long term without reflection on employees, community and the planet, and this also forms an essential part of the family and business ecosystem. For a family and its business and investment interests to be sustainable, they need a sustainable world, and this includes care for employees, communities and the planet. For a family business to contribute to the sustainability of our world, the family and its business need to be sustainable. There is huge *positive* symbiosis to be achieved.

For the Birds and the Cranes, an important element of the ecosystem will be to have clarity on who a family member actually is. This will mean that the family agrees on definitions of 'family'—perhaps the inclusion of adopted children, if adopted before a certain age, and maybe, for some purposes but not all, spouses and other partners of family members. With the definition of 'family' agreed, this will link into benefits family members might get, as well as into governance arrangements, including who makes what decisions and who chooses those who are then in a position of stewarding both the family and its 'engine'.

Extreme balance is also relevant to the question of whether it is better for assets to be owned by individual family members or to be stewarded for the benefit of multiple generations of family members and other stakeholders. In my experience, the more of a balance there is between individual wealth in younger generations, supporting the self-actualization of each family member, and assets to be stewarded for the long term, the more can be achieved for the family, both in terms of the objective of confident and self-sufficient individual family members and in terms of how those family members work together to steward assets for the benefit of future generations. This might, for the Bird and Crane families, mean that there is a focus on ensuring a transparent approach to succession—an approach that allows individual family members to benefit from assets that come into their individual ownership and reduce their dependence on family assets. This might mean that some assets passing from older generations go directly into the ownership of the younger generation, while other assets may be designated as assets to be stewarded for the long term. And for both the Birds and the Cranes, this might be done in a way that combines some elements of the 'engine' to be stewarded for the longer term with individual ownership. An example of this might be that Sara Crane transfers to her three children equal amounts—perhaps some during Sara's lifetime, and other assets only on her passing. But part of what is transferred to the children can include a stake in the family investment and business 'engine'—and one that is designed to reflect both the intended stewardship of the engine for the long term and direct participation of family members in reward systems designed to encourage engagement.

There are any number of structures that can be used for the family business and investment 'engine', and only one possibility would be to have the engine take the form of a limited partnership with interests that, perhaps, can only be owned by family members. Limited partnership interests can be linked to investment time commitments, limiting possibilities of exit and thereby contributing to long-term stewardship. Sara Crane, for example, can transfer to each of her three children assets that include limited partnership interests in the family investment and business engine, which interests are dedicated to remaining in the collective investment approach of the engine for fixed periods. The idea here would be to allow for exits, but for these to be controlled in terms of timing, ensuring the continuity that the family believes is needed. This can be combined with a philosophy of allowing for 'generational harvests' and rewards for those in the family who prepare themselves for, and undertake, important stewardship roles.

Ed, Sam and Syd, Sara Crane's three children, might thereby receive certain assets from their mother, during her lifetime and on her passing, that allow each to have independence and clarity regarding what they have. Apart from this individual wealth (distributed on a family 'branch' basis), as members of the 'family', each would be clear on other benefits and protections the family provides—perhaps coverage of health insurance, education for the younger generations and some basic housing ... and maybe even a minimum income for those who are 'family' and who adhere to the family constitution and approaches. These benefits are provided not on a family 'branch' basis, but on a 'per-capita' basis.

In relation to the family business and investment 'engine', while the Bird and Crane families might increasingly be relying on professional non-family managers, as part of a solid, long-term ecosystem, family members might be part of an 'autopilot' approach that ensures safety and security of the engine over time. As discussed earlier, the 'autopilot' approach to things does not mean that family members do not need to be prepared. Like pilots of an airplane, while the business and investment engine may be on autopilot, the pilots need to be in a position to steer the plane, set the direction and have the ability to take the controls if and when needed. Well-prepared family members can take a helicopter view of things and have the ability to take a deep dive into issues that arise. An effective autopilot approach will have family choosing the right teams of professionals in place to run things.[2]

Governance is a key element of the ecosystem and of the autopilot approach. And linked to this governance need is how family members are attracted to and prepared for their governance and other roles. For the Birds and the Cranes, providing clarity to younger generations early on in relation to the *opportunities* the family offers to those who are ready to prepare themselves for key roles will be important. The families might put in place and reflect in their family constitutions a variety of governance bodies. A *family assembly* might include all adult members of the 'family', including spouses, who have the ability to vote in members of a *family council*. Perhaps also open to spouses, the family council can be the body that makes decisions in relation to *family* issues—questions regarding qualification for the education, housing and other benefits family members are assured if they support the family constitution and endeavours. The family council might also be represented on a second governance body that acts as a *bridge* between 'family' and the business and investment 'engine'. Jay Hughes has written about the concept of a 'Council of Elders' as a third mediative (never judicial) branch of family governance. This can be part of the concept of a *bridge* between 'family' and 'business' and benefit from the opportunity to take advantage of the wisdom and experience of family elders and to provide them with a meaningful role as younger family members take more active roles in the family ecosystem. As Jay says, '*social anthropologies' discerning view is that without elders, human communities cannot flourish*'.[3]

The engine will be providing flows of income to fund the family expenditures, and these can extend to philanthropic and other endeavours of the families. And on the supervision and stewardship of the engine, a *business council* might be made up of qualifying family members who have prepared themselves for roles within the autopilot system. The business council might be the body to which professional managers report and which has the responsibility to develop the teams on which the family relies. But the business council needs the skills and ability to always take a helicopter view of things, undertake a deep dive where necessary and keep the engine running well. Perhaps in the case of the Birds and the Cranes, family members qualifying for a seat on the business council have the opportunity to buy interests in the business and investment engine that they then have to sell back on retirement. The idea is to encourage long-term multi-generational stewardship, but to provide entrepreneurial incentives that will have individual family members benefit financially to the extent there is growth in value over the time of their watch.

In a well-functioning ecosystem, the *values* of the family will help guide decision-making. Reflected, ideally, in the family constitution and regularly discussed, values will set out what the family stands for; the behaviours that are valued; how the family will work towards achieving their mission and vision.

The *mission* of families relates to what they are doing today and what they are trying to accomplish. For the Birds and the Cranes, this might include the fact that they are building for the future of their families, their mission being to be a multi-generational family with strong and self-actualized individuals supported by a business and investment engine designed to sustain the family and other stakeholders for the very long term.

The *vision* of the families relates to where the family is going; what the family wants to achieve in the future; the role of the family in society and the family's vision of future society.

In deciding on the structuring of the different components of their business and investment engines, the Birds and the Cranes can reflect on a variety of potential derailers and how bridges and tunnels can be found to navigate them. Some derailers will be external—tax and political risk challenges would be examples. Others will be internal—mental health challenges, divorces, family disputes and otherwise.

In the case of the Birds, George, ninety-one, has begun a relationship with Giselle, who is fifty. Alfred, who is sixty-five, has developed a relationship with Sophie, who is younger than any of his children. Sophie and Giselle are, of course, potential derailers. They also have the potential to be positive contributors to the happiness of George and Alfred and, as a result, to the family as a whole. Perhaps the more upfront clarity for Sophie and Giselle on what they might get and what they will not get if relationships are maintained is important. And from a legal perspective, pre- and post-nuptial agreements, well-considered trusts or similar arrangements, and perhaps early gifting by George and Alfred, can be part of a plan that ensures these relationships do not jeopardize the impact goals of the families.

There are many, many '*what-ifs?*' the Birds and Cranes should regularly consider. Political risk, taxation and other external derailers can and must be navigated through, among others, well-chosen structures and the use of investment protection agreements and the like, topics covered earlier. The diversification of ownership that extreme balance of *I* and *we* results in—the independent wealth of each family member and the diversification within the business and investment engine—can all contribute to the families navigating political risk and other challenges.

In the case of both the Birds and the Cranes, philanthropy may be an important element of the impact goal and envisioned future ecosystems of the families. This might take the form of a foundation or trust that is governed by approaches designed to introduce family members to collaborative responsibility for family endeavours, perhaps allowing family members to start with involvement in philanthropy and then move to governance roles within the family business and investment engine. And this philanthropy might itself be linked to the investment engine through the philanthropic structure maintaining part of its investments as a stake, perhaps a limited partnership interest, in the engine.

Reflecting on how families can benefit from circular economy approaches, the Birds and the Cranes might adopt an attitude of encouraging rather than discouraging family members from pursuing their own areas of interest and careers—and their own interests in where they might live. In simple terms, to avoid wasting family human resources, the families might celebrate diversity, recognizing that the future needs of the family, both in relation to the 'family' side of things and in relation to the business and investment 'engine', may need skills and abilities different than those of the past.

In the case of the Birds, the chain of hardware stores may or may not reflect the future of the family business and investment engine; in the case of the Cranes, the tech company that Sara Crane established has been sold—both families cannot be sure what businesses and investments will drive their futures. Having a diverse family can help, not hurt, resilience and adaptability. But there will be a need for family members to understand the mix of skills that will be needed in future and what needs to be done in terms of development to ensure that there are always family members available to play the roles they need to play in relation to governance and otherwise.

As mentioned, clarity on rewards is important. The earlier family members are aware of what support they can expect in relation to housing, education and otherwise, the better. And clarity as well on 'harvests' that might be enjoyed, such as on an exit through a sale of a stake in the family business and investment engine, will come into the picture. For the Birds and the Cranes, perhaps this is done in a way that reflects circularity and not wasting resources ... there are exits in a limited way available for family members, but linked to an open door to return—the door is a *revolving door*. As an example, Sam Crane might inherit a stake in the family business and investment engine from Sara, but the stake can only be owned by family members and can only be sold at set times (in part, designed to ensure the continuity of the engine) and at terms that facilitate the long-term success of the engine. Perhaps there is a valuation formula that applies on the exit, and the payout on a sale of interests to the engine itself is made over a period of, say, ten years. The same valuation formula might be open to family members seeking to re-enter through the revolving door. If my father sold his stake in the family business, as a family member I can buy my way back in—through the revolving door.

Many of the approaches and concepts that would be considered by families such as the Birds and the Cranes might seem too complex to be needed by families with less in the way of complex assets, such as the Apple family. But some of the ideas, including clarity on rewards and navigation of internal and external derailers, can be of use to those families. And for all families, understanding their dependence on the sustainability of employees, community and planet are key. Short-term thinking that society is somehow optional is only that—short-term thinking that leads to long-term negative outcomes.

As part of their impact goals and future ecosystems, the Birds and the Cranes might set out in their family constitutions and/or family guides regular meetings of family and non-family stakeholders. Perhaps once a year a meeting of the entire family assembly, in a meeting organized by the family council, and with an emphasis on the family rather than on the business and investment engine. But as structures that benefit the family with educational, health, housing and other support is funded by the engine, and given that family members may have their own stakes in the engine, the meeting would also be able to provide snapshots on the performance of the family business and investment engine and on the opportunities for family members to prepare themselves for governance and other roles relating to the engine.

Other meetings on a regular schedule might include the business council and the bridge—perhaps the Council of Elders—between the engine and the family.

Meetings can also include steps to be taken in developing the family constitution and all of its elements.

For success, good parenting comes into the picture, as does very early introduction to both family opportunities and what it will take to benefit from those opportunities. It is unfair for the next generation to learn of these when they are in their twenties or thirties and having already made decisions about their education and profession. If the opportunities are highlighted early, the younger generation can be supported in developing themselves in ways that can balance their individual interests with what the family as a whole needs in terms of skills and otherwise.

Recognizing the challenges of ever-changing tax systems and attitudes, the Birds and the Cranes might maintain flexibility on places of residence and perhaps even citizenship, but with mindfulness of the need to balance this with what it takes to be responsible business and wealth owners.

Once the impact goal is clear, we move to the left of the chart—looking not at the future but at the present and the steps necessary to get to the planned destination.

Inputs and Resources

As part of the *Theory of Change*, once the three families have developed and articulated their impact goals, they can reflect on the *inputs and resources* they have and need to orient to their strategic roadmap. In all three families, there will be family values, history and other resources that can and should be brought into the planning process. This can be something that is developed formally or informally, but the key is to ensure that family values, history and other

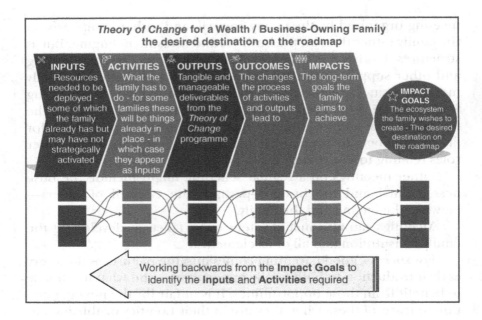

resources that will be helpful are cherished and developed and not lost. Part of the process here will also be to reflect on what else is needed in the way of inputs and resources. In the case of the Birds and the Cranes in particular, all family members having a good understanding of the past will help them to create a positive present and a successful future.

This first step after developing the impact goals of the families will include identifying the investments the family may need to make towards their future, as well as identification of the right people, in and out of the family, with the skills necessary to help. In relation to expert support, in some families, the right experts may already be in place—in which case they are an input that the family will bring to the table. If the right experts are not yet identified, then the needed input may be to allocate a budget for hiring the right experts, and a necessary next step *activity* will be to identify the right experts.

Activities, Outputs, Outcomes and Impacts

With the impact goal and the ultimate ecosystems each family is working towards being clear, it becomes easier to prioritize activities the family needs to undertake with a view to achieving outputs, outcomes and impacts that lead to the destination.

The *Theories of Change* for each family provide a strategic roadmap—and on that roadmap are activities that need to be undertaken. These can include analysis of ownership, stewardship and succession structures; ongoing '*what-if?*' analyses that allow for testing ownership and stewardship structures for necessary resilience; work on the family and its business and investment engine being clear on mission, values and vision; putting in place and testing the right decision-making and governance strategies; engaging in internal and external dialogue and learning; finding and using the right experts to support the objectives of the family; networking with peer families and more.

The outcomes of these activities can and should be measured. The programme should be designed to help the family ecosystem become a learning organization and one which is increasingly aligned, minimizing disruptive disputes and encouraging collective decision-making. Outcomes can include well-prepared family members who are socially and environmentally aware; financial rewards that are clear so that family members can commit to developing themselves in preparation for interesting and necessary roles.

And all on the strategic roadmap leads to impacts—impacts that collectively make up the overall destination, and the starting point of the families developing their *Theories of Change*. The long-term vision of what success looks like—success in terms of family happiness and wellbeing and how it and the communities around it can achieve this with the support of a financially sound business and investment engine.

Some examples using our fictional families. In the case of the Birds and the Cranes in particular, reaching their impact goals will require that assets not only remain largely intact and in place over time, but grow, as the family and its ecosystem do. Once the decision is made that this is a desired outcome, planning activities in and around the objective would take place.

This can include obtaining and following advice in relation to minimizing taxation, both in relation to earnings and particularly in relation to transfers by gift or on death—a matter that will depend on the countries whose tax laws are in issue given the location of assets and the residences (and possibly citizenships) of family members. In the case of the Apples, the approaches to tax minimization might be straightforward—perhaps there are exemptions in the country of residence of Reginald and Martha on transfers between spouses, and this can be combined with reliance on exemptions on other transfers to be made within the family. But if there are advantages in the relevant country to early gifting (such as in the United Kingdom at present, where gifts made earlier than within seven years of death are free of inheritance tax), advances made to some of the Apple children, such as Brenda and David, might be treated as gifts that reduce further inheritance rather than as advances.

Common to all three families will be the activity of meeting and discussing the future impact goals and how the families plan to reach their destinations. This in and of itself is a healthy step in families and can lead to the clarity necessary to avoid mismatched expectations, which are so often a derailer on many fronts. If the Apple children all know that there is a safe and fair approach in place regarding early advances to support the living needs of two of the three children, there will (hopefully) be less in the way of risk of a sense of unfairness. If there is clarity that the **main priority** in the impact goals of the family is to provide for the retirement needs of Reginald and Martha Apple, this might provide an agreed cap on what any child can get as an early advance—say, a limit of 50% of what they might ultimately inherit. Early action and activity on what it takes to get to the ultimate impact goal is what use of the *Theory of Change* as a planning methodology is all about.

The Approach for Dagland and the Opportunity for a Country to Establish Itself as a Forward-Looking Centre for Responsible Wealth and Business Owners

Taxation is a complex subject, particularly when dealing with the income and assets of global wealth and business owners whose businesses, holdings and places of residence almost always cross borders. But current tax systems are not fit for purpose in a world of mobility and choice, and for a country like Dagland to thrive, it would likely need to undertake radical tax reform. It will also be important for Dagland to understand that it is not just taxation that comes into the mix when wealth and business owners make decisions about where to live and invest.

A first step, as fits with the *Theory of Change*, is for Dagland to be very clear about what the country's impact goal is. Addressing income and wealth inequality can be part of the impact goal, but so might be the development of a *regenerative* tax system. What if Dagland is sincere about and committed to providing an attractive long-term home to global wealth and business owners—attractive enough for them to not only spend time there, but raise their families and grow and run their businesses from the country?

Were Dagland to offer something more than low or moderate taxation, would wealth and business owners be happy to contribute to the economy, not only through taxation but in a number of other important ways? And if the system were designed to focus on *place*—the physical and non-physical attributes of Dagland—improving the environment, developing better healthcare and education and creating a safe and secure country of opportunity for all, would this be a move towards a tax and legal system that is regenerative? Could Dagland offer a Nordic approach to society but with much lower headline tax rates?

With a focus on its impact goal, Dagland could move back to focusing on the inputs—the resources it needs to put the plan in place—and on the actions that it needs to take to achieve the outcomes that can lead to the impact goal.

- Dagland can take the opportunity to carve out an important global role as a future-oriented safe centre for **responsible** wealth and business owners. This is *not* the replication of a territorial tax system with a narrow tax base like Hong Kong or Singapore, or the creation of a new tax haven attracting the wealthy to a sandy beach in the Caribbean, but rather a thoughtful reflection of the real needs of wealth and business owners and how these can be addressed symbiotically—in ways that accelerate the move to a fairer society with real opportunity for all.
- The approach Dagland adopts can take into account the realities of the weaknesses of traditional 'offshore' wealth management centres, the failure of Swiss bank secrecy and the need for a global leader in providing what responsible business and wealth owners need. This includes, for those who are compliant with all relevant tax and other laws, the human right to privacy, protection against part or complete confiscation of their assets and more. The initiative might not only be oriented to Dagland as a place business and wealth owners might live and invest in, but also to the global role Dagland can take as a voice of responsible business and wealth ownership.

- Wealth and business owners have much to contribute to economies. In many countries, the approach to taxation as it impacts wealth owners has been chaotic, overly complex and filled with unacceptable loopholes. In the example of the United Kingdom, the non-domiciliary rules described earlier in this book were changed over the years such as to **reduce**, not enhance, the attractiveness of the United Kingdom to wealth and business owners.
- There are many options for a simplified and fairer approach to be taken that would attract rather than repel wealth and business owners to a country. Where headline rates for income and inheritance tax are misleadingly high, they need to be reduced. What is the point of advertising a 40% inheritance tax rate when the reality is that through careful (though sometimes complex) planning, the tax can be legally avoided?
- The headline rate can and should decline significantly while raising substantially more revenue if the system is simple and comprehensive.
- Another way of putting this is to say that a country can achieve higher revenues by everyone simply paying a low-rate inheritance tax, recognizing this to be in the interests of both their families and their community. A system that has only those who fail to take advice and do their planning paying, for instance, a crushingly high rate of inheritance tax does not work.
- For a country looking to focus on wealth and business owners as a means of strengthening its economy and benefiting all in society, understanding the benefits that wealth and business owners could bring and communicating this well requires some focus. There is considerable and compelling research available on how family wealth and business owners can and do contribute to economies. Effort is needed for a government to be convinced of this and to then use this knowledge to help educate its population about the opportunity for everyone if policies are well executed. This means a different political discourse from bashing the wealthy and promising to tax them more vigorously. Part of the activities and actions that the relevant government would need to take is to also help journalists and others understand better that there is a way to address

inequality and the societal needs of all through a more wealth-owner-friendly dialogue and collaboration designed to achieve real symbiosis.
- Linked to how wealth and business owners living in a country are taxed is the question of residence rules and otherwise. There is much room for broadening the tax base in strategic ways in and around the realities of how global wealth and business owners live and operate, and in ways that seek to be *win–win–win*—reflecting the needs of global wealth and business owners and all stakeholders, including government and the general population.
- Apart from wealth and business owners who may choose to live in Dagland, there are many initiatives the country could take to support its development as a future-oriented centre for responsible wealth and business owners. These can include the support and conduct of well-designed disclosure facilities for developing countries in particular, with a focus on the realities associated with tax evasion and corruption in too many places, including a number of countries in Africa and Latin America. Perhaps Dagland can be an ideal trusted financial centre that facilitates confidential approaches to voluntary disclosure accompanied by trusted approaches to ensuring that tax revenues of developing countries in particular can be monitored in their application to the real needs of the countries involved.[4]
- Dagland can offer advance rulings to wealth and business owners that if strategic in approach can be part of a programme designed to develop Dagland as the future safe haven for responsible business and wealth owners. The idea here is simply to offer predictability to wealth and business owners, something that can be done in a way that might produce upfront revenue for Dagland through charges it imposes for such certifying rulings. In a world of complexity, dealing with multijurisdictional compliance and disclosure requirements can not only be burdensome and costly, but also result in uncertainty and loss of privacy. Dagland might consider initiating approaches, sometimes working with the tax authorities of other countries, to determine, on a joint basis, whether a wealth or business-owning family, individually or through

trusts, partnerships or otherwise, is in full compliance with their tax obligations, in which case compliance requirements can be much simplified and privacy enhanced. An approach such as this can reduce costs and risks for both the governments involved and the taxpayer.[5]

- Dagland might consider its approach to inheritance taxation, noting that there are some countries, like the United Kingdom and the United States, that continue to have high headline inheritance or estate tax rates while permitting a variety of techniques to be employed to bring the actual rate down dramatically (even to zero).
- Combined with this should be consideration of a controversial area—the question of wealth taxation. On the latter, this is a tax on the value of assets the taxpayer owns—not a tax on income and capital gains generated from investing those assets. Any consideration of wealth taxation should also focus on the realities of what today's global wealth and business owners need, and how Dagland can deliver on these needs. Where needs are met, the resistance to taxation in any form declines, particularly where headline rates are low, systems simple and governments avoid the desire to 'chop and change' and make things overly complex. Dagland might consider wealth taxation, and without a sense that there is an *either/or* between wealth taxation and inheritance taxation. Broadening the tax base requires an open mind on the kind of taxes that can be imposed.
- Wealth taxes are not necessarily taxes that should be imposed only on 'billionaires' as part of a move to address the realities of income and wealth inequality. There are countries that impose wealth taxes successfully (Switzerland is an example) at relatively low levels of wealth, and simply as a way of reflecting the **reality** that not every individual lives from earned income. Regardless of how one comes into capital (whether by inheritance, the sale of a business or otherwise), is it not fair to tax such individual on the basis of the capital they are living from if their neighbour, working a full-time job, is taxed on her salary and other work-related earnings?
- Dagland could review the role it can play as a global centre of philanthropy. Together with blended value or impact investing, this is also a part of how it can become the future safe haven for

responsible global business and wealth owners. Dagland can and should take a leadership role in helping to align private wealth with international development and sustainability priorities.
- Tax evasion is less of a problem than it was for the world only a few years ago, and this as a result of important developments associated with automatic information exchange. There are, however, gaps, and some of these can be addressed through strategic approaches to enforce the rights of Dagland against enablers of tax evasion, such as aggressive tax advisors, private banks and others. It would be interesting to consider how Dagland's own initiatives in this area can be part of a programme under which Dagland coordinates, for the developing world in particular, similar strategies.
- In seeking to develop itself as a financial centre of choice for global wealth and business owners, Dagland can take steps to encourage the use of Dagland trusts, partnerships and other ownership vehicles. Interesting for Dagland is to observe that the United Kingdom, through its tax regime and otherwise, gave up its leading role in the trust world to other financial centres, including the offshore world, the United States, Switzerland, Singapore and others. It would be easy for Dagland if—as we can imagine for the purposes of the example—it has a solid infrastructure, respected legal system and leadership in trust law, to capture business that can be valuable to the economy.
- Perhaps requiring some effort on various fronts, Dagland citizenship could be developed to provide safety and security for wealth and business owners living around the world. While I would not be an advocate of Dagland shifting to a system of taxing citizens on the same basis as it taxes residents, there is room for consideration of an alignment of the benefits of a country's citizenship and the revenue needs of that country with simple approaches to having wealth and business owners pay for the value they receive as citizens. Additional services and value afforded to those who are Dagland citizens can be part of what Dagland develops as part of a forward-looking strategy, including enhancing the coverage of investment protection agreements where appropriate and otherwise.

- Consumption taxes are also an area Dagland can focus on. A consumption tax is common in the European context, as well as in a number of other parts of the world. Tax is imposed on the consumption of goods and/or services. Put more simply, whereas an income tax is imposed on what is earned and a wealth or transfer tax on the value of an asset owned or transferred, a consumption tax is based on what the taxpayer *spends*. Value-added taxes (VAT) are a common form of consumption tax. In focusing on creating a *regenerative* tax system, Dagland might reflect on the possibility of orienting consumption taxes to some very specific objectives, including addressing income and wealth inequality and encouraging a symbiotic relationship with wealth and business owners.
- Some consumption taxes might be oriented particularly to the wealthy and in relation to expenditures that contribute to 'costs' borne by others in society. This type of tax is known as a *Pigouvian* tax, named after Arthur Pigou, a 1920s British economist. Fuel for a private jet or a yacht is purchased by a wealth owner but results in costs to our global climate. Consumption taxes should well reflect this societal cost. The whole area of carbon and similar taxation is one that Dagland can carefully review and tailor to the society it envisions creating.
- Towards the objective of broadening the tax system, permitting headline rates in all areas to drop in the longer term, Dagland might focus on increases of consumption taxation on 'luxury' expenditures. But to more clearly address the needs of society, there may be a form of 'hypothecation' of the luxury tax, with a set portion of the proceeds going directly to offset consumption taxes otherwise imposed on necessities. The idea here would, for example, have a portion of the tax collected on the purchase of yachts or luxury cars go directly to the reduction and eventual elimination of consumption taxes on groceries and other necessities, lowering the cost of necessities to the general population.
- Focusing on 'place' and the desire to have the tax system be regenerative might have a portion of the extra revenue going to improve facilities that are of direct interest to the wealth and business owner—investments in educational programmes reflecting the need for skilled employees may mean that

wealth owners will become more active in the country; even investments in 'place' reflecting natural environmental benefits enjoyed by all the population, as well as the wealth and business owner. If Dagland has waterside elements in need of upgrading, orienting expenditures to new public spaces, clean-up of pollution and new dock facilities for yacht owners might make those paying the luxury tax feel better about it.

- Hypothecation of taxes—dedicating all or a portion of a particular tax to a particular use—is something that is criticized by economists, the view being that governments should be the ones in the best position to determine how tax revenues should be used at any given time. But have governments shown trustworthiness on this front? Around the world, there are dramatic examples of why taxpayers *cannot* trust governments. From corruption to waste, we have seen the misapplication of tax revenues in virtually all countries. While governments try to earn back trust, which they sorely need to do, hypothecation of at least some taxes might be something Dagland employs as a way to improve its relationship with wealth and business owners and the entire population.
- Dagland might also explore using hypothecation in other areas. Wealth and business owners might well resist a wealth tax, but what if the proceeds of the wealth tax go directly to approved funds that the taxpayer can choose between? The taxpayer might even get units in the fund that give them governance rights—the ability to be part of the oversight and possibly even the management of a fund that, say, has as its mission eliminating the cost of university education for those who cannot afford it. Dagland might even experiment with having its taxpayers *initiate* for approval hypothecation possibilities that taxpayers can get more excited about contributing to. Considering that wealth and business owners are major supporters of philanthropic initiatives that they are passionate about, why not have elements of taxation that bring out this passion and engagement?

… but why should taxpayers not demand a say in how individual taxes are spent beyond the funding of basics? Why must discretionary spending be decided by central edict, rather than by choice of the individual taxpayer? How could this work? Parliament could put forward a list of projects to be funded—with its own priority listing. More

projects than could be funded would be put forward. A fixed percentage of taxes would be reserved for the individual taxpayer to allocate to the projects of their preference.[6]

- Dagland's focus on 'place' and its other impact goals will likely include the issue of security—safety and protection afforded to all in Dagland society, not just wealth and business owners. Just one of many areas that can be a focus of broadened tax bases and hypothecation would be dedication to providing a safe and secure country for all—regenerative, as this would have been one of the reasons for a wealth owner to choose to reside in Dagland. More investment in 'place' from the proceeds of success would mean making Dagland even safer—through effective security mechanisms but also through the creation of a fairer society of opportunity for all—with excellent health care, free education and more helping to avoid the lost generations in so many parts of today's world.
- The objective for Dagland should be to attract **and retain** wealth and business owners, and this for the long term. It would make sense for tax rates to be discussed among all stakeholders, including wealth and business owners, and for these to be graduated in a way that encourages those at all levels of wealth and income to be attracted to what Dagland offers. What Dagland should consider offering is *not* a tax benefit for the wealthy—the reality is that the wealthy have many planning options, including the option of mobility, that offer far lower tax costs to them.
- Would wealth and business owners be attracted to an approach that involves a broad range of simple, low-rate taxes if these are combined with assurances that the system will not be the subject of constant chopping and changing and will include a focus on the security and safety of the taxpaying wealth owner's family and financial interests? Among the benefits to the wealth and business owner would be simplicity and comfort that the rules would not be constantly changing. As the wealth owner would be taxable on worldwide income, the full benefit of Dagland tax treaties, important to global wealth and business owners (and not always available to those who choose to be taxed under 'special' tax regimes, such as the soon to be historical UK non-dom system), would be available. For example, protection

from being treated as a resident of other countries under treaty tie-breaker rules would arise, as would reduced withholding taxes imposed by other countries. As a Dagland resident, the wealth owner would benefit from other Dagland international agreements, including investment protection treaties. Simplification, certainty and trust are key. And in relation to the last, with global reporting under the CRS, information comes to Dagland, a trusted government.

Dagland's *Theory of Change*

Dagland has much that it can achieve. The *Theory of Change* can offer Dagland a methodology to achieving its impact goal. For now, that impact goal might be articulated as Dagland, in a set number of years (say ten) having established itself as the country of choice for global wealth and business owners seeking not only a place of residence, but a place to establish holding companies and both non-operating and operating investment and management vehicles. Importantly, apart from the economic contributions wealth and business owners would be making by virtue of this activity, there would be tax and related approaches in place that provide for a long-term synergistic collaboration between the country and wealth and business owners.

Tax policies, among others, would seek to achieve, again, extreme balance between ensuring taxation that is fair—not only to the wealth and business-owning families involved, but to the overall population—addressing present and real income and wealth inequality, *together* with maintaining the country as a destination of choice for well-advised wealth and business owners.

In developing its impact goal, Dagland may add to the vision a tax system that applies without discrimination. The ultimate destination for Dagland might be for the tax system to offer all residents the same transparent, simple approach—say a top tax rate of 15% on all realized income, whether on capital (e.g., a sale of shares) or on earned income (e.g., a salary). This might be combined with a top transfer tax rate (e.g., on gifts and transfers on death) of 7.5%. And to broaden the tax base, Dagland might envision a wealth tax based on the value of assets, but with a focus on a rate that reflects that Dagland wants to attract and retain wealth owners for the long term and at least in part on the basis of a regenerative and collaborative approach to taxation. Other taxes Dagland envisions as part of a broad system will be consumption taxes designed to generate revenue for Dagland while exempting, where possible, purchases of necessities.

As part of its impact goal, Dagland might focus on the regenerative aspects of taxation that it wants to encourage. Dagland might earmark elements of taxation, say half of revenues, to go to priority areas for its envisioned future—education, housing and healthcare. The impact goal could envision free education for Dagland residents, combined with an approach allowing for families to voluntarily pay fees if they can afford them, helping Dagland to provide the free education it wants to provide as part of a regenerative system oriented to addressing societal needs and mobility. The healthcare system would be similarly aligned with an approach that seeks to provide high-quality healthcare to residents for free, with a private option that is designed to support, not undermine, public, free access to healthcare. Those who can afford to pay for their healthcare do; those who cannot obtain high-quality care without cost. Support on public housing adds to the creation of a society everyone wants to be part of, including the wealth and business owner benefiting from policies and approaches that help families achieve their own long-term impact goals of ensuring sustainability of their own families and business and investment interests.

In order to protect revenue as Dagland moves towards its impact goal, Dagland might adopt a voluntary opt-in tax system that initially offers wealth and business owners certainty in exchange for, perhaps, an upfront 'ruling'. A safety feature for Dagland in implementing the approach might be not to accept into the opt-in system any taxpayers whose tax expenditure might decrease rather than increase. For a new resident to Dagland, the tax take to Dagland will increase given that a taxpayer is being added; for an existing Dagland taxpayer, the existing tax system, if producing a higher actual tax, would continue to apply unless and until the tax system as a whole is changed (as might be the case once Dagland has clear evidence of the overall revenues produced).

For a new resident looking at Dagland as a possible place of residence, a ruling might be obtained regarding taxation, promising the new resident the 15% capped rate and otherwise. The new resident, perhaps on paying the tax in advance for the first year as a 'fee', plus the annual tax going forward, gets assurance regarding taxation. Dagland gets advance revenue.

Dagland's approach would be to focus its own policies on enhancing its attraction to wealth and business owners. In negotiating investment protection and tax treaties, among others, Dagland would seek to protect the interests of its taxpayers using Dagland investment vehicles such as companies, trusts and otherwise. And with its simple tax system, Dagland would have as a focus transparency—as much as possible the tax system would ignore the interposition of legal vehicles such as companies, trusts and otherwise, attributing income and assets to individuals and taxing them at their level. This can encourage activity and investment in Dagland and the use of trusts and other succession vehicles in simple ways that are not driven by tax objectives but by asset-protection and succession needs of the relevant family.

Dagland, like the families in the examples discussed, starts at the end—developing its impact goal and articulating it in detail. Dagland then works back, identifying the inputs and resources needed to develop a strategic roadmap on reaching the impact goal. This involves Dagland undertaking activities: benchmarking other countries; understanding the real needs of wealth and business owners; helping the Dagland population understand and support the move to a regenerative tax system; developing clear treaty and other policies oriented to the impact goal of being the country of choice for well-informed and responsible wealth and business owners.

Some Final Thoughts on the *Theory of Change* and its Use in Family Business and Wealth Continuity Planning

The *Theory of Change* provides a framework for planning, implementing and measuring strategies adopted by families to achieve their longer-term goals. Inputs and resources needed are identified, as are the activities necessary to get to the impact goal. Also identified are expected outputs and their outcomes, permitting a measurement of the impact of steps taken to help the family reach its impact goal.

Families can and should decide on their long-term goals. This can include the family vision for its business and wealth and desired impacts on family harmony, business success and community contributions. Business growth and sustainability can be planned with reference to leadership transitions and operational resilience.

In the process, families can review the assumptions behind their long-term goals—such as an assumption that the younger generation will be willing to take on leadership roles. This leads to an understanding of a precondition to the assumption—that there will be governance, communication and development within the family ecosystem to ensure that the assumption is a safe one for the family to make.

Activities will include succession and financial planning, family governance meetings, work on philanthropy and other joint activities, all leading to the identification of well-prepared successors in the younger generation, established governance bodies and successfully implemented financial strategies.

In the shorter term, immediate changes such as improved communication and financial literacy among family members might be measured as an outcome. Medium and longer-term outcomes and impacts might be identified and measured, including leadership transitions, business and investment growth and solidified governance structures. Longer term, the impact goals of the family and of its business and investment interests can be measured and evaluated.

Use of the *Theory of Change* can help families become *responsible* wealth and business stewards who understand that exercising their *moral* responsibilities in ways that benefit society and planet benefit the family and help ensure that the family can safely reach its destination and achieve its impact goal.

Notes

1. The diagrams that I have used in this book were developed with the kind and thoughtful help of Nicolette Fourie, the Chief Administrative Officer of Ispahani Advisory (https://www.ispahaniadvisory.com/the-team/leadership/nicolette-fourie-2/). I have worked closely with Nicky and her colleague, Iraj Ispahani, in teaching and consulting engagements involving the *Theory of Change* and the diagrams reflect our collective thinking.
2. As mentioned earlier in this book, autopilot leadership is one of the many great ideas I have learned from Sammy Lee, the Executive Chairman of the Lee Kum Kee Group, in my view a top thinker on family business. Sammy is a fourth-generation member of the Hong Kong-based Lee family, with interests in a variety of sectors including the manufacture and distribution of delicious Chinese sauces and Chinese health products carrying the Lee Kum Kee and Infinitus brands. Among Sammy's writings are

Lee, S., *The Autopilot Leadership Model* (McGraw-Hill Education (Asia), 2016) and Lee, S., *We are Greater than I: The Path to a Happier Life* (Co-Creating Happiness Limited, 2021). I use many of Sammy's ideas in my work and writing, including in my development of his ideas on autopilot leadership and on the need for *extreme balance* in managing the interaction between family and business.

3. Mentioned in earlier notes, James (Jay) E. Hughes Jr. is the author of *Family Wealth: Keeping It in the Family* and co-author of *The Cycle of the Gift* and *Family Trusts*. Papers on the concept of a Council of Elders can be found at www.jehjf.org.
4. I have written on this topic. See Marcovici, P., Developments in global tax transparency and the need for effective dialogue (Parts 1 and 2), *The World Financial Review*, May/June and July/August 2017.
5. See Marcovici, P. and Noked, N., Cooperative compliance program for individuals and trusts: A proposal for a compliance passport, *Journal of Tax Administration*, **6**(2) (2021).
6. Hulsroj, P. and Aliberti, M., *Essays on the Optional Society—and a Letter Concerning Inclusion* (ExTuto Publishing, 2021), pp. 229 and 230.

A Few Extracts From *The Transformative Power of Family Wealth*

On the Application of Circular Economy Principles to Family Business and Wealth Stewardship While wealth and business-owning families increasingly embrace sustainability as an area of focus, most of the dialogue on sustainability relates to areas external to the family and the governance of family and business interests. But is enough thought being given by families to the sustainability of the family itself, both as a family and in relation to the family's wealth and business interests?

Circularity means avoiding waste and finding value in it—not just of natural resources but of the human resources within families, including family members not directly involved in the family business, but who have a stake in the future and who need to support those in more active roles. In evaluating the resources of a family, these extend well beyond physical assets such as interests in wealth and businesses. The experience of the family, its reputation and standing in the community and more are all part of the resources a family seeking real continuity needs to avoid wasting.

On the Needs of Wealth Owners Wealth owners have latent needs—they have needs, but don't know what they are. Knowing the right questions to ask is the key—no one has all the answers, but if a wealth owner does not understand their own succession plan, whether this involves the use of wills, trusts or otherwise, it can be very dangerous. Who has the power to make decisions if we are disabled or die? Who can replace the trustee? Who will monitor conflicts of interest, including how asset managers and others charge for their services? What can be done to manage the risks of divorce and other risks to wealth?

On Succession Planning and Asset Protection The first step in succession planning is to understand that having no succession plan in place is a succession plan. If I die, something will happen to my assets, and this notwithstanding that I may not have actually thought about my succession and planned it.

I have run into a number of cases over the years where trusts and foundations established by wealth owners were not disclosed to family members, something quite common in times when wealth owners in Europe and elsewhere were led to believe that good planning involved hiding their assets from tax authorities and others. In too many situations, advisors ranging from lawyers to trustees to protectors and others ended up helping themselves to all or part of the assets involved. When families finally discovered the structures their deceased parent had created, it was often too late to recover the full value involved.

On Changing Demographics and Ageing Do failing memories put assets at risk? It is wonderful that we are all living longer, but is it not the case that dementia and even simple forgetfulness that comes with ageing put assets at risk if no one knows where they are? Early succession and asset-protection planning is the key, and families increasingly need to consider the ageing process and its effect on the safety of family assets and the maintenance of harmony within the family for the long term.

On 'Gold-Diggers' I am often asked by families I work with about the risk of in-laws or others being gold-diggers, more interested in the wealth of the family than they should be. This is not a difficult evaluation to make, and my answer is always 'Of course your son-in-law or daughter-in-law is a gold-digger!' This is not because everyone is evil, but because money comes into every relationship—if not at the start of the relationship, then at some point in the future. I always advise families to hope for the best, but plan for the worst.

On Mistresses and Paramours Mistresses are not an Asian concept. They are a global concept. Mistresses, paramours and other relationships all too often move into situations of blackmail, and there are approaches that wealth owners falling into common traps can employ to manage things effectively. One golden rule is to never give a mistress a lump sum of money—before long, she is back for more. Why not use a trust or annuity that is designed to make payments over her lifetime, but conditioned on her keeping things quiet?

A mistress or paramour will often come to realize that they had better get hold of some assets while wealth is still in the hands of the wealth owner, creating issues as the wealth owner ages and as the relationship moves, as it too often does, from excitement to blackmail.

On Divorce In the case of divorce, community property, co-habitation and otherwise, it is easy to say that the rights of the spouse or other party are there because they need to be protected. And this is often the case, and why laws are in place to provide this protection. But for a wealth-owning family, and particularly where wealth is at the higher level, it is critical to understand how laws designed to protect a spouse can be abused to provide a spouse with rights to family businesses and wealth that by no stretch of the imagination should they have access to. And with lawyers charging on contingency, getting paid on the success of their efforts, is it fair that family wealth falls into the hands of those who fuel the flames of marital disputes?

On Second (and Subsequent) Marriages Second and further marriages often cause more issues within families than the wealth owner establishing the new relationship thinks. The wealth owner often ends up in a difficult situation that jeopardizes not only the wellbeing of his children, but also the chances of success in his new relationship. As a believer that money comes into the picture in every relationship (because everyone is a gold-digger, at least to some extent), recognizing this is a first step towards finding approaches to help the process not be a destructive one.

On the Need for Women to Understand Their Rights and Financial Position There is one very important reality about women and wealth. Chances are that they will end up with the money, one way or another—so they better know where it is and how to deal with it. Women live longer than men, and in a marriage, it is likely that they will outlive their husband. And if the marriage fails, which many do, the wife will and should end up with something—so everyone needs to be prepared.

On Whom You Can Trust Trust no one. This is not because no one can be trusted, but because the safest approach is to ensure that the right checks and balances are in place to deal with the reality that everybody has conflicts of interest. And for trustees, bankers and others, there is no client better than a dead client—dead clients do not complain about fees and do not fire you. Key is to ensure that those who succeed to your assets are able to properly keep an eye on trustees and others and remove and replace them when necessary.

On Family Business Succession and a 'Revolving Door' Families that manage to keep their businesses intact over the generations tend to be families that are flexible in their understanding that it is inevitable that not everyone in the younger generation will see things the same way.

Allowing for the likelihood that there will be family members who will not want to participate in and support the family business, and having clear procedures for how to buy out their interests and at what price, has been a key way successful families have managed to keep businesses in family hands over the generations. Having the ability to 'prune' the family tree has been viewed as important to the long-term success of a family business.

But buying out family members is not only expensive, it can be wasteful. Pruning denotes a permanent separation. A 'revolving door' is an approach that reflects circularity and celebrates the *both/and* choice that can be made. Yes, there is an approach that allows a family member to temporarily distance themselves from the family business but there are terms for how they and their children can return or be involved in the future.

On Tax-Advantaged Investing There are many facets to tax-advantaged investing, but in the simplest terms, to invest on a tax-advantaged basis means focusing on the after-tax and not the pre-tax return on an investment. It is very easy to get into an investment, but often not enough attention is paid to the question of how one will exit from the investment, and what the tax consequences of this might be.

On Taxation In a world where disparities of wealth are increasingly at the forefront of the political and social agenda, is 'hiding the money' either an option or the right thing to do? Advisors and wealth-owning families have to change their ways, and in many cases, the ways of the past were not something to be proud of.

The only certainty in the tax world is that the laws will change, and constantly do. The wealth-owning family does not need to become expert in the tax laws of every country that affects them and their investments. Rather, the wealth-owning family needs to be able to understand the advice they receive and be able to challenge that advice, and ask the right questions. Being aware of how tax systems work can help families stay in control of the succession and asset-protection planning put in place for their families.

On the Move to Tax Transparency and Automatic Information Exchange Is transparency in the tax world a rocky road that is creating a new kind of refugee problem and a drain of capital and entrepreneurship from countries most in need? I worry that many developing countries are simply not ready for automatic information exchange. Politically motivated use of tax information, corruption, leakage of tax information to kidnappers and more is leading to entrepreneurs desperately needed by their economies realizing that they only have two choices—play by the rules or get out. And to play by the rules does not work if the tax system does not adequately protect taxpayer interests, so getting out is sometimes the only choice. Who will replace the lost jobs and revenues of the developing countries involved?

On Mobility Play by the rules or get out. These are the only choices wealth owners have—the third choice of staying connected to a country by residence, domicile, citizenship or otherwise and hoping that no one will find out is simply not an option in a world of growing transparency and where tax laws are increasingly and more aggressively enforced. Tax laws are laws, and there is no choice but for compliance with them.

One simple guideline on mobility planning is that the best time to consider leaving a country is before that country begins to impose an exit tax. As the world moves to greater tax transparency and tax laws are enforced more vigorously, it is likely that more wealth owners will be using mobility as part of their planning, attracting more high-tax countries to consider barriers to mobility, including exit taxes and tougher rules in relation to the question of who is and who is not a tax resident, particularly among those who were previously taxable residents of the country.

Is Society Optional? There is a very simple reality that no wealth or business-owning family will survive for the long term if our planet does not survive for the long term. More specifically, the challenges of climate change, migration, instability, poverty, inequality and more are not ones that a family can escape for the long term by moving from one country to another. The family is part of a connected ecosystem that also has to thrive for the family to thrive. So no, society is not optional.

On Tax Planning, Tax Avoidance and Tax Evasion As a tax lawyer, my job has been to work with wealth owners and to help them legally plan their affairs such as to minimize tax exposures. But how far should one go to pay the least amount of tax possible? Is it an ethical obligation of wealth owners to pay headline rates of tax to help address wealth and income inequality and to not take steps to reduce tax exposures? Where is the line between legal tax planning and illegal tax evasion ... and what of tax avoidance, something that used to be considered legal and appropriate, but which is increasingly condemned by tax authorities and others?

On Political Risk There are many risks that a wealth owner is subject to that can fall under the heading of 'political' risk, including changes in the tax landscape, perhaps in part as a result of a new focus on income and wealth inequality ... Addressing political risk will be an increasing need of wealth-owning families worldwide. The current focus on income and wealth inequality, increasing populism in the political sphere and the difficult financial position of many countries is increasing risk, and not only in parts of the world one normally thinks of as unstable.

On the Wealth Management Industry Wealth management is a knowledge business, but sadly run by many who are more focused on their own interests than on the need to invest in and manage knowledge for the benefit of their clients. A wealth owner has little choice but to get a handle on what is relevant to their own situation and be in a position to ask the right questions that will lead them to the right advisors. And for the wealth manager who gets it right, the opportunity to excel and attract clients is significant.

Today, around the world, there are increasing regulations that require asset managers to provide transparency on charges to their clients, but there continue to be many circumstances of hidden charges that asset managers, such as private banks, impose on their clients. Is the client aware that the bank may have made arrangements to receive 'retrocessions' or kickbacks from investment funds in which they may invest the client money they have under discretionary management?

On Independent Asset Managers and Family Offices Interesting to observe is that the independent asset manager and single and multi-family offices usually come into the picture when the wealth-owning family gets fed up with the poor service they get from their traditional private bank. And while the private bank ends up being nothing more than a custodian, the independent asset manager or family office begins to focus on negotiating even these fees on behalf of the wealth owner, putting more pressure on the private banks.

On Compliance as a Client Need Compliance is a client need. Tax and related reporting requirements are only part of the picture, and too few banks realize that families need help to understand the choices they have on how to structure their affairs and ensure that they know who has what information on their family and assets and where that information is going to go. Delegating these things to the compliance department is not enough—helping clients deal with increasing compliance is part of the service an effective bank or trust company needs to provide.

On Inequality and Sustainability It is my hope that this book will be read not only by wealth owners and their advisors, but also by those concerned about growing inequality and sustainability generally and who might benefit from a better understanding of the positive contributions wealth and business owners can make to societal wellbeing.

Wealth and business-owning families have much to contribute to society and where the family itself is strong and sustainable over generations, this contribution can be all the greater. The synergies that can be enjoyed where a family works on its own sustainability through a focus on what the family can do for others—stakeholders including employees, community and society—are exciting and real.

On the *Theory of Change* The *Theory of Change* is about working hard to develop a clear vision for the future and to then work backwards to identify the steps necessary to ensure that the desired outcome and destination will be reached. In the context of families, this means developing clarity on the envisioned ecosystem for both the family and its business and investment 'engine' in the future. We then work backwards, identifying the derailers that can block the progress of the family—internal disputes, political risk, taxation, lack of adequate preparation of family members for their roles, poor succession planning and many other challenges. The focus is then on the actions, inputs and outcomes that can lead to long-term positive outcomes for both the family and its wealth and business interests.

On the Opportunity for Tax Systems to be Regenerative But the tax world is fast changing, and in the next years, more and more difficulties will be faced by the world's wealth owners as the rough road to transparency leads governments to be better able to enforce their tax laws. I have a vision of a world in which tax laws can be simple and predictable, with modest tax rates, and where full compliance results in a significantly higher level of tax revenues for countries that can efficiently and transparently administer a tax system that addresses income and wealth inequality and the needs of a fair society, while attracting to it for the long term wealth and business owners who invest and are otherwise locally active.

True regeneration might involve a focus on tax systems being designed not only to attract and keep wealth owners connected to the country, but to help create new wealth and business owners. A stable, fair, broad and predictable tax system that reflects the realities of healthy global tax competition combined with a focus on implementing policies that support wealth and business owners is feasible.

Glossary

Annuity There are many kinds of annuities, but the term usually refers to an insurance product designed to provide annual payments. These can be associated with retirement products but can also be customized annuity arrangements.

Anti-Deferral Rules Anti-deferral rules are tax rules that seek to stop taxpayers from being able to delay when they pay tax on particular income items. A common example would be where a country taxes residents of the country on a worldwide basis, and the taxpayer uses a company or other structure to earn income outside the country. Anti-deferral rules might cause the income of the company to be taxed to the resident as if that income was earned directly by the resident, without the interposition of the company.

Anti-Money Laundering Rules There are a variety of laws that seek to uncover funds associated with illegal activity. Increasingly, these laws, which deal with money laundering, require the filing of *suspicious activity reports* with relevant authorities where a financial intermediary, such as a bank, real estate broker or other party, handles funds that they suspect have an illegal origin. The owner of the assets is usually not notified that the reports are being filed, and the 'crimes' that can trigger such reports often include tax crimes, meaning that undeclared funds can be identified by tax authorities through these reports.

Asset Protection Asset protection is a very broad term that can cover all elements of planning that is undertaken by wealth-owning families. More specifically, asset-protection structures focus on the protection of assets from the claims of creditors and are used by those in high-risk activities, such as medical practitioners and others who may become subject to legal claims.

Assets Under Management (AUM) Asset managers generally earn fees based on the quantum of assets held under management, or AUM. Where assets are held in trusts and other structures, and the assets may not be managed directly by the trustee or other legal owner, the reference can be to *assets under administration*.

Automatic Exchange of Information Led by the OECD, the common reporting standard is the basis on which countries will be *automatically* sharing a wide range of information regarding the income and assets of wealth owners. Automatic exchange of information contrasts dramatically with previous forms of exchange of information between countries, which was, largely, information exchange on request. Countries will now receive information on the assets and income of their taxpayers outside the home country without making any request for such information.

Bank Secrecy The laws of many countries provide varying degrees of confidentiality associated with banking relationships, including bank deposits. Bank secrecy has come under considerable attack given the misuse of bank secrecy rules.

Beneficiary The beneficiaries of a will, trust, foundation, insurance policy or other structures and succession strategies are the individuals or entities that benefit on a particular event happening. In the case of a trust, the beneficiaries can be named and have fixed interests or may simply be members of a class of potential beneficiaries who may or may not actually benefit, depending on the exercise of discretion by the trustee or other fiduciary.

Bequest When a gift is to be made on death, such as under a will, the gift is often referred to as a bequest.

Bilateral Treaties and Other Agreements Bilateral treaties are agreements between two countries. In relation to the interests of wealth-owning families, such agreements include tax treaties, covering a number of issues that can help address the tax exposures of families living and investing on a cross-border basis, as well as investment protection agreements, which address, among others, expropriation of assets and political risk.

Blended Value Investments This broadly refers to *impact investing*, where investments are made with a view to providing blended value—returns to the investor, but also benefits to multiple stakeholders, including employees, communities and others. Rather than giving money away through philanthropy, a number of wealth owners seek to make investments that can provide returns on capital and also have a positive impact.

Capital Gain A capital gain is the profit on selling an asset, such as arises where real estate or shares are sold at a profit. Capital gains may be tax-free or taxed more favourably than ordinary income, depending on the tax regime. Where a wealth owner is actively trading assets, the gains may be characterized as trading income rather than as capital gains, and may thereby be subject to a higher level of taxation, depending on the country the laws of which have application.

Captive Insurance A captive insurance company is an insurance company that is owned, in whole or in part, by the person who is insured. Sometimes captive insurance arrangements are designed to provide tax benefits by creating tax deductions for premiums paid on what would otherwise be self-insured risks.

Civil Law The civil law derives from Roman law, and is largely based on statutes rather than on case law. This contrasts with the common law, which, while featuring laws provided in statutes, focuses more on laws developed through judicial decisions. The common law derives from England and applies in countries such as the United States, Canada and others, the laws of which are generally based on English law.

Common Law See definition of civil law and the contrasts between civil and common law.

Common Reporting Standard The common reporting standard (CRS) was developed largely by the OECD in relation to the implementation of automatic information exchange between countries, and is designed to assist in the enforcement of tax laws. Considerable information on the CRS and implementation of automatic information exchange is available on the website of the OECD. The CRS is designed to set out rules for determining information that needs to be reported and how determinations on beneficial ownership are made.

Controlled Foreign Corporations (CFCs) Many countries that impose taxation on a worldwide basis have anti-deferral rules in their tax legislation. Among these are rules that focus on foreign corporations controlled by residents, and provide for current taxation of the earnings of such companies despite the fact that no dividends are distributed. These rules prevent taxpayers from being able to delay payment of tax in their home countries by accumulating income in offshore companies.

Direct Taxation Direct taxes are taxes imposed directly on an individual or company, and would include income, wealth and capital gains taxes, among others.

Discretionary Trust or Foundation Where a fiduciary structure such as a trust or foundation is discretionary, the trustee or others have a discretion regarding the exercise of their powers, such as a power to make distributions. If the trust is discretionary, the trustee, for example, does not have to distribute to a beneficiary a certain amount at a certain time, but may have a discretion to decide whether or not to do so. This can allow the trustee to consider whether it is appropriate to make the distribution, and also means that the beneficiary does not have a legal right to the assets involved, something which may provide tax and asset-protection benefits.

Dividends A dividend is a payment made by a company to shareholders out of the profits of the company.

Domicile Some countries have tax and other laws that focus on the 'domicile' of an individual. This concept is different from the question of residence and citizenship, and often includes elements of intention regarding where a person plans to remain indefinitely, making it possible for a person to be resident in a place other than their 'domicile', which, in effect, is their permanent home. In the United Kingdom, under laws that are about to be dramatically changed, individuals have 'domiciles of origin' (usually their father's domicile, or intended permanent home), which can be affected by a subsequent 'domicile of choice'.

Donation A donation is a gratuitous transfer and can be a gift to a family member or to a charity or other recipient meant to benefit. Donation taxes apply in some countries, often imposed on the donor rather than the recipient of the donation. In some countries, the recipient is taxable on the donation in certain circumstances. Charitable donations are often tax-free.

Estate The estate often refers to the assets of an individual at the time of death, and in some countries the estate itself may become a taxable person during the time of administration of the estate.

Executor The executor is an individual or entity charged with putting into effect the intentions of the deceased, and most often refers to a person appointed to the function under the will of the deceased.

Exit Tax In a number of countries, where an individual (and sometimes a company) moves out of the country, ceasing to be taxable there, an exit tax applies. Often, the exit tax is calculated by deeming the individual to have sold their assets at fair market value, exposing any gains to taxation despite the fact that the assets are not actually sold.

Expropriation Under international law, countries have the sovereign right to expropriate, or take away, assets under their jurisdiction. While compensation may have to be paid in relation to the expropriated assets of foreigners, in political risk planning, dealing with the risk of expropriation is a key issue.

Family Constitution A family constitution is generally a non-binding document that sets out a variety of things relating to how the family operates, its values, how disputes will be resolved and how succession and other arrangements will be made. Many of the provisions of a family constitution become binding by being included in related documents, such as trust deeds, shareholders' agreements and other governance arrangements.

Family Office A family office refers to the functions undertaken for wealth-owning families in relation to investments, maintenance of assets—including holiday homes and otherwise—supervision of advisors and succession arrangements, and many other possible functions. Single-family offices look after single families; multi-family offices resemble private banks and independent asset managers in providing services to multiple families.

Family Retreat Communication within families about succession, family values, safety and security and more are all valuable means of helping in the succession process. Family retreats are gatherings of families, annually or otherwise, providing an opportunity for the review of succession and other arrangements, the review or creation of family constitutions and otherwise. These can be formal or informal and can be organized by the family alone or with the help of outside advisors.

FATCA The Foreign Account Tax Compliance Act (FATCA) is US legislation designed to close loopholes that existed under the US Qualified Intermediary rules and requiring financial institutions and others to automatically exchange information with the United States regarding the interests of US taxpayers, including residents and citizens, where US persons are considered to beneficially own the assets and income involved. The relevant rules pierce corporate, trust and other structures and provide strong disincentives to banks and others who fail to cooperate with the United States.

Forced Heirship A number of countries have laws requiring that those who die transfer at least a portion of their assets to specified family members in specific shares. These rules, which can also affect lifetime gifts, generally apply in civil law countries as opposed to common law countries, but are not applicable in all civil law countries, and apply in very different ways. Forced heirship also appears in *Sharia* law, which is Islamic law applying to Muslims and is part of the laws of many Muslim countries.

Foundations Foundations are generally the civil law equivalent of trusts, albeit with a number of important differences, such as the fact that foundations are separate legal entities, while trusts are not. In general, foundations can often be used interchangeably with trusts and operate in many similar ways.

Freezing of Assets In political risk planning, expropriation of assets is a key risk. Also part of the risk is the freezing of assets that can arise in a number of circumstances. This relates to assets not actually being 'vested' or taken away, but 'frozen', such that the owner is unable to make use of the assets or deal with them.

378 Glossary

Gift A gift is a gratuitous transfer, such as where a parent makes a gift to a child or a spouse makes a gift to their spouse. A sale of an asset at an undervalue may carry with it elements of a gift, and where gift or donation taxes apply, can also attract such taxation.

Global Custodian A custodian of assets usually refers to a bank that holds equities and other investments, often in the name of the custodian (which is referred to as 'street name'). A variety of banks provide global custody services to family offices and other wealth owners.

Governance Governance refers to the approaches in place to deal with how assets and structures are administered. As assets move from one generation to the next, it is very important to consider how decisions will be made when there are several in the younger generation who will become owners of assets, whether or not including family businesses. Decision-making, dispute resolution, buy–sell arrangements and many other issues are part of governance, and can be provided for in shareholder agreements, trust arrangements, partnership agreements and otherwise.

Green Card A 'green card' is an informal reference to US permanent resident status under US immigration rules. Green card status carries with it a number of US tax exposures and while not exactly the same as citizenship given exceptions under tax treaties, can also cause the holder to be taxable on a worldwide basis regardless of actual time spent in the United States.

Guardian The term 'guardian' is used in many different ways, and can include the individual charged with supervising the affairs of a minor or of someone who is under a disability. The term can also apply to a 'protector' under a trust and to many other functions that are part of governance structures adopted by wealth-owning families.

Headline Tax Rates Top tax rates in countries are sometimes referred to as 'headline tax rates', as these are the tax rates that are focused on—say a top rate of 50%. The reality, however, is that the actual tax that wealth owners pay may be far, far lower given legitimate planning approaches adopted, tax deductions and otherwise.

Income Tax An income tax is a direct tax imposed on individuals or entities relating to the taxable income of that individual or entity. Salaries, dividends, revenues from sales of goods and many other such items may be subject to income tax.

Independent Asset Manager An independent asset manager (IAM) is usually an asset manager who does not retain custody of the investment portfolio involved. Quite commonly, the assets themselves will be with a custodian bank, and a limited power of attorney will be provided to the investment manager, who is independent of the bank, to provide input on how the assets are to be managed.

Independent Trustee Trustees can be individuals or companies, and many banks own trust companies that offer trust services to both bank and non-bank clients. An independent trust company is a trust company that is independent of a bank, meaning that it is not bank owned.

Indirect Tax An indirect tax includes value-added taxes, sales taxes, customs duties, stamp duties and other taxes that are not directly imposed on the income of an individual, but rather on other items, such as consumption.

Information Exchange There are a variety of ways information is exchanged between countries, including information exchange on request, which is contained in Tax Information Exchange Agreements (TIEAs) and in comprehensive tax treaties. Through FATCA and the CRS and related steps encouraged by the OECD, information exchange has moved towards being *automatic*, meaning that information will be exchanged even where *no request* for the information is made by the receiving country. Other forms of information exchange include *spontaneous* information exchange, which a country can perform on its own initiative, providing information to treaty partners on their taxpayers. Information exchange also takes place where there are no tax treaties in place, as might arise through anti-money laundering reports and otherwise.

Inheritance Inheritance refers to the succession of assets and otherwise on death. In relation to taxation, the term is widely used in a loose way, whereas more technically, taxes are more often applied to the estate of the deceased (estate taxes) as opposed to being applied to the recipient of the assets. There are, however, countries where the recipient of an inheritance is the person to be taxed, particularly where the deceased was not taxed.

Intestacy Intestacy refers to an individual dying without having left a valid will or other instrument that sets out how the assets will pass. Where an individual dies intestate, his assets pass under the laws relevant to his estate, which may be a combination of the laws of his place of nationality, residence or domicile at death, and the laws applying where assets are located at death. Most countries have intestacy laws that have the assets of an intestate pass to family members of specified degrees in specified shares, and if there are no such family members, to the state. In some jurisdictions, however, such as India, Lebanon and Singapore, the applicable laws governing the devolution of a person's estate may also depend on the religion of the deceased.

Letter of Wishes Where a trustee or executor or other person is provided with discretion, such as the power to determine at what age a beneficiary should benefit, or who among a class of beneficiaries can benefit, a letter of wishes may be provided to guide the trustee or executor on the wishes of the person whose assets are the subject of the arrangement. Letters of wishes and similar documents are usually not binding, and are in place only to provide guidance and suggestions.

Life Insurance Life insurance is insurance that is designed to provide payment to surviving family members on the death of the life assured. There are many kinds of life insurance, and some policies can allow for investment features that allow the owner of the policy to access the investment monies in a variety of ways. A number of tax and asset-protection benefits can be obtained through the use of certain life insurance arrangements, depending on the countries involved and the circumstances.

Limited Liability Companies (LLCs) Most countries have corporate laws that allow for the formation of companies that offer limited liability in the sense that shareholders are not personally liable for the debts of the company—the liability of the company is limited to the assets that are owned by the company itself, and such liability does not extend to the assets of shareholders. As separate entities, tax laws usually tax companies separately from their shareholders, but in the United States, LLCs (as opposed to corporations) are treated as 'flow-through' entities, meaning that taxation is at the level of the shareholder, avoiding a second level of corporate tax. While an election for treatment to the contrary can be made, LLCs can offer tax and reporting advantages given the mix of limited liability and flow-through treatment.

Living Will A living will refers to the documenting of one's wishes regarding medical and other care in the event they are unable to make decisions on their own. In a number of countries, there are formal procedures for living wills that need to be followed.

Midshore Midshore is not a formal term, but with increasing attacks on the use of 'offshore' tax haven companies, there is a move to the use of corporate and other vehicles that are either located in 'onshore' home countries or in 'midshore' countries, being countries with meaningful infrastructure in terms of legal, accounting and other support, access to a wide employment pool and, importantly, access to tax and other bilateral and multilateral treaties.

Multilateral Agreements and Treaties In contrast to bilateral treaties, which are agreements between two countries, there are a growing number of tax and other agreements that are entered into by multiple countries. These are multilateral agreements. Cross-border activity requires a good understanding of the bilateral and multilateral treaties that may have application.

OECD   The Organisation for Economic Co-operation and Development has both member and non-member countries that contribute to the development of economic and social policies. Critically important to wealth owners is the involvement of the OECD in encouraging tax compliance and the adoption of automatic information exchange to facilitate this, as well as other initiatives relating to helping address tax enforcement, inequality and other economic needs. The United Nations, interestingly, is becoming more involved in tax policy, in part on the basis of views that the OECD has been unable to properly reflect the needs of less-developed countries.

Offshore   'Offshore' is most commonly a reference to the world of tax havens. Usually, these include zero-tax countries where companies, trusts and other vehicles can operate with no taxation and little in the way of interference. Moves towards tax transparency and enforcement of tax laws are reducing the role of offshore havens substantially.

Onshore   'Onshore' generally refers to activities and structures that take place and are located in the country of residence of the investor and in the countries in which the investor is investing. If an investor lives in country X, a company in country X is an onshore company, whereas if the investor uses a company in a different country, say a tax haven, to hold assets, the company would be located in an 'offshore' location. If the investor invests in country Y and uses a country Y company to hold the investment, that would generally also be considered to be the use of an 'onshore' vehicle. If, instead, the investment is held by a company in an offshore tax haven, albeit that the investment were made in country Y, the investment vehicle would be considered to be 'offshore'.

Partnerships   Partnerships are business organizations that have more than one owner or interest holder, and are generally taxed not as separate entities, but as 'flow-through' vehicles. This means that the profits and losses of the partnership are taxed not at the level of the partnership, but at the level of the individual partners. Partners are generally liable for the debts of the partnership, but limited liability partnerships also exist, which allow limited partners to participate without becoming liable for the debts of the partnership.

Post-Nuptial Agreement   A post-nuptial agreement is an agreement entered into between spouses *after* the marriage takes place, and generally covers economic and other agreements regarding what happens in the event of a break-up of the marriage. A post-nuptial agreement may be entered into where no pre-nuptial agreement was made, but may also supplement a pre-nuptial agreement, particularly where the circumstances of the marriage change, such as through a change of domicile, a change in assets and income or a number of other circumstances.

Pre-Nuptial Agreement A pre-nuptial agreement is an agreement entered into between individuals *prior* to a marriage taking place. In some countries, such an agreement is binding in relation to economic and other areas of the marriage; in others, the pre-nuptial agreement may only be persuasive in the event of dissolution of the marriage. In some countries, pre-nuptial agreements are not respected by the courts.

Predicate Offence A predicate offence refers to an offence which must first occur to trigger a reporting or other requirement. In the case of anti-money laundering rules, these generally require that suspicious activities be reported to the authorities. What constitutes a suspicious activity relates to 'predicate' offences. Where tax is a predicate offence, funds that may not have properly been taxed, when handled by an intermediary, may thereby give rise to the obligation for a suspicious activity report to be filed, which may then lead to the tax obligation being enforced.

Private Trust Company A private trust company (PTC) is generally a trust company that has been established for use by only one family in relation to one or more trusts that the family may put in place. PTCs can take many forms, and are often administered by professional trustees or by directors who are appointed for the purpose.

Probate Where a will is in place, it is not automatic that the assets of a deceased go to those specified as beneficiaries under the will. Probate is the legal procedure for legally proving the will is the valid last will of the deceased.

Retrocession The term retrocession is a nice word for 'kickback'. Increasingly prohibited under laws protecting the interests of clients of banks and other asset managers, unless specifically approved by the client, retrocessions refer to payments asset managers receive from third parties, such as managers of investment funds the asset manager orients investments towards. It has not been uncommon for banks and other asset managers to receive retrocessions and to have kept these amounts without informing their clients of them. In other words, the investment manager makes investments on behalf of their client and receives compensation as an encouragement to make the investment over and above the fees the client pays to the investment manager. Clearly a conflict of interest, many jurisdictions now prohibit retrocessions that the client has not specifically approved. Sadly, the approvals from clients often appear in small print that the clients do not focus on.

Rule Against Perpetuities Under the common law, it is possible for assets to be legally owned by someone, but for someone else to have the beneficial ownership of the assets. In a trust, the trustee is the legal owner, and the beneficiaries have the beneficial ownership. The rule against perpetuities is a legal concept that requires that there be a time limit within which the legal ownership of assets passes to the beneficiaries, meaning that, at least traditionally, a trust cannot last forever. This rule, however, has now been replaced by legislation in many countries that allows trusts to last indefinitely, without a time limit. The traditional rule against perpetuities required that assets vest within 'a life in being plus 21 years'.

Shareholders' Agreements Where there are shareholders of a company, a shareholders' agreement is an important governance document that provides for many eventualities, including procedures on decisions being made, how shares are bought and sold, financing of the company, dispute resolution and more.

***Sharia* Law** *Sharia* law, otherwise known as Islamic law, derives from the *Quran*, which may form the basis of the legal system in many Muslim countries and includes, among other things, forced heirship principles that affect how assets pass on death and otherwise within families.

Tax Avoidance Unlike tax evasion, which refers to the illegal activity of not paying a tax that is legally due, tax avoidance generally refers to finding a 'loophole' that allows for the tax to be avoided. Countries can attack such avoidance using anti-avoidance rules, such as a general anti-avoidance rule (GAAR) and in other ways. Tax avoidance is also increasingly coming under attack on moral grounds, both in the corporate and individual tax area.

Tax Evasion Tax evasion is the crime of not paying a tax that is legally required to be paid.

Tax Planning Tax planning means understanding the tax laws that have application, and undertaking a course of action designed to legally allow for tax exposures to be mitigated.

Tax Residence Most countries have rules that determine when a taxpayer, whether an individual, a company, a trust or other vehicle, is a resident for tax purposes. In the case of individuals, these rules are usually either or both of objective and subjective. Objective residence rules would include residence rules that focus on days of presence. Subjective residence rules would include references to the intentions of the individual regarding where the individual lives. Residence rules are also affected by the possible application of tax treaties, which commonly contain residence 'tie-breaker' rules designed to address double taxation that could arise where an individual or entity is considered to be resident in more than one country at the same time.

Tax Treaty Tax treaties include comprehensive bilateral agreements between countries that deal with a number of areas of taxation, including information exchange, the avoidance of double taxation, reductions in withholding taxes on dividends, interest, royalties and other amounts, residence 'tie-breaker' rules and protections from taxation on business profits in the absence of the maintenance of a permanent establishment in other than one's country of residence.

Territorial Tax System In a territorial tax system, it is generally only locally sourced income that is taxed. A territorial tax system can be contrasted to a worldwide tax system, where a resident is taxed on worldwide income, including both locally sourced and foreign-sourced income.

Tie-Breaker Rules Tax treaties commonly contain 'tie-breaker' rules designed to determine which of two countries has the right to tax a taxpayer—whether an individual or an entity—as a resident. These rules can be very important in tax planning, particularly where there is physical presence in more than one country and/or other cross-border activity.

Transfer Pricing Transfer pricing refers to the allocation of revenues and costs between related entities. If a taxpayer conducts business activities in several countries and has companies in each country that are involved in the conduct of business, how prices are set between related entities will affect tax exposures. There is currently considerable focus by tax authorities and international bodies on the abuse of transfer pricing rules as a means of improperly reducing tax exposures.

Transfer Taxes Transfer tax is a general term covering gifts and bequests. Where there is a tax on gifts and bequests, these can generally be referred to as transfer taxes.

Trusts and Parties to a Trust A trust is a very flexible arrangement that involves a 'settlor' transferring assets to a 'trustee', who becomes the legal owner of the assets, holding the assets for 'beneficiaries', who are the beneficial owners. An optional party to a trust may be a 'protector', who has certain oversight over the trustee. There are many, many forms of trust, making them flexible wealth planning tools.

Wills A will is a document that sets out the intentions of an individual regarding what should happen to assets owned by the individual on his death. Whether a will is valid depends on the laws having application to the assets of the individual, and it is not uncommon for individuals to have more than one will where they own assets in various countries.

Withholding Taxes Withholding taxes are taxes that are imposed at the source of income, and designed to ensure that tax laws are complied with. One form of withholding tax applies when certain types of payments are made to foreigners, such as dividends, interest and royalties, and whether the payer of such amounts is required to withhold tax from the payment made. In some circumstances, the taxpayer may be able to obtain a refund of all or part of the withholding tax given the application of a tax treaty, or the filing of a tax return or otherwise.

Worldwide Taxation A majority of countries tax individuals and companies that are resident in those countries on their worldwide income. Residence rules determine who is a taxable resident, and the tax system usually provides for reliefs, in the form of tax credits or exemptions, for foreign taxes paid so as to reduce the possible impact of double taxation. In the case of the United States, worldwide taxation is not only based on residence, but also on citizenship and the holding of a right to permanent residence ('green card' status).

Index

A

activities, *Theory of Change*, 2–3, 11–12, 348–350
advisors, 287
   accountants, 289–295
   conflicts of interest, 304–307
   IAMs (independent asset managers), 302–304
   lawyers, 289–295
   private banking, 295–302, 316–329
   relationship manager, 299
   succession plan and, 288
   trust, 288
   trust officers, 299
   wealth planners, 299
aging wealth owners, 159–161, 366
Apple family, 4–5, 333–334, 350–361
Ashby, Ross, 34
asset protection, 44–45, 237–242, 312–314, 365–366
   succession planning, 183–189
   taxation and, 75–79
   trusts, 262–263
Astor, Brooke, 160, 205–206
automatic information exchange, 67–75, 136–137, 142–143, 368

B

bank secrecy, 54–56. *See also* taxation
   proactive approaches, 64–65
   secrecy-based financial centres, 60–61
banking
   abuses, 56–59
   offshore, 55
   private banking, 295–302, 316–329
Bird family, 5, 334, 350–361
Birkenfeld, Bradley, 65, 110n
Buffet, Warren, 298

Bush, George H.W., 245
business succession, 208–221

C

capital gains, 117
capitalism, regenerative, 18–19, 118–121
CFC (controlled foreign corporation) rules, 92–93
circular economy principles, 17, 365
   elders of family, 34–35
   governance and, 37–38
   opportunities with, 19–23
   paradox thinking, 31–34
   succession planning, 35–48
   sustainability, 17–18
   taxation, 52
   waste and, 29–31
citizenship planning, 99–110
Colbert, Jean-Baptiste, 110n
company ownership, 275–278
Crane family, 5, 334, 350–361

D

Dagland, 6–7, 18, 350–361
derailers, 181. *See also* succession planning; tunnels and bridges
   business succession, 208–221
   confidentiality, 227–229
   demographics changes, 205–207, 366
   divorces, 193–199, 366
   family conflicts, 207–208
   inheritance, 181–182, 188–193
   investments, 229–237
   kidnapping, 248–250
   multi-jurisdictional families, 204–205
   philanthropy, 221–227
   political risk, 242–248
   privacy rights, 227–229
   second families, 199–204

Index

diversification of ownership, 143–144, 229–231
divorces, 38, 193–199, 366
donation duties, 131–135

E

Emerson, Jed, 227, 252n, 252n
estate duties, 131–135
estate planning, taxation and, 75–79

F

families
    children of second marriage, 165–176
    conflict, 207–208
    daughters, 168–170
    friends of, 176–177
    governance, 29
    grandchildren, 174–175
    high-functioning, sustainability, 23–24
    I and we alignment, 26–28
    in-laws, 170–173
    individualism, unity and, 28
    kidnapping risk, 248–250
    mistresses/paramours, 162–165
    multi-jurisdictional, 204–205
    second marriages, 161–162, 199–204
    security, 248–250
    siblings, 175–176
    sons, 166–168
    sustainability, 18–19
    third culture kids, 177–180
family bank, 41–43, 278–279
family constitutions, 208–221
family office, 311, 370
Fan, Joseph, 167
FATCA (Foreign Tax Compliance Act), 56–57, 68
forced heirship, 190–191
foundations, 269–271
Fourie, Nicolette, 362n
Fullerton, John, 118–122

G

Gartner, Gary, 18
GILTI (global intangible low-taxed income), 141
global minimum tax, 139–147
global tax systems, 81–82, 127–131, 138

GloBE (Global Anti-Base Erosion) rules, 139–141
Goh, Kenneth, 18, 48n
gold-diggers, 157–158, 366
grandchildren, 174–175

H

Haeri, Hussein, 252n
Haley, Alex, 27
Halkyard, Andrew, 149n
Healey, Denis, 79
Helmsley, Harry, 255
Helmsley, Leona, 255
Hughes, Jay, 26, 49n, 285n, 331n, 343, 363n
Hulsroj, Peter, 22, 25, 113, 116, 149n, 150n, 153, 363n

I

IAMs (independent asset managers), 302–304, 370
IIR (income inclusion rule), 140
IMF (International Monetary Fund), 132
impact goal, *Theory of Change*, 2–3, 6–9, 13–14, 337–347
impacts, *Theory of Change*, 2–3, 13–14
in-laws, 170–173
income tax, 82
inheritance, 181–182, 188–193
inheritance taxes, 114–122, 131–133
inputs, *Theory of Change*, 2–3, 9–10, 347–348
insurance products, 279–284
investments, 229–237
Ispahani, Iraj, 1, 14n, 17, 48n, 252n, 362n

J–K

Johnson, Boris, 95–96
kidnapping risk, 248–250
King, Roger, 46, 167

L

Lagarde, Christine, 132
Lee, Sammy, 14n, 362n
Lewis, Lesley, 177
Liniger, Stefan, 110n, 252n

liquidity, 229–231
living wills, 192–193

M

Le Maire, Bruno, 146
Mariani, Stefano, 149n
marriage
    gold-diggers, 157–158, 366
    pre-nuptial agreements, 196–197
    second marriage children, 165–166
    second marriages, 161–162, 367
mistresses/paramours, 162–165, 366
mobile wealth, 125–127, 369
money laundering, anti-money laundering rules, 67–70
Morgan, Samantha, 149n

N

Noriega, Manuel, 245

O

OECD (Organisation for Economic Co-Operation and Development), 55–56, 68, 139–141
offshore banking, 55
optional society, 54, 113, 369
    capital gains, 117
    global minimum tax, 139–147
    global tax systems, 127–131
    Hong Kong duties, 131–135
    inheritance taxes, 114–122
    regenerative capitalism, 118–121
    Singapore, 131–135
    UK tax policy, 123–127
outcomes, *Theory of Change*, 2–3, 12–13, 348–350
outputs, *Theory of Change*, 2–3, 12–13, 348–350

P

partnerships, 272–275
philanthropy, 221–227
Picketty, Thomas, 115–116, 226, 248
Pigou, Arthur, 356
political risk, 44–45, 242–248, 370
privacy rights, 227–229

private banking, 295–302, 316–329
probate, 188–193
psychology of wealth, 151
    aging wealth owner, 159–161
    children of second marriage, 165–166
    friends, 176–177
    gold-diggers, 157–158, 366
    grandchildren, 174–175
    in-laws, 170–173
    marriages, second marriages, 161–162
    mental health challenges, 156
    mistresses/paramours, 162–165, 366
    siblings, 175–176
    spouses of wealth creator, 157–159
    third culture kids, 177–180
    wealth creator, 154–156

Q–R

QI (Qualified Intermediary) system, 54–56
Rauschenberg, Robert, 264
regenerative capitalism, 18–19, 118–121, 126
regenerative tax system, 9, 177–121, 371
religious influences, 181, 188–189, 195

S

Saint-Amans, Pascal, 147
security, 248–250
Ser, Sharon, 194
stakeholders, *Theory of Change*, 4
succession planning, 365–366
    advisors and, 288
    business succession, 208–221
    circular economy and, 35–48
    communication, 311–312, 315
    continuity audit, 310, 335–336
    cultural and religious approaches, 45–48
    demographics changes, 205–207, 366
    education and, 329–330
    family conflicts, 207–208
    multi-jurisdictional families, 204–205
    plan necessity, 182–187
    pre-nuptial agreements, 196–197
    probate, 192–193
    stress tests, 309–310
    taxation and, 53
    trusts, 191
    wills, 188–193
    women and, 314–315

Sunak, Rishi, 124
sustainability, 371
  circular economy and, 17–18
  families, 18–19, 24–26
  governance and, 29

T

tax avoidance, 79–81, 369
tax evasion, 59–62, 79–81, 369
tax planning, 79–81, 369
tax transparency, 53–54, 62–64,
    229–231, 368
  automatic information exchange, 67–75
  proactive approaches, 64–70
tax treaties, 86–88
tax-advantaged investing, 231–237, 368
taxation, 368
  advisors and, 290–292
  asset protection and, 75–79
  circular economy principles and, 52
  common reporting standard, 57
  competition, 81–82
  estate planning and, 75–79
  FATCA (Foreign Tax Compliance Act),
    56–57, 68
  global tax, 81–82, 127–131
  income tax, 82
  inheritance taxes, 114–122
  minimizing taxes, 312–314
  optional society and, 54
  privacy rights, 227–229
  regenerative taxation, 117–121
  residence based, 85–86, 89–91
  succession planning and, 53
  system types, 81
  territorial systems, 83–85
  trusts, 257–258
  types of taxes, 97–99
  undeclared, 99–101
  undeclared money, 65–67, 101–103
  worldwide, 91–96

Theory of Change, 1–14
  Dagland, 350–361
  example families, 337–350
third culture kids, 177–180
trust officers, 299
trusts, 191, 257–269
tunnels and bridges, 253
  company ownership, 275–278
  derivative products, 284–285
  family bank, 278–279
  foundations, 269–271
  insurance products, 279–284
  partnerships, 272–275
  wills, 254–257

U–V

undeclared money, 65–67, 101–103
UTPR (undertaxed profit rule), 140
VanderWolk, Jefferson, 149n

W–Z

wealth
  costs of, 153
  definition, 152–153
  sources, 151–152
wealth creators, 154–156
  aging, 159–161
  daughters, 168–170
  mental health challenges, 156
  mistresses/paramours, 162–165
  sons, 166–168
  spouses, 157–159
wealth planners, 299
Wilkinson, Abi, 115
wills, 188–193, 254–257
women, planning and,
    314–315, 367
worldwide taxation, 91–96,
    125–131
Zucman, Gabriel, 145